I0800260

GHOSTS OF ORTONA

GHOSTS OF ORTONA

Reckoning with the Traumas of Canadian World War II Veterans

IAN COSH

sh.
SUTHERLAND HOUSE

TORONTO, 2026

Sutherland House
416 Moore Ave., Suite 304
Toronto, ON M4G 1C9

Copyright © 2026 by Ian Cosh

All rights reserved, including the right to reproduce this book or portions thereof in any form whatsoever. For information on rights and permissions or to request a special discount for bulk purchases, please contact Sutherland House at sutherlandhousebooks@gmail.com.

Sutherland House and logo are registered trademarks of The Sutherland House Inc.

First edition, March 2026

If you are interested in inviting one of our authors to a live event or media appearance, please contact sranasinghe@sutherlandhousebooks.com and visit our website at sutherlandhousebooks.com for more information about our authors and their schedules.

We acknowledge the support of the Government of Canada.

Manufactured in India
Cover designed by Lena Yang

Front cover image: Bill McConville, "All that remains of one of Ortona's finest churches." Imperial War Museum, NA–10389.
Back cover image: Terry Rowe, "Ruins of unidentified church."
Library and Archives Canada, PA–136308.
Front endpaper: Charles F. Comfort, Via Dolorosa, Ortona.
Canadian War Museum, 19710261-2308.
Back endpaper: Charles F. Comfort, Boschink. Winnipeg Art Gallery,
Gift of Robert and Margaret Hucal, 2005–68.

Book composed by Karl Hunt

Library and Archives Canada Cataloguing in Publication
Title: Ghosts of Ortona : reckoning with the traumas of
Canadian WWII veterans / Ian Cosh.
Names: Cosh, Ian, author.
Description: Includes bibliographical references and index.
Identifiers: Canadiana (print) 20250281619 | Canadiana (ebook) 20250281899 |
ISBN 9781998365968 (hardcover) | ISBN 9781998365975 (EPUB)
Subjects: LCSH: Ortona, Battle of, Ortona, Italy, 1943. | LCSH: World War, 1939-1945—Personal narratives, Canadian. | LCSH: World War, 1939-1945—Psychological aspects. |
LCSH: World War, 1939-1945—Veterans—Canada—Psychology. |
LCSH: World War, 1939-1945—Veterans—Canada. | LCSH: World War,
1939-1945—Veterans—Italy—Ortona. | LCGFT: Personal narratives.
Classification: LCC D763.I82 O77 2026 | DDC 940.54/215713—dc23

ISBN 978-1-998365-96-8
eBook 978-1-998365-97-5

For my parents and my sister

I wish I could explain the desperate sense of isolation, of not belonging to my own past . . .

—Farley Mowat, in a letter to his parents from San Leonardo, Italy, December 19, 1943, quoted in *And No Birds Sang*

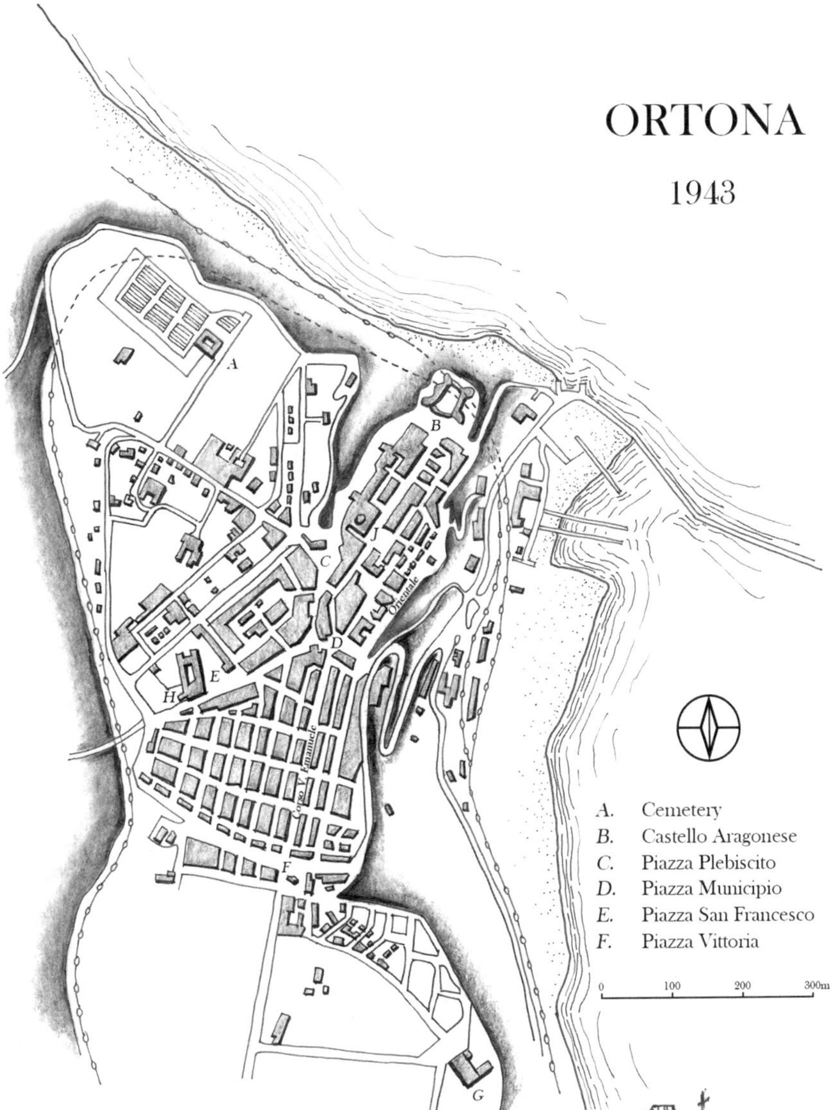

G. Santa Maria di Costantinopoli

H. Santa Maria delle Grazie

J. San Tommaso

Contents

ORTONA TODAY IS A PEACEFUL LIKE PLACE,
WITH ITS BEACHES A TOURISTS DELIGHT.
ITS HISTORY LIKELY UNKNOWN TO ALL THEM
OF THE ARMIES THAT CAME HERE TO FIGHT

BUT JUST SOUTH OF TOWN IS A GRAVEYARD STILL,
FILLED WITH MARKERS OF BOYS AND OF MEN
THOUGH TIMES ENDLESS MARCH HAS RENDERED US OLD
WE SHALL REMEMBER THEM.

ORTONA — ORTONA A'MARE — ORTONA BY THE SEA

'Doggerel'

This was unexpected. I was looking for something else.

Far away and in a distant land
And so many years ago,
Canadas youth were asked to engage
A very formidable foe

I'm sitting on the floor beside the box holding these four sheets of lined paper. Hand-printed, all capital letters. It's a poem by—

"Not a poem."

That's right. I remember now.

They'd eaten the dust of Sicily,
Felt the heat of scorching sun,
Marched up the toe of Italy
Always facing the Jerries guns

When he handed me these pages, I saw the title—"Ortona"—followed by lines of rhyming verse. I remarked that he'd written a poem.

"Not a poem," he said. "Just some doggerel I wrote."

Rearguard actions they were called,
Although many men had died,
For the German sought the best terrain
Where he could maybe turn the tide

He would make his stand, delay his war
Slow up the bitter attacks
Make sure the enemy pays the price
Stop him dead in his bloody tracks.

Doggerel—I didn't know the word. I asked him what it meant.

He looked at me, startled.

I was startled that he was startled. Was it so strange that I didn't know?

Late in the fall the Canadians moved
To blue Adriatics fair shore
Halfway up the Italian boot
Still knocking on Jerries door

Fording rivers high and incessant mud,
They nipped at Tedeschi's heels,
And on 'Vino Ridge' a price was paid
With the fate of brave men sealed.

Eva, his wife, broke the awkward silence. She had been sitting quietly by the door of the study listening to us talk. Now, smiling brightly, she spoke.

"There's a dictionary on the shelf behind you there," she said.

Then we all shared a laugh as I reached for the shelf, took out the dictionary, and looked up the word. He had learned it, he said, from a crossword puzzle.

Soon after that lay another town,
Just one of so many they'd seen,
A little port in Decembers cool sun,
Looking placid, quiet serene.

Ortona it's called, but hold on a minute,
We cant just walk on through,
And a machine gun stutters its greeting now,
Hey Eddy, this ones labelled for you

Every day, he did a crossword. It was his method of self-study. As he'd told me before, he'd quit school at grade nine and hadn't gone back after the war. His lack of education was a lifelong regret. But he'd found that by doing a daily crossword puzzle he could improve himself bit by bit. When *doggerel* had come up one day as the answer to a clue, he'd liked the word, reckoned it was useful, and added it to his vocabulary.

"But if a PhD student doesn't know it," he sighed, "maybe it's not so useful as I thought."

"Over on the left, on the edge of that coulee,
That house. The firings from there,"
"Stretcher bearer"! Someone now called
"Theres wounded men over here"

A tank is sent up and soon got the range,
And blew the house all to the hell,
And that was the start of the Ortona stand,
But the end of some comrades as well.

It's undated. He must have written it after one of his return trips. Maybe on that first time back when he went there with Eva. They had stopped at the sign on the road, got out of the car, and sat for a while looking across the valley at the town.

The fighting was carried from house to house
Blowing holes in walls to get in
With dynamite, guns and the hand grenade
Both sides were desperate to win.

Blow up my house and Ill blow up yours
Was a game that was soon to be played
And the cost in lives was heavy indeed
Looking now at so many graves.

Painstaking work. Here and there, his lack of formal education shows. But the penmanship is perfect. Four pages. It would take me ages to handwrite anything this long and keep it so neat and clean.

How many drafts did he write before he was done? How many thoughts were put in, didn't work, and were cut? How many words were looked up and replaced?

I think of his struggle with his stomach—

"But see even now, talking about this, this churns up, any food that I've got, churns it up."

The flip book of pictures in his mind—

"There's pretty well a constant picture in there. Not one, one picture, but flip to, you know, it's like one of these things that you flip."

His crossword companion dictionary beside him as he works.

Back then as you lay on a huge rubble pile
With your rifle loaded and cocked,
Your sights on the dome of Ortonas church
Overlooking the length of the block

San Tomasso the church, was a sniper up there?
Who could see every move that was made
Better not take any chances my friend
And so the tower was sprayed.

The battle continued in terrible force,
Every inch of Ortona saw red
And Hitlers division of parachute troops
Were beaten by the blood that was shed.

They called it the western Stalingrad,
And some history's say this is so,
This fight that raged through Christmas'es days
Before Jerry was made to let go.

Actually, in his penmanship, he has made one mistake. Near the very end, just seven words from the finish, he's left out the auxiliary "has." Then, noticing his error, he's written the word above the line with a caret below to show its place. A rough fix, but it does the job. God knows, he made it this far—second last line of the page—and didn't want to do the whole thing over. I can relate.

Ortona today is a peaceful like place,
With its beaches a tourists delight,
Its history likely unknown to all them
Of the armies that came here to fight

But just south of town is a graveyard still,
Filled with markers of boys and of men
v HAS
Though times endless march rendered us old
We shall remember them.

At the poem's end, he's written three names for the place, including how it appeared on postcards before the war.

Ortona—Ortona a' Mare—Ortona-by-the-Sea

Not a poem, he said.
It was doggerel.
Trivial or badly written verse.

CHAPTER 1

Safe Conduct

SOMETIMES I WONDER WHAT might have happened if I'd taken the military historian's advice. No doubt, this box would be different. My life might be better as a result.

But there's not much point in wondering. The box is what it is. And that advice wasn't really for me.

I mean that in both senses. First, I didn't agree with it—I'd been trained to see things differently. Second—in a manner of speaking—the historian had me mistaken for somebody else.

This tends to happen when people learn that my research involved World War II veterans. For many—experts and non-experts alike—the mere mention of *war* and *veteran* is enough: no matter what I say next, my work has already been pegged as military history.

In this case, however, I'd introduced myself as an anthropologist from the start. In my letter, I explained that I was a PhD student in anthropology and that I was planning to interview World War II veterans. I was seeking his advice partly for his expertise on the topic of war, but more so for his experience working with veterans. He was a senior scholar with many demands on his time, so I was pleasantly surprised when he agreed to meet. A few weeks later, when I arrived at his office, I assumed he would remember the context.

He didn't beat around the bush. Within moments of my taking a seat, he told me I was setting myself up for failure.

"There's not much value in talking to veterans."

His message was blunt, but not disrespectful. Having served in the military himself, he clearly didn't mean to put veterans down. However, perhaps also due to his military background, he wasn't one for sugarcoating the truth. Especially because I was at a key point in my scholarly career, he wanted me to be forewarned. He pointed out that almost all of the men who'd been officers in World War II were now dead. The veterans still living had mostly served in the army's junior ranks. As low-ranking and very young soldiers, those guys had rarely had a good grasp of what was going on. Even among the better-informed officers, historians had found memories to be unreliable. Now that the only veterans remaining were basically guys who'd been teenagers and privates, and now that so many more years had passed since the events I planned to ask them about—he was sorry to say, but for scholarly purposes, it was pretty much a waste of time.

He leaned back in his chair with a sigh.

"The guy will be able to tell you, probably very reliably, that old sergeant so-and-so was a mean son of a bitch. But he'll be hopelessly unreliable in anything he tells you about what he did, where, on what day."

Looking back now, the historian's words seem almost prophetic. In the course of my travels and interviews with veterans, I really did hear a lot about a son-of-a-bitch sergeant. And when it came time for me to analyze the men's stories, I discovered many problems with the facts.

That patrol with Sam, Gus, Rollie, and Bill, for example—was that in Guardiaregia? Vinchiaturo? October the third? Fifth? Eighteenth? Did they take five prisoners, one prisoner, or none? Were these guys even on the same patrol?

Then there was Mel, telling me about shooting the church, while pointing at a photo of the municipal building. Bill's entire story was off by a day. Ted's was significantly out of alignment.

And those were just issues that I was able to identify because there were other sources to check the stories against. For most of what the men told me, there were no other sources. Between what actually happened and how they remembered it, there were surely more discrepancies that couldn't be known.

When I was still sitting across from the historian, I had yet to hear any of the stories. However, I was familiar with the fallibility of memory, and I knew that, for my research, it wasn't a problem. The historian's warning was sensible for his own line of work; the aim of most historical research is to reconstruct the past. With that agenda, if you interview someone, you're aiming to get accurate insight about things that really happened. The subjectivity of the person you're interviewing, including their personal ways of remembering, is tangential to your purpose. If anything, it's an encumbrance. You might still want to know about subjective influences on the storytelling, but only insofar as it helps you to separate the "fictive" elements from the facts.

In my work, however, the personal *was* the purpose.[1] My goal was not to reconstruct the past; it was to understand the meanings of the past for the people who had experienced it. My work belonged to a research paradigm that's interested in how people and societies remember. The basic premise of such work is that the stories people tell about the past, and the manner of their storytelling, shed light on what's important to them and their relationships to their societies. In this paradigm, it's still valuable to notice mistakes and contradictions; however, far from regarding these as regrettable symptoms of unreliable memories, the researcher treats them as clues for understanding people's efforts to find comfort and meaning in the stories of their lives.[2]

So I wasn't going to heed the historian's advice—but that wasn't something I needed to say. I was there to get his perspective, not to argue for my own. After predicting what I should expect from interviewing veterans, he shifted to suggesting other ways I could pursue my topic. He offered tips for searching the national archives, pointed me to collections in the Canadian War Museum, and explained how some of these primary sources had come into being. It was all useful. He was an expert in the field, and I was getting a valuable orientation to the terrain.

We were about to wrap up the meeting when he asked me, "So who are you working with?"

This caught me a little off guard. We weren't at my home university, and in contemporary anthropology, there are hardly any household names. I didn't see how the names of my professors were going to mean anything to him. For some reason, though, he seemed to think that they should. As I recited the names, he began to frown. By the time I was done, he looked absolutely appalled. If there was still any doubt that my answer hadn't met his expectations, his next words offered more than a clue.

"Who the *hell* are *they*?"

I struggled to think for a moment. Why was he so put out?

"Um . . . Anthropology professors?"

"*Anthropology?!*"

In my description of my research paradigm in the paragraphs above, I've explained it a fair bit better than I could have done at the time. Back then, I certainly knew the gist of it, but there was still a lot that I had to learn. Moreover, what I did know about narrative and memory was mostly from reading books. It's one thing to have intellectual knowledge of a subject; it's very different to have to navigate that subject while it's coming at you in real life. When you're sitting in front of a real person, and they are talking to you, or they've just gone silent; and you have to discern what they mean, what they want, and whether or not you might be crossing a sensitive line; and meanwhile you're trying to remember where you're going and how much time you have; and all of this has to factor into what you decide to say or ask them next—in the midst of all that, it's easy to forget what you read in the books.[3] Even without opening this box here in front of me, I can think of some of my early mistakes.

The first that comes to mind was in my interview with Norman.

It was quiet enough to hear the turning of the tape recorder. From his seat on the opposite sofa, Norman watched me with a look of apprehension. He was a small man in an oversized plaid shirt, well-pressed pants, and thick-cushioned sneakers. He kept clasping and unclasping his hands. Was it nervousness that was making him do it—or just the tremors of age?

In my hands, between thumbs and forefingers, I was holding a leaflet. A moment ago, this had been inside Norman's box of what he called his war souvenirs. He'd opened the box, taken it out, and handed it to me without a word. Now he was watching—maybe waiting for me to say something, maybe hoping the thing would speak for itself.

On it were just a few lines of text. At the top, in bold type, were the words *SAFE CONDUCT.* Below that was a message in English and German. It promised safety and good treatment to the German soldier who carried this leaflet and surrendered.

Shadows of birds moved across the carpeted floor. Outside the window was a bird feeder. The silence between Norman and me continued. Then we both spoke at once.

"That's the—" Norman said.

"Safe conduct," I read aloud.

"—things they fired over," Norman said, "in an artillery shell to the German lines. Offering them, uh—"[4]

"Oh I see."

"—their chance to surrender."

"Did any of them do it?"

Our voices were muted, although we were alone in the house. Norman paused frequently, shifting his hands, but his words came out quickly when he spoke.

"Some did."

"Really."

"Yeah. Some did. But uh, not many."

"Did they fire similar things at you?"

"No. No. But uh, they had lots of broadcasts, you know, radio broadcasts, that they would, uh, tell us what we were missing."

"Really. How great it was over there."

"Yeah! Yeah!"

Norman chuckled slightly but his face remained tense. I tried again to lighten the mood.

"Did that have any effect on guys?"

"No, not really."

"Any of that German propaganda?"

"No. No. But uh, I can remember uh, Chris Vokes. You've heard of him, have you?"

"Chris Vokes?"

"Chris Vokes."

"Yeah."

"The general."

This was puzzling. Vokes had been the commander of the 1st Canadian Infantry Division. Why was Norman all of a sudden talking about him?

"Anyway, his—, he gave us a talk, and he said uh, the more Germans you k—"

Norman's voice tripped on the word. He tried again to say it.

"—you *kill*, he said, the quicker you're gonna get home."

Norman went quiet. I wasn't sure what to say.

After a short silence, he spoke again.

"So that was the, his, approach."

"That was pretty harsh."

"Yeah, that's hard. Yeah. But, I guess it was a fact."

The square of paper in my hands was clean and flat, though a few crease marks hinted at hard times in its past. Many years ago, somewhere in Italy, a twenty-year-old Norman had found this, held it in his fingers as I was doing now, and decided to keep it. *Safe conduct.* I imagined it tucked away inside his pack through the rest of the war. Now it was in the living room of his Vancouver Island home.

Why had Norman picked it up?

Why had he kept it?

Why did it remind him of his general's words?

I should have asked him. But I didn't. I thought the leaflet was off-topic, and I was worried about the time. I wanted to get on with my questions about Ortona.

> Ortonium is in the country of the Frentani, a cliff-town belonging to pirates, whose dwellings are pieced together from the wreckage of ships . . .
>
> —Strabo, 7 BC

> Ortona gleamed white like a fiery Asian city on a hill in Palestine, carved into the blue, all in parallel lines, without minarets.
>
> —Gabriele D'Annunzio, 1894

> *May Ortona be blessed,*
> *This beautiful sea and this air so fine!*
> *These young girls, roses of the gardens,*
> *May Ortona be blessed.*
>
> —Luigi Dommarco, 1914

ORTONA IS AN ANCIENT town on Italy's Adriatic coast. Today, it's home to about twenty thousand people; for most of its history it's been much smaller.

In Italian terms, it's actually a city (*Città di Ortona*). Like many Canadians, however, I'm in the habit of calling it a town—a habit I probably picked up from the veterans.

In any case, city or town, it's rare that Ortona is called anything. It isn't a well-known place. Even among Italians, many have never heard of it. There was a time, however, when it was the linchpin of a nation. The ancient Greek geographer Strabo included the town in his map of the world, and identified it as the key port and arsenal of the Frentani, an Italic people who were once powerful rivals to early Rome.

The town is narrowly perched on an escarpment overlooking the sea. Some of its streets are medieval and labyrinthine; others are laid out in a grid. From the promenade along the cliff edge, a winding road and switchback stairway descend to a harbour, train station, and beach. The rail line hugs the coast, passing through a tunnel under the town's northeastern point. Steep slopes into valleys of orchards and vineyards mark Ortona's boundaries to the west and south.

Many eras and empires have left their traces in the town. At the northeastern tip of the promontory, a thick-walled fifteenth-century castle is seated upon the remains of a Bronze Age settlement. Named *Castello Aragonese* after the Spanish royals who built it, the castle is a reminder of how Ortona was once strategic enough to be the target of Venetian raids. Near the Orientale (the sea-facing promenade) there's the *Palazzo Farnese*, a sixteenth-century palace that formerly belonged (as did the whole town) to the Habsburg archduchess Margaret of Austria. On the west side of town, the triangular Piazza San Francesco is named for the Franciscan friars whose church, Santa Maria delle Grazie, has stood in the square for more than five hundred years.

At the escarpment's southeastern corner, the church of Santa Maria di Costantinopoli is even older. Founded in 1280 by Celestine monks, it has a curious story behind its name. In 1500, a Turkish convert to Christianity disembarked from a ship in Ortona's harbour, carrying with him an effigy of Our Lady of Constantinople, the Byzantine advocation of the Virgin Mary. He claimed to have discovered the effigy in his house, and that the effigy had spoken to him, exhorting him to take her to safety in Ortona and place her in the Celestine church. As for the gully that the church overlooks, there's also a Turkish connection—but not a positive one. In 1566, an Ottoman fleet led by Grand Admiral Piyale Pasha raided Ortona as part of their war with the Habsburg Empire. Santa Maria di Costantinopoli was one of the raid's targets, and the gully below it came to be known as *Fosso Saraceni*—Saracens Ditch.[5]

Ortona's tallest and most sacred building is the domed Basilica and Cathedral of San Tommaso. The cultural and spiritual heart of the town has always been in this cathedral's place. Prior to Christianity, it was the site of a pagan Roman temple and a statue to the god Janus. The cathedral that replaced the temple was originally dedicated to the Virgin Mary.

During Marco Polo's time, the relics of Saint Thomas the Apostle were taken from the Greek island of Chios by an Ortona fleet as spoils of war and were placed in the cathedral, which was later renamed for the saint. In the fourteenth century, Pope Innocent VI decreed that Ortona's San Tommaso was a site for plenary indulgence, a place where Christians could be granted full remission of their sins. Ever since, it's been a destination for pilgrims, especially during the annual *Festa del Perdono* (Feast of Forgiveness) when a silver bust of the saint containing his relics is paraded through the streets.

For millennia, Ortona has been a centre of fishing, farming, viniculture, shipbuilding, and seafaring trade. In the nineteenth and early twentieth centuries, new industries appeared, including factories producing yarn, soap, cured meats, and bricks. In the surrounding countryside, sharecropping farmers produced wine, olive oil, and fruit, much of which was traded through Ortona's port. A shipbuilding academy operated in town. With no deep-water dock, large ships anchored offshore, and local barbers, cobblers, and other tradespeople would row out to offer their services to the visiting sailors. As for the fishermen, they and their families saw themselves as the bedrock of Ortona—its main provisioners and the custodians of its traditions. They mostly lived in the oldest and poorest neighbourhood, *Terravecchia* (Old Town), which includes the castle and cathedral. Their fishing boats were known for their many-coloured sails, and their defiant spirit was captured in the Latin words—*NAVIGARE NECESSE EST*—painted on the fish market wall. The words are from a story by Plutarch that tells of ancient Roman sailors whose city's survival depended on the arrival of their cargo of grain. When their ship encountered a violent storm, their commander urged them on with the words: "Navigare necesse est, vivere non est necesse"—sailing is necessary; living is not.

Ortona a Mare - Panorama

" Chi scià bbindette Urtona,
Stu mère belle e st'aria accușcì fine ! „
L. DOMMARCO

At the turn of the twentieth century, Ortona became a fulcrum of traditional and rebellious arts. Among its hometown heroes and lifelong patrons was Sir Francesco Paolo Tosti, a composer of salon music, teacher of Caruso, and singing master to the British royal family. Although Tosti spent most of his time in London (and was eventually knighted by King Edward VII) he returned often to Ortona to promote and take part in cultural events. On one occasion, when he learned that his fellow Ortonesi were unhappy that he'd become a British citizen, he went home to give an intimate performance in Santa Maria delle Grazie to reassure the people (and perhaps himself) that he still belonged to them. Another famous (or for some, notorious) figure who frequented Ortona was Gabriele D'Annunzio—decadent poet, World War I hero, nationalist firebrand, and role model to Mussolini. Nicknamed *il Vate* (the title for prophetic poets in ancient Rome), D'Annunzio considered Ortona his second home; it was dear to him from childhood as his mother's hometown, and for three years he represented it as an elected member of national parliament.

A more humble but no less spirited group of artists created Ortona's annual *Maggiolata*, a rowdy festival of folkloristic music, poetry, and dance. During the festival, carts and oxen were decorated with flowers, pianos were placed on the carts, and musicians performed while the oxen trundled them up and down the streets. One of the poems that was put to music was "Che Scià Bbindette Urtone" ("May Ortona Be Blessed"). The song describes a day in the life of Ortona and was adopted as its official hymn.

When the sun shines on the sea
And the Eastern winds blow from the shore,
The boats with their sails all raised
Wave to the town and go on their way.

The young girls fitfully sleep,
Dreaming that their bridegroom is near;
The morning bells ring in San Tommaso;
Already the people are starting to work.
May Ortona be blessed . . .

Meanwhile, and more prosaically, the Franciscans ran a popular soup kitchen for the poor (which was also celebrated by *Maggiolata* artists). Their former convent, attached to Santa Maria delle Grazie, became the town's hospital. Across from the church and hospital, forming the other long side of the triangular Piazza San Francesco, stood the new residence of the Franciscan Sisters of the Infant Jesus. In this solid two-storey stone edifice, the sisters managed the San Tommaso Institute, which included a kindergarten, an elementary school, and a craft school for young women. The building also accommodated over two hundred orphans who were cared for by the sisters.

During Italy's fascist era in the 1920s and 30s, the town of ten thousand inhabitants grew into a flourishing tourist resort. The population tripled in summertime. Restaurants and hotels were packed, and locals rented spare rooms to vacationers. A funicular provided easy passage between the upper town and the beach. Beside San Tommaso, the medieval clock tower (dating back to 1255) was modernized by the Italian Navy, gaining a new lookout post and a signal light for ships. The town hall was renovated to include a balcony, a third storey, and a small clock tower. Life in the town was enhanced with a movie cinema, a concert hall, and public gardens with enclosures in which exotic birds and monkeys were kept. A popular pastime was to gather at sunset on the Orientale and watch the fishing boats coming home. Tourists could buy postcards of these and other pleasant scenes from the photography studio on the Corso, the main commercial street.

That same studio on the Corso gained Fascist Party favour by making cards celebrating Italy's imperial conquests. One of those products, showing a local boy urinating on the sanctions imposed by the League of Nations, was turned into a nationwide propaganda poster.[6] Reminders of the Fascist state were omnipresent in Ortona. The Fascist Party symbol, the fascio (a bundle of rods with an axe) loomed above the balcony of the municipal building overlooking Piazza Municipio, the town's main square. Also on the square stood the Casa del Fascio, the local Fascist Party headquarters. Phrases from Mussolini's speeches were inscribed on walls throughout the town. In the school, Mussolini's portrait hung high in every classroom on the wall behind the teacher's desk. In gym class, the children wore shirts emblazoned with the letter M. It's impossible to know how many in Ortona genuinely supported the fascist regime. Any sign of dissent could result in beatings from Mussolini's Blackshirts, loss of employment, and arrest and imprisonment.

It was Mussolini who coined the term "Axis" to describe the alliance he forged with Hitler. In 1940, Italy entered World War II on Germany's side. By then, however, the country had already been weakened by sanctions and imperial overreach. The war soon brought further economic austerity, mounting military defeats, and growing civil and military discontent. By July 1943, when Allied armies landed in Sicily, most of the defending was carried out by German forces, as few Italian soldiers still wanted to fight.

The rapid conquest of Sicily by the Allies triggered a palace coup in Rome. On July 25, King Vittorio Emanuele III and the Army Chief of Staff deposed Mussolini, had him imprisoned, and dissolved the National Fascist Party. That evening in Ortona, as in many places across Italy, people gathered in the Corso to celebrate the fall of the regime. In Piazza Municipio, they climbed the town hall's balcony, tore the fascio from the wall, and sent it crashing to the street. Portraits of Mussolini were hurled from windows; his words on walls were hastily painted over; the Casa del Fascio was attacked and ransacked. Amid the joy, a few revenge beatings were meted out against the Fascist Party's local street-level enforcers.

In early September, people rejoiced again when the new government signed an armistice with the Allies. Their joy, however, was short-lived. Hitler immediately sent an invading force to occupy Italy, liberate Mussolini, reinstate a fascist government in the north, and block the Allies in the south. Members of Italy's new government and royal family fled overland from Rome to Ortona, and with help from Ortona's fishermen, they escaped through the harbour to a navy corvette. All over the country, leaderless and confused, the Italian army collapsed. More than six hundred thousand Italian soldiers were captured and taken to work as slave labourers in Germany (where many thousands of them died). Soldiers tried to evade that fate by donning civilian clothing. When German units passed through Ortona heading south to confront the Allies, rifles and uniforms of fleeing Italian soldiers lay in heaps at the foot of the escarpment.[7]

For three months, the Germans fought rearguard actions in southern Italy while across the country's mid-point they prepared a defensive line. The eastern anchor of that "Winter Line" line was Ortona.[8] In November, the occupying German army ordered all the town's residents to leave. Many sought shelter in the countryside; some defied the Germans and remained in town, hiding in churches, the hospital, and house basements.

Meanwhile, the British Eighth Army was approaching. Led by General Bernard Montgomery, their objective was not Ortona, but the coastal city of Pescara, twenty kilometres to the north. From there, they would gain access to a route across the interior mountains to Rome. At the same time, on the western side of Italy, the US Fifth Army was advancing north towards Rome from Naples. In late November, at the start of their push up the Adriatic coast, General Montgomery rallied his troops with the words: "We will now hit the Germans a colossal crack!"

In early December, the mission of delivering that crack was handed over to the Eighth Army's New Zealand, Indian, and Canadian divisions. Between the Maiella Mountains and the sea, the front was twenty kilometres wide. The 1st Canadian Infantry Division led by Major-General Chris Vokes was responsible for the easternmost, coastal side of the attack.

The progress of all three Commonwealth units was hindered not only by strong German resistance but also by the landscape and weather; the terrain of tightly folded hills and gullies favoured defenders, and persistent rains limited the Allies' air support and mired their tanks in mud. After nearly three weeks of hard fighting, the Canadians, Indians, and New Zealanders had advanced only a few kilometres. The Canadians drew up to the crest of San Donato hill, from where they looked across the *Fosso Saraceni*—known to them as "The Gully"—toward Ortona. Vokes gave the task of attacking the town to regiments from the Canadian west. On December 20, men of the Loyal Edmonton Regiment and Vancouver's Seaforth Highlanders descended into the gully and fought their way up Ortona's southern slopes.[9]

The Canadians were not expecting the Germans to make a stand in the town. From prior experience, it was assumed the enemy would only briefly defend before withdrawing north to the next river. However, the German defenders had been ordered to hold the line by Hitler. They belonged to the German 1st Parachute Division, the *Fallschirmjäger* (literally, "parachute hunters"), an elite, all-volunteer force renowned for their airborne assault on Crete. Mythologized in Nazi propaganda as "the Führer's boldest elite unit," the *Fallschirmjäger* were considered the epitome of German manhood, fighting lightly armed with great courage and ingenuity against the Allied armies' so-called debased "mixture of peoples."

Apart from the obnoxious racism of this myth, it also somewhat (though not entirely) exaggerated the paratroopers' abilities. By the time they reached Ortona, many of their best soldiers had been lost on the Russian front. Their reinforcements were young and inexperienced; many were not qualified to parachute.[10] Nevertheless, the *Fallschirmjäger* remained a skilled and dedicated unit. Preparing to hold Ortona, they demolished buildings and created rubble piles designed to channel the enemy into "killing zones." In key positions, they placed heavy machine guns, snipers, mines, and booby traps.

When the Edmontons and Seaforths entered the town, they found themselves in an unexpectedly fierce fight.

The westerners quickly devised a tactic to avoid the killing zones in the streets: blasting through walls in the upper stories of connected buildings. They called it "mouse-holing." In this way, they fought the Germans house by house and block by block through Ortona. Where the streets were wide enough and could be cleared of rubble, tanks from Canada's Three Rivers Regiment provided support. The battle continued for seven days with no break for Christmas. In a radio broadcast from Ortona, Matthew Halton of the Canadian Broadcasting Corporation described it to his audience at home:

> An epic thing is happening amid the crumbling and burning walls of the compact town . . . For seven days and seven nights the Canadians have been trying to clear the town and the action is as fierce as perhaps modern man has ever fought. For seven days and seven nights the Canadians have been attacking in Ortona, yard by yard, building by building, window by window. And for seven days and seven nights the sullen young zealots of a crack German parachute division have been defending like demons. Canadian

> and German seem to be both beyond exhaustion and beyond fear. The battle has the quality of a nightmare. It has a special quality of it own, like . . . the fight at Stalingrad . . . the same apocalyptic pall of smoke and fire and maniacal determination . . . The splitting steel storm never stops and the men in there are as if possessed.

And then, in the early morning of December 28, the air in Ortona was strangely quiet. The Canadians advanced and met no resistance. The Germans had left in the night.

Ortona was the hardest battle the Canadian army had fought to this point in the war. Canadian losses in the town were 108 killed and 191 wounded. Soldiers taken out of battle and treated for psychological distress were not counted as wounded, but the divisional psychiatrist reported a sharp increase in their number during the week of December 22–29, totalling 237 across the division. German commanders recorded their losses as 68 killed, 159 wounded, 205 missing, and 23 sick. Many of those Germans counted as missing must have been killed, as the Canadians discovered and buried more than a hundred bodies of paratroopers while clearing the wreckage after the battle. An estimated two hundred Italian civilians were also killed in the crossfire of bullets, shells, and exploded buildings. An uncounted number were left with permanent disabilities, and at least forty children were orphaned. Ortona was left in ruins, entire blocks reduced to rubble. The port, its boats, and all public buildings were destroyed. More than half of the residences in town were unliveable and damaged beyond repair. The medieval church of Santa Maria delle Grazie was blasted through from front to back, and the cathedral of San Tommaso lost its entire facade and half its dome. Even the cemetery was desecrated, with graves blown open by bombs.[11]

Among the dead and debris on the Corso, the Canadians picked up postcards of Ortona that had been blasted from shops and scattered all around. At the town's entrance, the Canadians put up a sign:[12]

THIS IS ORTONA
A WEST CANADIAN TOWN

More than a half century later, I travelled across western Canada seeking the men who had fought in Ortona. When I met them, these men were in their seventies; at the time of the battle, they had been as young as eighteen. I was a twenty-nine-year-old student pursuing my PhD in anthropology. This journey among the veterans was the fieldwork for my dissertation.

I WOULDN'T SAY THAT I had a personal connection to the topic. None of my close family members had served in the war. Growing up, I learned about World War II from the culture around me—movies, comic books, toy soldiers, and the annual November 11 Remembrance Day activities at school. The Italian Campaign was rarely mentioned. The stories were about other events in the war—D-Day, the Battle of Britain, the liberation of the Netherlands. In Canada at the time, Ortona was mostly unknown.

I learned about Ortona quite early in my life, without knowing it was Ortona I was learning about. This happened through the work of one of my favourite childhood authors. I was an avid reader of Farley Mowat, a writer of sympathetic and scientific tales of animals and people in the northern Canadian wilderness. *The Dog Who Wouldn't Be. Lost in the Barrens. Never Cry Wolf.* Mowat seemed the kind of man I could imagine one day becoming myself. When I picked up his book *And No Birds Sang*, I was surprised to find it was a memoir of war. From this, I discovered there had been fighting in Italy and that Canadians had been part of it. I was a bit too young to fully comprehend, but I understood enough to realize that Mowat's war story was unlike any others I'd encountered. The story ended unexpectedly, not with the author returning home, but on the front line with his mental breakdown. Mowat didn't explain, but I pieced together that it was a short time after the end of this story that he'd gone into the Canadian north to do the work that inspired me. Learning this left me with a deep impression, a feeling I couldn't name.

As I got older, I had other interests and didn't read Mowat anymore. However, when I was starting my PhD fieldwork, I remembered *And No Birds Sang*. I looked back at the book. The place where the story ended was a hill outside Ortona.[13]

Another way in which the war in Italy cropped up earlier in my life was a curious conversation I had one day with a man I'd known since childhood. This was a carpenter who sometimes did work on my family's eastern Ontario farm. I say I knew him, but up to this point I really knew nothing about him. He was an older man of few words, polite but serious, and for a bookish kid like me he seemed unapproachable, tough as nails. One day when I was eighteen, he came by the farm to do a job. This time when he saw me, he paused, unusually, to talk. I'd been attending an international school in Italy and was home now on summer break. He'd heard about my foreign travels and was curious to know what I'd seen. His questions became more and more detailed. *Had I been to Sicily? Had I been to Mount Etna? Was there still a bar on the mountain? Did it still serve this drink?* I was startled that this local guy, whom I'd only ever seen cutting two-by-fours and putting new roofs onto barns, knew all of this Italian geography and culture that I had only just discovered for myself. Obviously he had been to that country—as a tourist, I assumed. I asked him when he'd been. *Nineteen forty-three*, he said. After a moment, I connected the dots. He had been there as a soldier. But when I remarked that he was a veteran, he seemed to recoil at the word. He didn't think of himself that way, he said—and then he left me to get on with his job.

If those moments played any role in how I arrived at my PhD topic, however, I certainly wasn't aware of it. At the age of twenty-nine, I was hardly going around with the feeling that life was calling me to Ortona. When I was starting the doctoral program and casting about for ideas on what to do, this was not the first—nor the second or third—topic that came to mind. My initial research proposals had nothing even to do with war; if one of those earlier funding requests had succeeded, I would have gone off to study a different topic in a different part of the world. When eventually I landed on the idea of research related to war veterans, in some ways I was simply riding one of the currents of the time. In the 1990s there was a surge of interest in war commemoration. There were public ceremonies of the fiftieth anniversaries of D-Day and the Liberation of the Netherlands. One of the sensational films of the decade was *Saving Private Ryan*. The veterans of World War II were very much on people's minds—due in no small part to the fact that the "war generation" was aging and soon would no longer be around. When I proposed a project that spoke to these themes, I got the funding to support it.[14]

What were my research objectives? What exactly did I set out to learn? That's hard for me to remember now—and I'm happy to forget. If I were faced now with that project proposal from twenty-seven years ago, I'm sure I'd wince like the old carpenter—I don't think of myself that way. At the time when I planned the project, I was working in a small and hyper-critical corner of academia, aiming to make a career in that world, and drawn especially to the most difficult and enigmatic French and German theorists; there was cachet in mastering their ideas. My project was set up to advance and critique those and other theories that were cutting edge in cultural anthropology. As for the battle of Ortona, I came upon it quite randomly when I read a small news item about a group of veterans who were going to commemorate it.[15] The contrast between the battle's original intensity and its present-day obscurity made it a conceptually interesting case study in social memory, or how groups and nations recall the past. This is not to say that I wasn't genuinely interested in the topic. But I went into it with a mind that was busy and anxious, preoccupied with how I was going to excel intellectually and distinguish myself in the highly competitive job market of Canadian universities.

All of that changed when I met the veterans. Within weeks—maybe even within the first days—the theory-driven framing of my project faded away.

In the first few encounters, I tried to explain myself to them in precise and accurate terms. This was important, I believed, for the "informed" part of getting my research participants' informed consent. The participants should know that I was a PhD student in anthropology, and what "anthropology" meant. They should know that this was a case study in . . . something I was finding harder and harder to say. Eyes were glazing over. The veterans were hardly listening. They regarded my project description, I think, as some kind of red tape that I sadly had to run through. In their minds they already knew what I was about. My purpose was self-evident. It needed no justification. To the veterans, there was nothing complicated about me at all.

Mel and Sam took me to the Edmonton Kingsway Legion. Around the tables in the dining hall, the introductions went like this:

"He's the guy who wants to know about Ortona."

It was the second or third day of my fieldwork and I was in the City of Edmonton Archives, inside the Prince of Wales Armouries Heritage Centre, turning the pages of a thick records file. The file's label was interesting—"War of '39" not "World War II" as you might expect. At the time when the file was created, I guessed, people hadn't settled on a name; they didn't yet know how big this war was going to be.

The pages in the file were pasted with newspaper clippings relating to the men of the Loyal Edmonton Regiment. The men were overseas. There were stories of them training in England, and then—deeper in the file—stories of them fighting in Italy. For many readers of these stories, maybe including the archivist who had cut and pasted them, these men were their sons, husbands, brothers, and fathers.

Here was a newspaper clipping from Christmas Eve, 1943. It was the first Christmas that the men were in combat.

> December 25 is Christmas in Ortona, Italy, as it is in Canada. For the battle-weary Canadians pushing their way through its tattered streets it will be another day of fighting, of killing, and of dying. Still it will be Christmas for them, too, symbol of the universal peace for which they fight.

Turning the page, I was jolted by the headline.

> CANADIANS DIG LAST NAZIS
> OUT WITH BAYONETS

Feeling a slight discomfort in my gut, I continued reading.

> A military commentator said that the enemy still held one corner of Ortona and that many of the Germans were sticking to the

> death rather than retreat. This had turned the Canadians' struggle for the city into a house-to-house campaign with bayonets and small arms.

Another page. The battle was over. Here was an article telling how it had been won by western Canadian regiments. The article celebrated the character of the men.

> These prairie farmers are the men who blasted and sniped their way through Ortona. The great majority of them have shooting for their hobby in peacetime and have camped in the Rockies and foothills. Maj. Stone, for instance, carries a rifle rather than the regulation officer's pistol. He has hunted moose in the Peace River country for 15 years and has no time for toys like pistols.

That must have been a comforting message for the people who were reading at home, a reassurance that their men were strong and spirited and that, whatever the war was doing to them, these were still the men you knew, the men who had camped and farmed in peacetime.

I would come back to make copies of the articles. For now, though, I closed the file and returned it to the desk. I had an appointment for my first interview. I went down to the ground floor of the atrium to meet Mel.

A few days earlier at the Legion, I'd observed that Mel was well respected. He was tall, soft-spoken, and youthful for his seventy-seven years. He didn't have a formal leadership role—and during the war he'd only been a private, the army's lowest rank—but going around the hall, he was frequently stopped and held in conversation by many of the men. He was modest and a careful listener; perhaps that's what made him popular. When conversations among the veterans sometimes turned raucous and off-colour, Mel appeared comfortable in their midst, but his own manner remained unswervingly quiet and polite.

I learned more about him while he was driving me to his place. He'd grown up in a coal mining town called Wayne in southern Alberta. Before the war, he said, life had been hard. He'd quit school after grade nine to join his father and his brother in the mines. After the war, he'd gone back to the same job as before, the only difference being that now he wore his old army uniform as his work clothes. Then the mines shut down. Wayne became a ghost town. Mel moved to Edmonton and found new work, first in an auto parts department, then in a road sign factory for the Alberta Ministry of Highways.

I asked him what that had been like. It was good, he said, paid the bills, and was even interesting sometimes. He recalled how busy the factory got when Canada switched to the metric system from imperial. Not only did the factory have to make all new metric road signs; they also had to keep replacing them. That's because people kept shooting them. Especially down around Red Deer, Mel said. "There were some real wingnuts down there." Replacing all those shot-up signs cost the province fifty thousand dollars, which was a lot of money back then. As for the old imperial signs, Mel decided to keep a collection. He put them up on the factory wall and joked that it was a "sign museum." Word got around that Mel was "creative" and his managers started asking him to work on designs. He enjoyed doing that, but really, he said, the factory should have hired a real designer. One of his designs, a sign for farmer's markets, was trashed by the *Edmonton Journal*. Imagine—a road sign so bad it got reviewed in the newspaper. Mel couldn't argue with the review. What did he know about design? But still today—he said with a smirk—every farmer's market in Alberta was signposted by his own badly done handiwork.

Mel and his wife Eva lived in a condominium community for seniors. When Mel and I arrived at the apartment, Eva was making us lunch. The dish she was cooking, she said, was called *won ton soup*, something she'd learned from the Chinese lady next door. It was a very mild dish, good for Mel's sensitive stomach—but she could make me a sandwich if I didn't like Chinese. Mel said that this couple from China had recently moved into the community and it was great—he and Eva were learning so many new things.

After lunch, it was time for the interview.

I followed Mel into his study. He closed the door and went behind his desk, taking a seat in a high-backed swivel chair. I sat in an armchair, took my clipboard from my bag, and set up my tape recorder. Mel remarked that he felt strange behind the desk. With a slight chuckle, he got up, wheeled his chair around to my side, and sat down again, hands resting on his stomach.

I didn't need to explain. Mel knew my topic.

The cheer on his face rapidly faded.

"That's uh, yeah, there was some awful experiences there. Uh . . ."

He paused.

"Not so much tales of derring-do but, uh, more surviving than, than . . ."

He paused again.

"Mind you, you had a gun and you used it whenever you could."

IT WAS EASY TO become that person, the guy who wanted to know. Maybe it was the effect of their stories. Maybe it was something deep in my nature brought to life by their expectations. In a short time, I found myself wanting to know all that I could about Ortona. I didn't pause to wonder why.

The more that I learned, the more gaps became apparent in my picture of the battle. I wanted to fill all of them. This guy who was mentioned—was he still alive? Could I find him and interview him? This incident in this story—was there anyone who could tell me more? Could someone explain a curious detail in this photograph? What might it mean to this veteran? What memories might it stir? One man put me in touch with another who put me in touch with another, and so it went. I found other men's names in archives and regimental lists, looked for their names in phone directories, and called them up. I went to archives in Edmonton, Vancouver, Victoria, and Ottawa, studying and copying army records, newspaper clippings, oral history recordings, maps, and photographs. I went to Ortona and lived there for three months to see what insights that might bring. For a year and more, my life was immersed in the time and space of the battle.

I was going with the flow, following the stories, behaving like a collector or maybe an obsessive artist. But I was supposed to be on the path to becoming an anthropologist. Out of all this material that I was gathering, I was going to have to build an intellectual argument, something that could be credited as a contribution to anthropological knowledge. And yet I'd gone so far and still couldn't explain to myself the larger purpose of my work. Having abandoned my original objective, I hadn't come up with a new one, apart from this impulse to be what the veterans thought I was: the guy who wants to know.

This did worry me a little.

However, I reassured myself that it would not remain a problem. In the fieldwork tradition of anthropology, it was normal, even expected, for your plans to be overturned. Many of the legendary works by anthropologists told stories of this happening. The fieldworker goes to that Pacific island with a set of carefully developed research questions, all of which become irrelevant on arrival when it's learned that the islanders have completely different things going on. My first anthropology professor had even been forced by circumstances to alter his plans while he was still on the ship, moving to a different island than the one he'd prepared to study. Another emphasis of the traditional method is deep immersion in unfamiliar ways of living. In the early stages there's culture shock, and little of what's happening around the fieldworker makes sense to them; however, with time and effort comes understanding, as does empathy for the lives of others. Those stories had inspired me. Those scholars had been disoriented, yet followed their intuition, and worked it out. I would do the same.[16]

Furthermore, I felt intuitively that in the course of talking with the veterans, I was tracking something substantial. Something was beneath the surface details of the stories of Ortona. I couldn't tell what it was, but I knew it when I encountered it. Its presence was felt in certain moments when the stories weren't making sense—or when the stories were going on as usual but there was a mysterious alteration in the narrator's voice. It was felt in momentary breakdowns in my comprehension when I lost my bearings while listening and I instinctively felt something at risk. Was I the only one experiencing this? Or were the veterans aware of it too? It was never brought into the open. I wouldn't know how to begin to discuss it. But whatever this phenomenon was, I sensed there was a pattern to its occurrence. It had some kind of meaning and I was sure it was important somehow.

I came home from fieldwork, transcribed all of the interviews, and examined all of my material.

Nothing came.

I looked for guidance and insight in the literature of my discipline.

Still nothing. I was no further ahead.

This wasn't working out like the stories of the legendary scholars.

The enormity of my plight began to dawn on me. I was lost, without a clue to what my research had been about.

Whatever it was that I had naively tracked in my fieldwork, it had not been covered by my training. Worse, I couldn't even guess what sort of training I would have required. I couldn't name the problem. What was the nature of this phenomenon that I was trying to interpret? Was it just some trivial personal feeling that I had got? Surely I wasn't that foolish; there must be more to it than that. But I lacked the words, the concepts, that would allow me to think my way further.

It was a dead-end struggle that continued for two years. Every path I took led me to a cul-de-sac. Then the money ran out. In order to stay close to my goals, I got onto the hamster wheel of low-paid university contract teaching. On the side, whenever I could make the time (which wasn't often) I spun the other hamster wheel of trying to write up what I had done. More years passed with no progress. Eight. Nine. The life consequences of getting nowhere started adding up. In desperation, I tried to cease caring what I wrote for the dissertation. Any argument, I told myself, any interpretation that could earn me a pass, would do. Even that didn't work. Maybe it was integrity, maybe some other affliction, but I just couldn't put words together for what I didn't feel was right. How had I got myself into this hole? I had always been a good student. I'd been told my future was bright.

The angst became all-encompassing. Even my dreams went in hopeless rounds.

Shooting at the bell tower. Leaning on the wall. German prisoners singing. The Indian sniper losing hope. Strange death in the olive grove.

The gift from the little Italian girl whose words he didn't understand. The imploring look on his face. His struggle to get the words out. My sudden feeling of shame. Mel's narratives had conjured so many mysterious images and sensations, I felt I'd spent the whole day in a dream.

Now I was coming back to reality. At the tables around me, young people were drinking chais and lattes, doing homework, and chatting in small groups. The usual coffeehouse music was playing, well suited to the evening and the university crowd. The upper-level café overlooked the bookstore's main floor and big front windows. On the busy avenue outside it was cold, dark, and snowing. It was good to be here under warm lights in this world of books.

I had just purchased one. By incredible coincidence, I'd found on the new releases table a title on the very topic of my research: *Ortona: Canada's Epic World War II Battle*.[17] On the front cover was an image of Canadian soldiers and tanks on a street among ruined buildings. The hardcover's jacket copy foretold that this reading experience would be intense.

> In one blood-soaked, furious week of fighting, from December 20 to December 27, 1943, the 1st Canadian Infantry Division took the town of Ortona, Italy, from elite German paratroopers ordered to hold the medieval port town at all costs. Infantrymen serving in the Loyal Edmonton Regiment and the Seaforth Highlanders, supported by tankers of the Three Rivers Regiment, moved from house to house in hand-to-hand combat amid heavy shelling and wrested the town from the grip of the fierce German defenders.

That tone of grim ferocity reminded me of newspaper clippings I'd read in the archives earlier that day. I skimmed the book, looking for more descriptions of the action.

Here was a moment from early in the battle. The Edmontons had gained the upper floor of a house, surprising the Germans who were outdoors below.

> Rifles, Bren guns, and Thompson submachine guns poked out of the windows and opened fire as one. The Germans died in place.

Aha. Now here was an explanation of the house-to-house fighting. The Canadians had made their way down a street by blasting through walls of attached buildings. I'd heard the veterans refer to this tactic as "house-clearing" or sometimes as "mouse-holing." Here was my first clear description of it.

> The process of clearing floors was dangerous and bloody business. When a hole had been breached in the wall, the first section hurled a few grenades through. After these exploded, one or two men would jump into the smoke- and dust-filled room and rake it with Thompson submachine-gun fire. If there were any paratroopers in the room, they usually died before they could react.

Something felt odd as I read. What was it?

> Guns poked out. Germans died.

Something in the text was being hidden from view, conspicuously unspoken, held strenuously at bay like a tight, repressed coil.

The moment with Mel came to mind.

Mel had started out by telling me about his struggle with his stomach. He predicted that during the interview his stomach would start acting up.

He told me this in order to tell me not to worry about it; he was used to it; he didn't want it to stop us from talking about anything that mattered. His troubles with his stomach had started during the war, he said, beginning in Ortona—when he was "in the line," the term that he and others used for being in combat. Ortona had been his first real battle and it had gone on for days and days.

"You know, whenever you're in the line, you're on two hours and off two hours, and my two hours off I was either heavin' my guts or, I couldn't sleep or, just like a, like an iron poker, a hot poker in your stomach, you know?"[18]

"You were two hours on and two hours off?"

"Two hours on. Yeah. We were relieved every once in a while by another company, you know."

"What was it that you'd do when you were on? Would you be led up the street somewhere, or—"

"Yeah, yeah, you'd go up the street and uh, go into the next house, you know, and uh, throw a hand grenade first and go in with your gun and, you know. So—"

Mel paused. He had just begun to answer my question. Something was putting him off track.

"Yeah, these, these, these are things that I, that I say I was trying to erase from—and I did a fairly good job I guess but uh—but things that you try and erase from your memory because how much good does it do you to recall it."

He paused again. Suddenly he seemed overcome by a thought that he urgently needed to share.

"I—I don't think—I don't think any veteran wants—wants the schoolkids today to—to glamorize war or anything. It's a terrible thing. Nobody should have to go through it."

His stammer worsened. His face was pained.

"What—what—what—what fun is there, what—what is there to killing each other? You know? And really, the only thing we've learned over these wars is how better to kill each other, and how—how many more people we can kill at the one time, you know."

I observed him in stunned silence. A wave of shame went through me. This was the answer to my question about house clearing. What a thing to want to know. What on earth was I doing, asking this kind old man to tell me how he had killed?

Mel concluded.

"That's the only thing that we've learned over wars."

THERAPY WASN'T REALLY A decision, more like something I fell into. By the time that happened, the dissertation was only one of the issues. It didn't even top the list.

However, as I worked through my problems as a client in psychotherapy, one of the positive outcomes was a new perspective on the PhD. This new perspective was that I could simply give it up.

After so much work, of course, it would be a shame not to get the degree; but it would be a greater shame to carry on stubbornly and be ruined by the effort. This decision not to finish didn't have to be a tragedy. For too long, I'd been narrowly focused on academia. High hopes had got me into that world, but the wrong reasons were keeping me in. There was more to life than this.

But if I abandoned the project—I wondered—would I be letting down the men who had told me their stories? This concerned me. But it also occurred to me that none of the men had ever signalled that they expected anything more. In all of the time since I'd concluded my fieldwork, I'd never heard again from a single one of them. In the interviews, they had talked; I had listened. They had been helpful to me; maybe they felt that whatever they got from doing so was good enough. Even so, however, on the edge of my decision to quit, I wished that I could do more. The veterans had told me so much. I wondered if I might still manage to write something—nothing academic, to be sure, but something—provided that I could bear to live with the topic a little more. It was in that spirit, ready to say farewell, that I went back for a final look at the transcripts. I hadn't looked at them for years.

I was astonished by what I found. It was like a fog had lifted, revealing whole new vistas—hills, trees, islands, an ocean horizon. The difference in comprehension was akin to returning to read a book as an adult that you'd struggled with as a child. What made the difference in reading was my new awareness of psychodynamics in narrative. As a client in therapy, I had learned to identify this in myself; now I could see it happening between myself and others on the page. Those moments in the interviews where I had vaguely sensed something beyond the words, now I was able to discern. I had the vocabulary, the concepts; they came to me naturally. Here was an instance of rumination or obsessional review. Here was a sudden topic shift, possibly motivated by a hidden association. Here was a recurring, unusual metaphor—some kind of personal symbol. Here was a false start and pronoun shift that might be a clue to implicit meaning.

That's not to say that I saw through to all of the answers. But I knew these phenomena were real, they mattered, and there were sound methods for examining them. I knew what interpretive tools I needed, what training I had been lacking. These were in areas of scholarship—psychoanalysis, sociolinguistics, conversation analysis—that I hadn't previously known how to read selectively, nor grasped their relevance to my work. Now I did.[19]

Furthermore, my intuition during my fieldwork had been correct—there was indeed a pattern to these moments of narrative mystery. These were symptoms of mental struggles to repress or heal emotional wounds. The struggles took different forms for different men. Sam had been trying to find peace by compulsively searching for vindicating details. Mel was committed to remembering others who had been wounded worse than him. Bill had been deeply traumatized by a moment of empathy that got violently upended. Ted was spiritually troubled and seeking atonement through public ritual. Maurice was also trying to atone through his private searching for a lost place. The contexts varied, but the struggles all had a common theme. Indeed, this theme had been in front of me all along. It was in the word that Norman had tripped on. It was Mel's "only thing that we've learned."

I could make an intellectual argument from this. A lot more work was ahead, but the way forward was finally clear.

I wrote the dissertation, passed the defence, got the degree.

It was done.

Then, having done it, I was desperate to get away.

For fourteen years, I'd been stuck in this topic. It wasn't uplifting—it was dragging me down. I needed to get it out of my life.

A deep aversion to your PhD material is not conducive to an academic career. The dissertation is typically the basis for your first scholarly publications. It's your resource, your capital, for establishing your authority, expertise, and the reasons for anyone to hire you. But the very last thing I wanted was to be an authority on this dissertation. Teaching about it, writing about it, arguing about it with others—that was not who I wanted to be. It had never been my plan to be an expert in this area. I had stumbled into it unwittingly. Certainly, I'd made the best of it and grown wiser from the experience. But I was spent. To live with it any longer would not feel like living at all.

So I left. There were other lines of work where it was useful to have this degree and where there was also no need to talk about it. There were places where I could apply my skills without it mattering how I had learned them. The unwelcome past didn't follow me. No one knew or cared to ask. I could do my job, accomplish new things, and that was good enough.

IT'S TWENTY-FIVE YEARS since my fieldwork. Eighty-two years since the event that the fieldwork was somehow about. The men I interviewed are all dead.

And in the middle of my living room floor, I'm looking at this box.

I carried it up here from storage.

It makes me think of Norman. The box where he kept his "Safe Conduct."

It also makes me think of Sam. He had a lot of these boxes. We spent a whole weekend going through them. I think he had three at least.

Sam was an exception. No one else had that many. But many of the veterans had a box like this, and they all described it the same way. It was the box of their war souvenirs.

Do I call my box anything? I've never had reason to speak of it. Box of my fieldwork, I guess.

I know what's inside. Field notes, cassette tapes, documents, address lists, copies from the archives, photographs, maps, and the odd thing that's a sort of souvenir of the road.

Memories of their memories.

He's the guy who wants to know.

Do I want to be that guy again?

What am I doing with this box?

CHAPTER 2

Boots and Souvenirs

I REMEMBER THE SOUND of the wipers on the windshield of Sam's car. We were driving up the northern highway in the early winter darkness. The road was wet from gently falling snow. Huge trucks blew spray onto our windshield as they thundered past, hauling loads of gigantic logs. Somewhere to the north, forests of massive trees were being harvested. Here, where we were driving, there were just a few plots of woods among the low barren hills. In the distance I could see the silhouette of a working pumpjack and the light of a gas flare.

We stopped at a gas station. While filling the tank, Sam remembered that he had a friend nearby who'd been a sniper in Ortona. He said this would be a good guy for me to meet. If I didn't mind delaying our dinner at the restaurant, maybe he'd call the guy and ask if we could drop in. I said sure, let's do it. Sam went to use the payphone and came back with the word that we were invited over right away.

A dirt road took us into an evergreen forest where the branches were laden with snow. The trees cleared briefly when the road crossed some train tracks, and then came thick around us again. We arrived at a clearing where there was a little wooden house with smoke rising from its chimney. It had a brightly lit window, and a brightly lit doorway that was open with a man standing in it. We got out of the car and Sam said some words of greeting. His friend Jim answered with a muttered word and a nod.

Jim was short and stocky with baggy eyes and a gruff, grey-whiskered face. He was in a plaid shirt, cardigan with holes in it, loose jeans, and puffy slippers—quite a contrast to Sam, who was skinny and extra clean-cut after shaving, combing his hair, and dressing up for the restaurant. When I started to remove my boots at the door, Jim brusquely grumbled that he didn't follow that "stupid rule"—I should leave my boots on.

We went to the Formica kitchen table where there was a choice of mismatching chairs. I started to take an old wooden one, but Jim pushed a chair on wheels my way, saying this would be more comfortable. On the table stood three mugs with images of Alberta and the Calgary Olympics, and an ashtray. Sam started introducing me, saying that I was a student from Toronto. Jim shuffled to the stove, came back with a steaming pot, poured oily black tea into the mugs, and sat down with a cigarette, all while listening to Sam telling him about our work on Sam's war souvenirs. The refrigerator was humming. A bulletin board on the wall had pinned to it a drugstore calendar, receipts, handwritten notes, and a war remembrance red poppy. I took my tape recorder from my bag and started to say my usual words to introduce my research.

Suddenly Jim was staring at me, panic-stricken.

"I can't talk about those things," he gasped.

He turned to Sam. "I can't talk about those things."

He turned back to me. "I'm sorry."

I said it was fine, no problem. Hurriedly, I tucked my recorder back into my bag. This was awkward. It had happened so quickly. I had assumed that, in his phone call, Sam had told Jim about my research and Jim had agreed to be interviewed. Stupid of me. Poor Jim had been caught completely unawares.

Sam didn't seem the least bit troubled.

"Well," he said, "it's easier to remember the good times."

And then Sam carried right on talking about the war.

I wanted to tell Sam that this really wasn't necessary. Jim was staring at him helplessly. His cigarette hand was shaking. I was wishing that Sam would stop.

Sam asked Jim if he remembered the women in England. "It was amazing," Sam said. "All they wanted to do was get married." Jim nodded. Sam continued. "I told some of the girls that I owned a gopher farm back in Alberta. And goddamn it, they believed me!" Jim grinned and took an unsteady puff of his cigarette.

Sam asked Jim if he remembered going through that town in Italy where they'd seen the cathouse. Later, when they got some time off, some of the guys had gone back to it. "They just walked in the cathouse door and right away they were grabbed by the MPs [military police] who had been there waitin' for them!" Jim nodded, grinned, and muttered. "Yeah, those MPs, they knew someone would be tryin' that."

I had been silent all this time after giving that fright to Jim. Now I spoke up.

"Sorry, what—what's a cathouse?"

Sam and Jim both froze, looking at me. Maybe they'd forgotten I was there.

Then they erupted in laughter.

"That's another word for a whorehouse," Sam said.

Jim was cackling, his whole body shaking. He wiped tears from his eyes.

Sam continued with the funny stories, asking Jim, did he remember this, did he remember that. Jim relaxed with his elbows on the table, grunting, grinning, nodding along. Did Jim remember the old Italian asking them if they knew Joe DiMaggio. Did Jim remember stepping in shit from the donkey trains. Did Jim remember the sergeant liberating wine and chickens from the farms. Yep, yep, Jim muttered, puffing on his cigarette, tapping out the ashes.

Sam asked, "Do you remember landing in Sicily and jumping into six feet of water?" Jim nodded vigorously. Sam went on. "And we had those goddamn heavy packs on our backs."[1]

Sam turned to me. "You see how short Jim is. Can you imagine?"

Jim muttered something about the guy next to him telling him to put his arm around his shoulder, the guy helping him to keep his head above the water.

Sam said, "I remember this big Scottish sergeant, when I went under, he grabbed me and he pulled me along, and he was yelling, '*Come on, Canada, you can make it!*'"

Jim cackled again, shaking with laughter, but his face was turning red in a grimace. His lip quivered. A tear streamed down his cheek. He stubbed his cigarette and wiped his wet eyes with his calloused hand.

Sam went on remembering this, remembering that, while Jim listened and agreed. Then the house began to vibrate. Through the forest outside came a slow thumping mechanical sound. It was the approach of a freight train. The noise grew louder and louder, to the point that I felt the train was going right through us. The little house reverberated to the rhythmic squeaks and bangs. Sam continued talking as if nothing were happening. I could barely make out his words.

Gradually the sounds of the train receded. The house became very still. Sam paused at the end of a story.

"Well," he said.

He sat up straight. It was time for us to be going.

Snow crunched under our feet as we walked outside to the car. Sam stopped in front of a tree and took a long, loud piss on its trunk. I looked up. The snow had stopped falling. It was a clear, moonless, starry night. I could smell the smoke from the wood burning in Jim's stove.

We got into Sam's car. As he put it in reverse, Sam said to me, "I'm sorry that wasn't very useful."

In the window of Jim's house, brightly lit, I saw the whiskered face watching our departure. Then the face, window, and house disappeared behind trees as we turned onto the road. I said no, no, it was useful. It was good to meet Jim, interesting to hear the stories.

We drove across the train tracks and down the dirt road. "Jim drank a lot after the war," Sam said, "and it affected his memory. He was a sniper, so he saw a lot of the action. But he lost his memory from drinking."

That got Sam onto the topic of his own methods for remembering—"See, I never drank. This is how I can remember in such good detail"—as he steered the car onto the paved highway and started us back on our way.

But I was thinking about something else as I got my recorder back out to resume taping. I was thinking that Jim's problem with memory was not really that he had lost it.

I SPENT A WEEKEND with Sam. He lived in a modest bungalow in a village north of Edmonton with his wife and a little white dog. On this weekend, his wife had gone into the city to play bingo and was staying there overnight—it was her regular bingo weekend with friends—so Sam had said it was a good time for me to visit and for us to "work," as he called it, on his "war souvenirs." He brought his cardboard boxes into the living room and for two days we went through them, sitting on the sofa together with the dog, removing papers and photographs and medals and books, examining it all on the coffee table and on the floor in front of the television. Sam was serious about remembering. He carried on telling stories about the war while making our lunch of canned soup and sandwiches, and while driving us around, going out in his car to run errands.

He took me to see one of his gravel pits. "I'm just making rock," he told me with a mischievous grin. That manner of grinning was characteristic of Sam. His resting face was a look of mild amusement, with keen eyes behind his wire-frame glasses. He was skinny, with buzz-cut hair. His fashion—always with multiple pens and a notebook tucked into his shirt's chest pocket—reminded me of my high-school science teachers. His business was supplying gravel for the expansions of the northern highways. Standing in a plot of dug-out land surrounded by birch trees, among piles of dirt and front-end loaders that were resting quiet for the weekend, Sam told me that he didn't really need the money. "It keeps me busy," he said. He believed in always working, keeping busy.

"I just keep puttin' one foot in front of the other."

He'd grown up in a small rural community of German immigrants in Alberta. He was fluent in German, having learnt it from his parents and from the German Saturday school he'd attended as a boy. Attended, that is, until one day the school's principal kicked him out for bringing a chipmunk to class. "That guy was a real Nazi." When the war started in 1939, Sam was an eighteen-year-old barber working on a boat in the Northwest Territories. He enlisted in the army because all the other guys from the boat were going. "It was the thing to do." After the war, he'd returned to being a barber, but started investing in land. He'd purchased cheap, rocky plots that everyone else thought were useless. People had laughed at him, he said, but he knew he could somehow profit. He credited his war experience with giving him this wisdom about the land.

"I was on that road just outside of Ortona, on the crossroads, eh? And that's when that Italian came along."

It was a story he'd told me already at his home. Now he was reminded of it as we stood in the middle of his gravel pit under a beautiful sunny sky.

"And, I said to him, *buon giorno*. And he says, hello. And uh, yeah, he spoke to me, he could speak in English, eh? And then he asked me, he says uh, do you guys know what you're doing over here? And I says yeah, if it wasn't for you bastards and Mussolini, and you'd have been on the right side, we wouldn't have been here. And then he says no that's not what I mean. He says look at that land. It's all holes in the ground. Trees are destroyed. Houses are destroyed. And he said, here, you're on it now, bleeding, urinating on it, dying on it. And he says, you'll always remember, when the land—when you're dead and gone—the land is still gonna be here. You know, like the land is gonna be producing again."

"Yeah," I said.

"And that's how come I got interested, and always after that, thought I would like to own a piece of land in my name. And I did accomplish that."

I wondered. Had this encounter at the Ortona crossroads really happened that way? Or had Sam dreamt it, and later mistaken it for real? Many of his stories had these cryptic qualities of dreams—rich in natural metaphors, colours, sounds, and uncanny coincidences. And yet Sam seemed to pride himself on being a man who was resolutely practical and objective. We went to the local land office, where he studied maps, thinking about future investments. We went to post a letter to his lawyer—he was fighting the rail company for putting a track through his land without permission. As for his war stories, Sam wanted them to be established on facts. His boxes were full of notes he had made while doing research to that end. In all of this activity, keeping busy, he rarely showed or admitted to any feelings. The notable exception was when, on returning to his house from these errands, he effusively greeted his dog, picking it up, hugging it. We'd been gone for maybe two hours.

"I missed you!" he cried.

SAM HAD INTERPRETED JIM'S refusal to tell stories as if it was masking an absence, as if Jim simply had nothing that he could recall. Remembering was so important to Sam that perhaps he could not conceive of anyone not wanting to do it. It didn't seem to occur to him that remembering the war could be painful, and that others might want to avoid that pain. This emotional burden was perhaps not something that he could relate to. Sam remembered so much, with so much enthusiasm, but with little apparent feeling. He had an intellectual sort of relationship to his war memories, treating them as artefacts to be collected, organized, preserved—rather like his wife's collection of souvenir teaspoons that were mounted and covered an entire living room wall.

Among the souvenirs in Sam's boxes was a small red hardcover book, *In Memoriam*. This contained the names of all the World War II dead from Sam's regiment, listed with the dates and locations of their deaths. When I remarked, "It's quite something that you can just kind of flip through the list and you see all these names," Sam took this as a utilitarian rather than emotional observation, as he answered, "Yeah, well, see, this is why I can remember so easy. Because I know the dates. If I want to check anything I just check the date of when one of the guys was killed, eh? Yeah. And uh, it gives me, terrific information." *Information*. He spoke about this memorial book of the dead as if its value was merely data.

And yet the stories that he told, informed by that data, were vivid, conveying a sense of wonder and beauty in small, even violent things. Describing how one of his comrades had been killed, he compared the German bombs with flowers.

"They'd land, they'd explode, they'd uh, uncurl, a lot, the metal would uncurl like a dandelion, eh? You know how a dandelion—"

"Yeah?"

"Push your finger on a dandelion, how it curls down?"

In another of his stories, he depicted soldiers taking shelter from bombardment as if they were birds.

"We went up a little further, and I come and, there was a bank here, and open ground here, and uh, like these guys were in there like swallows in these holes that were dug in, and I think it was C company that was there . . ."

He described gruesome human outcomes with no affect. However, the fact that he dwelled on them so much suggested that he cared.

"Oh yeah, here was where, twentieth of October, was when that guy I was telling you, the most highly trained officer in the Canadian Army, and he wouldn't listen to us how to get out. He started showin' us fieldcraft and he got his head blown off with one of them fast-firing German machine guns. Captain Taylor. We took him out to an Italian cemetery to bury him. And when we were diggin' down, we didn't go down so far and we hit bones. So we dug the bones out, went down a little further and there was more bones. We threw them out, so then we thought we'd better lay him to rest in there. But he didn't stay there long, I guess they took him out and he was put in the, he was put in the uh, yeah he's in the cemetery at Agira, in Italy. Yeah. Where they put a Canadian cemetery up on this mountain. I went there once when I went back."

Sam had gone back to find the grave of Captain Taylor. He was not indifferent; he just appeared, in his storytelling, to be untroubled by the physical details that he remembered so well: the wounds, the bones, the beheadings. At most, he would describe something as "strange." He would say, "it was the strangest thing" and pause for a moment, never finishing the thought. In these moments, somehow, I imagined him as if he were holding a piece of a jigsaw puzzle, bewildered, because he thought the puzzle had already been finished.

It was impossible for me to see it at the time—I lacked the psychological insight and was overwhelmed by the torrent of details in Sam's energetic storytelling—but looking back, it seems to me that Sam had experienced a painful crisis in the war, and what he called his "work" on his "souvenirs" was an unconscious strategy for managing it. His way of remembering was symptomatic of an intellectualizing response to trauma, whereby traumatized individuals review their experience as an intellectual problem, detaching themselves from it, working on it—sometimes obsessively—as a curiosity while denying or never acknowledging that it has any emotional significance.[2] Sam displayed little emotion, but his obsessional review of one violent event in particular suggested that he remained profoundly affected and wounded.

Between his sergeant and his enemies, Sam had experienced a breakdown in his understanding of himself and his moral character. Many of Sam's stories were about his sergeant Sam Hately, with whom he shared his first name. The one occasion when I witnessed strong emotion in Sam's voice and on his face was when he imitated the harsh and violent speech of this other Sam who had commanded him throughout the war. Meanwhile, Sam also shared an identity with his German enemies. He spoke the language well enough that he could interview German prisoners—and sometimes torment them. By Sam's account, his namesake Sergeant Hately had encouraged this heartless approach to the enemy. And after all, the point of the war, as Sam understood it, was to kill Germans. This is what it meant for him to be a good man during the war. On one occasion Sam described another man in his regiment in these terms:

"He was considered a good man, well, like he—"

"What did that mean, that he was a good man?"

"Well, well he, he killed them Germans, he was killing Germans, and—and he was a good guy. He, he was doing his job."

The moral certainty that Sam applied to this fellow soldier was lacking, however, with respect to himself. When it came to his own actions, Sam wasn't actually sure that they were good. His uncertainty was never openly expressed, but it was evident in his repeated efforts to organize and narrate his experiences. There was one story in particular to which he kept returning. This was a story of how he had killed, or thought he had killed, "them Germans." Deeply unsettled questions about his life—*Who am I?—Am I a good man?*—were hidden inside his intellectual-style pursuit of the facts about this story. Years after my interviews with Sam, I noticed that the questions had nevertheless been raised, surreptitiously, in the symbolism that Sam had attached to soldiers' boots.

THERE WAS "ONE PARTICULAR DAY" that Sam was working on. He had pages of notes about it in his box.

"What's all that?" I asked.

"It's uh, the stories. Oh, I got this book *A City Goes to War* and I'll cross reference it with what happened that one particular day."

"And what are those notes that you wrote there?"

"Ah, just some notations with regard to that."

"Just something you wrote out for yourself?"

"Yeah."

He was working on his memory of a small battle—most people would call it a skirmish, really, but Sam called it a battle—at a white house on a hill somewhere in southern Italy. He had got the book, *A City Goes to War* by George Roy Stevens—the official history of his regiment in World War II—to help him understand that day. All weekend of my visit, through the stream of so many stories, he kept returning to this one, of that one particular day, telling it slightly differently every time, so that it often took me a while to realize that we were back at it again: the white house; Sergeant Hately's aggression; the death of Corporal Frew; and the killing of four Germans, with a fifth German taken prisoner. Those were the details that remained constant in Sam's story.

One of the paths that led into this story was the reading of that little red book, *In Memoriam*. When the book came out of the box, Sam got excited and wanted to read me all the names. This was the book that, he'd told me, helped him to "remember so easy" because it listed the dates and places of all the men killed.

"But uh, this book gives all the guys from the time we went on, eh? Okay . . . Here's the Sicilian Campaign. Robinson, Rasmussen, Brimacombe. They got killed on the fourteenth of July. That was about the first time we ever met the Germans. And then Piazza Armerina. Munro, McLeod, Masters, Huff, Buxton. Yeah, Buxton, uh, we went ahead, and we picked him up, and he had his jaw shot off, eh? He died of wounds after we got there. Hell of a nice guy . . . And here's Leonforte. The guys who were killed there. Gill, Atkinson, Baxter, Harris, Smith, Cameron, Blaylock. Some of these I don't know. Bryant. I knew Bryant really well. Agira. That was in the cemetery there. Major Bury got killed, and Private Davison, and Pat O'Coffey. Pat come from Fort McMurray, and his dad owned the hotel up there. And then, this is the Salsio River, when we crossed that. Hill 736. Bud Craney. He got hit, and, you know he was an awful brave guy and he, he says I know I'm dying he says, I can smell myself. Never forget that. You know. Could smell himself. Sergeant Hammell. He got killed. Walker. McEwan, Sergeant McEwan. Yeah, he come from Barrhead. Uh, Wabisca. He was a Métis, he was in our outfit. Lieutenant Pratley. He died of wounds at Debolt. Italian Campaign. Lieutenant Donald. Oh, here was where we had that battle. Frew. Where, we uh, we went on a, like we went on a patrol ahead of the regiment—"

This was the start of Sam's story. Notice that, from the start of the story, he questioned the judgement of his sergeant, Sam Hately.

"—we went on a patrol ahead of the regiment—"

"Yeah?"

"To try and contact the enemy. We weren't supposed to, uh, engage in any shooting or anything but just scout and find out. But we had a couple of pioneers with us to lift mines off the roads or anything. And we come ahead to this town."

In the town, a civilian told them there were Germans in a house up on a hill.

"Sam Hately right away said well let's, let's go out and get 'em, you know? First thing, he wanted to goddamn fight. So we went through the town past, up on the hill, and uh. Well this guy [the civilian] come with us, he pointed the house out, he says they're in there, so we crept forward, and the only cover there was that ditch up on one side, and where I was, where the well was. And I got behind the well. But when they shot, the bullets were bouncing off that goddamn well. But I was layin' low and just on the edge, and I had the Bren gun[3] around the corner, eh? And I remember Hately here and someone here. And then the shootin' started, well we—"

"When did you start shooting?"

"Right away. Right into the building."

"Soon as you got there."

"Well soon as uh, we heard them shoot, we started shootin' into the building."

"Oh yeah."

"'Cause they must have shot here, and that's when they got Frew, and they got Giesbrecht through the lung, eh? But uh, we had peppered in there. And then they come out of the house, and they had white shirts on. And they were runnin' across this field. Well can you imagine what kind of a target they made?"

"Hm."

"I know uh, Hately and I were both firing, I wouldn't say who got him but, one guy I'll bet he jumped as high as this ceiling. Screaming, eh?"

"When he got hit."

"He went down, yeah. Others fell. They, they were killed. But the sergeant then, I forget—, Gus Campbell. Yeah, Gus was here. He went in, and he brought this guy out, and then that's when he asked him uh, me, what, what do you think, what, what are, what are we going to do with him? And I says well we give him a chance to run down the road. And uh—"

"Run down the road?"

"Yeah. And when I asked him, he couldn't run, and he showed where he'd been shot through the leg on the Russian front. He said, '*Ich kann nicht laufen*,' I can't run. Well then, that's when we put him in jail. But otherwise. He had the chance to run, but he didn't take it. We used to give quite a few of them the chance. But it was, when you think of it, it's cruel, isn't it? The guy had no chance, really, when it come down to it."

Later I understood the meaning of "run down the road." Sam was referring to a practice of telling a prisoner to run away so that the captors would be justified in shooting him. Presumably, in this circumstance, the prisoner did have a chance to escape with his life—if none of the shots fired at him found their mark. The German's chance to run was the Canadians' chance to kill him without committing a war crime. The fact that Sam suggested giving the German this "chance" reveals what Sam had really wanted to do to him.

But then the German showed Sam his wound. Told him about the Russian front. And Sam changed his mind. Did Sam relent only because the German couldn't play by the rules of the "run down the road" game? Or did something more happen in Sam's heart as he and the German spoke together in their mutual language which none of the other Canadians could comprehend?

We got to talking about how Sam had learned German from his immigrant parents, and other encounters he had with German prisoners during the war. It seems that, because he knew their language, he was given frequent prisoner guard duty. I wonder if he also sought it out because he enjoyed it. He had many stories of eavesdropping on the prisoners who didn't know that he could understand them. In these stories it was evident that Sam was often inclined to be kind to them. But he could easily flip to cruelty, following the examples of his sergeant and other officers. There was the time he was guarding prisoners in a cemetery outside the town of Cattolica.

"Like uh, where I was telling you where we had these paratroopers in these crypts? This uh—"

"What was that again?"

"We had these paratroopers as prisoners, laying in the crypts where we took the coffins out."

"Oh yeah."

"Yeah, we pulled the coffins out and had the prisoners in."

"Where was that?"

"That was up near Cattolica."

"Yeah."

"But uh, there was one German was standing up and he was a big bugger, eh? And this [Canadian] officer come along that I knew well, and we'd given the German a cigarette and he was smoking, and the officer looked at that and he said, 'Get that cigarette out.' And went up to him and he took it out of his mouth and twisted it. And the officer was small and this guy was a big bugger."

"Yeah?"

"He was looking! I'll, I'll never forget that! Uh. Yeah, that was the same spot, the one was there, and he didn't know I could speak German or anything, and he made a remark, if he could get hold of that rifle, they could get away or something like that. And uh, yeah I had my rifle, I went fooling around then with it. Like that—"

Sam imitated holding a rifle loosely and tossing it from hand to hand in an absent-minded manner.

"—and right close to the guy, and you know he was looking like this."

Sam imitated the man's burning stare.

"And uh, so finally I told him. I says, '*Warum greifen sie das nicht?*' Well you should have seen him, he just, *hurrr!*"

Sam imitated a wide-eyed gasp and sigh.

"He knew he was set up, eh?"

"Oh."

"Yeah. I told him, 'Why don't you grab it?' Well, he knew better than to grab it."

Having given the German prisoner a cigarette and then witnessing the Canadian officer snatch it angrily from the prisoner's mouth, Sam had then decided to toy with the German, setting the German up to make a move that, had he fallen for it, would have got the German killed.

We came to another paper in Sam's box, a sheet of blue graph paper on which he had printed the title, "Rough Map of Recollection of October 3, 1943." This was the battle at the white house again. Sam had sketched a map of it. He had drawn the walls of the house, the ditch, the well in the yard; he had drawn Xs to mark the spots of the Canadian soldiers, with their names labelled, including his own. Xs also marked the spots of the Germans where they had fallen, shot dead, in the field to the left of the house. Dotted lines traced the lines of fire between Germans and Canadians, and differently dotted lines traced the path of the Germans' flight from the house to spots where they fell.

"Oh here was where, yeah that one place where we captured that one German, this is where, the ditch, and I, where Frew was killed."

Sam was excited to see the map and describe it to me.

"Sam Hately was here," he continued, with his finger on the map. "I was here with the Bren gun. And there was someone here, firing that way. And when these guys were running out this way, uh, that's when we were nailing them, eh? And that's where—" Sam put his finger on some words he'd written on the map, and read them out loud—"'House Jerries were in.' Well we captured that one there."

I made a clumsy attempt to ask Sam what was motivating his efforts to organize this memory—all of his intensive notetaking, book reading, and map-making.

"Who did, when did, why did you write this?"

"Well I had this story on it, eh? Yeah. It happened in—" Sam paused, and then read the title of his map out loud—"'Rough map of recollection, recollection of October the third, 1943.' Yeah that's when we must have had that battle with them guys. 'Cause see in October, the weather's nice there yet. 'Cause the weather was good."

"Yeah?"

"When we were there. Yeah, I haven't published this yet, but Gus Campbell wants me to publish it, and I think I will."[4]

"So when, why did you write this down?"

"Well I sent it to this friend of mine that got shot through the lung here where Frew was killed. Frew, and Henry, like, and Gus, Gus Campbell. See them three were there. Well, Frew got killed, he got shot through the lung, and I wanted to know if I was, I couldn't figure out what these guys were doing over there and how that happened. He was killed without us even knowing it, eh? But you know the way the firing were, we were firing from here but I don't think they were really firing from that angle."

"Yeah?"

"Because I was right behind the well here."

"Yeah."

"Yeah. But I mean, once we started bouncing the bullets into that house, I guess they got outa there pretty fast 'cause uh, we put a lot of rounds in through the windows, through the doors."

I never got a clear answer from Sam to my questions about his purpose. At first, it seemed that the problem he wanted to solve was how exactly Frew was killed. The way that Sam described it, Frew's death was not witnessed by anyone; they only found him dead when the battle was over. "He was killed without us even knowing it, eh?" And Sam was puzzled as to how the Germans could have shot him. This seemed to be the purpose of the map: to determine the lines of fire. "I don't think they were really firing from that angle."

And then there was this suggestive, unfinished thought in Sam's narrative, a significant false start and correction[5] that I only noticed years later when I was re-reading my transcripts: "And I wanted to know if I was, I couldn't figure out what these guys were doing . . ." Sam had wanted to know if he was—what, exactly? I wonder if he was worried, and wanted to know, if he had been the one who shot Frew, by mistake, when he was shooting from behind the well at the Germans as they ran. From my own recollection of Sam's map, the angle did not seem right for that: Frew's trench was to the right; the Germans fled from the house in the opposite direction, towards the left. So Sam would have been shooting to the left, away from Frew not towards him. Of course, Sam's map may have been inaccurate. And of course, I am only guessing what Sam was thinking when he made that false start and correction in his narrative. Sam's thought remained unfinished, and I did not notice it in time to ask him.

What he did make clear to me, later, was that he had wondered if it was right to kill the Germans. He also had the contradictory thought that the Canadians should have killed them *all*, including the prisoner. He shared these thoughts during another moment, when we were sitting on the sofa with the souvenirs all around. More of his notes on the battle came out of the box.

"About five years ago, I started writing this up. You know?"

"Yeah."

"But you'll see, by reading them two, it's uh. You can ask any questions on that. Then I can answer them. I'll want to publish that one, 'cause Gus Campbell would like to see it printed, 'cause Gus's name is mentioned there, he was the one who was laying in that ditch where Frew was killed, eh? And they must have been all right close together in the, and the German that got him must have been a terrific sharpshooter. But maybe they stuck their heads up a little too high, even though they were in a ditch. Well that's why, actually, I'm glad we got them. And uh—"

"Got who?"

"Got them uh, Germans, that were running out of the house."

"Yeah?"

"'Cause one of them killed Frew. And killed, and shot Giesbrecht up. You know. And who knows. I'd hate to think it was that guy we let get away."

"Oh, the guy with the penny?" Earlier, in one of his many iterations of this story, Sam had mentioned that the German they took prisoner had been carrying a lucky penny.

"Yeah with the bullet in the leg that was shot on the Russian front."

An important clue to Sam's conflicted feelings about this event was his use of the word *actually*. Sam said "actually" he was glad they killed the Germans. *Actually*—as if he was responding to an opposing idea, or an unspoken question to himself: *How do I feel about killing the Germans? Was it the right thing to do?* Sam's feeling that the whole battle was unnecessary was implied in his complaint against his sergeant, Sam Hately, in another telling of the story (in a passage quoted earlier): "We went on a patrol . . . We weren't supposed to engage in any shooting or anything . . . Sam Hately right away said well let's, let's go out and get 'em, you know? First thing, he wanted to goddamn fight." The sergeant had led them out of their way to attack the Germans in the white house. Then the Germans were running out of the house—running away. Had it been right to kill them?

"Actually, I'm glad we got them," Sam said, I think in answer to that unspoken question. "'Cause one of them killed Frew." He was trying to use Frew's death to justify the killing. But this logic of justice created another problem, because Sam didn't know which of the Germans had killed Frew (or if it was even a German who had fired the shot). What if the German who had done it was the only German that they *didn't* kill, the one who surrendered, the prisoner who Sam had at first wanted to kill but then relented? "I'd hate to think it was that guy we let get away." Sam's effort to justify the killing led him to question his own compassion in sparing the German prisoner who could not run. "He said, '*Ich kann nicht laufen,*' I can't run."

Furthermore, Sam's feeling that it was cruel to shoot a prisoner who was running away—"When you think of it, it's cruel, isn't it? The guy had no chance, really, when it come down to it"—might apply just as well to the Germans that he and his comrades did kill. Those Germans had been running away, too, fleeing the house. Sam's description of their flight implied that those men had no chance either.

"They had white shirts on. And they were runnin' across this field. Well can you imagine what kind of a target they made?"

Easy targets, white shirts running across a field on a clear October day; and when hit, went screaming into the air.

"I know uh, Hately and I were both firing, I wouldn't say who got him but, one guy I'll bet he jumped as high as this ceiling. Screaming, eh?"

Sam never expressed any feeling about this; he just asked me to imagine.

On a few other occasions when Sam returned to this story, I tried to understand why it was so important to him, why it was worth so much of his effort to figure this out. I never got a clear answer.

"And what made you write this up?"

"Well I, just to remember that and, with Frew getting killed and, and with Hately being there and uh, it was an action. And like, as I said next day was when White and uh, Ernie, White, and the other guy, three of us went downtown. And that's when the officer told me, make sure you take your weapon, so I never took my weapon, and uh, that's when we were in the barber shop and . . ."

And so began another story. Was he avoiding the question? I tried on another occasion.

"When did you sit down to write up this thing?"

"Quite a while ago. Yeah."

"What made you do that? Like what inspired you to—"

"Oh I was just—"

"—to write it out?"

"I was just remembering this uh, episode, 'cause uh. Being able to get away again, and live. And then, losing Frew, and Giesbrecht, knowing Giesbrecht really well, and Gus Campbell. Good friend. And then uh, like being with Hately again, you see again, out on a god damn patrol with Hately. You, you didn't, no life insurance company would issue life insurance if a guy was with Sam Hately."

Sam was at his most emotional when he talked about his sergeant. "Right away he wanted to goddamn fight." "Out on a goddamn patrol with Hately." He often cursed when he remembered Hately, like how a man curses when he hits his thumb with a hammer—the curse releases and assuages the pain. One might think that he was angry about the sergeant provoking an unnecessary battle that had risked Sam's life and cost the life of Frew. Surely this was one source of anger.

But then this detail came up, suddenly, when I asked a clarifying question about the sergeant.

"And this is Sam Hately, the guy that was—"

"Yeah that was the guy I was telling you about, that uh, one of them Germans was laying here that was shot through the belly and, and, uh. And Hately says, 'Well he don't need no fucking doctor.'"

Sam spoke the words of his sergeant in a suddenly different, angry voice—as if he were becoming, for a moment, this other Sam. Then, back to himself, with a pained look on his face, he swore.

"Jesus Christ."

He looked down at the blue graph paper, his sketch of the battle that was in his hands again. In a quiet tone, staring at the graph paper, he continued.

"So, actually that was over with. But next day we went out there and took a look again. The bodies were still there and the Italians had drove the pigs out there, and the pigs were eatin' them."

"Oh my god."

"Yeah. Oh I'll tell ya. Well of course the boots was gone, the Italians had all that, they were real thieves. No uh, it's a horrible thing sometime, when you look at it, and, it's not nice. At all."

Pigs eating the bootless bodies. The killing was harsh: white shirts, jumping, screaming; the sergeant cursing the mortally wounded German who *don't need no fucking doctor*; the horrible sight of the bodies the next day. This, I think, is what Sam was trying to rationalize, to justify, through his "work" on the story. His work of organizing, mapping, searching for data in books, was also an effort to manage these troubling memories; if he could not suppress them, then this work was at least a way to busy himself with the memories in a manner that protected him from feeling. He had to do something to tame this past. Whereas his friend Jim the sniper had tried to erase his memories (according to Sam) with alcohol, Sam had sought comfort by working on his like they were a research problem—as if what he needed in order to conclude all of this, and put it to rest, was just to find and fill in a few missing facts.

For all of Sam's work on the story, he seemed unfamiliar with the version of his friend Gus, which was so divergent from his own. Sam had marked Gus on his map, and told me that Gus had been there. Yet when I interviewed Gus, the story took such a different form that I did not at the time recognize it as having anything to do with Sam's story at all.

I met Gus together with three of his friends, Rollie, Jack, and Bill. The four veterans gathered to meet me one evening at Gus's daughter's suburban Edmonton home. They had a weekly routine of getting together, and there was a lot of banter between them. At one point, they told the following story about an action they had participated in together, and they mentioned that Sam had been there too. It began with their sergeant, Sam Hately, leading them up a hill towards a white house; but in this story, before getting to the white house, their sergeant sent them back down the hill where they went into town and attacked Germans in a different house. And in this story, no Canadians died, and no Germans were killed; all Germans were taken prisoner, including one from the Russian front who they remember had talked to Sam. The story was led by Gus, with the other friends joining in.

"We were on a patrol, this was way before Ortona, it was at uh, Colle d'Anchise. We'd been sent on a static patrol out about three miles to a little village called Guardiaregia. We got up in there, and there was a white house up on the hill. White house up on the hill, and Sam [Hately] says, 'That's an observation post, mark my words.' He says, 'Come on guys, let's go up and take 'em out.' So one guy says, yeah I'll go with you, when, if you can get anybody to volunteer then they'll, if Jones is goin' I'm goin'—"

"Yeah, we all went."

"He went, and I went."

"Sam Lenko."

"Sam and, anyhow, we tried to go around the back. There was a great big crevasse there, and we couldn't get across it. Anyhow, we got as far as, oh about half a mile of the place, and here's another great big ravine so Sam [Hately] says, 'Well I'm not going to get across there with you guys,' so what did—"

"Sandford. Norm Sandford."

"Normie Sandford volunteered to go with him. So he told me to take the rest of the guys down to Campochiaro and wait for him. We get to

Campochiaro and here's one of our scouts and he told us he'd been talkin' to a wop [derogatory term for an Italian] and there was four Germans in the town looting the town, would we come and chase them out. So we had about nine men left, sure we could go and chase them out sure we'll go and chase them out. So remember, I think you were right in front of me—"

"Yeah, you and I were right together there!"

"And anyhow we're sneaking along the ditch and out of the window comes a potato masher [German hand grenade]. Just the one, just the one. And it didn't get a damn one of us."

"Well we rolled into the ditch there, yeah."

"So I told DeLorme to smarten them up there with that Bren gun. So we started shooting into the house there with this Bren gun and pretty soon this white flag come out."

"And they all come out."

"And we come in the, but the thing about it was, there wasn't four Germans—"

"There was more than that!"

"There was five Germans, and he went and got help, and, I tell you—"

"We just got out in time!"

"We just got out in time."

"I remember Sam Len—, Sam, he could speak pretty good German there, and he had, we had those guys carryin' the heavy equipment—"

"Yeah!"

"One guy said he was wounded in Russia, so, Lenko was just a-talking to him in German, telling him—"

"Well who went back with, did you come back with me to take them to company headquarters?"

"No."

"Well we got back, I know I took them back, just four of them you know but they weren't armed."

"Yeah. Yeah."

"But I was sure somebody else came with me."

"Well I went back with those two pilots that came walking in."

"Oh yeah. But anyhow we fed these guys. And I heard somehow that one of these guys could sing 'Lili Marleen' in English. I said, 'Before you get any supper, you sing us 'Lili Marleen.' And he could sing like a lark!"[6]

"Oh yeah!"

"He'd been wounded in Russia."

"They were Desert Air Force, weren't they?"

In this story, they had killed no one, and no Canadians died, and they said that Sam had been there, talking to the prisoner. None of the others could speak German, so it would have been Sam who told them about the prisoner's wound and the prisoner's ability to sing. It would have been Sam who translated Gus's command to the prisoner, making him sing for his supper.

So was Sam mistaken in his memory of the battle at the white house? Was he trying to find meaning in events that had never happened?

Sam certainly believed in his memories strongly enough that he had been working on them, to the point of mapping them, for years. Perhaps during that work, in his effort to find the missing pieces of his story in history books and other accounts, he had unconsciously woven together into his story an assemblage of details that really belonged to other events. (That is, perhaps everything in Sam's story had truly happened, but it didn't all happen on that same day at the white house.) Or perhaps it was Gus and his friends who were mistaken. The numbers might suggest otherwise—four men remembering against one—but it's possible that Gus and friends did not realize that when they went back down to the town,

Sam had stayed with Sergeant Hately, proceeding with Hately up the hill to the white house. But then Sam must have been mistaken in remembering that Gus had been there in the battle with him and Hately.

And yet they all remembered the German prisoner with the wound from the Russian front.

Certainly there was no mistaking Sam's rare display of emotion as he recalled witnessing the white shirts screaming, the harsh words of his sergeant, and the terrible scene later of the dead bootless bodies. There was also no mistaking Sam's feeling of responsibility for what he had (or believed he had) participated in, and no mistaking that he felt the need to explain it, to provide a clear account of who had killed and who had died. While his friends told the story as if they and Sam had not killed anyone, Sam clearly felt implicated in some kind of urgent moral problem. Disturbed by his sergeant's violence, he also felt he was part of it ("Hately and I were both firing, I wouldn't say who got him") and while his sergeant had spoken cruelly about the dying man, Sam by his own account had also been merciless in his original intent to kill the prisoner. "I says well we give him a chance to run down the road."

Sam associated all of these events with the death of Corporal Frew and the wounding of Henry Giesbrecht. These casualties are recorded in the War Diary of the Loyal Edmonton Regiment for October 3, 1943.[7] The Diary reports that during a reconnaissance patrol—

> . . . the enemy consisting of 12 All Ranks, likely to be a German Demolition Party, were engaged in a cemetery near their present area at 1430hrs yesterday. One of the enemy was killed, 2 were wounded and a Sgt was taken prisoner. This engagement unfortunately cost the Regt M16639 Cpl Frew, J.M., killed, and M65392 Pte Giesbrecht, H., wounded.

The Diary says this happened in a cemetery, and does not mention a house. However, this doesn't mean that no house was there. As for the story told by Gus and friends, those events might be what the official history reports happening two days following the death of Frew, on October 5, when the Edmontons suffered no casualties while taking German prisoners during a raid in the town of Baselice.[8]

In any case, apart from the death of Frew for which there is a definite record, all of these details that were remembered by Sam and Gus and friends might have happened on any number of different occasions. There were countless patrols in which Germans were killed or taken prisoner. As Gus and friends told me—

"But we had the patrol sergeant of all patrol sergeants. Sam."

"Sam Hately."

"He would come in to where we were stationed, and he'd say, 'Which one of you yellow bastards wants to die tonight?'"

"That was Sam."

"And then he'd say, 'You'd better write your letters home.'"

And as Sam told me, about his namesake sergeant Sam—

"—out on a goddamn patrol with Hately."

We were sitting on the sofa in Sam's living room. The little white dog was sleeping on Sam's lap. Somehow it came into my mind to ask Sam a more personal question about his sergeant.

"Did he like you?"

Sam paused in thought, with his characteristic, resting-face grin. He seemed to find the question interesting.

"I don't know."

He thought some more.

"I don't know, really, you know. Actually, I considered him a friend. In a funny way. He was a tough bugger and you had to keep up with him. That were the thing. Because if you slacked, he'd make it rough for you."

"Do you think he knew that you didn't always approve of what he was doing?"

I felt my question was risky. Sam didn't seem to mind.

"Well, no, I don't know, I don't think he realized that. I wasn't too happy with what he'd done, and what I'd seen and uh, that, but yet, that's one of them things that I guess you accept. Because you don't want to be a blockard [sic] either, you know. You, you are either with him or you're not."[9]

Later, while researching in the Edmonton archives, I came across something that brought Sam's troubled story back to mind: an article in an old issue of the regimental journal *The Forty-Niner*, written by the regiment's padre. The padre described an attack by Sergeant Hately and his men on a German-occupied house, near the town of Vinchiaturo—in the vicinity of Guardiaregia, Campochiaro, and the place of Frew's death.

> I think it was at Vinchiaturo I first saw that redoubtable soldier, Sgt Sam Hately. He was in action with his pal Cpl Channel, plus some other fierce battle competitors. We were situated on a hill overlooking a large plain and valley and we could therefore see all the action clearly. There was a well placed farmhouse and we saw that it had two armoured vehicles near it as well as some dozen Germans going in and out of the house. Sam took out a group to 'clean up' this nest of snipers and machine gunners. We couldn't follow too well the progress of the group as they crawled on their stomachs as near as they could to the farmhouse but we heard the gunfire and saw one of the vehicles drive away while the other vehicle remained stationary. Presently we could see Sam's

> group checking the house and it was assumed that the crew of the vehicle that remained behind had been eliminated. We could then see our bunch of men returning to their base and in the distance the vehicle that had previously taken off was seen to be edging its way back. The next thing we knew all of a sudden Sam's bunch sat down, except for Sam that is. He hurried back to the house and we who were watching were a bit disturbed since we could see in the distance the German vehicle on its way back. However, Sam was soon back with his crew with something under his arm. When they had all returned to our base we questioned Sam as to why he had gone back to the house. He at once brought out a lovely pair of long boots, brown ones, that he had 'liberated' from a German officer who it is assumed was no longer in need of them. This was only one of Sam's many escapades.

The padre told the tale with an approving, almost jovial tone—calling it an "escapade." What a striking contrast to Sam's memory of a similar event—or perhaps the very same one—which he recalled with shock and disgust. The image that stuck with him was seeing the dead German bodies without their boots. "The boots was gone, the Italians had all that, they were real thieves." Was it possible that Sam didn't know, or didn't remember, that his own sergeant had sometimes stolen German boots?

Whoever took them, the boots clearly meant something to Sam. Even months before that violent episode, boots had already taken on a personal significance for him. He didn't seem to know this. I didn't notice it myself until many years later when I was studying the transcript. Sam revealed it that night when we were leaving Jim's place and he was steering the car back onto the main road.

We were en route to Sam's favourite restaurant. After telling me he'd worked hard to preserve his memories—whereas Jim had drunk his to oblivion—Sam fell quiet. I took out my tape recorder and turned it on.

A logging truck surged out of the night, its beams cutting through the darkness. It roared past, blasting us with spray from the wet road. Sam flicked on the wipers. Then the road ahead was clear and dark again. Some day, I thought, this highway would be widened—and made safer—with a little help from Sam's gravel.

"Jim was mentioning about us, uh, landing in Sicily."

It was actually Sam who had mentioned it to Jim, but I didn't correct him. I waited, expecting him to continue, but he fell quiet again.

After a while, I said, "Yeah."

"'Cause uh," Sam said right away, as if he'd just been waiting for my cue, "that day a storm come up before we land. We went around Malta I think about two or three times, eh? And, Jesus. Like on the ship we were on, the *Empress of* uh—"

He paused a moment, then corrected himself.

"No, no, it was a Union of South African liner, the *Durban Castle*, that we went to Sicily on.[10] And uh. No, we got in the Mediterranean there, and that storm come up. And we, like, the bow of the ship down in the water, when it was clear, was about thirty feet, eh? And the waves were washing over the bow, eh? When we were getting ready to kinda land. But that night, I think it was about one o'clock in the morning, we had to go on the side of the ship and jump in the landing craft tanks, eh? And the water was just swirling."

I wondered where all this was going. Sam was speaking carefully, pausing between thoughts like he was working hard on them. His mood had changed. At Jim's house, he'd bantered easily, telling funny stories, trying to lift Jim's faltering spirits like the Scottish sergeant had once lifted him out of deep water in Sicily. Now, in the dark car, it felt like he was speaking from somewhere else. His eyes stayed on the road ahead, his voice slower, more distant.

"The barge would come right up near the door and then you jump. And then it would go way down. And I didn't get the first jump. And I looked, the black water just swirling down below there, oh my god. But the second time it come up, I jumped. I landed way out in there. And I had a rifle, ammunition on me and, you know. Pack loaded. Uh, but we finally got near the shore and it was just starting to break. Daylight a little bit. Dusk yet. So, I, and you just get out of the water and the water's pouring off you, you know? And it's hard to move, you've got all that weight. And then you're getting on round rocks, and uh, we had uh, well good heavy boots on, with cleats, and steel. Corks. And uh, try and run on them rocks, and you know it just seems like we had to run maybe two hundred feet to get up to the tree line. And it just seemed to be one of the longest miles I've ever run in my life."

"Were you nervous?"

"Well, no, I had my rifle ready and everything. And I come into the bush, and this was the odd part. There was an Italian standing there, and I come up on him with the rifle, and I was flabbergasted what I seen. He had a torn jacket, green, torn pants, no helmet, but he had a rifle taller than himself. It was one of these, I guess they brought it back from the Abyssinian war. And there the guy was on the beach. And I looked down. And the goddamn, he had no boots on."

"Oh god!"

"Yeah. And uh, you know, if he'd have been well dressed, I'd have killed him."

His voice hadn't changed—still slow, steady, and tinged with wonder.

"But I was stunned when I seen this. I thought my god, is this what we're going to fight? You know. And the sergeant, that sergeant, Sergeant Hately, run up beside me. And I had the rifle on the guy and the guy of course threw his hands, and his rifle flew way over, eh?"

"Yeah."

"And the sergeant come up running. He says, 'Shoot him, shoot him, shoot him!' And I says, 'But he's got no shoes on.' That made a difference. I wouldn't shoot him because he had no shoes on."

"That's funny."

"Well, Jesus. You know when you think of it afterwards, such a thing, that kind of a thought enter your mind, so fast, eh? That he had no boots on. But uh, then I told the sergeant, 'Well, you shoot him.' And he says, 'No.' He says, 'What in the hell are we going to do with him?' And I says, 'Well, let him go back to where the ships were.' You know. And that's the last I seen of that guy. Then we went forward."

Sam was quiet for a moment. Then he concluded.

"Poor bloody Italian. He was an old man standing there. Jesus. But you know I had the rifle cocked, safety off, ready and, and, it would have been, if he'd have had good clothes on, and boots on, he'd have been dead. There's no two ways about it."

SAM HAD REFUSED TO kill a man with no boots. Whatever boots symbolized for him, the meaning was so deep that he'd even defied a direct order from his sergeant.

Earlier in his story, he'd unknowingly foreshadowed this moment. As he described his landing, he emphasized his own "good heavy boots . . . with cleats, and steel." They were good—but also heavy with power. And then, on that beach, in his first encounter with an enemy soldier, he had discovered in himself an unexpected instinct: a force of compassion he hadn't anticipated and still didn't fully understand. Who could have predicted that a bootless enemy would stop him in his tracks?

This was not a story that Sam had chosen to work on. I don't think he'd considered it important, until now. He might never have thought to tell it to me if we hadn't stopped, on his impulse, to visit Jim.

As for the story that Sam *had* been working on, very hard—the battle at the white house—despite all his effort, this was still in hopeless disarray. Maybe he had the dates wrong. Maybe he had the number of Germans wrong. Maybe some of it had happened elsewhere at other times.

Maybe some of it had never happened at all.

But something had definitely happened to Sam. I don't think he understood what it was, and in this way his confusion over the details of his story might have been the symptom, not just the cause, of his deeper unease. Sam did not know if he had personally killed those Germans who went running across the field with white shirts on. But he did know that in *some* places at *some* times he had wanted and tried to kill Germans, and even if he couldn't know if he was the one who'd fired the killing shots, he knew that he had helped to achieve the deadly result. In his work of mapping, organizing, cross-referencing, and revising, he was trying to compose a story that would justify the end.

Justify—to himself. Only to himself. No one else was arguing that anything was wrong. Who thought it was a crime to kill enemy soldiers in a battle? Especially when it's a battle against soldiers of Nazi Germany? You'd be hard pressed to find anyone in Canada who would question that. This effort to justify was a struggle within Sam, with his own conscience, with his own understanding of himself. He maintained out loud that he was glad the Germans were killed. "Actually, I'm glad we got them." But the fact that he had continued to work on the story, never managing to finish it, for years, suggests that his gladness was not settled. He remembered the voice of his sergeant; he cursed it; and I think he worried he was too good at imitating it—that he'd become too much like his namesake, his sergeant who was also named Sam. And I wonder if the sight of the bootless German bodies had been all the more troubling because it had triggered the memory of that morning in Sicily just three months previously, when he'd felt a resistance to killing that was so strong that he'd rejected his sergeant's command. I think the story that Sam was struggling to compose, through the details of the white house, was about how he had, at different times, been different Sams—and what that meant for his conscience and his desire to be a good man.

"He was considered a good man, well, like he—he killed them Germans, he was killing Germans, and—and he was a good guy."

"I know uh, Hately and I were both firing, I wouldn't say who got him—"

I don't think his method of working on his story could ever find the answer to the real question that was inside him. Indeed, his method was probably keeping him from ever knowing the question. On one hand, I regret that it took me so long to grasp what his work might be about—and that I could not offer him this thought. On the other hand, I'm not sure it would have been my place to tell him. I was there to learn what it was like to remember the war. Sam, more than he realized, was showing me.

We arrived at the restaurant. The waitress who took us to our table knew Sam by name. She knew his usual order as well—quarter chicken with fries. I ordered the same.

It was a cosy place with lots of families at the tables all around us. Our paper placemats said "Welcome" and featured illustrations of local industry, forests, a moose with antlers, and a giant roadside chipmunk. I thought of keeping mine as a souvenir of my weekend with Sam.

"Darn it," I heard him say.

I looked up. He had his finger on his nose, and it was bloody. His nose had started to bleed.

He tried to stop it with his napkin. Blood soaked through it. He dropped the napkin and took another one. That got bloody, too. Then he grabbed his placemat from the table and wrapped it around his nose.

Finally, the bleeding started to slow.

Tentatively, he removed the crumpled paper. Dabbed it on his nose. The bleed was coming to an end, but still added red spots to the paper with every touch.

He studied the balled-up placemat, turning it round in his fingers, with that characteristic look of wonder on his face.

“Sometimes,” he said, “it’s hard to make it stop.”

CHAPTER 3

These Prairie Farmers Are the Men

"MIND YOU, YOU HAD a gun and you used it whenever you could."

That was how Mel began to tell me about Ortona. The battle had been Mel's first experience of combat. He had joined the regiment as a new recruit just a few months before. Apart from the army training he'd just received, the battle had also been Mel's first experience with shooting a gun. Growing up in a coal mining town, he had never learned about guns. "I'd never hunted before. And we'd never had guns in our house before."

For many of Mel's comrades, however, shooting was a familiar activity that reminded them of home. As boys, they had learned to use rifles on their farms and gone hunting with their fathers. The pride these men took in their heritage was conveyed by the newspaper report on the conclusion of the battle.

> These prairie farmers are the men who blasted and sniped their way through Ortona. The great majority of them have shooting

> for their hobby in peacetime and have camped in the Rockies and foothills. Maj. Stone, for instance, carries a rifle rather than the regulation officer's pistol. He has hunted moose in the Peace River country for 15 years and has no time for toys like pistols.

For men who had lived this way before the war, it was perhaps natural for them at times to be reminded of hunting while using their rifles to shoot their German enemies. The archives contain traces of such associations. These show up, for example, in some narratives describing the initial attack on Ortona.

Approaching Ortona from the south, the Edmonton regiment's first objective was to capture a three-storey building on the edge of the town. To do so, they had to advance through what some recalled as an orchard, others as open ground. In a recorded interview preserved in the University of Victoria archives, Major Jim Stone recalled the action, starting with his instruction to his lieutenant, John Dougan.

"I said to Dougan we'll put down a couple of smoke bombs from our two-inch mortar and we'll run across this open ground. Which we did. And most successfully, it was quite a surprise to all the Germans, and they were dug in just in front of us, and which we hadn't seen, but who had raised Cain with us."

In a separate interview preserved in the same archive, John Dougan described the surprise encounter with the Germans. "They had a system of sort of zig zag trenches and uh, and uh, they'd pop out of there like bloody jack rabbits and you know you had to be, you had to had to have a shot gun to uh, to get 'em I guess. But uh, not many, and we, we, we pressed right on."

The Edmontons gained the upper floor of the building overlooking the German trenches. Jim Stone recalled what happened next. "And then we had fun shooting them, like they were a bunch of deer when they started to move away."

In the regimental archives of the Seaforth Highlanders, I found the transcript of an interview with Don Harley and Clifford Wood. The two of them described the actions of the next day, after the Edmontons had captured the first building, as the Canadians made their way into the narrow streets of the medieval town.

> Then we moved up the main street about one block . . . And we moved down, we were each given a street to move down . . . Most of our work was done by mouse-holing from one place to another, but I suppose if anybody stood out in my mind at that time it was Jim Baldwin who was just a crazy man . . . Jim would rush down the street, you know how narrow they were, he'd just push his foot in, almost a Hollywood character, he was just mad and going from place to place shooting himself in . . . I think the first man I'd ever seen really killed up close was at that point where we were sitting up sniping down the street, and Jim was driving them out of one building to the other, and they'd rush across, these paratroopers, and one of my men got this fellow completely through the neck, and it was like shooting ducks.

Sitting in the archives, reading and listening to the veterans' stories, I felt something uncanny every time I encountered these deer, rabbits, and ducks. The animals of my familiar wilderness were conjured in my mind's eye amid the scenes of the battle. I had never hunted, but I knew the life of farming and camping on the land. If projecting this life onto Ortona felt strange and haunting to me now, had it felt that way for these men also? Farming men who had hunted in quiet boreal forests, lakes, and foothills of the Rocky Mountains had become soldiers and found themselves in a Mediterranean landscape of vineyards and olive groves, a landscape in which (I had been told) men got their jaws and their heads and their limbs torn off by heavy machine-gun fire and (as Sam recalled) could smell themselves dying. In the narrow streets of the coastal town of Ortona, doors and rubble piles were rigged with explosives, while tanks and mortars blew the walls out of apartment buildings, blowing beds and furniture and dishes and photographs into the streets, cutting church domes in half, bringing down entire houses with men inside. In the midst of this carnage, did the men actually *want* to associate their actions here with the lives they had lived at home? Were their memories of hunting a comfort to them, protecting them from possible trauma as they suffered and did violence to other men? Or would they rather not have made these connections—deer, rabbits, ducks—were these thoughts unwelcome to them, because once connected to this violence, hunting might forever be a reminder of it; nature itself might be a reminder of it; terrible experiences of war might be woven into their cherished landscapes of home.

It was a dark winter evening. We were gathered on comfortable sofas around a fireplace in the large living room of Gus's daughter's suburban house. Gus had invited Rollie, Jack, and Bill here to meet me. The four friends often gathered like this on weekends, Gus's daughter told me, and they all golfed together in the summertime. She brought us tea and biscuits and then left us alone to talk.

Gus had a calm, serious demeanour. He was tall and lanky, a bit frail in his movements, with sagging skin and bags under his eyes. The other men were more energetic, but it was clear they looked up to Gus and followed his lead. Rollie and Bill had been young privates during the war; Gus had been their twenty-seven-year-old corporal. (Jack was a bit more independent; in Ortona, he'd been a twenty-two-year-old sergeant of a mortar platoon.) But Gus didn't use his authority to talk about himself. He was always thinking about what he figured I needed to know and who was the best person to tell me. At times when he believed his friends' stories were veering too far from my topic, he'd intervene to put them back on track: "But he just wants to hear about the battle of Ortona." Sometimes, though, it was Gus who veered off. When that happened, no one corrected him.

I asked the friends to tell me about mouse-holing.

"Well when you mouse-holed of course you made a hole in the wall, and you didn't take the stairs," Gus explained slowly, with his index finger raised. "They used to use an antitank weapon, you know? And they'd stick it against the wall there"—he pointed—"and prop it up there, and just as soon blow it, blow a small hole, not a small hole but, about that big eh? And then throw a grenade in there and go in." Gus gestured at Rollie. "That's, I never did that, Rollie'd know more about that than I do."

Rollie was a small man with sharp bright eyes behind a long nose. His speech had a melodic quality and a slight accent that hinted at his French Canadian roots.

"A lot of this is hard to remember," Rollie said, "because you're just going into buildings and you're firing a few shots and guys just, make a dash, you know what I mean?" The other men nodded. Rollie continued. "You may not have found a target to shoot at but you were shooting down there anyway so that no German would be there, eh?"

"Did you ever actually see a German?" I asked.

"Oh yeah," Rollie said, "we saw them but they were very good soldiers, they didn't make a target of themselves unnecessarily."

"We had some very good looks at dead ones," Gus said.

At this point, Jack interjected.

"The thing about mortars—"

Jack's face was plump and round with red cheeks. He had a jovial manner, and his deep voice had a lilt that might have come from his northern English coal-mining father.

"The thing about mortars, I fired four thousand and fifty rounds of ten-pound bombs in Ortona, but you can say like, in Ortona, I never killed a soul."

The room was quiet for a moment.

Then Rollie spoke.

"I was just going to tell him about Norman Letendre."

"Letendre?" Jack said.

"Yep."

Rollie turned to me.

"Well Norm's number is 30851. Mine is 30848. We joined up the same day back in August 15th, 1940. But he got fourteen German paratroopers in Ortona. With a sniper rifle."

"Was he with you?" I asked.

"No," Rollie said.

"He was a sniper," Gus said.

"He was with the sniper section," Rollie said.

"So did you talk to him after the battle?" I asked. "Did you know him?"

"Yeah," Rollie said. "I didn't talk to him after the battle. I didn't talk to him till we got back in Holland, and we were going into action, crossing the IJssel River. That's when I saw Norm. We shook hands. He said, 'I'm not coming back.'"

"Is that right!" Jack gasped.

"He told me," Rollie said. "He says, 'I'm not coming back.'"

"A lot of guys knew that!" Jack said. "I used to say that every time I went in, but I made it out."

"I never did," Gus said, gravely.

"What?" Jack looked puzzled.

"I always thought the other guy's going to get it but I'm not," Gus said.

Jack chuckled. Rollie looked pensive. The conversation moved on.

When I look back on this with the benefit of time to study the transcript, it occurs to me that Rollie must have had a point that he wanted to make with his story about Norman Letendre, but he had been interrupted before he could make it. What was it that Rollie had really wanted me to know? What had brought this man, Letendre, into his mind? Rollie had been telling me how rare it was to see any Germans. Even though Rollie was in the thick of the action in Ortona, he could rarely see the target of all his shooting. Gus mentioned seeing dead Germans. Jack spoke of how, as a mortar man, his distance from his targets allowed him to pretend that he had never killed a soul. Somewhere in all of this talk, Rollie thought of Letendre, the sniper who had killed so many. This was a man Rollie seemed to feel close to, a man whose number he knew, whose story he knew and cared about; yet Rollie had not spoken to him after the battle. Somehow, he had not even seen Norman Letendre until sixteen months later when the regiment was going into battle in Holland and Norman told Rollie his premonition—or was it actually his wish?—that he was not coming back.

Later in the conversation, I learned that this deceased friend of Rollie's was Indigenous. It came up when I asked, using a then unexceptional term, if there had been any Native men in the regiment.[1]

"Now were there, were there Native guys, in uh—"

Gus, Jack, and Bill all began speaking at once, with a bit of confusion about the topic.

"Yes."

"Indians, you mean our Indians?"

"Like uh, Canadian Indians?"

Rollie said to me, "Oh yes, this Norman Letendre I was talking about, he was a Native."

"We had one, a sniper," Jack said.

"And he was really good," Gus added.

"Atkinson, was it?" Bill said.

Once again Rollie had mentioned Norman Letendre but the others had moved on.

"Smokey," Jack said.

"Smokey."

"Smokey Atkinson."

Jack began a story about Smokey Atkinson the "Indian" sniper.

"You know, I'd be in the OP [observation post for directing mortar fire] and I'd, I'd feel a presence behind me, you know? And I'd look around and he'd be there, and I'd be busy with something else, and I'd look around, and he'd be gone. He'd just come in like a, and, if he, he'd shoot out the window of the OP you know, and he'd have the rifle there like this—"

Jack raised his hands and bent his arms to hold an imaginary rifle, his eyes peering through the sights.

"And, he'd fire like this, then he'd lever around in. But if he hit something, he'd put his head down on his, on his arms and, stay there for a minute—"

Jack lowered his face, closed his eyes, and folded his arms over his chest. He held the pose for a moment. Then he released the pose and faced us once again as himself.

"—and then look up. And I said to him, 'Smokey, how do you know you've hit something?' 'Well,' he says, 'it's just like killing a moose,' he said.

He says, 'When I hit, kill a moose,' he says, 'I can feel the shock from the moose to my shoulder.' He says, 'I know I've hit something solid but, when I miss,' he says, 'I, I can't feel that.' That's what he told me."

There was a brief silence in the room. Then Gus spoke.

"Talking about Indians. There used to be this Indian that was quite a runner."

Looking to me across the room, Jack said again, "That's, that's what he told me." I nodded my acknowledgement.

"Real good runner," Gus said. "Little Chief."

"Yeah," Bill said. "Little Chief."

"He became the chief of the Wabamun reserve while we were overseas," Gus went on. "His dad died. And the colonel put on a bit of a show for him. And he was a runner on that cross country running team when we had six guys . . ."

In the rapid ebb and flow of the group storytelling, there seemed to be a collective force keeping the conversation light and pulling it back from any emotional depths. When one man struck a sensitive note, the other men would change the topic, raising the tempo and restoring the lighter tone. Perhaps they were mindful of Gus's daughter in the kitchen. Perhaps they were mindful that I was recording this. But even if we had been alone in the house, and no recording, it might have been the same. This tacit agreement to avoid talking about feelings is a common dynamic among men.

And there seemed to be a tacit agreement to avoid talk about one topic in particular—even though each man seemed to have something he wanted to say, or couldn't help saying, about it. Throughout this winter evening gathering, amid the banter about larger-than-life sergeants, mysterious moments, and hard times, there was a question that kept returning, always implicit, never spoken out loud. That question was about killing. None of the men here seemed to have experienced it directly. While they did not disavow having done it, they maintained that they had not been able to see it as an outcome of their own actions. Rollie knew only that he had shot in the directions where the Germans might have been. Jack had been too far away. When they told stories about other men—Norman Letendre, Smokey Atkinson—this seemed to be a way for them to pose the question: *What is it like to know that you killed? What does that do to a man?* But the stories always remained unfinished, the question never really explored.

At one point in the conversation, the topic was broached by Bill, and the way he did it was particularly unwelcome to the others. This happened in the context of talking about Rollie's sergeant who had been awarded the "MM" or Military Medal for bravery in Ortona.

"Another little story about Sergeant Dick," Rollie was telling us. "We'd taken this building and he was going to put the platoon down for the night because uh, I guess one, one of the other platoons had gone further than we could. Anyway we get this, he's assigning everybody to these bunks, because this had been a German spot. So he kept one bunk for himself, but he was looking after everybody else. The 88 shell come through the wall and landed right where his bed, right on, where his bed was."

"Is that right," Gus said.

"Didn't explode."

"Strange."

"Real good fellow."

"Oh yeah."

"Was he your sergeant?" Jack asked.

"Yeah."

BLASTAWAY

"Was he the runner?" Jack asked. "The cross-country runner?"

"Oh no," Gus said. "No, no."

"He uh, he went to North Africa," Rollie said, "with Clark and a few others, you know, when the troops landed in North Africa."

"I think he got the MM there, didn't he?" said Bill.

"I don't know if he got the MM there, he got it in Ortona I think. Because he got the MM when he scrambled up that pipe I think, and cleared that building with the rest of us—"[2]

Bill cut in. "But where the heck did Charlie Rattray get the, he got the MM in, in Ortona—"

"It's in the book."

"Oh Rattray," Bill continued, showing no interest in consulting the book. "He was a, he was the damnedest poor soldier I ever seen. When he marched, his right arm would go with his right leg—"

"Yep."

"And they'd try and break him of that and they'd get him doing it and then next time he got up he'd do it again. I remember big Step there in Currie Barracks—"

"Yep. Sergeant Step."

"He'd come in and grab him by the scruff of the neck"—Bill raised his voice, imitating the angry sergeant—"'*Are you gonna stay in step, you!?*'"

Everyone laughed.

"Yep. And he became the uh—"

"And he got an MM, yeah."

"But he was the uh, latrine man."

"No that's the other guy."

Suddenly Jack launched into a story.

"The last time I saw Charlie Rattray," Jack said, "was in Ortona and he was walking around with this bottle of green stuff in a bottle and he was drinking it. 'Boy this is sure good,' he said and he offered it, I said no thanks, I said you never know what you're drinking. Anyway he got a hold of Pete Lintrus and Pete could read Italian and on the bottle he read it, 'for pregnant women.'"

Everyone burst out laughing.

"Yeah!" Jack continued, "And Charlie drinking this bottle of green stuff! I never saw him after that."

"That, that must have been after the battle," I said.

"That was after the battle."

"He disappeared in a hurry," Bill said, "but I know he got the MM." Turning to me, Bill added, "He was a bad son of a gun who if a guy, if a German was wounded, he'd bayonet him, you know? He was—"

"Really?"

"Oh yeah. So they were . . ."

Bill hesitated, his voice faltering.

"Yeah."

The levity in the room had been broken. The men had gone quiet and looked uncomfortable.

"When did that happen?" Rollie said.

Bill didn't answer.

"So he was," I ventured, tentatively, "he was a tough guy I guess."

"Yeah," Bill replied, feebly. "Tough. Yeah."

"Never heard of that," Rollie said.

Suddenly, his voice picking up, Bill said, "And yet he was slow, and easy going—"

"Yeah," Jack chimed in, cheerfully, "he was so easy going and slow and—"

"Yeah," Bill said. Looking at Rollie, he added, "I never saw him do it but the guys said he'd done it."

No one seemed to pay attention to that last remark. Gus was already talking over Bill, asking him a question.

"Do you ever think about Harold McMasters?"

"Yeah," Bill said. "Goofy. Yeah."

"I don't know why we called him that," Rollie said.

"Called him what?" Jack said.

"Goofy."

"Goofy." Jack was about to launch into another one of his stories.

"He, he used to run up and down Jasper with these placards you know and, him and I became real good friends . . ."

It was a story about how this hard-luck Harold, formerly a human billboard in the Rocky Mountain resort town of Jasper, had always been assigned to latrine duty with the regiment in Italy. The man's cartoonish complaints about life had been a source of humour to his comrades throughout the war.

THE OUTPOURING OF NAMES and stories was overwhelming. I often failed to notice that I was hearing about the same men and events in stories told by different veterans on different occasions. This was the case when I was sitting there in Gus's living room and Rollie was talking about Norman Letendre. I didn't connect the name and story with what I'd heard just a few days earlier from Sam.

We'd returned from driving around to visit some of Sam's gravel pits. Now Sam was tired. He was watching the news on TV while the dog slept on his lap. On the couch in between us was one of Sam's war souvenir boxes. He'd invited me to dig into it and let him know if I had any questions. Inside, among more sheets of graph paper and Sam's handwritten notes, there was a hardcover book, *A City Goes to War*. This was the book he'd referred to earlier, the official history of the Loyal Edmonton Regiment in World War II. I opened it, looked for the section on Ortona, and scanned the pages for any details that might be interesting to read to Sam. I found a passage that quoted the renowned Matthew Halton from the CBC.

"It says here uh, Matthew Halton said after Ortona that uh, 'Sergeant Hately had left his Bren carrier to snipe. He broke his rifle over a German's head and now carried a German one.'"

Without moving his gaze from the television, Sam said, "Yeah! Well that's Sam all right, boy! Like I was telling you before. You can see what I meant with him."

Sam went quiet. His attention seemed to be held by the television news report about banking fees.

Don't normally . . . the bank machines . . . CIBC says it doesn't matter. Everyone gets charged, even CIBC customers . . .

I scanned the page some more.

"Did you know either of these two guys, Ted Botley, and uh, Norman Letendre?"

Sam replied immediately. "Oh yeah, Norman Letendre." He pronounced the man's name in the French Canadian way. "I knew him quite well. He come from uh, Alberta Beach, down there."

"Really. Alberta Beach," I said. I had no idea where it was.

"Yeah," Sam said, still looking at the television. "Yeah he uh—" Sam paused for a moment, still staring at the television. "He got a, charge against him, for rape I think. After he was in jail. And I think, when this friend of mine from uh, Nanook, was bringing him into the line, that's when he got killed."

"Oh really."

"Letendre, yeah."

The TV news item continued.

But the Royal Bank says that it's not charging its own customers extra fees . . .

Sam appeared to be watching. I looked again at the book in my hands.

Suddenly Sam spoke.

"Norman Letendre, you know, god I can't remember really when did he come to us? He might have come out of the, out of the Fusiliers." Sam turned his face to me. "Does that mention he was killed or something?"

"Not here, here it just says, this is, during the battle of Ortona."

"Oh."

"It says Norman Letendre had killed fourteen, fourteen Germans. He said, 'I used to like hunting, but when I get home I never want to see a rifle again.'"

"Is that right, eh?"

"Yeah."

"Well I'm sure Norman Letendre got killed."

"Yeah?"

"You'll find that, he's in the casualty list."

"Think he got killed?"

"Yeah he did. Got killed by a moaning minnie."

"A moaning minnie. What's that?"

"Well that was, what they called them a *Wienenwerfel*, it was a five barrel mortar, a big one, it had shells that were about that big and, about that long. And when they fired up, you'd hear, *roo-roo-roo!*"

The dog opened its eyes and looked up at Sam.

"And uh, they, they threw them, eh, and, if you happened to be anywhere near. And they'd land, they'd explode, they'd uncurl a lot, the metal would uncurl like a dandelion, eh? You know how a dandelion—"

"Yeah?"

"Push your finger on a dandelion, how it curls down? But they, they had an awful percussion."

"Percussion."

"Yeah, a boom, eh? Just a, I guess it was more than a person could stand. The uh, concussion—"

"Oh."

"—would kill you, you know."

The dog was slowly closing its eyes, going back to sleep.

"Really."

"Yeah."

"And that's—"

"If you were too close."

"And that's how he got—"

"I'm sure that's how he got 'er, 'cause he, I think Norman Miller was bringing him up the line. He was released from jail with some other guys, and he was bringing 'em up to get 'em in. Because the colonel asked to have him back out, because you don't put a good man like him away in jail."

"Yeah?"

"You know."

"He was—"

"He was considered a good man, well, like he—"

"What did that mean, that he was a good man?"

"Well, well he, he killed them Germans, he was killing Germans, and, and he was a good guy."

"Yeah."

"Yeah. He, he was doing his job."

The TV news had moved on to another story.

At the head of that labour protest . . .

Sam stirred from his repose, slowly sat up straight, and reached to the side table for his red memorial book, taking care not to disturb the dog.

"If I take a look at the book, I can tell you which action it was."

I waited while he turned the pages, scanning the names of the dead.

. . . with us now to talk about today's events. Mr Giorgetti, what do you make of the strength and vigour of today's protest?

"Here it is right here," Sam said, with his finger on the place. "He was killed on the IJssel River, in Holland, N.J. Letendre, twelfth of April 1945."

Sam studied the page for a moment. Then he exclaimed, in the slow, animated voice that he used when something really mystified him, "I don't know how else he could have come to us! 'Cause see right here the number he's got, M30851. He might have come from the uh, he might have come from the uh . . . Oh shit . . . Edmonton Fusiliers. I'm trying to find that—"

He left his thought hanging there, incomplete. Whatever it was that he was trying to find, his voice trailed off without naming it. His attention remained fixed on something in his book. I felt that he had half-forgotten me. I couldn't fathom what could be so interesting about Norman's number and how Norman had joined the regiment. And I had reached a point where I didn't have the energy to care.

Well our rally was in excess of thirty thousand people and when we marched I think we picked up another ten . . .

There could have been so many more questions to put to Sam about Norman. But I was tired. I needed a break. Perhaps it was the mention of rape that had turned me off. Now I was the one watching the television, while Sam studied his memorial book.

The views and desires of many working Canadians . . .

By the time that Sam and I eventually broke our silence, Norman Letendre had been forgotten.

When I met Gus and Rollie for the second time, it was in the atrium of the Prince of Wales Armouries Heritage Centre in Edmonton. It was early autumn, ten months since our meeting on that previous winter evening. I was passing through Edmonton on my way home from interviewing veterans in British Columbia.

We sat at one of the tables on the second-floor indoor patio, drinking tea from Styrofoam cups. On the far brick wall, almost level with us, under the large sun-filled windows and the ceiling's arched steel beams, was the *Battle of Ortona* mural, a massive depiction of Edmonton infantrymen shooting and running for cover among tanks and piles of rubble on a ruined street.[3] I asked Gus and Rollie their opinion of the mural. They said it was realistic. Then they started asking each other about an incident at the rubble pile when they were first going into Ortona. They were trying to remember who were the other guys that went with Charlie Rattray when Charlie went over the rubble pile into that house and cleared all the Germans out. Charlie had got the MM for that.[4] While they talked about Charlie, I heard them use a phrase that piqued my curiosity. Although I was feeling done with my interviews, I got out my tape recorder. By the time I started recording, they were talking about another detail on the mural.

"I know of one tank we lost that way anyway. But that doesn't look like a Sherman to me."

"Oh yeah that's a Sherman, Angus. No doubt about that."

"I think the turret they got—"

"'Cause that's a short barrel."

"The turret on the Sherman tank joined the, you know uh, was moulding like that, with the tank. But anyhow, and like my memory's getting pretty dim."

I asked about the term that I had heard them use a minute earlier.

"When you say Charlie was a real killer, does that mean that he had a lot of anger in him, do you think?"

"Well, he—" Gus paused and thought for a moment. "He wasn't afraid to go around that corner there and *pop-pop-pop-pop,* you know?"

Using thumb and forefinger of both hands, Gus imitated taking rapid shots from a rifle. He continued his explanation.

"He was a fighting man. You know. Yeah he was, I shouldn't say a killer I think, he was there to do away with Germans and so he did. You know, he had to win a war, get out of here, go back to his farm."

"Did he, did he go back?"

"I don't know whether Charlie made it all the way or not."

They had called the man a "real killer" but now Gus was retracting it. Perhaps he was concerned that I, and any future audience of my work, would misunderstand and unfairly judge the man. I recalled a story that I had been told a few days earlier on the other side of the Rocky Mountains.

"'Cause I heard a story of how the, uh, there was a German officer who tried to surrender and this guy shot him and it was explained to me that well he was a real German hater."

"Well that could be Charlie too," Gus said. "That's what I mean about it, he's, he was uh, I don't . . ."

Gus was struggling to choose his words. Having just accepted this ruthless description of the man, he immediately wanted to retract it.

"I wouldn't say he was murderous type or anything like that. He'd come over there to fight and that's what he was doing. That's, I don't know whether he's still alive or not. He had a farm or something out, away east of town somewhere."

Perhaps as a way to change the topic, they started talking about other men whom they recalled, men who had made it all the way home and men who had not made it. One of those who had not made it was Norman Letendre.

Gus turned to face me and his tone became very serious.

"But that Norman Letendre, and he, I think he's dead, yes he is dead now. So you're supposed to speak well of the dead but, he got into some trouble with some women in Ortona."

Rollie added, "Norm at the end of it yeah he got into some wine, and uh, that cost him a—"

"And he was in jail for a while," Gus said.

Rollie added, "A time in the castle for quite a while."[5]

And then Rollie shared a thought, which was maybe what he had really wanted to tell me about Norman on that winter's evening ten months ago.

"If he hadn't have got into wine, well, the pressure must have been pretty terrible because he killed a number of snipers, and uh, probably that's when he got drinking at the end of it. The fighting was just about over."

The point of Rollie's story had been the pressure of killing, what killing had done to Norman. And now I knew why Rollie hadn't spoken to his friend Norman after the battle. They hadn't met again until—Rollie had been unable to tell me the reason, but Sam had told me—Norman was released from jail by the colonel because he was needed for the battle in Holland. The regiment needed "good men" like him—as Sam said—men who were good at their job, killing Germans.

But as Norman had told the CBC correspondent Matthew Halton, he didn't like what that job was doing to him. Norman told Halton that he used to like hunting, but now when he thought of going home he hoped to never see a rifle again. Maybe he told Rollie that, too—or Rollie had sensed it—when they shook hands on April 12 as they were going up the line in Holland. Maybe that was on Norman's mind when he told Rollie that he was never coming home.

THE ARMY SERVICE FILES of the Canadian World War II dead are open to the public. It's not hard to retrieve a file. But in all of these years during and after my fieldwork, I have never wanted to look up Norman's.

I'm doing that now. Filling in the search fields on the online form.

Name. Date of Death.

Search results. There he is. That's his number. M30851.

Here's his army enlistment form. He joined the Edmonton Fusiliers, as Sam had figured. It's dated August 15, 1940. That's the date that Rollie remembered. I'm picturing Rollie there, the third guy ahead of Norman in the line, signing up.

It says Norman's nineteen years old. Left school at age fourteen. Completed up to Grade Ten. Occupation, farm work on father's 320 acre farm. Home is Lac Ste. Anne. I Google that. Yes, it's near Alberta Beach, as Sam had told me. Not that I doubted it. Next of kin is his mother, Mary. Curious that he'd put his mother as next of kin, when it says on the form that his father is still alive. Languages, English and Cree. Says he can speak and read both, fluently. Religion, Roman Catholic. Physical description, health good, complexion dark, hair black, eyes brown, height five foot ten and a half, weight one hundred forty-two pounds. A tall, skinny guy.

For the next year of his service record, he's stationed in Alberta. There's a long list of transgressions—absent without leave, breaking out of barracks, refusal to obey an order—for which he's repeatedly confined to barracks and docked his pay. Then there's the paperwork for a discharge. July 16, 1941. He's convicted of "improper possession of a sum of money belonging to a comrade." He's kicked out of the army.

Here's a letter, handwritten by Norman. "Dear sirs . . ." He's writing from Lac Ste. Anne to the headquarters in Calgary, requesting to be readmitted. Apologizes for his actions. Says he tried to re-enlist but the recruiting office told him he needs permission from higher up. "Please give me instructions on how to get back to the service of my country. Thanking you in advance. Norman J. Letendre." For a guy who left school at fourteen, this is pretty well written.

His request is rejected. The army's internal review of his application doesn't mince words. "It is the opinion of this Headquarters that Letendre should definitely NOT be re-enlisted." The decision quotes a report from his former commanding officer. "This soldier is a halfbreed Indian of very little education and less than average intelligence. He has been a continual source of trouble since his enlistment . . . This man is unlikely ever to become an efficient soldier."

There's nothing here showing how that news was conveyed to Norman.

Next document in the file. It's another army enlistment form. February 18, 1942. The name of this new recruit is Norman Joseph Collahan. His home is Lac Ste. Anne. Left school at age fourteen. Father's still alive. Next of kin is his mother, Mary. Fluent in English and Cree. Religion, Roman Catholic. Physical description, health good, complexion dark, hair black, eyes brown, height five foot ten and a half, weight one hundred fifty pounds. Number M35164.

During the first months of Collahan's service, there are a few minor transgressions. Absent without leave now and then.

Five months into service. June 29, 1942. Private N.J. Collahan is court martialled. His crime is giving a false name on enlistment. His real name is Letendre. He's sentenced to forty-two days detention. On the service record they've crossed out Collahan, typed Letendre over it, and replaced the number given to Collahan with the old one belonging to Letendre. It's back to M30851.

But it looks like, after serving his punishment, he's going to stay in the army. There's nothing in here about kicking him out.

So his little trick has worked.

Next in the file.

> Dear Sir

It's a typed letter from Mrs. Marie Anettainte Letendre.

> Just a few lines to let you know that I would like to know about my son Pte. Norman J. Callahan.

She wants to know why he's in jail and for how long.

> Please give me answered by return mail I nearly went craizzy when I heard that because poor kid as I did in know where he was for long time.

Unlike her son, Marie is clearly not fluent in English. To make sense of her letter, in some places, it helps to read it out loud. It goes on and on, a full page as one single paragraph, very loosely punctuated. It's like a stream of consciousness. The poor woman is in distress.

> He did in not steal that name is father's name was Sam J. Callahan and he died when he was a baby. then when he was small I got married to Norman Letendre from Wabumun. And had three kid from him so he ues to be so mean to my son Norm J.C. at last one day he kick him out so so poor kid never had a home and had to make is leaving till after my husband left me with the kid's so my son come back home . . . and help me to make my leaving with is step sisters. You know now dear sir if you don't want him in the armie please sent him home because I need.

She is having a hard time. She's ill. Can't pay for—something. And it's haying season and there's no one to help. Norman has been sending her the money he earns but she'd rather have him on the farm.

> He should never joiejent the armie because I have so much work for me to around place. And is just a kid to and foolish no body to adives him xesept is poor mother . . . I guiss if he dadd was still leaving he wont be like that.

She begs the dear sir, if the army doesn't want her son, would they please just send him home. But most of all, she wants her son to be free.

> I prayed to god in heaven poor son of mine would be free . . . Yes I would rather like to see him to be sent over seas then to be in jail poor kid . . . He said he like the army but I would rather have him home.

From army headquarters, there's a short, polite reply to Marie. They say that her son must serve out his sentence. Norman can request compassionate leave to visit her, but the request needs to come from him. Marie is advised to write to her son and tell him to make that request.

Did it happen? I can't tell. By the time his mother heard about his detention and then these letters went back and forth, Norman's forty-two days of punishment might have been nearly over.

And then he's overseas. The record shows him taken on strength by the Edmonton regiment in England. He catches up with the regiment in April 1943, which is just a few months before they left England and went into action in Italy.

So maybe this is why his number was such a puzzle to Sam. Rollie could remember Norman from the beginning when they first signed up. But then Norman had been kicked out, had taken time trying to re-enlist, and got held back from the regiment during his time in detention. To other guys in the regiment, like Sam, Norman might have appeared to be a new recruit who had joined after they did, who showed up in England just before the action started. When Sam looked up Norman in the memorial book on the couch with me that day, it surprised him to see that Norman had the number of an early recruit.

Next item. June 15, 1943. Embarkation, United Kingdom.

July 10, 1943. Disembarked. That's the date of the Sicily landing.

August 5, 1943, he's promoted to the rank of corporal. That's a few days after the battle of Agira.

October 29, 1943, he's reverted to the rank of private. The record notes, "at own request." So he didn't want to be a corporal anymore. I wonder what he didn't like about it. This was a few days after the battle of Colle D'Anchise.

Next item is January 10, 1944. That's after Ortona. He's awarded the Canadian Volunteer Service Medal.

And now here's his crime and conviction.

Date of offence: December 28, 1943.

Trial: January 26, 1944.

> The evidence of the prosecution is somewhat confusing . . .

The trial is summarized in a few pages. It says that the original military court documents were lost in transit from Italy to England. It doesn't say how, but that's easy to imagine. There was a war going on all around them.

The truck carrying the originals was destroyed. The plane carrying them crashed and burned. The ship carrying them sank. Or, they were lost in a very ordinary way, misplaced or cast away somehow in all of the confusion.

So the crime happened in a house in Ortona. Norman pleaded not guilty. Said he was very drunk at the time. He thought the woman had invited him into the house. He thought the woman had consented. The woman and her family testified, as did a Canadian soldier who intervened. The military court ruled that while "a very confused state of affairs seems to have existed," the woman's testimony was more plausible than Norman's. It was inconceivable that a woman, who it was noted had recently given birth, would consent to intercourse with a stranger while her husband and entire family were in the house. And even if it were accepted as true that no physical force had been used, the court noted the woman's testimony that she had been intimidated by Norman's rifle.

> Evidence was given, by two officers, of the accused's good character as a soldier. He was said to have an exceptionally good record in action.

Norman was convicted and sentenced to three years of detention in military prison barracks.

There's a letter from Norman appealing his conviction. Repeats his claim that he didn't use force, was very drunk, and thought there was consent.

> I would like very much to go back to the front line and serve my country as I have already done willingly and to the best of my ability.

The appeal is rejected.

This is now July 1944. He's in Canadian military prison in Italy.

February 7, 1945. Sentence suspended.

Embarked Italy, disembarked France, March 6, 1945.

March 28, 1945. Taken on strength, Loyal Edmonton Regiment. He joined the regiment at a staging area near Antwerp, Belgium. They were about to go into action for the liberation of the Netherlands.

The next item, of April 12, 1945, is the last.

`Killed in Action.`

The regiment had crossed the IJssel in amphibious vehicles during the middle of the night. On the morning of the twelfth, they were fighting to establish a bridgehead. The engineers putting in the pontoon bridge were under fire from the Germans who were behind a dyke 600 yards from the river. Norman's company was sent forward to push the Germans back.

He was buried temporarily in the nearby town of Zutphen.

There's an inventory of what they found in Norman's kit. This was to be sent to his next of kin.

```
newspaper clipping
souvenir bank note and coin
snapshots
pocket book
sport medal
prayer pamphlet
rosary
cig. case (leather)
pair of moccasins
```

There's a Canadian Pacific telegram:

> Ottawa
>
> April 20, 1945
>
> To Mrs Mary Anne Letendre. General Delivery. Lake Ste. Anne, Alberta.
>
> Regret deeply M30861 Private Norman Letendre has been officially reported killed in action twelfth April 1945.

Lastly, there's a form that Norman's mother had to fill out and send in to claim her son's army service estate.

On the form, she's put May 5, 1923 as Norman's birth date. This is curious. It's not what Norman had told the army. On his enlistment form, his year of birth is 1921. That made him nineteen years old at the time of enlistment. Perhaps not coincidentally, nineteen was the minimum age to join the army. But if his mother was correct—and how could she be not—then Norman was only seventeen when he joined.

I remember something from way back during my fieldwork when I had been reading through files in the Edmonton archives. In some copies of the regimental journal from the war years, I'd seen notices of the deaths of the regiment's overseas soldiers, complete with their photographs. Had I made copies of these pages? Was Norman's image within them?

I'm searching through the box on my living room floor.

I have it. On a page of the journal from July 1945, here is Norman. He's in his army dress uniform. Yes, he sure does look like a kid aged seventeen. I guess you could say that he's smiling in the picture, but you could also say that his eyes aren't smiling. At the time of this picture, Norman still liked hunting. And he must have been good at it—a great shot. I wonder who he learned it from, this kid without a father, around the shores of Lac Ste. Anne.

"I WAS TWENTY-ONE YEARS old and, I didn't know what the hell was botherin' me."

We had moved from the study to the kitchen to make ourselves some tea. Mel's wife had gone out to do some shopping. Mel was telling me about his agonizing struggles with his stomach which had started during the war.

"And at the time," I said, "you just thought it was 'cause you were—"

"Scared. Yeah."

"Were the other guys scared too?"

"I don't know anybody who wasn't. If you weren't scared, you were dead."

A low rumble started rising from the kettle on the counter.

"Yes," Mel continued. "And there was guys, there was a fellow by the name of Sam Hately. I used to hear great tales about him. If they needed a prisoner he'd go out and get one. Uh, I think he's still alive out in BC someplace."

"And what makes you think of him?"

"Well, just the tales that I used to hear about him. He, he didn't seem to be afraid of anything, you know?"

"You heard stories about him?"

"Yeah."

There was a click from the roaring kettle as it switched itself off. Mel poured the hot water into two mugs with tea bags. I looked around the kitchen.

"Do you have sugar?"

"Oh yeah," Mel said, directing me. "Just in the corner. Yeah. Next one. Should be the second bowl in, on the bottom. Spoons right there."

I sat on a stool and stirred my tea at the kitchen island across from Mel.

"You never actually were with him, were you?"

"Who, Hately? No, just heard about him. Knew him to see him but I didn't know him."

"Were there other guys like him? Like, was that a certain kind of soldier that you could—"

"Yeah, I think so."

"Like a category?"

"Oh I think, exceptional, you know. I think exceptional. Because, like I say, uh, I don't think you'd find me volunteering to go on a patrol. But uh. What would you like to eat with that. I don't think there's much. There's some cookies here, but, they might be kinda crunchy."

He held an open bag of cookies in my direction. I took one.

"People like that were probably a minority, eh?"

"I think so. There was a fellow by the name of Norm Letendre who was a sniper with the regiment. And Norm I think—" Mel paused for thought. "He had about seventeen to his credit. Whether he had notches on his gun or not I don't know but, how he kept track I don't know that either. He was an Indian too. A good f—"

"Was he a friend of yours?"

"No. Not really. But a friend of mine by the name of Barney Pellowe was also a sniper and, and Barney was never the type of guy that told you how many, but, how I found out that uh, that Norm Letendre had seventeen to his credit, I forget how that come about, but he said—*I never want to see a gun after this war.*"

Mel lowered his voice and shook his head gently when speaking Norman's words, as if he had tried to imitate how he figured Norman would have said that. Then, back in his own voice, still quietly, Mel continued.

"But he was, he wouldn't either, because he was killed in Germany after the regiment moved on, you know."

Mel was silent. He sipped his tea. I sipped mine. I wondered what to ask.

As I write this now, I wish that I had asked Mel to tell me more about the connection in his mind between Hately and Letendre. How had one man reminded him of the other? On one hand, he seemed to regard them both as exceptional in terms of their courage and ability to capture and kill so many Germans. On the other hand, he had described Hately as someone who relished the task, whereas he remembered Letendre—to the point of becoming him, in that moment—as someone who felt revolted by it.

Mel broke the silence. "But Sam Hately. Let me see if—" He left the kitchen island, went to his study, and came back with his regimental association's members list. He turned its pages, sipping his tea, scanning the list—but to no avail. Later we learned that Hately had died a few years before.

AFTER THE BATTLE OF Ortona, Mel had started wishing for an injury that would get him sent home. He finally experienced a breakdown in the next combat action after Ortona.

"I got through, I got through Ortona there was, I think, I'm not sure eleven or twelve of us left after the battle in Ortona, in my company."

"How many were there to begin with?"

"Oh I would say about a hundred and, a company runs between 120 and 130."

"So you were brought down from about 120 to, to twelve?"

"Yeah. Yeah, yeah. Yeah, some taken prisoner, some wounded, some killed. So there wasn't uh, it got to the uh, so that you were wonderin' just when your time was up, you know? And, which was always, always kind of stressful, but you were there, what are you going to do about it, you know? So, guys, some guys had premonitions of what, you know, and I think each of us, after a while I think you got to think to yourself, well, uh, if I get hit I want a good one, you know. I want to get out of this."

He described the guilt that he felt for wishing this, and for the fact that he had indeed made it home safely when others had not.

"And, of course ever since then I've had this sense of, I think everybody that come home, and come home with all their limbs, had a, had a certain sense of guilt, with, and I, I think everybody has carried that, to some extent. Uh, the fact that, how is it that guys can be shot and killed on both sides of you, you know, and, and nothing happens to you."

As often happened while we were talking, Mel recalled a troubling episode and got carried away in the momentum of telling it.

"Like Buck Holder, standing next to me when he got it, you know. I can still see the look of uh, uh, amazement on his face, you know. In fact, somebody said *Buck you crazy bugger you shot somebody*. And Buck said *I didn't do anythin'!* and all of a sudden, bang. He's got it, you know.[6] We come under machine gun fire, it was off to our left, just starting in to Ortona, we were going through a, I don't know whether it was a olive grove, or a grove of some kind, and so we all just hit the dirt. All of us dug in and they called up a tank and eventually the tank come up and blew the house, the machine gun fire was coming from a house on the edge of the ravine that separates Ortona that was on the other side of Ortona. And uh, but anyway, blew the house all to hell."

Later that winter, north of Ortona, Mel suffered his breakdown that led him to be taken out of action.

"It was a static sort of winter line, and we were on one side of the canal and the Germans were on the other and we could hear each other talking, we were that close."

During the nights on the line, Mel was two hours on duty and two hours off.

"So, my two hours off as I say I was just heavin' my guts, and listening to somebody else snore, and that sort of thing, and finally I just went haywire. I, I went out and uh, started walkin' around, just, you know, and there's the odd shell coming over and that sort of thing. I just absolutely had as much as I could take, so my nerves were shot. They sent me out to what they call a 'bomb happy' place, you know. I didn't think, I thought I was more sick than I was 'bomb happy' but, my nerves had just given out entirely. So I never went back to the front after that."

Mel didn't mention seeing a Canadian army psychiatrist but it seems that he was diagnosed with what they called at the time "battle exhaustion."[7] This was the injury that finally got him out of the war. It was the reason that he wasn't with the regiment in Holland when Norman Letendre was killed. Many years later, back home in Edmonton, he was diagnosed with severe stomach ulcers for which he had received surgery—and was still receiving treatment.

"This was all a part of what I'm being paid attention now for, is the fact that I had these stomach ulcers."

He seemed relieved that he could attribute his wartime breakdown to a physical illness rather than something which had happened in his mind. However, sometimes while talking with me, Mel reported symptoms of post-traumatic stress disorder, though he didn't seem to recognize them as such.

"But see even now, talking about this, this churns up, any food that I've got, churns it up. But it wouldn't matter. It wouldn't matter anyway. Because I'm, you know, I'd probably think about something, something that would remind me. There's always a constant, there's pretty well a constant picture in there. Not one, one picture, but flip to, you know, it's like one of these things that you flip, and you see movement, it's almost like that, different pictures. They go through my mind. I don't know whether, if that's the case with anybody else. I never talk to anybody about it."

MEL HAD A BOOK about Ortona containing many pictures from the battle.[8] We were looking at it together.

"Oh, here's the wall. And it's still there, I went back to see it twice now. Because that's one of the walls that I remember when we first started in. Now, you see, you were walkin' along like that. One of these guys could be me."

In the photograph, down a sloping street strewn with rubble, there was a long brick wall. A number of Canadian soldiers were standing and leaning against it with their backs to the camera. Furthest from the camera, two of the soldiers were crossing the street, heading into a gap between buildings, about to disappear from view.

"Because like those guys in that picture I was leanin' up against it for a time. You're waitin' to, you know, as your corporal or sergeant motioned you on."

"Did you pass by that wall often during the battle?"

"Oh no, no, just that once."

"Just that one time."

"Yeah, but it stands out in my mind."

"Why did you go back to find it again?"

After retirement, Mel and Eva had taken holiday tours of Europe during which they had visited Ortona.

"Just because it's a landmark that I remember. See when you go back to Ortona today it's built up. It's not the pile of rubble that we knew, you know. But this was one of the things that I recalled. And another thing that I recall was San Tommaso church itself."

Mel turned some pages of the book to find another picture he wanted to show me. I hadn't really got an answer to my question about the wall. It seemed that Mel didn't know why the wall mattered to him. Perhaps it stuck in his mind because it was a last place of safety, in fearful anticipation, before the signal to move in.

"And I can remember, uh, lying. Here."

In the picture was a narrow street framed by damaged and ruined buildings. The street opened onto a square overlooked by an imposing building with a small tower—somewhat blurry in the photo, perhaps from smoke or dust.

"Lying on a pile of rubble, way back this way, and firing up into here, into the bell tower. 'Cause I thought Jesus that's a good place for a sniper to be, you know. But I guess everybody else thought so too. And I think there was a bell up there, but I'm not sure whether I was ringing it or not. You couldn't hear. Because, you know, there was firing going on all around you, and coming from the other direction too. So, how are you going to know if there's a bell being rung."

Turning more pages, looking at the narrow streets and alleys, Mel recalled another moment.

"Going into Ortona, this is probably about the second day going in. Went along the street, and uh, I ducked into another bit of an alcove but there was no way out of this one. This one was just a kind of a storage place. And uh, Jesus, there must have been a German, just on the first floor above me, because there was a spattering of Schmeisser machine gun fire, right at the entrance there, you know.[9] And every once in a while a potato masher, what you call their hand grenades you know? Potato masher. So there was no way, no way, there wasn't any way out the other way and, this guy kept firing bullets down in front, the front entrance to this thing, you know? And uh, so I was kept there, it must, it seemed like an eternity but eventually somebody must have got him or else he moved because eventually when there was a little bit of quiet I got out of there."

He paused in thought. We turned some more pages. There was a picture of Canadians sitting down in a courtyard, eating a Christmas meal.

"Do you remember what you did on Christmas Day?" I asked.

"I don't remember sittin' down to a dinner. I remember a bottle of beer, I, that, but it's not a clear, it's not a clear, I can't see me standing here having a bottle of beer."

"What do you see?"

"I see, I see being up on about the third floor of a building and uh, I see me peeking around a window and firing a shot at this window or that door, or, you know, periodically, and then going from, from that window to another, another window."

"How did you do that? Inside—"

"Yeah inside the house. And uh—"

"What were you shooting at?"

"Windows."

"Other windows."

"Yeah. Well, there's nobody standing there to take a shot at."

My momentary confusion about the target of his shooting prompted Mel to carry on with a more general description of the experience of battle.

"You know a lot of people think war is a guy standin' up and uh, if I shoot first, why, I'll get him. Well sometimes that does happen when you come around a corner and you startle somebody, then of course, the first one to fire is the one who stays alive. But uh, but when you're, when you're standing guard and you're just shooting at windows and open, open doors and, wherever you think there might be somebody, you know, and uh, you fire away at that and you just keep up a, at a, not a constant fire but periodic, you know. Just to keep everybody on their toes, that sort of thing. And if you're in a house then of course there's a, if you're heading downstairs you throw a hand grenade down first, you know. If you're going upstairs you use, you use your gun and uh, if you can, yeah, you gotta be very careful about using a hand grenade there because it might come down the stairs after you, you know!"

He stopped. A puzzled look came over his face, as if surprised at where his own talk had taken him. His description had slipped into a sort of lesson, a set of urgent reminders that he was giving me on how to survive the battle, when to use the gun, when to use the grenade. We were sitting in his study, his bookshelf behind me, framed pictures on the walls.

He regained his composure.

"But uh, there's so many different ways that a person has of killing and being killed, you know."

Mel had no personal stories about killing. His stories from personal experiences—the pictures in his mental flip book that he said was always moving in his mind—were of sudden deaths of men beside him, of shooting his rifle into empty spaces, of finding himself lost in the maze of medieval alleyways being stalked by unseen enemies. For all the traumatic shock that Mel had suffered, however, he seemed to feel that he was one of the fortunate ones. Explicitly, of course, as he told me, he was fortunate in making it through without being killed. Implicitly, he also considered himself fortunate in making it through without killing—or more precisely, without having knowledge of it. Mel might have killed; he just hadn't witnessed it. He'd shot at windows, doors, bell towers; he'd shot up stairs; thrown grenades down; but he'd never seen a man die as a result of his actions. Nevertheless, the moral problem of killing seemed to weigh on him. The question of killing was part of his mental flip book of Ortona that still disturbed him in his sleep.

"You were always busy, you were running from window to door to window and, and uh, you know you're firing shots. There's nobody up there. The odd time you see a guy running from one, and maybe half a dozen guys will take a shot, you know. So did you get him or did, did the guy next to you, or somebody at a window further down get him. So. But. And you always wonder about that too, you know. Whose, whose life did I end."

Mel often criticized war, and every time he did so, his point was not only that war makes us suffer; his point was always, also, that war makes us kill.

He never stated it directly, but many of his stories conveyed his belief that killing can have terrible consequences for the soldier who kills. One such story was about a much-celebrated Canadian hero of the Italian Campaign. Mel was reminded of it while talking about the terror of anticipating his own death and wishing for an injury that would send him home.

"No human being should be in that kinda, I, I know they praise war and uh, and a lot of guys maybe, well not a lot of guys, there wasn't too many that really relished it, but there were guys that did things under stress, did heroic things you know, and not everybody had seen these things, you know, and it was just some guys like [name redacted], his was very obvious because they were a couple of tanks that attacked his position, I guess. He just grabbed a PIAT gun[10] and knocked out both tanks and then I don't know how many Germans he killed—"

As sometimes happened, Mel's mind and discourse were racing from one thought to another, and it was hard for me to keep up. With the benefit of time to read the transcript, I can see that he began with the point that war does terrible things to people. He then took issue with the celebration of war, and started to say that some men "relished" it, which he immediately retracted or downplayed. This got him onto the topic of heroism. He suggested that many heroic actions did not get to be well-known ("not everybody had seen these things") and then he shared a troubling secret—what the Canadian public had not seen—about one celebrated war hero.

"But as they piled out of the tanks, and there was Germans along with the tanks too. How he got away with it I don't know, but he knocked out the two tanks and I think there was twenty some Germans that he killed at the same time. I can understand him being a drunkard, which is pretty much what he is."

Mel responded to my raised eyebrows, the startled look on my face.

"Oh, he drinks constantly. From the time he gets up in the morning, and I can understand that."

"You think because of something to do with that experience?"

"I think so. There's a certain amount of hatred that you harbour while you're there on the line, you know. I can remember once in Ortona—"

Once again, Mel was moving from point to point faster than I could follow. In this instance, he went from the hero killing twenty Germans, to the hero constantly drinking, to the feeling of hatred which Mel indicated that Mel himself had also felt. Amid these interconnected thoughts that seemed to be coming all at once—killing, drinking, hating—Mel remembered and shared with me one of his most traumatic experiences of the war.

"When I was standing guard. And uh, I was in a, there was just a bit of an alcove there, but it was leading out to a street, maybe fifteen feet away. I was standing there with a Tommy gun.[11] And I could, this was in the early part of the morning and I could hear this, somebody coming from the

German side. And I just had the nose of the Tommy gun on, on this thing, and I could see this, to me it looked like an officer. But as soon as he come into view, and there's only, you know, so much that you can see there in the early morning light, I pulled the trigger, and nothing happened. And had he looked, had he looked toward me, I was dead."

It was the thought of hatred associated with killing (and drinking) which had reminded Mel of this moment. He had been standing guard, on night duty. He heard somebody coming from the enemy side of the street. He readied his gun to shoot the source of that sound and movement. In the vague pre-dawn light, he first perceived it as "this thing." In the moment that it took shape in his eye as a German—and this was his first good look at a German, only fifteen feet away—he pulled the trigger. In that moment—the context of his story suggests—he was feeling hatred. No doubt in that moment he was also feeling terror. He hated that thing which was terrorizing him. He believed, and hoped, he was about to kill the hated object. And he surely would have killed—but his gun inexplicably failed him. Then, on that failure of his gun, Mel was suddenly defenceless. His inner state must have jolted wildly from anticipation of killing to the terror of being about to be killed.

"But, he didn't. He looked straight ahead and went that, and went by me, you know."

The German had crept past the alcove in which Mel was hiding, without seeing Mel, without hearing the click of Mel's impotent gun. The German would never know that Mel had almost killed him. Mel would never know why the German had failed to know.

"So jeez I got out of there, and I went back, and I got a rifle. 'Cause the Tommy gun was jammed, and I got a rifle, and I went back to position but, he never showed up again. So, I didn't go after him."

"No? Were you, were you thinking that he might come back?"

"Well I thought uh, maybe he's just uh, just seeing what the hell is out there. So, but he went, why, why he didn't look in I'm, I, to this day I've never known this."

For the rest of his life, Mel was left wondering how he had got away with living. But his story of the German at the alcove was not just a story about a narrow escape from death. It was also a story about a narrow escape from killing. If his gun had worked, if he had succeeded in shooting the German, then perhaps Mel might have lived out his life "drinking constantly" as he had observed was the fate of other veterans. His belief in this possible fate was implicit in the stories that he told about heroes. In Mel's view, it seemed, the more that a man was personally involved in killing, the more that he risked doing lifelong damage to his psyche—or, perhaps, to his soul.

This was how I came to understand Mel's remembrance of Norman Letendre.

"I THINK I TOLD you when we first started talking, I spent the first forty years tryin to forget about a lot of that stuff."

It was late on the second day of our interviews in the study room of his condo. Mel was telling me about the dilemma of remembering.

"Because a lot of it is, is, well, death and destruction, you know, so those are things that you don't want to keep in mind. But, god there isn't too many days go by that I don't think about the war."

"Really."

"Oh yeah. Yeah."

Mel paused in thought for a moment.

"Certainly it shouldn't be forgotten. But by the same token it shouldn't be, it shouldn't be a thing that, say hey, we're going to do better next time.

You know, that, that kind of thing. I knew one fellow, he was an Indian fellow, he was with the regiment, a sniper with, and he uh—"

"Was he at Ortona?"

"Yes. He, eventually he was killed in uh, when the regiment, I wasn't with the regiment then, when the regiment moved to Holland. He was killed in one of the last actions that they had. But he'd al—, he was a sniper and he already had seventeen Germans to his credit. He said I never see or want a rifle again in my life. He, he was an Indian."

"So he was going ahead, but, but felt bad about—"

"Yeah. Oh yeah. A lot of them were, I guess, sittin' ducks, you know."

It was the second time that Mel told me about Norman Letendre. Mel had said that he knew Letendre, but he'd also said that he hadn't known him well. Why was the memory of Letendre so important to Mel? What made Letendre a symbol, for him, of why we should not celebrate war?

On both occasions when Mel remembered Letendre, the elements of the memory were the same. Letendre was a sniper. An "Indian." Had killed seventeen Germans. Had come to hate his rifle. Didn't make it home. Most of these elements—sniping, the kill count, hating the rifle—are consistent with Mel's belief in the damaging effects of killing. As for Norman being Indigenous, why was Mel so emphatic on that point? "I knew one fellow, he was an Indian fellow . . . He, he was an Indian."

It could be that Mel was simply fascinated by this example of an Indigenous person who despite his marginalization had chosen to serve his country. But I think Norman's "Indianness" was especially noteworthy to Mel because of Norman's turn against his rifle. In white Canadian imagination, the "Indian" has historically symbolized a mode of existence that is at one with nature, a way of living in which hunting animals is essential for both material and spiritual sustenance. From this vantage point, when Mel heard that Norman never wanted to see a rifle again, this signalled to Mel that Norman had lost something vital, perhaps the very meaning of Norman's life. Norman could never return to his way of living on the land. Norman had lost the very essence of who he was.[12]

When Mel described Norman's victims as ducks, this animal imagery may have come to him because he associated Norman with hunting. But Mel had his own experiences of duck hunting which he associated with bad feelings about the gun. I learned about this when I asked if there were things in his life after the war that had caused him to remember.

"Would things happen that would remind you, like, make you think, what sorts of things would make you think about Italy?"

"Oh, when you hear a gun bein' fired off, you know."

"When would you hear that?"

"Oh, any time you're out hunting, or anything like that, you know."

"Oh right, you used to go duck hunting, eh?"

"Yeah, shotgun, yeah."

"Was it hard to start hunting again after the war?"

"I'd never, I'd never hunted before. And we'd never had guns in our house before."

"When did you start hunting?"

"Oh I started hunting I guess when I first could afford a shotgun, and that would be about, ah, let's see. I joined the Edmonton parachute club in 1964. So it'd be about 1961, somewhere in that time. You know, you're busy trying to make a living in those years, you know and uh, it wasn't much of a living because I worked in a parts department, and the only way we could make it was both of us working, my wife and I."

Norman Letendre had been an avid hunter before the war, but after Ortona he wished to never see a rifle again. Mel had never hunted before the war, but came home from Ortona and became a hunter.

"So you finally got a chance to take up a hobby—"

"Yeah, I uh, guys were going out hunting, they'd say, how come you don't hunt? Well, okay, I'll buy a shotgun. So I bought an Ithaca lightweight I can remember that, and uh. And this one time when I was out hunting ducks I was laying by a swim [pond] waiting for a duck to come over and, and across the way, some distance away but he come down so easily, a guy in a parachute. And I thought jeez that looks neat, because he landed standing up, he didn't, no roll or anything, you know. So when I got back to town, I was forty-five years old, forty-two years old then and when I got back to town I, without telling my wife, I made a few phone calls and found out there was a club, and I went out and joined them."

His new hobby was hard on his marriage. He told me that Eva hated it. She thought it was dangerous. He did it anyways. He couldn't explain why. It was just something that he needed to do.

An obvious explanation for Mel's sudden passion for skydiving would be that he wanted to test his courage, to prove to himself that he could be strong against his fears, his lasting traumas. But I sense that it had more meaning for him than just testing himself. Aiming at ducks in the sky one day, he had seen a man come into view instead.

"But I never got any pleasure out of knocking birds out of the sky, you know."

I remember those words and how he said them.

"Never did."

I remember the first thing Mel told me about Ortona.

"Mind you, you had a gun and you used it as much as you could."

And his memory of Norman Letendre.

"He said I never see or want a rifle again in my life."

Mel had finally given up the gun. He had given up shooting forever, replacing it with an activity in which he risked his own life while never taking another's. It was a way of relating to the land of his home without a rifle.

When I think of Mel, I often think of him skydiving. I picture him going up in the plane, removing himself from the land. Seeing the land from the vantage point of a bird. Then from a great height, letting himself go. No need to fight his way home. Gravity taking him there. No sound but the rushing of the air. Falling down to the land to which he and his comrades had so desperately hoped to return.

These prairie farmers are the men . . .

Remembering those who had lost their hope.

CHAPTER 4

From Harley Church to Dead Horse Square

SHELVES FULL OF BOXES lined the walls of the little room. In the centre was a small table with a mechanical desk lamp and chair. Mounted high up on one of the walls was the antlered head of a stag. The brown eyes of this mascot of the regiment gazed mutely over the room towards the window that was turning dark, beginning to mirror the scene inside. Muffled sounds of voices bellowing orders came through the thick stone walls and floor. The army cadets were practicing drill. Up here, in what felt like a forgotten attic of the Armoury, I was in the archive of the Seaforth Highlanders.[1]

Elsewhere in the building, the regimental association was holding a meeting. A few of the members had shown me around. They weren't sure what was in the archive, but said I was welcome to stay a while and have a look. Before leaving me to go back to their meeting, they had given me this card from their most recent Men's Annual Ortona Dinner.

The regiment's crest was on the front of the card. There was that stag's head again, under a crown, with the Scots Gaelic motto *Cuidich 'n Righ*, "Help the King." The card opened up into a menu. "That's exactly what they ate in 1943," I was told. Nuts and raisins, vegetable soup, roast pork, mashed potatoes with peas and carrots, mincemeat pie, oranges and chocolate bars, and beer.

> Toast List.
> Introduction of Head Table and Other Ortona Veterans.
> Entertainment, Seaforth Pipes and Drums in Attendance.

On the back of the card, under the heading *Ortona, December 20th to 28th, 1943*, there was this text.

> Ortona. Who shall forget it? Its tall narrow houses and dark cramped streets huddled against the massive 15th Century medieval castle which crowned the high promontory thrusting squarely into the sea. And the newer part of the town, laid out in a system of rectangular blocks, with only the main thoroughfares wide enough to allow passage of a tank. And the skilful demolitions designed to lead to the killing ground in the Piazza Municipale. And the fanatical defense by the 1st German Parachute Division of the 76th corps, defeated only by initiative and the 'mousehole' technique of house clearing. And the stinking 'Dead Horse Square' which we dominated by the 24th. And the 'Padre' Major Durnford and his unforgettable umbrella and the 'uplift in spirits' wherever he visited. And the wonderful Christmas dinner served by Captain Cameron and his staff in the church of Santa Maria di Costantinopoli, where the Companies took turns to feed their men, for many of whom it was the last meal.

That Christmas dinner in the church in Ortona had become a legend for the Seaforth Highlanders. Every year, the regiment re-enacted it, honouring their veterans of Ortona who were still alive, and remembering those who were not. Every year, there were fewer veterans in attendance. Soon the dinner would be re-enacted only by the cadets.

I turned my attention to the shelves around me. I hadn't expected an archive. The purpose of my visit to the Armoury was to get tips from the association about Ortona veterans whom I might interview. Thinking how different this was from the strictly controlled procedure at the National Archives in Ottawa, I started taking boxes down one at a time, rifling through the contents, and returning them to their place. I found a box with files inside that were marked from 1943. I took out a thick folder, placed it on the table, and opened it under the lamp.

> Diary of Major Roy C.H. Durnford, Chaplain (P).

Padre Durnford's diary! I turned its pages to December.

> 7—Tues. Gregg & I make tea surreptitiously & talk of better things . . .

> 8—Wed. Mud is terrific. A Esch. is a sea of mud. Get some writing done in a feverish haste.

A prayer.

> Loving Father we thank Thee for this feast of Remembrance & for the memory of those of our members who now feast with Thee. Amen.

Notes of words in Italian.

Chicken - gallina. Egg - uova-ovi. vegetables - verdura. Swop - Cambiamo.

Names of Men Personally Buried by Me.

A long list of names, dates, map coordinates.

25th—Sat. Xmas Day. Red Cross Jeep to Ortona . . . Jerry sending shells over . . .

Amazing. I would come back to this later. I was in a hurry to see what else was in this box.

Journal of H7551 Pte. McKay, A.J.

This appeared to be a guy from the signals unit.

Interview with Al Mercer, Northwest Bay, 18 July, 1960.

There were pages and pages here of typed interview transcripts. Someone had done a ton of interviews with Seaforth veterans in the early 1960s.[2]

This one caught my attention.

Interview with Don Harley and Clifford Wood, Toronto, June 7, 1961.

Harley. I knew that name.

Where had I heard it before?

"THE FIRST TIME I ever touched an organ with the Seaforths was at Harley Church."

It was in the living room of Wilf's home in North Vancouver. Wilf was telling me how he had played the church organ during the Christmas dinner. Seated in a large leather armchair, he spoke calmly, with a gentlemanly manner. He was a tall, lanky man with a long, friendly face and moustache.

"I can't really remember too much about the details of the church except it was fairly small, and it had several shell holes in the wall and maybe one or two in the roof. But it was a church and it had good masonry, thick wall, so it was reasonably bomb-proof you might say. The padre was a little bit scared to set up the carol singing and so on but we did manage to find an organ of some kind and I just happened to have my little music book, I always kept it in my pack because I had studied organ and I knew darn well that probably somewhere along the line I'd have to play hymns or something like that."

He had called it Harley Church so naturally. I had never heard it called that way before. The real name of the church where the Seaforths held their Christmas dinner was Santa Maria di Costantinopoli. Had Wilf assumed that I knew this insider name for the church, the name that would only be familiar to him and other Ortona veterans? More likely, it was just a slip on Wilf's part—natural for him, when returning to these events in his mind, to name the church as he had known it then. In his experience, nothing had happened in a church called Santa Maria.

"And the padre had a good voice so he led the singing, and I had my book of notes, and we managed to get the fellows to sing. And this was, this was just great. Gave a little attitude, and they could, we could see from the start of things that it would be a company at a time. We had seating for about sixty men, and they were seated in tables, alongside each other . . ."

I never made it back to ask why they had called it Harley.

"FROM THE POSITION WE had we could look over the brick factory and across this valley with Ortona and the church on the other side . . ."

Don Harley was on the hill of San Donato, looking north towards Ortona, and feeling—as he put it—"the jitters." He'd just come from an Orders Group meeting of senior officers with their colonel, Syd Thomson. Moments earlier, he'd been feeling relieved that, as captain of Seaforth A company, he wasn't going to be leading the attack. Then he'd learned otherwise.

> I was told that C coy [company] was to make an attack from the high ground on the coast, down across the gully, through the brick factory, and up to Ortona, which meant scaling the cliffs and getting up to Ortona in the neighbourhood but to the right, the seaward side of that church. Blackburn was in charge of C coy; and he was at this O[orders group meeting]; and having listened to the whole thing, and feeling very content that I was A coy in reserve, [Colonel] Syd Thompson suddenly turned to me and said, Oh, by the by, Don, you are in command of C coy . . . Blackburn is not well and he is going back. . . .
>
> I immediately got the jitters; however I had the orders, and I went to C coy and took command. . . . There was very limited time in which to form up and make the attack . . .

Indeed, the attack started almost immediately after the O Group. I had seen the story of it in the regiment's official War Diary.

This was in the National Archives in Ottawa. At a long table in the reading room, overlooking the rapids of the Ottawa River, I had spent a day with this thick stack of legal-sized pages that were typed in landscape form. These pages had once inched their way through the typewriter of one of Colonel Thomson's staff. The page in front of me had been typed by the war diarist on December 20, 1943, inside the house where they held that O Group in San Donato. The diarist described the house.

> The upstairs rooms of the house in which B.H.Q. had its Headquarters, were used by the artillery F.O.O.s [forward observation officers] as an O.P. [observation post] because a sweeping view of the approaches to ORTONA could be seen from the windows.

I could see the unevenness of the ink from the typewriter and the pressure of its letter strikes on the page. In places, two letters were superimposed on one another—the typewriter's strikers had stuck together due to a bit of dirt or the speed of the diarist's typing.

> 0930 The Brigade Commander, Brigadier. B.M. Hoffmeister, held an 'O' Group at the Seaforth B.H.Q. outlining the plan for attack of ORTONA . . .
>
> In the Field ITALY
> 20 DEC 44

Dec 44? But it was 1943. I looked at the previous page. The year there had been typed correctly. Starting on this day, however, the diarist had mistaken it, typing *44* instead. Maybe this was a symptom of the circumstance. As the diarist observed at 09L5 hours—typing an *L* there instead of the numeral *1*, and then also misspelling *battalion*—

> Enemy shells falling in and around the Batalion area.

Typing under bombardment, that was just the start of the Seaforth diarist's mistakes. Through all the next seven days of the Ortona battle, the diarist continued typing the year as *44*.

The attack on Ortona began. From the house on the hill under bombardment, the diarist typed its progress. (I'm keeping the typos that appear in the original War Diary so the reader can witness the diarist's struggle with his typewriter—and with his nerves.)

> 0930 A heavy arty [artillery] pprogramme [sic] was laid on to precede and continue during the attack. Zero hour was laid on for 1000 hrs.
>
> 1200 Companies reported areas heavily mined and it was hindering progress.

On this page from a box in the Seaforth archive, Don Harley was remembering it.

> I think it was [Sergeant] Ellaschuck [sic] who led us across; he led us down; there was no fire at all, except the supporting fire from D coy and the 25pdrs [artillery] as we went down into that valley. But Ellaschuck got into a minefield; there was quite a solid minefield in the bottom of the valley . . . he yelled back that he was in the mines; however, we had to go on, we were in open country, and therefore I remember saying we'd have to hurry . . .
>
> When we came into the open of that valley we could see the mines all around us; and I remember so well there were mutilated bodies of Germans in that valley and in the minefield; and the

miraculous part was that we weren't under fire then, that we got right through that minefield . . . we could see them [the mines], they were humped, and it was a question of stepping over them as you ran. We ran really very fast across that; when we got to the other side the minefield and the lay of the country forced us towards the coast, and forced us towards the steeper cliff . . . it got steeper and steeper . . . we came under fire from the cliff tops, and we began scrambling up. . . . I remember . . . having to put my rifle over my back with the sling and go up on all fours. . . . As we went up that cliff the Germans at the top were throwing grenades at us as we went up, and that's where we began getting our casualties. . . .

We got to the top of the cliff and we went over that top with our bayonets, and we cleared out the slit trenches on the perimeter of the cliff and we got into those. . . . We had this little perimeter with the cliff absolutely behind us, and the vineyards and a sort of open space in front of us. . . . And we then came under terrific fire. . . . [The church] was not more than 200 yards away. But there was a vineyard in front of us, with all the wires and things, not much foliage, so that you could see through it . . . and the other side of the vineyard was a hedge and the churchyard beyond that hedge. . . . and the Germans then made a pretty heavy counter attack on us . . . in other words the fire increased terrifically, and we were very much afraid that they would attack in force with a bayonet type of approach across the vineyard . . .

War Diary

20 DEC 44

1500 C Company reported that they were engaging the enemy, with the support of tanks, in the vicinity of the Church. They were making good progress.

1530 C Company reported that they had driven off a counter attack and were now being heavily shelled and mortared by the enemy. They asked for arty [artillery] fire to be laid on the enemy positions.

1535 C Company reported many enemy machine gun posts in the church firing on them.

I was in contact with [the colonel] Syd Thompson [sic] then by radio . . . I asked him for support, and he said, well I can give you the 25 pdrs [artillery], and I'll lay that down . . . and he called down the 25 pdrs, but unfortunately their shells fell short . . . Now under the cliff just below us there was a bank, a steep drop of about 10 or 15 feet, and then a little bank, and then it went on down . . . And the wounded, we'd collected all our wounded, underneath this bank . . . There must have been a dozen that we'd collected, and others who'd passed on down the slopes . . . This counterattack came in, by just firepower we were able to keep it off. And Syd and I talked regularly on the intercom through that night. I remember so well his making some crack, and I said, well I'd rather be at the Savoy [luxury hotel in London], Syd, than sitting up here . . . And he said well, you wouldn't see the fireworks at the Savoy that you're seeing there; and I said well I could sure do with a drink, chum, would you send one over. And he said, right, I'll arrange that.

But I'm getting out of sequence. Before nightfall, during that counterattack, the 25 pdrs let loose, our own; but their first salvo fell short . . . and they hit our wounded in the cliff-shelf; and we had a number of casualties there. The wounded, there may have been more, about 20 of them, took off back down the cliff to go across the minefields . . . and I don't think a single one got across . . . I think they were all killed going across in the dark. I know there was explosion after explosion behind us, and I remember going down to them and saying for God's sake don't move; everything's all right if you stay here; but the minute one's back was turned they began fading off into the darkness, back. The night . . . We went through the night . . .

War Diary

20 DEC 44

1800 During C Company's attack, on the Church, which was thwarted by M.G.s [machine guns], a tank, and many hand grenades extensively used and thrown over the cliff on to the forward platoons, Lieut. L. Robinson was killed, and Lieut. Hanbury wounded. C Company dug in for the night 300 yards below their objective undergoing constant mortar fire.

There was a wall in the churchyard, and I felt if I could get round I could get into the church, and if I could get into the tower of the church I felt that I was in command of the situation. . . . I said to [Sergeant] Mottle if you'll take your [platoon] . . . I think it consisted of 12 or 8 men at that time, very small . . . make the right hook down that wall into the churchyard and into the tower, you'll command the position, and we've won the battle; and I said the only way to do that is with fixed bayonets and at the double . . . we'll try to give you supporting fire with what's left. And it was then that Mottle made that charge, a real bayonet charge, and he was killed. I know the next day, when we were relieved . . . there were 86 [of us who] started, and 22, 24 [of us] were left. I think those were about the numbers. But the Edmontons came in, we consolidated at the Church, the Edmontons went on into the town, left me behind in the church, and Syd came up and made the church his HQ.

War Diary

21 DEC 44

0600 The Loyal Edmonton Regt and C Coy of the Seaforth of C advanced into the South and South East extremities of the town, the Edmontons advanced forward, and C company to the area of the Church. The fighting was stiff, but good progress was made and it appeared that the town might be cleared by night. However, the enemy Paratroopers soon showed their intention of holding what they had, when they were pushed back into the centre and heart of the town. There, the buildings were packed together and the streets were narrow, allowing the Germans to demolish the houses and by doing so, the streets were completely blocked.

1100 It was decided that the Seaforth of C would detach another company to the Loyal Edmonton Regt's command to relieve one of their own coys from the job of left flank protection, thus allowing their unit a committal of more strength for the task of house clearing.

"Do you remember when you first saw the city?"

Shadows of birds fluttered silently through the sunbeam on the carpet between us.

"Yeah," Norman said.

He clasped and unclasped his hands on his lap as he quietly spoke.

"I, uh. The first building I went into, the Loyal Edmonton Regiment were ahead of us. And the first building I went into I remember, it must have been their headquarters. But anyway they had a lot of their dead in the building, and that was quite a shocking experience, to see all of their, the casualties that they'd had, and they were all in one building."

"Was it shocking because there were so many of them, or uh—"

"Oh just the fact that they were, they were dead you know and uh. They look very different when they're dead. You know all the blood has drained away, and they're very white. Faces. And uh, yeah that was kind of hard to take."

War Diary

21 DEC 44

1600 The C.O.'s [commanding officer's] and I.O.'s [information officer's] jeep and the 22 set [signals radio] vehicle moved up to the church where B.H.Q. had joined C Coy H.Q. Then the evidence of C company's stiff fight remained, as they were busy burying their own and enemy dead. The companies [sic] casualties being 7 killed and many wounded during the attack on the church.

Journal of H70551 Pte. McKay, A.J.

The church proper consisted of three or more rooms and an attic. A very substantial building. The attic I learned about from necessity. It was our safest high level spot for the 18 [radio] set. . . . The walls were heavy enough that the ensuing battle only scratched upon its surface and chipped here and there as if by a hammer-happy mad-man. But the rafters soon showed through the crummy lead tiles padding the upper floor against further outbursts of cannonade. . . .

There were no quiet days nor still nights. The churchyard became a graveyard and the rectory became a little war office of 2nd Brigade 1st. Can. Div. Near the church mortars had blasted loose the covering of a cript [sic] and rattled the brown bones of several generations. . . .

Inside the hollow church proper among the pews every sound above a hand clap ricocheted from wall to wall. It was a poor place

> to rest. The rectory was worse. A small shed on the lea side, which signal personnel not on actual duty sat around looking out into the distance across a choppy Adriatic and dreamed of the salty old Atlantic. And this was as it was—the gun smoke mixed with fog, wet soldiers, sad faced men going forward, wounded patched up or dying. The dead buried. The crashing, horrible enormity of war. . . .
>
> One company was set up within sound of the Adriatic. Its pleasant oceanic roars and rumbles never quite obliterated the ripping screech of incoming shells.

"The weather was lousy," David told me. "It was overcast, and drizzly, not really raining but overcast, and fairly cold. I say fairly cold it was about uh, oh, forty degrees."

In Ortona, David was a twenty-four-year-old lieutenant with the Seaforths. He had just returned to the regiment from his officer training course in England.

"I was posted to D company when I rejoined the battalion. They had just worked their way into Ortona on or around the twentieth. So, my first two days, I was sent out on the, D company was on the left flank, on the west side of Ortona."

```
War Diary
22 Dec 44

0800   D Company was committed to the town fight and
       were pushing up on the left flank coming under
       heavy enemy M.G. [machine gun] fire . . .
1030   Mortar bombs ~~falling~~ fell in B.H.Q. area and
```

Instructions regarding preparation of War Diaries (which will be kept from first day of mobilization, creation or embodiment), are contained in F.S. Regs. Vol. 1.

Title pages will be prepared.

WAR DIARY
OR
INTELLIGENCE SUMMARY
(Erase heading not required)

M.F.M. 11
40/P & S/37 (9/42)

Original, duplicate and triplicate be forwarded to O. i/c 2nd Echelon for disposal.

Place	Date	Hour	Summary of Events and Information	Remarks, references to Appendices and initials
In the Field ITALY	22 Dec 44	0600	The Enemy still shelling and mortaring the Battalion area.	
		0800	D Company was committed to the town fight and were pushing up on the left flank coming under heavy enemy M.G. fire.	RB.
		0930	D Company reported enemy concentrations.	
		1030	Mortar bombs ~~falling~~ fell in B.H.Q. area and set fire to the ammunition truck belonging to the Anti tank platoon; the exploding ammunition set~~ting~~ fire to he jeep belonging to the I.O., Lieut. A.W. Gray, destroying same. A party, with the aid of a rope, dragged a carrier and the 22 Set vehicle to safety. the A/C.O. Major S.W. Thomson, at a great risk, drove his jeep out of the danger zone. Continuous enemy mortar fire in B.H.Q. area all the morning, one bomb striking the roof of the church which was occupied by B.H.Q., there were no casualties.	RB.
		1300	D Company reported they were advancing, but meeting with heavy enemy opposition all the way, he enemy being well entrenched in demolished buildings.	RB.
		1500	A Company reported that they had observed an enemy multiple mortar in acton approximatley 3/4 of a mile from heir O.P. During the day, the battalion A/Tk guns fired many rounds of H.E. and armour piercing shells into the enemy occupied houses in the town, and the Battalion 3" mortars did a splendid job on selected targets.	
		1800	A Company were warned by the A/C.O. Major S.W. Thomson to move at a minute's notice to the area that had been occupied by D coy the previous night. The enemy shelling and mortaring quietened down during the evening, and Coy carriers were sent forward from "F" Echelon with ammunition and rations.	RB.

> set fire to the ammunition truck . . . one bomb striking the roof of the church . . .
>
> 1300 D Company reported that they were advancing, but meeting with heavy enemy opposition all the way, the enemy being well entrenched in demolished buildings.

"So anyway," David continued, "the thing I soon came to realize was the number of snipers around, and also the fact that the town was pretty well booby trapped. I lost three men at one time to a booby trap. I had sent one of my sections around to uh, to take out, to go down a side alley, and to get into a block of houses that were down there. But unfortunately they kicked in the door and it blew on them and uh, I lost, lost three men. And later on I found out, I saw the evidence myself, but the town was pretty well booby trapped. And I know the Edmonton regiment lost a whole platoon to a house that went down. So we were very careful, very wary of where we went when we entered a house.

"Now in order to move through the town, we were assigned a section of the city, to clear it. And uh, a very close up, close built little town, all attached housing. And on three occasions, on the blocks that I had to take out, we made our way up to the top floor and then worked our way through . . . usually by breaking down a wall to get into the next room, which was very slow, and you had to watch the house across the street too because if the enemy were up on the top floor of the house across the street, any movement, they would fire. It was bloody dangerous."

"Were the Germans mostly waiting for you on the top floors of the houses?"

"No they were, not necessarily, I wouldn't say that, no."

"'Cause I can't imagine how you'd even get into the house. A house is so full of furnishing and so on, the Germans would have so many things to hide behind—"

"Yeah."

"Inside the house—"

"Mind you, any ex—, if you blow a wall in, the explosion would go in, would go forward. And uh, I don't, honestly, just on two occasions that we found uh, dead, dead Germans in the houses that we went through. That we blew into."

War Diary

22 Dec 44

1330 B Coy reported that they had advanced 50 yards and had encountered stiff enemy opposition all the way.

1400 A Company was warned to prepare their evening meal and to be ready to move off in an hour and a half.

"We were, I think everyone was, jittery. And uh, not jittery but nervous. Because of lack of sleep. Poor food. We lived on bully beef and uh, M and V, meat and vegetable, which came in cans, and uh, didn't get much, very little chance to boil up tea or coffee. We got, one hot meal was sent up to us, this was after the, on the twenty-eighth, after the battle was over, that's the first—"

"After the battle."

"That's the first hot meal we got other than that Christmas dinner."

"And the other days, did you just carry some food with you?"

"We carried M and, hard tack, bully beef and meat and vegetables, and our water bottles."

"And you survived on that."

"Yeah. And we carried, we would, we only carried, no blankets, we carried a gas cape up on our bag."

"How would you get to sit down and have a bite to eat and go to sleep?"

"There was no movement at night. When darkness came in everybody stayed where we were, because it was so noisy, you couldn't move up the street without making a noise in the dark. And any noise like that would draw machine gun fire or sniper fire. So the only break we got was at night, we might get a very troubled, six, seven hours sleep. Daylight was, well dark came in very early, I would say about five thirty, six o'clock. And dawn around seven."

"Now would you sleep very close to the front line?"

"Just where we were. We stopped where we were and bedded down the fort."

"Was there anything in the houses that you could use?"

"Well yeah we did use the odd bed that was available. Yeah we did make use of the beds. But we had to keep constant guards out all night long, so, I forget what we did was it two hours on two hours off? I only had sixteen men in my, I'm talking about my own platoon now, and this was pretty typical of all the other platoons in the battalion. So that's the reason we were so frazzled at the end of the battle, from overtiredness."

War Diary

24 Dec 44

0600 The companies were still holding same positions despite heavy enemy shell and mortar fire. . . .

0800 The night had been a very trying one for the companies, as the enemy were using demolitions extensivley and their patrols were quite acive [sic] with grenades and machine pistols. A number of houses blew up during the hours of darkness.

1000 Today, the objectives were, a large demolished church, the town school, and command of 'dead horse Square', so named because of a dead horse lying in the centre of the Square.

"Very important man in the company is a signaler," Wilf was telling me. Wilf had been the Seaforth regiment's signals officer. In Ortona, he was based at the headquarters in Harley Church.

"As signal officer it was my job to see that the communications were good, or operative, and I couldn't get one company, Don Company, on the air. I called out a sort of an all stations call from our headquarters which was in the church, and Don company didn't come back on the air. So, I knew probably their battery had failed, or had worn out. I popped a spare battery in my haversack and went over to try and locate them, which I did, right at Dead Horse Square, one of those houses there, and when I got to the top—they always worked from the top down, these houses, the top was where the two signalers were. They were both sound asleep, absolutely passed out, completely from fatigue. The set was still going, everything was working, but they had simply expired through straight tiredness. Couldn't stay awake any longer . . . They were sprawled out on the floor. And uh, the equipment was there with them. They were asleep."

"How did you react?"

"Well right away I saw, it was quite obvious, they were simply so tired they couldn't function, without sleep. They'd probably been going for at least three nights without any rest at all. And uh, you could pump them up with a little bit of rum, sometimes, but these chaps were just, just through. Actually it was the oldest man in the signals platoon, of which we had about thirty men, and also the youngest, his partner was the youngest. His partner, it was uh, Howard Wylie . . . He was seventeen years old . . . Pop Warner and Wylie."

"Was that the first time that you went into the city?"

"Pretty well, yes I think that was pretty well the first night."

"Were you surprised by what you saw?"

"It was dark. You know, pitch black. And the first thing that hit me when I got to the house was there was a sentry there. He stuck a Tommy gun into my stomach, and said, 'The password?' Fortunately I knew the password. Which was 'happiness'. They'd say 'Hello?' And you had to answer, 'Happiness.' If you didn't answer 'happiness' you weren't very happy about the result. Anyhow, that was the, no I really couldn't say that I had very much comprehension of what was happening, except that I knew this fighting was going on in the city. Very tough fighting."

"Now when you went to find Pop Warner and—"

"Wylie."

"Wylie, you knew that they were with D company, how did you know where D company was?"

"Well, I would ask the intelligence officer. 'Where's Don company?' He'd say well they're in the first big house on the corner by Dead Horse Square."

"Now was Dead Horse Square one of the code words?"

"No. No, it was just a common expression, because there was a dead horse there. And you had no doubt about it being dead. Your nose would tell you that."

War Diary

24 DEC 44

1300 The Q.M. [quartermaster] Capt. D.B. Cameron, and staff, brought cooking equipment and supplies up to B.H.Q. in the church, in preparation for Christmas Dinner.

1500 The Padre. Major R.C.H. Durnford, arrived at B.H.Q. pointedly remarking on on his entrance 'Well, at last I've got you all in Church' . . .

1600 Major T.C.B. Vance O.C. 'A' Coy was reported killed in action and Capt. Harley assumed Command of the Company . . .

1800 The Companies were ecountering [sic] heavy enemy opposition around 'Dead Horse Square' A Company reported that they had one section in the church bitterly fighting the Germans who were at one end of the church, the church now being in ruins.

The enemy the companies were encountering were a formidable foe, the Paratroopers the

> cream of the German Army, veterans on many wars: Russia, Africa, France Sicily, and were instructed by their Officers to fight to the last man. During the day, the companies had advanced very slowly, and at night were in the peculiar position of being in the same buildings as the enemy, small hand grenade sorties taking place all night.
>
> One section of A company gained control of the school, wiping out resistance, but the enemy blew prepared charges under the building, burying 6 of the men. Attempts to get the men out were unsuccessful.

"There was a big cathedral in the square."

June had been the twenty-nine-year-old captain of the Seaforths' A Company. We were talking in his home in Victoria.

"And a church. Uh, it's a school. Actually, the school, I lost some men there because I sent a section over, and the school was blown up."

"The Germans had set a trap there?"

"Yeah. Yeah, they set a prearranged, but uh, no we came down this very narrow alleyway, and the school was over here, just a little one, the cathedral was over here, and there was, the front of it was partially knocked down, but there was a sniper up on the, uh, up in the top, and anytime we moved, we'd get fired upon. So anyway, one of the tanks managed to come up behind me in this very narrow road, and I pointed out to him where this firing was coming from, and I asked him, I said look it's right up there in the steeple of the church, but that's where they're shooting from, with a machine gun and snipers, and I want you to blow them out

of there. But he hesitated because it was a church. And I had hesitations myself but there was no other way about it. So he did, he fired a couple of rounds and that fixed them, drove them out of there."[3]

But we got down to the end of that street, if you remember Donald—

Clifford Wood was talking with Don Harley and the interviewer about the battle in Dead Horse Square.

> And then there was a schoolhouse in a square, and a church across, a big piazza and a big schoolhouse, which they defended for some time; and there we stopped pretty well over Christmas, I think . . . That's where we blew ourselves into the basement of this house, and you could practically walk through all these houses, through the whole city block, because they were all joined together . . . And we got down to that point . . . And on that rubble pile there were a couple of Seaforths lying dead, which we could never reach, because they [Germans] were sniping from the front. And up above us they were throwing these grenades down all Christmas eve . . . down from the top these potato mashers, running across the roof, we couldn't get out, but we could walk anywhere in those buildings we wanted to. . . .
>
> And I still think of where Tommy Vance was killed. . . . I remember one corner building . . . an old woman had been killed and she was sitting there and the tanks were running back and forth across her . . .
>
> (*Don Harley interjects*) Before she was killed she was mad . . . she was in the middle of that square, wandering about with her hair down, yelling and screaming, and then she was shot . . .

> (*Clifford Wood continues*) Nobody could move her at that time . . . This was Christmas Day, now . . . because we must have moved from that on Christmas morning up this new position during Christmas Day, because we went over to the Church for Christmas dinner . . .

"Do you remember seeing any Italians during the battle?"

"Very, very few," June answered. "They were hiding down in the cellars."

"Were you fighting around furniture and people's belongings?"

"I don't recall."

"It must be quite strange, fighting inside a house."

"That sort of detail, you had to keep your eyes too busy, looking and watching, and where am I going to go next, what am I likely to run into, all this, such a mental strain of uh, trying to figure out where you can go and what you do next that you, that sort of thing I just don't recall at all. There must have been, and of course some of the buildings were shops and what have you . . ."

"But you said you found some old ladies hiding—"

"Oh they were hiding and uh—"

"That was during the battle?"

"Mm-hm."

"Did, and you found them?"

"Well they were just sitting in a, in a, or cowering in one of the houses that we went through on the way up. And I don't know why they were there, no idea why they, I understand there was quite a few caves outside in the, that the Ger—, that the Italian population had gone to."

```
War Diary

25 DEC 44

0900    The Q.M. Capt. D.B. Cameron spent a busy
        morning fixing up details for the Christmas
        Dinner to be held in the church occupied by
        B.H.Q. The Protective Group sent parties
        of men around ruined houses in the town
        collecting chinaware.
```

"You could see the devastation of the city and all of that."

In Ortona, Denis was a twenty-two-year-old signals corporal working with Wilf in the church. We were talking at the kitchen table of Denis's suburban Vancouver home.

"Whole wall of a building down and all the rooms like a dollhouse in there, bathtubs hanging up there, it was, uh—"

"Was it hard to walk on the streets?"

"Oh yeah, oh yeah, it was just sort of tracks through the rubble."

The thought of the tracks prompted another memory for Denis.

"The, I guess the other very vivid memory I have of Ortona, and I don't know whether it was the square, dead, what they call Dead Horse Square, or, and I guess it was, or, 'cause there were the two churches . . . and this square was full of rubble, and the dome of the church had been half blown away so that was exposed, and there was a track through the rubble . . . and on the road there, in front of that church in the rubble, there was—oh how quite to describe it. You know the way older Italian women are all dressed in black."

"Yeah. Yeah."

"Well, this woman had obviously been killed from something or other, shellfire, hit by a truck or blown up by a booby trap I don't know but it was, she was on the road and she had been run over until she was just flat like roadkill. I've never forgotten that my whole life. Terrible thing, you know."

"I guess there were a lot of—"

"Oh of course. Sure there were. Sure there were. But uh, you get inured, you get a little callous. I mean that obviously affected me because it still does, to think that, that a human life was so little valued that it would become road kill in effect, like a, like a raccoon that's been run over on a highway several times, you know. That was somebody's mother, or sister, or wife."

War Diary

25 DEC 44

0900 The setting for the dinner was complete, long rows of tables with white table cloths, and a bottle of beer per man, candies, cigarettes, nuts, oranges and apples and chocolate bars. . . . 2 hours was to be allowed for each company for dinner. The menu for the dinner being: Soup, Pork with apple sauce, cauliflour mixed vegatables [sic], mashed potatoes, gravy. Christmas pudding and mince pie.

1100 C Company was the first Coy to eat Dinner in the church, a dinner that no/one had felt possible under such conditions, but no one had truly tested the ingenuity and resourcefullness [sic] before of the Q.M. Capt. D.B. Cameron and staff. From 1100 hrs to 1900 hrs, when the last man of the Battalion reluctantly left the table to return to the grim realities of the day, there was an atmosphere of cheer and good fellowship in the church. A true Christmas spirit. The impossible had happened. No one had looked for a celebration this day, another day of war. The expression of the faces of the dirty bearddd [sic] men as they entered the building, was a reward that those responsible are never likely to forget.

When C Company had finished their dinner, they relieved A company so that they might come back the 300 or 400 yards for the same, and so A coy relieved B Coy and B, D Coy.

1930 The latter were to become reserve Company, but the situation had grown tense with C Company on the left flank. Capt. J. McLean tookmhis [sic] Company back into the fight. Christmas day was no less quiet than he [sic] preceding ones, but it is one that this Regiment will never forget. Pipe Major Esson played his Pipes several times throughout the meals. During the dinner, the Signal Officer, Lieut. W. Gildersleeve played the church organ, and, with the aid of an improvised choir, organized by the Padre, Carols rang out throughout the church.

"And they came up with a meal," Wilf said, "that was cooked right behind the church with roast pork, one or two pigs were involved, in liberating the Christmas dinner.[4] Then, it was amazing to see the fellows coming in. They couldn't believe that at ten o'clock there was going to be a Christmas dinner, and then another one at noon, another one at two, and another one at four. Between four and six, there were two hours allowed for each company.

"And you know they came in tired, absolutely grizzly, unshaven, had very little sleep, they came in all of a sudden they heard some music and they saw some goodies on the table. Roast pork and vegetables, apples and fruit, chocolate bar, a bottle of beer, and uh, that was the Christmas dinner for them and oh my god this is impossible but you know there it was.

"They managed to scrounge, the quartermaster's staff managed to prepare the food, get it served hot, and also get tablecloths and cutlery. It was liberated from somewhere. It was liberated from various homes I think, probably. And the padre first thing he said was, well at last I got all you guys all in church."

"Were you playing the organ the whole time?"

"Yeah."

Journal of H70551 Pte. McKay, A.J.

There was no lull, no cease fire, no truce. Early in the day Q.M. (quartermastery) [sic] broke out several wooden cases of beer. The ration control relaxed and great effort by the catering personnel kept the Christmas meals hot. Combat weary infantry turned up, ate quietly. One company in while the rest held, so that there was more fighting in the spirits than love and the enemy persisted. Lt. Gildersleeve pulled his long frame into the loft by the pipe organ

> keys, while a private pumped the bellows, rendered a sad piece of consolling [sic] Christmas music.

"It was something we were very grateful for," Denis told me, "no matter what our religion or anything else. Just the idea that we could get a really good meal after, you know, some of the guys had had nothing but corned beef and hard tack, water if they could get it and tea if they could brew it sort of thing, so they hadn't exactly been livin' high off the hog. And to come back here was a great contrast, great contrast. But I don't think anybody thought too much about the apparent celebration of the Prince of Peace birthday.[5] And uh, no, I don't know what other people think about that, but I know what you're saying, that it does seem—but what were we to do, what were we to do? Say hey, now we've sung some carols we don't want to kill anybody? I don't think anybody really—it—it was—it's a matter of survival! You know."

> *Diary of Major Roy C.H. Durnford, Chaplain (P)*
>
> 25th—Sat. Xmas Day . . . Deathly chatter of machine guns. Rumbling of falling buildings, roar of guns (ours). Church. The tables set for Coys. . . . Roses, violets. Tom Vance. . . . "Holy night". The meal for "C" Coy. Brigadier & Colonel Cheered., The faces of new recruits. Fine speech by Don Harley. Orders to leave for front - a few hundred yards forward. 'A' Coy returns from front. Weary, strained, dirty - Cpl. June Thomas. I collect them for carols in Cloister (careful to make all

voluntary). They cheer (?) & come & join me. Gildersleeve (Wilfred) on harmonium & I singing. Soon have about 35-40.

Dinner. Medals for Indian (Webster, M.M.) & his Tommy gun. Sitting with patience waiting for Parachuteur [sic] sniper to move first. . . . The order to return to front. Faces of boys new to warfare! The reluctance, the faraway look, the nervous strain, the slight inebriation in few cases. . . .

'B' Coy comes in from front. News of Seller's death. Germans mining houses & blowing them after our boys get in. . . . Carols from Pipe Organ loft. Postie, Gowan, & other officers & men are pumpers. Cooking goes on behind high Altar, men eat in main body of Church. Piled up plates cover the altar; fruit & tins of provisions cover side altars. Carols, guns, vibration of near explosions, laughter, news of deaths. Wine, vaults, mail from home; signals bell with urgent ringing, yelling conversations over sets. Reunion of cronies. Farewell to return, as darkness begins to fall.

Don Coy comes in at 5 PM (about). We organise singing in Candle light by harmonium near high altar. I sing solo for a while with Gildersleeve at organ. Anxious time with lights. In flickering light & shadows I meet the men at the tables.

"Did it feel like Christmas?"

"Oh yeah," Wilf answered without hesitation. "Yeah, because you know there's the spirit. The spirit of Christmas is love, and thanksgiving. And I always, sometimes I've compared it as a tremendous gift, the gift of that supper that was given on the inspiration of the CO [commanding officer] and put into effect by the staff, could be rather vaguely compared to the greatest gift ever given to mankind on that first Christmas, one thousand nine hundred and forty-three years earlier. If you want to get down to basics, that's the thought that occurred to me. That was a tremendous thing, that Christmas dinner."

"And you know," Wilf continued, "everyone's trying to compare the terrible sacrifices that are made, the killing that goes on, with Christmas, and oppose to man's idea of Christmas, of peace and goodwill throughout the world. How can you compare those two, ever? Well there's that very vague comparison that I made up in my mind and I thought well, yeah there is something to that. And instead of the star up there in the sky guiding the Wise Men it was a signal flash, a signal light, from one of the companies. They use varied signal missiles to signal, 'we have captured the enemy,' or 'we are—,' these signals had a meaning. Sometimes if patrols were out in the area you'd get, just a white light would be thrown up by the enemy. There's a very vague comparison there between the Star of Bethlehem and the star from the forces.

"And then you try to connect it up still more by singing carols. And the carols are all connected, aren't they, with the birth of Christ. A lot of men, we found later from letters that they had written, or even poems that they had written, just picked out of a trench, out of a body, and one or two of them began, 'Hello Lord, I've never met you before, but I got a feeling that I'm going probably going to meet you soon. I hope you'll recognize me.' Now, little poems like that would occur to a man and he'd write them down on paper. And this would happen at a moment that he believed could be his last night on this earth.

"So, those things existed, and let's say that miracles can happen. And I'm sure they do happen. That's pretty well all I have to say, Ian, on Ortona. We'll never forget it. It will live as long as we live."

David Fairweather, Letter to Reginald Roy, September 10, 1967

On the way into the fight after our Christmas dinner I lost 3 of the reinforcements to shell fire . . . Late afternoon of Dec 25 I lost a Cpl and 2 men when they dashed across a courtyard . . .

Interview in the Mess with Dave Fairweather, July 25, 1960

One of [my corporals] with two of his men, they went down this lane, and I was watching at the time, and they ran across the courtyard, and the corporal banged this door open with his rifle, and it just went up and it killed the whole three of them. . . . at the same time [the Germans] had it covered with Schmeizzer fire . . . all within 50 yards of where I was.

"But there was no celebration, no anticipation of Christmas that I can recall," David told me.

He didn't tell me that he had lost six of his men on Christmas Day.

"During the day, Christmas Day," I asked him, "do you recall if you were looking forward to this dinner? You and your men. "

"I think we were looking forward to being taken out of the line for a little while and getting a hot meal, we knew we had a hot meal coming up. But that's the only, uh, perception I had. I wasn't thinking of Christmas Day as a holy day of any kind."

"And what was it like when you got back to the church?"

"Oh, unreal. To sit down—we sat on tables, I forget if there was a tablecloth or not. I think so. But anyway it was a well laid on dinner with cutlery and dishes and uh, and we had a bottle of wine, a bottle of beer each."

"A bottle of beer."

"Mm-hm. Yeah that came up somehow. And they had the organ with Wilf Gildersleeve, you'll like to talk to him about this, he was playing the organ and they had a little sing-song going. But it was unreal, really."

"I have to—"

For a moment I thought that my tape recorder had stopped.

"Oh, it's still fine. Just checking. So you say it was unreal, what do you mean by that?"

"I mean it's, to come back out of action and sit down at a good dinner. People, Christmas, singing Christmas carols and Joy to the World, I thought oh, baloney. It was hard to realize what was going on, and it was even harder in a way to leave, go back in."

That was the best David could do in his effort to explain his "unreal" feeling. When I tried asking him about it again, he changed the topic

THE SEAFORTH HIGHLANDERS OF CANADA

CUIDICH'N RIGH

MEN'S ANNUAL

ORTONA DINNER

SEAFORTH ARMOURY
VANCOUVER, B.C.

THURSDAY, DECEMBER 17TH, 1998
1930 HOURS

from the original Christmas dinner in Ortona to the recent re-enactments of it.

"Do you remember any particulars of the Christmas dinner, like who you, did you chat with the guys next to you, or singing, or—"

"No we sat with our platoons, that's all I remember, we all sat together and uh—"

"Did anybody make a speech, or was there any ceremonial type of thing like that?"

"No, no, just the carols."

"Christmas carols."

"And actually I don't think the men were, no, we didn't do much singing. But Wilf and the padre and, I think Corporal Greg, did some warbling . . . It was sort of a unrealistic interlude in a way."

"Do you mean unrealistic as in it wasn't a wise thing to do, or do you mean just that it felt quite strange?"

"I don't know if it was a wise thing or not. I think it did give quite a few of the men a bit of a boost. I found it, I was two minds about it because, we lost so many men the next two days after the Christmas period."

"Did you notice a change in your men because of the Christmas dinner?"

"I can't say I did, no. It became quite a celebration in years afterward. You could say we're still celebrating it, or still commemorating it with a big dinner at the Armouries."

In his answer to my last question, David seemed to change the topic abruptly from past to present. Looking back at this moment years later, I noticed his meaning behind it. David had underlined his main point to me. The dinner had become a celebration, he said, in the years afterward. He knew the tradition well; after the war, he'd remained in the regiment, rising to the rank of colonel and serving two terms as the commanding officer. In retirement, he was an honoured guest at the annual Ortona commemorative dinner. But "there was no celebration"—that's how he had started his story of the dinner—the original event had not been a celebration of Christmas, for him, at the time.

"My recollection of it is so vague."

Of all the Seaforth veterans whom I interviewed, Norman was the most reluctant to tell me about Christmas. And yet Norman did more than anyone to put me there, at the tables in Harley Church, among the soldiers who had just walked back from the fighting in Dead Horse Square.

"I can remember the sing-alongs they had, and that sort of thing, to keep things in a cheerful sort of mood. But the rest of it is pretty vague."

He went silent. I waited.

"There wasn't really a Christmassy atmosphere," Norman continued. "But uh, I can remember the candles. Of course there were no lights, so they had all these candles placed around. Ah, I guess that's uh, that's about all."

His mention of candles made me wonder.

"Was it dark inside?"

"It was dark. Yep. It was, it was evening. So—"

He went quiet again.

"Was it actually inside the church?" I asked.

"Mm-hm. Yeah."

"So you could see the altar, you could see the uh—"

"Yes, the altar was still intact, but a lot of the roof was gone. I don't know if there was a picture somewhere of that church. It shows what was left of it."

Norman paused again.

"I remember, maybe thinking of home, at that time. How nice it would be to be home. Yeah."

"Did it feel like it was Christmas?"

I could barely finish the question before Norman shot back his reply.

"No."

His head shook as he snapped the word. A stern expression had crossed his face. His voice, still quiet, was possessed with a sudden force.

"Not at all. No, there was no atmosphere there to make it feel like Christmas."

I waited, feeling chastened, in silence.

He took a breath.

"Anyway," he said, more gently now, "I hope those things never happen again."

Don Harley's story moved on to the day after Christmas.

> . . . and I went forward with my runner at first light to make contact with him again, and came under terrific fire in that street and realized that the house that he had commanding that bit of area was in the hands of the Germans; and then we had one helluva scrap there, and we got them back. They were all uncaptured; they'd all been made prisoner, all that night they'd been prisoners . . .

Suddenly I felt the silence all around me. No more sounds were coming through the floor and walls. Looking up from the paper under the desk lamp, I found myself at the table, in this little room, reflected in the dark window.

The Seaforth Armoury archive. I had been here an astonishingly long time. Was the association still in their meeting? And the cadets? Was anyone still here? Surely they wouldn't have all forgotten me and left the building. I dismissed that as a ridiculous notion. This was a military place—they wouldn't be so careless. But in that silence, in that remote corner of the Armoury, I could almost believe it was true. The very thought of it unnerved me. Quickly, I put the folders back in the box and the box back on the shelf.

At the door, despite my haste, I paused to look back at the stag head. From its place high on the wall, it was still staring blankly over the room.

Of course it was. It could do nothing else. Eyes frozen in time, it would stare that way forever.

I clicked off the light.

CHAPTER 5

They Said He Was There

HE WOULD LIKE TO be helpful, he said in a slow, deep rumbling voice. But he didn't remember much. "This is the thing, you know."

That was okay, I said.

And his wife was in hospital, he added. She'd just gone the other day.

I was sorry to hear that, I said. I understood this was not a good time. I wished him and his wife all the best and thanked him for answering my call.

This wasn't a big disappointment. In fact, he was probably doing me a favour. I had done more than enough interviews already and it was past time to be getting home.

I shouldn't even have been pausing at this payphone. There was a long road ahead of me—six days of driving down the Trans-Canada Highway, all alone. This was supposed to be the first day of that journey. After getting my morning coffee, I had planned to get right back in the car and go. It would be wise to drive hard today, getting well out of the mountains while the weather was still good. But the start of this beautiful fall day had affected me. It felt good to be out of the city. The morning air was crisp and fresh. It was a shame to be in such a hurry. On a whim, I had pulled out my well-worn list of members of the regimental association to see if any addresses were more or less on my way.

Now the phone call was effectively over. He was going to say goodbye and then I would say the same. My thoughts were already turning to other ways to appreciate the day.

His question caught me off guard. Where was I anyway, he asked.

I told him. He hummed in thought for a moment. His voice was like the low growl of a bear.

From there, he reckoned, I would get to his place by afternoon.

BILL'S DIRECTIONS LED ME off the highway onto a dirt road into a mountain valley. Yellow leaves drifted gently across the windshield as I drove. Birch trees were showing their fall colours; the mostly evergreen hills were mottled with yellows and greys. Down in the pastureland, herds of Hereford cattle were grazing. I slowed down to cross the occasional cattle guard that rattled as the car went over it.

Somewhere deep in the valley, I pulled up at a gate and turned off the engine. I was at the top of a driveway that sloped down to a dilapidated barn, an old tractor, and an old square house made of wood.

As I stepped out of the car, a border collie came trotting up the drive. The dog wagged its tail, sniffing me, then went around me to inspect the car. Then I felt something at my feet. A small border collie puppy had appeared out of nowhere and was licking my shoes and prancing excitedly. The adult dog returned and stared at me, as if to ask, *what now*? Nothing else around us was stirring, although I figured the arrival of my car must have made a great rumble in this still and peaceful air. I started walking down the drive. The adult dog led the way. I had to take care not to step on the puppy that ambled clumsily in my path. As I descended towards the house, I began to hear the sound of an axe splitting wood.

The door of the house was slightly ajar but I decided to continue walking past it, following the sound. Around the back, beside a woodpile, a man was standing, holding an axe. His face was thickly bearded and he was wearing a plaid wool jacket. I greeted him.

"Hi! Mr.——?"

He stared at me blankly. Through the lenses of his glasses I saw what might be a cataract in one eye. For a moment, I felt extremely weird in this place.

Then the man said in a perfectly normal and friendly voice, "Oh, you must be here to see my father. He's inside."

I went and knocked at the open door of the house. From within, I could hear the sound of a television, then heavy steps approaching.

"Hello, Ian."

The greeting startled me. He'd said my name without any question or hesitation, even though we'd never met. But of course, his assumption made sense; in this remote place, knocking on his door, I would have to be the guy he was expecting.

Bill was a tall, hefty man with big, calloused hands, a large weather-worn face, weary eyes, and thinning black hair. He was wearing rubber boots and an old-fashioned winter coat over a plaid polyester shirt. He led me inside, moving as slowly as he spoke, asking if I would like some tea. The kitchen had a wood stove in the centre, a wooden table and chairs to the side, and 1970s-era cabinets in pastel colours. On the counter, resting in a huge cast-iron pan, was a massive leg of pork.

"Hello, sir."

Now a chubby young man was greeting me. He had entered the kitchen from the living room, which was the source of the television noise.

Meanwhile Bill was telling me that he had been wounded in Ortona. It wasn't much of a wound though, he added. It's a terrible thing, war, he said, but everyone wants to glorify it. They think it's an adventure. His father had fought in the First World War and that had been terrible too. We were still standing in the middle of the kitchen. I asked Bill if we could sit at the table, and if maybe I could record our conversation with my tape recorder, which I would have to go back and get from my car.

"All right, Ian."

It was a relief to step outside. I needed to gather my thoughts.

Right away, however, Bill's son with the axe at the wood pile was gesturing to get my attention. He pointed across the valley.

"Do you see them?" he asked.

I looked where he was pointing. On the opposite slope, some cattle were grazing. What was so interesting about that?

"Deer," he said.

Then I saw them. Beyond the cattle, threading in and out of the forest, a family of deer were moving slowly along the treeline. I could just barely discern white spots on their fur coats.

"Oh wow." I wasn't sure how I was supposed to react.

A sudden scuffle was at my feet. The border collie puppy was climbing onto my shoes and biting my laces. The older dog came up close beside me, wagging its tail. I gave the dog a pat. Bill's son grinned and shook his head.

"She's always trying to steal attention from the puppy," he said.

As I went to my car, I wondered what I had got myself into. From one moment to the next this place was comforting and bizarre. Was anything going to make sense? Was it even safe?

One thing reassured me—the dogs here were happy and good.

We sat across from one another at the kitchen table, each of us with a floral-patterned chinaware cup and saucer. Bill wrapped his large hand around his cup, ignoring its little handle, and lifted it that way to sip his tea. I noticed that his thumb was purple and swollen, badly bruised. His face was stubbled. He was still wearing his coat and rubber boots. A few steps away from the table, at the foot of the warm wood stove, the dog was lying flat on the floor. Occasionally, she turned one open eye to watch us.

"Uh, I just gotta get my notebook out," I said. "Yeah I know a lotta guys don't like talking about it but—"

"No."

"—it's like you said about how we don't want to glorify war."

"This is it."

"That's why I want to write about it in a way that doesn't make—"

"Ah okay, yeah, yeah."

"I want to write about it in a way that doesn't make it sound like it was just an adventure, you know."

"Yeah that's right."

"That it was all great stuff."

"Well it wasn't short enough, that's for sure."

"So, I'll just, I don't know how much I explained to you on the phone but uh—"

"Not too much."

"I'll just remind you what I'm doing is my PhD research at York University in Toronto."

I felt awkward. Bill was looking at me skeptically. Maybe he was just shy. He seemed awfully quick to agree with whatever I said before I had finished saying it. Meanwhile, in the next room, the volume of the television had been cranked up. The young man had gone back there, out of sight, and was watching an American sitcom. The voices, jingles, and canned laughter kept intruding on my thoughts.

"Oh I see," Bill remarked. "Okay."

"So I'm a student at the university, and I'm writing about Ortona, just, I want to interview the Canadians, and the Germans, and the Italians, so that we get to see the battle from all the different perspectives—"

"Yeah. Yeah."

"—and when I write my thesis I want to use the stories of the veterans themselves, so it's not just me talking."

"No. Yeah."

"Um, would it be okay with you if uh, when I'm writing, if, if I quote you, if some of your stories are useful?"

Useful?! Why on earth had I said that? If I worried him about being useful, he would find it harder to talk. I was nervous, making stupid mistakes, off to a terrible start.

"Yeah, okay," Bill said. "I'm trying to think of some stories though."

"Oh, well don't worry about that."

"Uh, mmm, most of them are not too nice, Ian, that's the thing, you know."

There was his use of my name again. That was reassuring. He was still friendly. Maybe now I could get a grip.

"But, I'm interested in that too," I said. "Because, uh, things—"

Darn it, still stumbling over my words. The television was blaring a commercial for a compilation album of love songs by Kenny Rogers. What was it that I was trying to say?

"Like I guess maybe it's not a good thing to, to talk about, but some, some guys talk a lot about war."

I wasn't sure where I was going with this but it seemed to touch a nerve.

"I know!" he said. "Maybe some of the guys that weren't in, into it!" He chuckled.

"That's what I've heard, you know." I was eager to affirm his point. "I heard that uh, that the guys who were on the front line don't, don't tell the stories."

"No. No. No. I know," he said. "Yeah I've seen a lot of it, you know, almost three years of it. Front line soldier, you know. Yeah. I was only down the line once with pneumonia. This grenade blast just gave me a few scratches on my left leg, you know."

Bill had started to tap the table with his hand, slowly, while he talked.

"Um, but it did knock me cold. It was a good thing it was a German grenade because they had their uh, the outside was light tin. If it had been one of ours, you know, there was a lot of heavy shrapnel to our grenades, you know. Yeah. The blast was terrific I guess."

He was talking about this grenade blast as if I already knew the story. Had I missed something? Maybe this was the wound that he'd mentioned to me when I'd first entered the house.

"How did it happen?" I asked.

"Well I was running across the street. I shouldn't say it, for a better shootin'. They were upstairs in the building, you know. And this guy tossed a grenade, I guess he tossed it, I don't know. Anyway I was out, completely out for a while. Hmmm."

He had this habit of making deep, growl-like hums when he paused between thoughts.

"And anyway I guess, when I come to, our guys had left, and the Germans had gone too, you know. They were upstairs but somehow they got down, I guess. Our guys were trying to get 'em down so they, hmmm—"

"You woke up and you were, there was nobody around?"

"Nobody around no, it was quiet you know. There had been a lot of shootin', you know, and, there was still shells falling, you know, and they were shelling us and we were shelling them, you know."

There was an eruption of canned laughter from the television. Slowly and rhythmically, Bill's right hand continued to tap the table. Sometimes he absent-mindedly handled his teacup and saucer. His story was confusing me—he was immersing me in details without any context. But instead of asking him to step back and clarify, I decided to stay with him, wherever he was, and see where it went.

"Was it dark when you woke up, was it night?"

"No, it was still light. It was Christmas Day in '43, mind you."

"Christmas Day."

"Yeah, Christmas Day, yeah. We didn't stop for Christmas Day."

"Really."

"No. Yeah. They pulled them out company by company to have Christmas dinner in this bombed out church, you know. Uhhh, the name of it escapes me but, um. And then they went back into, hmm, up front you know, as soon as they had dinner they went back. They had a bottle of beer, and roast pork, and uh. All the vegetables I forget. Yeah. They scrounged all this, uh, this meat from the Italians and vegetables and, yeah."

Now I was further disoriented. There was something odd about the way he was saying this. He had suddenly switched from talking about his regiment as an inclusive *we* to a distant *they*.

"But, you were, you were wounded, and you were left for dead on Christmas Day."

"Christmas Day."

"So did you make it back for the dinner that all the other guys were having?"

"They said I was there but you know I don't remember it? I guess I was kinda still dazed, you know, yeah."

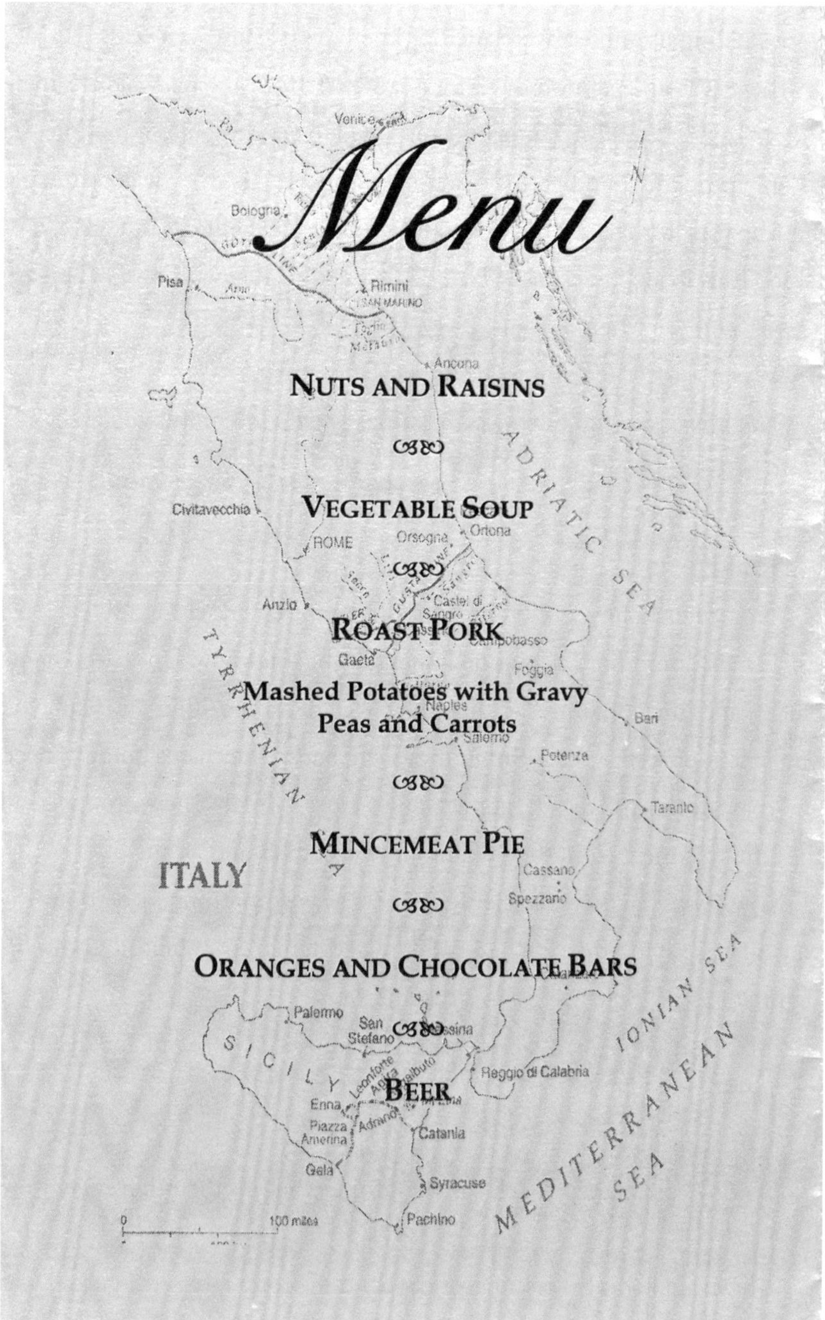

Menu

NUTS AND RAISINS

VEGETABLE SOUP

ROAST PORK

Mashed Potatoes with Gravy
Peas and Carrots

MINCEMEAT PIE

ORANGES AND CHOCOLATE BARS

BEER

Bill swept his arm back and forth on the surface of the table, making a swishing sound from the sleeve of his coat.

"Yeah, and uh, the postmaster, oh about three or four days after that. He kept track of the guys that were wounded and killed you know. He says we sent a telegram home. What was his last name. Sinclair? Sergeant Sinclair?"

"Oh yeah."

"Said we sent a telegram home there that you were killed in action. He says uh, we'd better send another one. They had called the roll you see? And I was there, you know. Odd, eh?"

"What did you think about—"

"Yeah it was down in my, I got my pension and it was down in my uh, uh, you know all the data on you, you know. Down there, you know. Hmmm."

"Did you write to your parents to tell them you were still alive?"

"They knew, they knew. Uh, sister said oh I knew you wouldn't be killed." Bill chuckled. "That's what she said when I got back, yeah."

"But how did you—" I decided to get back to the story of the wound. "So you woke up on the street, alone."

"Yeah."

"Do you remember how you got yourself out of there?"

Bill thought for a moment. Then with a start, like it was an amazing discovery, he exclaimed—

"I guess I walked out!"

His voice returned to its lower tone and rumbling pace.

"It was quiet, you know. There was no shootin' going on. Our guys had pulled out, and the Germans had left, you know. Yeah."

"And where were you wounded?"

"I wasn't wounded I was, just blast, you know. Yeah. I got a few scratches on my leg that's all. In fact I never even went and reported it you know."

"Just blast."

"Just blast."

"You mean just the blast will knock you out?"

"Yeah. Oh yeah it'll, you know. Yeah it will. From these German grenades, they were all blast just about, you know. Yeah. If you got a direct hit it would kill you all right. Or within ten or twelve feet, but it must have been, well I don't know how far it was. How would I know?"

"Yeah."

"Yeah."

"Right. Jeez."

"Yeah."

"What company were you in?"

I wasn't any wiser on the story of the wound. By asking about his company, maybe I could get onto some solid ground. Also, in this way, I might check the plausibility of his narrative. I was having doubts about the soundness of his mind.

"C Company then."

"C Company."

"Yeah."

"You were, so that was the one led by um, Don Harley, I heard. Do you remember him? I think he was the captain?"

"Captain Harley, yeah, that's right, yeah."

Bill paused in thought, and frowned. "I thought our company commander was wounded that day."

I waited for him to continue, but he was expecting a reply.

"No?" he said, looking troubled.

I shrugged.

"All right. What was his first name?"

"Don."

"Don Harley."

"I think his nickname was Lulu."

"Oh, okay. Yeah."

Bill paused again and furrowed his brow.

"Yeah the colonel was Thomson then in Ortona wasn't it?"

I nodded. Bill continued.

"Colonel Thomson, yeah. Hmmm. We called him Fartsack Thomson."

"What did you call him?"

Bill chuckled.

"Fartsack Thomson, yeah."

"Fard?"

"*Fart*-sack Thomson."

"Fartsack!"

Now we both laughed.

"Yeah," Bill said, calming back down into seriousness. "He was good though."

"Um, there was, I think in C Company there, I heard a story that a couple of guys got, captured, in a house, by the Germans."

"Mm-hm. Yeah."

Bill was nodding. His face took on a curious expression.

"Do you know that story?"

"Yeah," he said, dryly. "I was one of them."

"You were one of them!"

"Yeah, that's right, yeah."

"No kidding. Can you tell me about that?"

"Yeah, well anyway, we were, they put us right up front, you know—"

A FEW TIMES IN my research, I had come across this story, but never in any detail. My first encounter with it was in the National Archives. On the page of the Seaforth War Diary from Christmas Day, the diarist made this ominous observation as the last company was leaving the church.

> 25 DEC 44
>
> 1930 ... the situation had grown tense with C Company on the left flank.

This foreshadowed what the diarist was to learn the next morning.

> 26 DEC 44
>
> 0930 'C' Company reported that 2 sections of one of their platoons had been cut off and at the present time it was impossible for them to link up with the Coys.

Hours later, the crisis was resolved, and more was learned about what had happened.

> 1300 C Company reported they had recovered their 2 missing sections intact. Some of the missing men had been prisoners of the Germans in a house, but were turned over loose, when our troops captured the house, killing many and taking 16 prisoners.

I was curious to know more, but that was the end of it. I looked in history books for more of the story, but the only one that mentioned it had nothing more to add.

Months later, by the time I was in the Seaforth Armoury, I had almost forgotten about it. Then, while reading Captain Harley's narrative, it dawned on me—here was that story again.

> Ellaschuk still had his [platoon], and he was in a house and was . . . I remember warning him very carefully that there would be a curfew, and after nightfall we would not make contact with each other until the following day. But it was absolutely essential to keep a sentry at the door of the house he was in all night. And during that night he was attacked, the sentry had gone to sleep or they'd all gone to bed or something, and they were attacked, and I went forward with my runner at first light to make contact with him again, and came under terrific fire in that street and realized that the house that he had commanding that bit of area was in the hands of the Germans; and then we had one helluva scrap there, and we got them back. They were all uncaptured; they'd all been made prisoner, all that night they'd been prisoners, from about eleven o'clock on, but they hadn't been moved out . . .

Harley gave no further description. In the following weeks, in my interviews in Vancouver and Victoria with Seaforth veterans, I sometimes asked about this incident. Nobody had even heard of it.

Except for June. He mentioned it before I asked. It came to him while he was describing his experience of the battle.

"It was just going from one building to the next and we were gradually chasing the Germans out. And a lot of time we didn't even see the Germans. That was one of the strange parts of it. We very, very seldom actually saw them. Now there were times when some of our soldiers took prisoners, but I wasn't involved in that end of it. And they took some of us prisoners.

A matter of fact, on one occasion they took some of ours prisoners, we got them back and took *them*! I wasn't involved in that one."

June wasn't able to tell me anything more about the story. That was as much of it that he could remember, or had ever known. He had, however, put his finger on what made the story interesting. Whoever those Canadians were who had been captives of the Germans, they must have "seen" the Germans in a very exceptional way. As June had emphasized, the Germans were so rarely seen. The same point—how rare it was to actually see the Germans—had been emphasized by many of the Edmonton veterans.

> *What were you shooting at?*
> Windows.
> *Other windows.*
> Yeah. Well, there's nobody standing there to take a shot at.

> You're just going into buildings and, you're firing a few shots and guys just, make a dash, you know what I mean? You may not have found a target to shoot at but you were shooting down there anyway so that no German would be there, eh?

> We had some very good looks at dead ones.

In June's words, this was "one of the strange parts" of it. Even up close in the house-to-house fighting, the living enemy remained mysteriously invisible. Sometimes the Canadians could hear the enemy's steps and voices. Sometimes the Canadians got to see them dead. Sometimes they got good looks at the living, but those were usually Germans they had taken prisoner—and then, being prisoners, those Germans were disarmed and subdued. What the Canadians hardly ever got to see was the Germans in violent action. The Canadians were constantly experiencing that violence, pushing into it, fearing it, suffering it—the hail of bullets from a German machine gun; the sudden, bouncing arrival of a German hand grenade and its blast; the out-of-the-blue shot from a German sniper; the detonation of a doorway that the Germans must have booby-trapped. The Canadians saw the impact of all this on the bodies of their comrades. But as for the actual German men who were behind it, for the most part those men could only be imagined. Rarely, the Germans manifested as fleeting images, but little more.

Suddenly now, Bill was telling me he'd been a captive of those fleeting images.

I was taken aback. It was extraordinary. Surely, for Bill, this had been a profound experience. And he must have known that it was a rare story, one that he was uniquely positioned to tell. So why had he not mentioned it to me earlier? Why had he waited until, by pure chance, I happened to ask him directly about it? If I hadn't raised it myself, would he ever have got round to sharing it? Instead, he'd told me repeatedly about some wound that hadn't even hurt. What was going on in his head?

I had just started to get comfortable with Bill, but now, as before, I had doubts. I wondered about his grip on reality. He had, after all, told me at the outset that his memory was not very good. And then he'd told me he was trying to think of some stories. Perhaps he had meant that a little too literally. Perhaps that was why his storytelling was so confusing, so lacking in necessary context—he was just making it up. Was that possible? I couldn't rule it out. His manner and appearance, the purple bruise on his thumb, the TV blaring in the next room, the leg of ham on the counter, the guy outside chopping wood—this whole place was weird to me.

Except for the dog at the foot of the stove. She had closed her eyes and seemed to be smiling a bit as she slept.

"And we had fought for a while that day, you know. And they left us there, you know, they didn't bring us back. Anyway during the night the Germans closed in around us, you know? And we were more or less prisoners, you know? Well C Company attacked on Christmas Day, and uh, anyway we escaped in the counter attack, the Germans all went upstairs, you know. And uh, we were down below and we got out of there. We picked up some gun, I had a, well I was packin' a Bren gun and I got a hold of it you know. And uh, anyway. Uh. They were shootin', I was trying to get across the street, you know. For a better shot with the Bren gun? And this is what happened then, yeah."

"That's when you got wounded."

"Yeah, yeah. Well I wouldn't say, I guess—"

"Well, or when you got, knocked out, yeah."

"Yeah."

Now at last, here was the context for that wound he had been telling me about.

"Jeez. When the Germans had you surrounded, like, did they actually come in the house, and disarm you—"

"They, they just closed in. Corporal Deriter was doing guard duty. I guess it was just before daylight in the morning, you know. And uh, we heard him talking out there, you know. And he says, you better come out! So anyway, I didn't know it was Italians or what, you know I could hear jabbering out there you know. Anyway I went out and, and uh, a German shoved a Schmeisser in my ribs, you know, and, uh. Handy ho! He says, yeah."

"Handy?"

"Handy ho. It means hands up."

Bill chuckled.

"Oh I see."

This made sense. "Hands up" in German would be *Hände hoch*. The details of the story were starting to come together. I was doubting him less now.

"So I did of course, and I didn't know what the hell was going on you know. And then they took us back to this house and a German officer was there. He was the equivalent to our lieutenant, I forget what they call them. He could speak broken English, you know."

"Oh."

"Yeah. So he asked a few questions. Yeah they took our paybooks and everything, you know. Anyway, we were there for a few hours. It was, it got broad daylight, and we heard shootin' you know and guys hollerin' you know, and the German officer says, 'I want you guys to keep quiet,' he says, 'your, your men are attacking,' you know. And so they were all, they all went upstairs, you know. Yeah. Anyway, uh—"

"They left you there?"

"Oh yeah. Yeah. Yeah!"

Bill chuckled.

"What, did he trust you?"

"Well they, no." Bill became serious again. "You see, what could they do?"

He swept the table back and forth with his arm.

"They all went upstairs, this is it, what could they do, yeah?"

His tone was plaintive, as if he was sorry for them.

"They figured upstairs was better anyway, you know. And anyway uh—"

He stopped abruptly and looked down at the table.

After a moment, he broke his silence.

"Oh what the hell. We had a guy by the name of London [name changed, for reasons explained later] in the company, you know. And uh. Uhhhh, no I got to think about that."

He stopped again.

"Um."

He stared down at his china teacup.

"The German officer come down with his hands up. Yeah. For some reason."

He looked back up at me.

"And a sergeant, a German sergeant. Two. They both come down, you know. And uh, this London says—"

Bill's voice took on a barking aggressive tone.

"—'Are there any more Germans upstairs,' you know, 'any more upstairs? Come out of there!' And a grenade come down, you know. And of course London pulled the trigger and shot the German officer right in the heart, right dead centre you know."

"No kidding."

"Yeah. So he just keeled over and died. And they took the sergeant prisoner. And uh, this little guy, little German, shot one of our guys in the throat, as he come through the doorway, you know. With a Schmeisser. And anyway, Woody Taylor our first aid man is trying to, to stop the bleeding but he can't and, poor guy he died in his own blood, you know."

"Gee."

"Yeah I know. Yeah."

"The, the little German, you mean—"

"Yeah"

"—shot—"

"Okay."

"—shot the guy in the throat when—"

"Yeah."

"—when they attacked you the first time?"

"Okay. Yeah. Yeah. So anyway the little German guy had his, his uh, Schmeisser pointed right at my chest you know? And I don't know why he didn't pull the trigger. But he didn't. And anyway, Corporal Plant, who was around back of me, grabbed him and pulled him over. And I got the Schmeisser away from him, you know. And, so they took him prisoner, too, you know."

"My god."

Peals of sitcom laughter suddenly erupted from the television in the next room.

"But," I asked, "the, the, the officer got, got shot?"

"He got killed."

"But he was coming down the stairs with his hands up?"

"He had his hands up when he come down, yeah, and London shot him. Well, London was kind of that way, you know. He, he was killed a week or so after that anyway."

"Really."

"Yeah. He was a real German hater."

"Oh I see."

"Yeah. Hmm."

Both of us went silent. Bill lowered his eyes. He seemed deep in thought. I could see his chest moving under his plaid shirt and coat. I wondered what to say next.

"What was, when the Germans were holding you in the house that day, the officer spoke some broken English?"

"Mm-hm."

"Um, did he talk to you much? Like—"

"He asked—"

"—he took your paybooks, but was he curious about, you know, interested in talking to you about—"

"Well he, he asked how many Shermans there was in town, Sherman tanks, you know. And of course we didn't know. We wouldn't tell him anyway you know. Actually 'cause we didn't know, we weren't with the tanks, you know. We were with infantry."

"Hm."

Bill went quiet again. I considered my next question.

"What were the Germans like?"

"Treated us real good, mind you, yeah."

"Yeah?"

"Yeah. They gave us some of their cigarettes, and—"

He sighed.

"And they were terrible cigarettes, so anyway."

He lowered his eyes.

"Oh yeah?" I chuckled. "They weren't as good as yours?"

"No," he said, grimly, looking down into his teacup. His hand tapped the table.

Both of us were silent again. I wondered. How could I learn more about his experience with the Germans? I decided to ask for some descriptions.

"Do you remember what the officer looked like?"

"Oh god, no, no."

Bill's voice was pained. His face winced and he shook his head, still staring into his cup.

"Yeah," I said, awkwardly.

I worried that I had upset him. I tried to think of what to do next.

Bill broke the silence, speaking slowly, eyes still down.

"Anyway, somebody rifled his pockets. They usually did, you know. And they found a picture of his wife and a little girl, uh—"

"Oh."

"I know, this is what—terrible you know. Yeah."

"What did—?" I started to ask, but stopped. "Um—"

Bill's chest was heaving slowly. His face was grimacing and his eyes were squeezing shut. I felt an urgent need to give him something else to talk about. Something simple, unemotional, just the facts.

"Well how many were you that were taken prisoner? How many guys with you?"

"There was one section," he answered. "Uh, Corporal Deriter's section. I was the Bren gunner of his section. And uh, yeah."

"So a section had like uh, five guys?"

"No, more than—"

"Or ten guys?"

"Yeah seven or eight guys, yeah." Looking up from his cup, he added, "Depends. Sometimes we were understrength, you know."

He was perking up, his voice regaining its vigour.

"Yeah. Anyway we were up against that first German paratrooper division. I guess you heard that already, eh?"

Bill had suffered a traumatic experience that he'd been afraid to revisit and share. It was clearly not something he had worked through prior to this moment, not even in the privacy of his own mind. It was as if the grenade blast at the end had shattered and scattered the whole story. He was recovering it in bits and pieces and assembling it while we talked. One fragment led him to another, but he wasn't finding them in chronological order. I doubt that he'd ever narrated this experience; I was witnessing him put it together into a story probably for the very first time.

This was one reason that Bill's story had come out in such a disorderly, confusing manner. Another reason was his emotional ambivalence about telling it and his internal debate about how much to share. At the start, he was only prepared to tell me about the grenade blast. He hadn't wanted to go into what had happened in the house before that. But I was asking him how the blast had happened. In his effort to control his thoughts and speech while explaining the blast to me, there was a moment when he uttered part of his internal struggle out loud.

"I was running across the street. *I shouldn't say it*, for a better shootin'."

He didn't want to say where he was running from and why; he didn't want to take the narrative back into the house. But then, caught by surprise shortly afterwards by my direct question about the captured and rescued Canadians, he decided to tell me—or perhaps, against his will, he couldn't help blurting it out. Even then, however, after letting it slip, he was still conflicted as to how much he was going to share. As he approached the moment of the German officer's death, he stopped himself, then started, then stopped and started again.

"*Oh what the hell.* We had a guy by the name of London, in the company, you know. And uh. *Uhhhh, no I got to think about that.*"

This was why, at first, Bill had been so strange to me. Despite his warmth and friendliness, he had unsettled me with the apparent randomness of his speech, and I had intuited that his talking was sometimes not even directed at me. With my lack of experience, I wasn't able to comprehend this behaviour as symptomatic of trauma, nor did I know how to adequately respond. Bill must have seen that he was confusing me. When he made his decisions to share more of his story, he may have been driven by a desire to no longer be alone with it. He may also have been driven by a desire to help me out of the confusion that he had put me in—he wanted to help me understand.[1]

"THEY SEEN A LOT of action in North Africa, you know. We had a tough time with them, no foolin'. Yeah we took Ortona house by house, street by street, you know, yeah. And attacked just about every bloody day, you know."

Bill seemed to have cheered himself up. I thought maybe it was safe now to return to the topic of the Germans he had met.

"Now, I'm interested in the uh, you got such a close up look at the Germans, 'cause you were taken prisoner."

"Mm-hm."

"Um. What uh, did they seem like tough guys? They've been described as fanatic, or ferocious, in the battle."

"Hm. Well I guess I suppose they were, all right. They attacked. You know. They killed us. And we killed them. This is what it amounted to, you know. Yeah."

Bill went silent.

He had mentioned killing. This reminded me of a question I had thought of earlier.

"You said this guy London was a German hater. Was that, um—"

"Don't uh—"

"No I won't—"

"He's dead now, don't uh—"

"Yeah."

"Yeah I know."

Bill was clearly sensitive about the topic of London. Though he didn't spell it out, I understood *He's dead now, don't* as a request not to damage London's reputation by sharing what he'd done and repeating that he'd been a "German hater." Anyway, London wasn't really the subject of my question.

"Yeah. Um, does that mean that most, most guys weren't like that?"

"No I don't think we hated 'em. We used to say when we were down the line, 'Going up to meet the hated Hun,' but uh, I don't think that meant anything, you know. I don't think we hated them, no."

"Do you remember the names of the guys who were taken prisoner by the Germans with you? Aside from London, you said there was a corporal, and—"

"No London wasn't, no he was, they attacked, uh—"

"Oh that was the attack."

"Yeah that was the attack."

"With the other guys—"

"Yeah. Well, there was Corporal Deriter. There was only about five of us. God, do I remember the names. Yeah, the names escape me. He's dead anyway. Yeah, I think uh, well my memory is not good."

"Well it's hard to remember names too."

"Yeah. There was an Indian feller, I forget his name."

"Oh yeah?"

"Yeah."

Suddenly from the living room a voice called out. It was the young man.

"What about that guy Farley Mowat?" he hollered.

It was a jarring interruption. Despite the high volume of the television sitcom he was watching, the young man had evidently been eavesdropping on the conversation between me and Bill. He also seemed to be aware that Mowat was a veteran of Ortona. Was it possible that, like me, he'd read *And No Birds Sang*?

Bill was unfazed.

"No," he said loudly in the young man's direction. "Farley Mowat was with uh, Hasty P's [Hastings and Prince Edward Regiment] I think."

"Oh yeah," the young man hollered back.

"Yeah," Bill said.

"Yeah," I said.

"Yeah," Bill said in a normal volume, turning his attention back to me. "They were in Italy with us all right."

I thought of a new question.

"Were you guys scared, while you were—?"

"I'll say we were!"

"Yeah?"

"How could you be not? Yeah. Yeah."

"Could you talk to each other?"

"Yeah. Yeah. How do you mean talk?"

"Like I'm wondering how you spent that day, like it was a few hours that the Germans had you there in that house."

"Yeah about six, seven hours."

"Yeah so jeez I'm wondering what did you do?"

"Yeah we could talk to one another yeah, yeah, that's right."

"Was there a German watching you all the time?"

"Oh yeah, yeah."

Four chimes sounded from a clock on the wall.

"He ducked upstairs as soon as the shooting started though. It was a bet—, you know better, better shot, better shooting upstairs too. The guys are down below, you see, you know, yeah."

"Why did they keep you in the house? Why didn't they send you back to their—"

"Well the German officer said 'When it gets dark,' he says, 'we'll take you back, behind the lines,' you know. I guess they were afraid to move. Everybody was afraid to move there, I'm telling you."

Bill had been with the Germans when they came under attack by his fellow Canadians. He had watched the Germans up close as they defended themselves from the attack. He had witnessed his fellow Canadians get wounded and killed by German bullets. One Canadian was shot through the throat. Bill watched the man drown in his own blood. Bill watched the German officer drop dead when London shot him through the heart. And then the barrel of a German machine gun was pressed into Bill's chest. Just like the German officer, Bill was about to be shot through the heart. However, the "little German" holding the gun had hesitated to pull the trigger. All these years later, Bill still wondered why.

After witnessing this shocking violence, Bill refused to judge the Germans as any different from himself. He might not have been conscious of it, or not wanted to express it openly, but he revealed a feeling of empathy or shared suffering with his enemy. This was evident in his ways of talking about them, including his subtle rejection of demonizing portrayals of them. When I asked Bill whether the Germans had been "fanatic" or "ferocious" he didn't directly contradict the terms, but subtly undercut them. He began with a tactful concession—"I guess I suppose they were"—but then softened the claim in his own words: "They attacked." He immediately followed this with the levelling observation: "They killed us, and we killed them."

Bill's feeling of equivalence between Canadians and Germans was conveyed not only in the lexical content of his words but also in their poetic pattern. He made use of a symmetrical structure in which the word *killed* was repeated—and thereby emphasized—while the pronouns traded places (*they* killed *us* and *we* killed *them*). This wasn't a one-off turn of phrase; the same device had appeared earlier in our conversation when he described waking up alone in the street to the sound of the battle: "They were shelling us and we were shelling them." Not only was this an ingrained habit of speech; it pointed to an ingrained moral outlook. For Bill, there was symmetry in the actions on both sides.[2]

There was an undercurrent of empathy in the way Bill spoke about the Germans. He told me they were afraid to move, and added, "Everybody was afraid to move there." He did not say it directly, but when the attack came, he must have seen the fear on their faces. When he described the Germans running upstairs during the attack, he asked me, almost plaintively, "what could they do . . . what could they do, yeah?" He knew from his own experience in the house to house fighting that upstairs was a safer place to be. Now he was seeing the Germans in battle having the same needs and feelings as himself. And it must have been further disorienting for Bill when, in a way, he shared the German experience of being in a house that was attacked by Canadians. Was it *our* house or *theirs*? Were the attackers *they*, or were they *us*?

Beyond his captivity, Bill had other experiences that may have shaped his refusal to pass moral judgement. What strikes me in particular is his awareness of the suffering of Italian civilians during the battle. Looking back on the transcript, I notice what might even have been a subtle confession that he was directly involved in causing some of their deaths. At the time of the interview, however, this completely passed my attention. It was hard to keep up with Bill's storytelling. It was getting late in the day, I had forgotten to eat, and fatigue was setting in.

"Everybody was afraid to move there," he said.

On the television in the next room, a new show was loudly starting.

Wheel . . . of . . . Fortune!

"Really."

"Even Italians," he said, "yeah. Yeah."

And now, here are the stars of our show!

"So the German guy spoke pretty good English."

"Just the officer. A little bit. You would understand him and that's all, you know, yeah. The rest of the guys didn't."

"You mentioned the Italians. Did you ever see any Italians during the battle?"

"Oh yeah, they were in town. Yeah. Oh yeah. And quite a few of them were killed too, you know."

"Yeah?"

"Yeah, one poor old lady, she was laying on, they had to go out for water you know, she was laying half on the street and half out, and I didn't see this but they said the tanks were running over her feet, mind you. Nobody pulled her out. Well there was lots of snipers too you know, you'd have to not move around too much, yeah."

"Yeah. Did you ever, 'cause you were goin' in and out of houses all the time. Did you ever go into a house and find some Italians?"

"Yeah, sometimes, yeah, I know, most Italians killed too because—"

Bill paused. He took a deep sigh.

"I mean, what you done, you threw a grenade through a window if you could first, you know. You know."

I was confused. Bill seemed to have abruptly changed the topic. Whatever it was that had come into his mind, it had deeply depressed him. He was looking down at the table again.

"But you didn't know. You didn't know who was in there, actually, you know? Usually there was Germans in there but, uh. Yeah."

"Hm."

"There was no place to dig in. In a city, you had no slit trenches at all. You were just in the houses, you know. Yeah."

He took another deep breath and sighed.

"I'm going to get a drink of water."

Bill rose stiffly from his chair, teacup in his blemished hand, and walked to the kitchen sink in his rubber boots. Without stirring, the dog followed him with her eyes. From the television in the next room came the rapid ticking sound of the spinning wheel.

. . . buy another vowel. An A please . . . An M. Any Ms up here . . . Yeah.

IT WAS PAST FOUR o'clock. Bill had taken a break for water. I decided I should start wrapping the interview up.

"There are other guys that I'm looking for that I've read about."

I mentioned a few names. Bill didn't know them.

"You've heard of Plant then."

"Yeah. Yeah he was the guy that grabbed that little German with that Schmeisser from behind. Pulling him over and I got the Schmeisser away from him, was Corporal Plant, yeah. He was one of the, in the attacking, attackers, you know."

"Oh who came—"

"He wasn't with us as a prisoner. Yeah he was in the, it was London and, oh god I forget all the names."

"Did they know that you were prisoners?"

"No."

"Or were they just attacking?"

"No, they were just attacking, yeah. Yeah. Yeah there was shooting come, through the doorway and everything and of course then the Germans all run upstairs, you know. Yeah. But uh, this guy come through, one of our guys come through the doorway, and this German stayed down and he shot him in the throat as I was telling you."

"Gee. And you guys, like, I guess you were unarmed, right? The Germans took your guns away."

"Yeah that's right, yeah."

"So what were you doing while the Canadians were coming, and the—"

"As soon as the shooting started we were laying flat on the floor, I'm telling ya. Right through the doorway, yeah. They were using uh, oh about a 45 Browning, whatever they had, you know. Probably a Bren gun, probably rifles and everything, you know, yeah. And somebody started to holler, in English, and then they quit, you know. Yeah. Then they quit."

"Who quit?"

"The, our guys quit shooting through the doorway, yeah."

"Oh I see."

"They kinda figured that uh, you know—"

"You were inside."

"Yeah that's right, yeah."

I had intended to wrap up by asking about some names, but the name of Plant had got us back onto the story of what happened in the house. This reminded me that I was still missing some context, including what Bill had done after the attack.

"Now, after this whole fight for the house where you escaped from the Germans and you were knocked out, did you get to stay out of the battle after that?"

"No."

"You had to go right back in?"

"Uh, well, I didn't even report it, you know."

"Really."

"I could have been a bit woozy but, a lot of them, most of the guys were then, you know. Battle fatigue and everything you know, yeah. So they probably didn't notice it. Yeah."

"Jeez. Battle fatigue."

"Yeah."

"What was that?"

"Well, so much noise and shells and everything you know and, a lot of stress, you know. Terrible amount of stress, yeah. Some of the guys couldn't take it, and they sent 'em back behind the line, you know, and, like uh, you know they got jobs in echelons behind the line and, yeah."

"Do you remember how the rest of the battle went?"

"Yeah."

"After Christmas?"

"Yeah we uh, yeah we kept street cleaning or street fighting, whatever you want to call it, till the twenty-eighth of December I think it was, and then the Germans left overnight you know."

"How did you feel when the battle was over?"

"Well, of course I had to feel better all right. Yeah and we went out on rest for a little while, and then the Fifth Canadian Division come to Italy, you know. Anyway, they went through us and Pescara was the next . . ."

He began telling me about battles that came after Ortona. He didn't seem to be getting tired. On the contrary, he seemed energized. On a whim, I decided to ask him if he'd like to see pictures of Ortona.

"Yeah okay."

From my bag, I took out my book of old photographs from the battle and handed it to him. He laid it on the table and opened it. For a while, he said nothing as he slowly turned the pages. Some way into the book, he sighed.

"What a mess."

He paused on a picture of Canadian tanks.

"Who supported us? Calgary Tanks, I think it was?"

"Three Rivers," I answered.

"Three Rivers, was it? They had Sherman tanks, didn't they."

"Yeah."

"Yeah. Well, the streets were all blown up, you know, and rubble, all, you know. It was uh, ten, twelve feet of rubble, you know. Well I guess they'd knocked it all down, they shelled us hard you know, and steady."

He went back to turning the pages. A few photographs later, he stopped and stared a while. It was a picture of the church of Santa Maria di Costantinopoli.

"That's the church where you had Christmas," I said.

"Oh yeah. Christmas dinner, yeah." He hadn't looked up from the page. He continued staring at it a while longer.

"Hmmmmm."

"So you don't remember anything about that dinner."

"No," he replied in a tone of finality. "I don't."

"But they say that you were there."

"This is what uh, um, Bobby Frolick says. He was in the same company, you know."

He stared at the picture a bit more. Then he added, "They say that uh, when they knew they had to go back, you know, their faces didn't look too happy, you know. Of course they wouldn't be, you know."

The phone rang on the kitchen counter. Bill got up and went to answer.

From across the room, over the din of *Wheel of Fortune*, I could hear him telling the caller that his wife was away in hospital. He asked if he could take a message. I reminded myself once again that I should be going.

Bill returned to his seat. I was about to thank him for talking to me and signal my readiness to wrap things up, but right away he had something to say.

"We get together every December down at Vancouver. The Ortona veterans, you know. And there's only about—well we stand up."

He sat up straight in his chair, stiffly, imitating the ritual. Then he relaxed.

"All the other troops are there. The young guys, you know. And they have the Ortona veterans stand up and god there's only six or seven of us left you know."

"Gee."

"Yep."

Bill went quiet. I thought about what to do next. How to conclude the interview.

Somehow, the question came to me.

"Do you think—do you think it was worth it?"

Bill stared at me. His lips were pressed and his brow was drawn tight. He took a deep breath and uttered another one of his deep growling hums.

"Hmmmm."

He was quiet for a moment.

Slowly, with a grim look on his face, he said, "What can I say to that?"

"Yeah I don't know."

I was afraid now that my question had angered him.

"I'm just wondering," I said nervously, "because you told me how you got into it thinking it would be an adventure and—"

"Yeah well it was the thing to do then, you know. I don't know."

He shook his head and swept his arm back and forth on the table.

"Yeah. You know there was a war on, and uh, and uh, just about everybody was joining the army you know, first year of the war. A lot of them, you know. A lot of guys I knew. So—I joined up."

I nodded. We were both silent for a moment. Then he continued.

"And I guess the Germans had to be defeated I suppose. Yeah. I don't know who was wrong and who was right in that war but, all wars are the same aren't they?"

"Hm." I nodded. "A lot of guys—"

Bill cut me off.

"I don't think they need to happen at all, you know. Wars, you know. I don't think so."

I nodded. "I appreciate you talking to me about it."

"Yeah okay, Ian."

"'Cause it's not an easy thing."

"No. No."

"And some guys I've called have told me that they didn't want to talk about it."

"No. No. Yeah."

"But can I ask you one last question?"

"Mm-hm."

"I'm just curious why—I know it's not a nice or easy thing to talk about—what—why did you agree to talk to me? 'Cause you could have said I'm, you know I'm sorry, I'd rather not."

"Well I was going to say it but, I don't know, I kind of took a liking to you, so."

"Well I appreciate it."

"Yeah. I thought you were sincere you know. The thing is, uh, I wish you wouldn't quote all of this, you know."

"Okay."

"Yeah."

"Can I tell the story but I just don't mention your name?"

"Yeah okay."

"Is there just one thing in particular you don't want me to quote you? Or all of it?"

Bill thought for a moment.

"No." Then with a frown, he added, "Do you have to mention names?"

"You mean your name, or the others?"

Bill scowled. I reckoned it was a hard question. I was on the verge of saying no problem, I'd change all the names, but suddenly he shook his head and swept his arm back and forth across the table, as if to brush all his concerns away.

"It doesn't matter. It doesn't matter."

"I don't have to mention your name."

"No. Okay. Yeah."

"Would you rather, I'll just leave—"

"Yeah. Yeah. You can tell the story, yeah. Tell the story."

"I just won't say who told me."

"Okay. Yeah."

"'Cause for me it doesn't matter. I can make up a name too."

"Well the guys know about this grenade blast anyway, and uh, listed in, as killed in action, because they knew Sergeant Sinclair the postmaster of the regiment you know, and they knew that he sent a telegram saying that I was killed in action you know, yeah."

"Do they know the story of the, being prisoners?"

"Oh I think so, yeah. Yeah. Yeah that's down in the history of the Seaforths I think, that a section got cut off. You probably read it if you read the history."

"Yeah. But it's interesting because when you read the book, all that you read is just that a section got cut off."

"Yeah they don't mention any names."

And so, in my version of his story, London became London, and Bill became Bill, neither of them known by their real names. What seemed to worry Bill was the potential reaction of his regimental comrades, as he went on to explain what "the guys" already knew.

Evidently, they didn't already know Bill's story of what happened inside the house. In fact, they probably didn't even know that Bill had been a prisoner. If they had, surely one of them would have mentioned it. I had asked many of them if they knew the story of that section of their regiment that had been captured and rescued. Very few had heard of it, and no one could tell me who was involved or what exactly had occurred. Their lack of knowledge wasn't due to not knowing Bill. Though he lived in a remote area far from the city, he must have met "the guys" at least once a year at the Ortona dinner reenactments. And in all those gatherings, through all those shared evenings, apparently he'd never spoken of this.

Why not? He was reluctant to speak about London and the German officer, but he could have told the story without mentioning that part. If he chose to keep the whole experience to himself, it may have been because of an instinctive fear—not just of recounting what had happened, but of revealing how he felt about it. Perhaps, more than anything, he feared how those feelings would be judged.

In regretting the war and feeling compassion for the enemy, Bill was not as alone as he thought. I had interviewed some of "the guys" that Bill was worried about, and I knew that some at least shared the same feelings as him. If I'd been able to grasp the importance of the point and collect my thoughts at the time, I could have told him. Would that have been a wise thing to do? I don't know. In any case, I might not have done it well if I'd tried. I was exhausted and running out of time.

We stood up from the table. I was picking up my bag and clipboard, ready to go.

"*Harley*," Bill suddenly exclaimed. "Did he lose an eye that day?"

I had to think for a moment.

"*Did he?*" Bill repeated, a deep frown on his face.

"I don't know," I said. "I heard he was—"

"I thought our company comman—"

"I heard he was wounded."

"Yeah I thought our company commander was wounded."

I sensed that Bill wanted me to stay longer. Maybe more memories were coming to him, and he would have liked to share them and compare them with what I knew. I was probably a rare person who could keep him company in that way. I had an interest in his memories; I knew enough of the context so that he didn't need to explain; and I wasn't personally involved, so he had less fear of being judged.

But I couldn't do that for him. I needed to go. The young man who had been watching television in the next room had now entered the kitchen and was moving pots and pans around—maybe getting ready to make dinner. As for me, I was feeling the effects of forgetting to eat all day. My energy was flagging, the day was getting late, the sun would soon be setting, and it occurred to me that I was on a remote dirt road in the mountains and still had to find a place for the night.

I thanked Bill and said farewell.

He was right about Captain Harley. The company commander was indeed wounded on "that day"—the day Bill was held captive and was later rescued. A few hours after reporting the rescue of the prisoners, the Seaforth war diarist wrote: "1700—Capt. D.S. Harley, O.C. C Coy was severely wounded." As for Don Harley losing an eye, I haven't been able to confirm that, but according to Padre Durnford's diary, he did suffer a head wound.

> 5—Weds. [January 1944] Have visited Don Harley at St. Vieto [sic]. Doing well but miracle he is alive. Back & head wounds. I write his wife.

On one significant point, however, Bill's memory was mistaken. He remembered all of this as happening on Christmas Day. He was quite sure of this. "It was Christmas Day in '43, mind you. We didn't stop for Christmas Day." In fact, it wasn't Christmas. It was the day after—December 26.

This is evident in the War Diary. It is also evident from another source which I found in the Edmonton archives after interviewing Bill. That source is a newspaper article by a Canadian war correspondent filed from Ortona shortly after the battle.

The correspondent's story relied largely on the testimony of Sergeant Elaschuk who had been one of the prisoners. While Elaschuk's account makes it clear that Bill was mistaken about when these things happened, the account does corroborate much of what Bill remembered.

> **15 Canadian Captives of Germans in Peril as Own Men Raid House**
>
> By DOUGLAS AMARON
>
> With the Canadians in Italy, January 10, 1944.
>
> Captured in street fighting for the Adriatic coast town of Ortona late in December, 15 Canadian soldiers were released by

a patrol from their own battalion after several harrowing hours in a house with the Germans.

Their captors whistled the Lambeth Walk, dance tune fashionable several years ago, and wanted the 'true story' of Rudolf Hess, Nazi leader who landed by parachute in Scotland in May, 1941 after flying from Germany and has been a prisoner since.

The enemy, commanded by a youthful paratroop lieutenant, treated the Canadians well and, when the tables were turned by the arrival of the patrol, surrendered their weapons and left the house as prisoners of their erstwhile captives.

CSM. [Company Sergeant Major] John Elaschuk of Turin, Alta., pieced together the story as he enjoyed a rest at Company headquarters. Elaschuk, promoted from sergeant only Saturday, was getting his first respite from forward company duties since the Canadians entered the Mediterranean fighting.

'An hour after Christmas dinner we went back into action and during the night took out two sniper posts,' said the slim N.C.O.

Elaschuk had a rendezvous with the corporal in charge of this section and, not knowing he was a prisoner, made his way through holes in buildings to the appointed spot. Pte. Wilfrid Haimes of Vancouver was with him, following a few yards behind.

'I crossed the yard and went through the gate to join a group of men I thought were the corporal's section and the first thing I knew three German automatics and a machine-gun were pointing right at me,' Elaschuk said.

The Germans whispered words he could not understand but which he took to mean 'keep quiet.' Then they led him to a house where the other Canadians already were being held prisoner. The soldiers there included Cpls. Alex Ray, Vancouver, T.R. Plant,

Calgary; Ptes. Stan Simon, Creston, B.C., George Cunningham, Joussard, Alta., Wilfrid Etue, Goderich, Ont., G.S. Gilmour, Toronto, V.A. Murphy, Vancouver, B.C., and H.A. Hudson, Gogama, Ont.

'The Germans didn't search—just told me to empty my pockets, which I did,' Elaschuk related. 'They took away any government issue stuff such as knife and compass but returned all my personal belongings including my watch.'

There were twice as many Germans in the building as Canadians and only two loaves of bread. The only order was that the men keep quiet and muffle their coughs.

None of the Germans was more than 24 and Elaschuk said one of them was 'not a day over 17.' Their officer, who spoke French and English, was about 20.

The Germans were wearing spotlessly clean, well-pressed uniforms for they had just returned from leave. They tried hard to pump information from the Canadians, using indirect methods of interrogation which had little effect on the wary Westerners.

'They asked us about Sherman tanks and we told them we knew nothing,' Elaschuk continued. 'We gave them the same answer when they wanted to know how many Canadians had been killed in Ortona.

'They knew Mr. Churchill had been sick and were especially keen to hear the true story of Hess. They wanted all the details but as I didn't know much about him I couldn't give them information even had I wanted to.'

The Germans were all ardent Nazis and all carried pictures of Hitler. They hadn't much to say about the war except for a comment by the officer that 'win or lose, you Canadians can return to Canada and be happy—if we lose, we lose everything.'

The Germans whistled bars of the Lambeth Walk and the Blue Danube waltz. Elaschuk said he was almost tempted to join in himself.

The number of Canadian prisoners, only seven or eight at the start, increased to 15 as it became lighter. When Elaschuk was captured two Germans had taken Haimes to another house and asked him where his section was quartered.

'I told them I didn't know,' said Haimes. 'After they had finished with me they took me back to the street. We passed a house and one German wanted to throw a grenade through the door but the other stopped him, shone a flashlight in instead.

'Just then a gramophone in the house started playing (it was a record from the opera Carmen) and the door opened. A corporal came out and the German grabbed him. Then they went in and brought out the others.'

The Canadians were brought together in the same house and 15 were in one small room with a guard which varied from six to eight Germans. Other enemy troops were in upstairs rooms overlooking the street.

'About 12.30 a.m., the Canadians went into the attack and were coming to our building,' Elaschuk said. 'The German officer took me aside and told me all the men must keep very quiet.

'Then he went upstairs and as soon as he had gone the six Germans in the room turned their weapons over to me—all but the youngest who held on to his automatic until a Jerry sergeant-major took it away from him.'

Things began to happen fast. The Canadians in the street let

> loose everything they had at the house and Elaschuk said 'All you could see in the room was feet flying as the Jerry soldiers tried to get away from the firing.'
>
> Elaschuk and the other Canadians started shouting and only their yells prevented them from being mortared. Some of the prisoners and the Germans, who by this time were prisoners of the Canadians, started across the street. The Germans upstairs opened fire, killing a Canadian and wounding the German sergeant-major.
>
> The German officer came downstairs to surrender and a German upstairs fired after him, wounding a Canadian Bren gunner. In the scramble which followed the officer was killed.
>
> It was not very clear what happened after that for, said Elaschuk, 'it was just a case of Germans and Canadians scrambling from one building to another until we reached our headquarters.'
>
> 'The Jerries were just as anxious to get away from that place as we were and they were genuinely glad to be our prisoners.'
>
> Before the afternoon ended 20 prisoners had been brought in and four Germans killed. Elaschuk returned to action that night and helped to round up the eight enemy of the original 32. Three of them were killed and the other five taken prisoner.

Padre Durnford seems to have heard the same story, possibly at the same time as it was told to the war correspondent. In Durnford's diary entry on January 7, 1944—three days before the news article was published—he noted the curious detail of the *Carmen* records, plus another curious detail that was not in the news article: the German officer had asked the Canadian prisoners not only about tanks, but also about Christmas dinner.

> 7—Fri. 14 of our boys caught playing records of Carmen opera. Questioned by Jerry officer about Xmas day meals. About 'Sherman tanks' then spoke English. Then later he and his were captured & shot. (Pity).

If only I had been able to share these accounts with Bill. I wonder what more they might have prompted him to remember and share.

Might he have remembered the music from *Carmen*? Might he have been able to tell me who, among his comrades, had put that record into the gramophone, and what that man was thinking when he did? (Might that actually have been Bill?)

Might he have remembered the tunes the Germans whistled while guarding the house, with their Canadian captives, during the quiet hours before the Canadians attacked? (One of those tunes, "Lambeth Walk," was a hit song from an English musical. In the years just before the war, the song had started a dance craze across Europe and North America. If the Germans had just returned from leave, then perhaps the tune was on their lips because they had just been dancing to it.) Might Bill have remembered the German officer asking questions about their Christmas dinner? And the officer telling them that he had more to lose in this war than they did?

These details might have reminded Bill of more that he'd seen, thought, and felt. On the other hand, much of what happened in the house might have been forever lost from Bill's memory—or never held. On that morning as he sat helpless in that house with the Germans, he must have been shocked, frightened, and sleep-deprived. As a member of C Company, he had been in house to house combat for days without a break. He told me about battle fatigue, "so much noise and shells and everything you know and, a lot of stress, you know. Terrible amount of stress." By the time he was being held prisoner and smoking a terrible enemy cigarette, how much capacity did he have left in him to observe, listen, and remember?

There was much that Bill had undoubtedly forgotten from his time in the house. Tunes that were whistled, words that were spoken—for Bill, these and many more aspects of the experience may have slipped away. And yet something had left its mark: a lasting trace, a feeling of sympathy for the German officer. It was an emotional residue that he wanted to suppress. Others might not have understood why he felt it. Perhaps he did not fully understand it himself.

And there was one key detail Bill remembered that was missing from the other accounts. This was Bill's observation about how the officer was killed. The war correspondent's article was vague on this point. While acknowledging that the officer had attempted to surrender, the article attributed his killing to the "scramble" which followed, as if it had happened by chance. The padre's diary entry hinted at a more unjustified shooting—"he [the German officer] and his were captured & shot." But the padre was writing loosely, making rapid notes to himself. The padre surely didn't mean that the officer was first captured, then shot. That would be a blatant war crime. The padre would hardly jot down such a thing and then call it a mere pity.[3]

Unlike those other accounts, Bill was convinced that the officer's killing was unjustified. "He had his hands up when he come down, yeah, and London shot him . . . right in the heart, right dead centre." Bill's conviction that it was wrong was implied in the way that he talked about it, including his wish to protect London from being named and his suggestion that it was best not to speak ill of the dead ("don't . . . he's dead now, don't . . ."). And yet it was never all that clear to me what was wrong about London's action. Whether there was a shot fired by the Germans upstairs (according to the newspaper account) or a grenade which the Germans threw down (according to Bill), in either case it seems that as the officer was coming down the stairs, the Canadians were suddenly threatened by an attack that came from behind him. In that circumstance, even if some Germans had their hands up, was it not instinctual that London would pull the trigger?

Perhaps Bill's judgement of London wasn't really based on London's actions. Perhaps what it really came down to for Bill was London's attitude—he felt that London had wanted to do it anyways and was happy to be given a reason.

Or perhaps there were important details still missing from the story which would explain why Bill felt the way he did. This might include the location of London and the officer in relation to the attack from upstairs. Perhaps London had no need to shoot in the officer's direction. Furthermore, perhaps some elements of the story as it was reported in the newspaper did not actually happen, or not in the order in which they were told. Had there really been a shot fired or grenade thrown by the Germans from upstairs? If so, had that actually come before London shot the officer—or had it come *after* the officer was shot, as a reaction, not the provocation? After the fact, there could have been an understanding among Bill and his comrades that they would tell the story in a way that protected London. Such an understanding could even have been silent, never spoken. In the context of a protective group narrative with shared silence about certain details, Bill might never have known if his comrades had seen the same things that he did. In his way of remembering and feeling about the incident, Bill may have felt forever alone.[4]

He was certainly isolated from his comrades in his experiential absence from Christmas. They said he was there at the dinner. He had no memory of it. This was the famous meal which, in the words of the war diarist, "this regiment will never forget." Bill had forgotten. So what was it like

for him, after the war, to attend all those re-enactments as it became a public tradition? He was one of the dwindling number of veterans who were honoured for having been there—yet he carried no trace of it within.

To explain that glaring gap in his memory, Bill had turned to the grenade blast that had knocked him unconscious. He remembered waking up alone in the street but had no recollection of how he got out and found his company. "I guess I walked out!" He reasoned that the physical shock of the blast—its impact on his brain—could explain why he had no memory of making his way to the church, eating dinner, and celebrating Christmas with his comrades. "I guess I was kinda still dazed, you know."

However, in order for this post-blast "daze" to work as an explanation for his memory gap, the blast needed to have happened before the dinner. And for this to be true, the events leading up to the blast needed to have happened on Christmas morning. And so, working backwards from his need to explain his memory gap, Bill may have reasoned that it was during Christmas Eve and Christmas morning that he'd been a captive of the Germans.

As we know, that's not when it actually happened. The War Diary, Don Harley's testimony, the newspaper article, and Padre Durnford's diary all place the captivity and rescue during the night *after* Christmas dinner and in the morning of the next day. But those are all archived materials. The one place where Bill might have noticed a discrepancy between his story and other accounts was in his regimental history, which briefly mentions the event:

> Early on Boxing Day the enemy managed to surprise this small group of Seaforths and capture them. For about seven hours the Germans held them until the rest of the company recaptured the house and the Seaforths were released.

It's possible that Bill never read the regimental history. And if he did, he might not have noticed how the incident was dated—or if he did notice, he might have thought it was wrong. After all, the author could only write what he'd been told, and when it came to this story in particular, Bill probably felt that not everything that was told had been true.

There may be another and more important reason that Bill placed his story on Christmas Day. Beneath the surface, there was an emotional logic to that choice—it aligned with his belief in what Christmas is meant to be. His expectation of peace on that day was implicit when he told me the timing of his bomb blast: "It was Christmas Day in '43, mind you. We didn't stop for Christmas Day." That remark is only meaningful if it's grounded in the unspoken belief that they *should have* stopped.

During Bill's time as a captive in the house, there was the hint of a stop—a brief moment of peace and, if not fellowship, then at least friendliness. The conditions were unequal, of course, and imposed by force; the Canadians were being held against their will. But the Germans "treated us real good." There were gestures of reciprocity, not only in the gift of cigarettes, but perhaps in other things Bill no longer remembered—things that nonetheless may have left an impression on him. According to the newspaper article, the German officer didn't just "pump" the Canadians for tactical information; he also wanted to know what they had heard about Hess, the Nazi leader officially branded a traitor.[5] And according to the padre, the officer inquired about Christmas dinner. Perhaps he was being strategic—hoping that a show of friendliness might get the Canadians to let something slip. But he might just as easily have been curious: eager to learn something about these men who, until now, had been as ghostly to him as the Germans had been to the Canadians. His interest in what they knew about Hess suggests that he wasn't blindly loyal; he had doubts about his own government's version of events.

In any case, it's impossible to know whether the officer and the other Germans in the house were sincere when they were being amicable. They may not even have known that themselves. By all accounts, they were as mentally and physically exhausted as the Canadians. That's certainly how Bill saw them—tired and frightened like him. In this, and in other ways, Bill had an experience of their shared humanity. It made sense to him that such a moment would happen on Christmas Day.[6]

So this was Bill's story of Christmas in Ortona—the story he kept hidden. It's what he truly remembered—even as he upheld his regiment's tradition of commemorating the "unforgettable" Christmas dinner, the public memory that he stood for ("We all stand up") but didn't share.

In the end, he chose not to hide it anymore.

"It doesn't matter . . . Tell the story . . . Tell the story."

To the world, it may not mean much. But to him, it was no small thing to give away. I can't say for certain that I've understood what it really meant to him. I don't know how it will be received. He took the risk of letting me tell it—releasing it, so it would no longer be his alone.

THE WORLD OUTSIDE WAS quiet. The sun had dropped below the mountain tops, and long shadows spread over the valley. The cattle were gone from the pasture. There was no sign of Bill's son, nor the puppy.

As I walked up the gravel driveway, the older dog suddenly appeared beside me and trotted ahead. She led me as far as the top of the driveway, then stopped and watched as I went through the gate. Before getting into my car, I stood for a moment, looking back. Far across the valley, where the pasture met the forest, nothing was stirring—nothing, at least, as far as my eyes could tell. I opened the car door. The dog turned and trotted back down to the house.

Driving slowly down the dirt road, rattling once more over the cattle guards, I wondered how it was going to be for Bill now that he had told his story. He and the young man would be eating dinner now, and then probably they'd watch whatever was on the TV. I remembered Bill squeezing his eyes shut when he recalled the picture that was found in the officer's pocket. As brown leaves drifted from the forest canopy across my windshield, I thought of how a feeling for an unknown man and his wife and daughter had travelled to a place that was so remote from them, and had survived for so many years. I thought of how that feeling had outlived them, perhaps even the little girl. I thought of how in this quiet mountain valley those unknown lives had been a memory. The fact that they were remembered here was something they would never know.

CHAPTER 6

Weihnacht Means Christmas

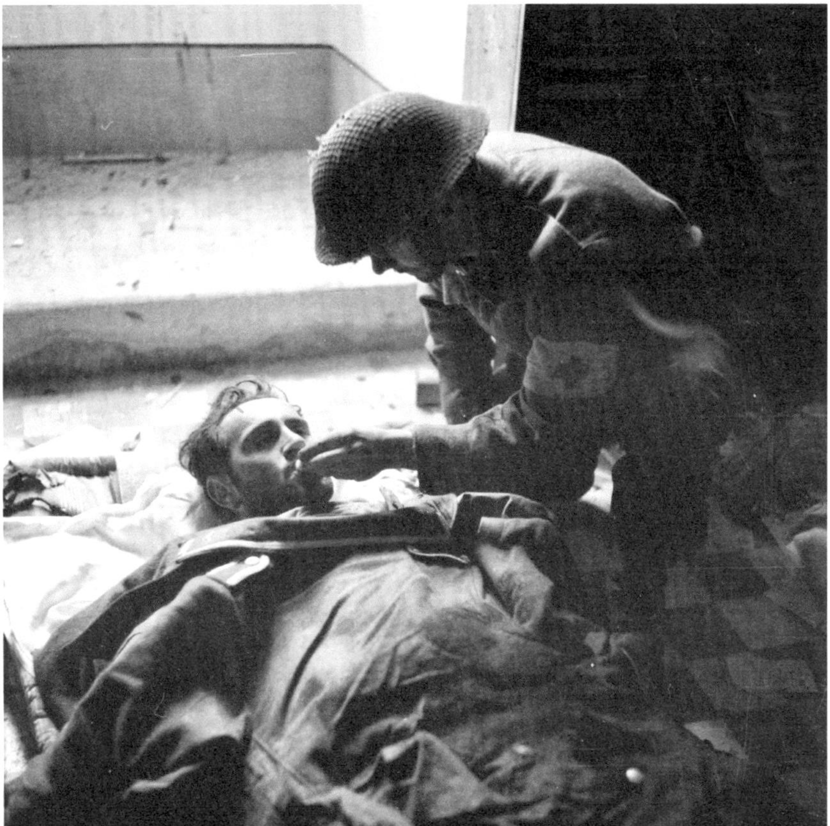

IT WAS DRIZZLING RAIN when I stepped out onto the Corso. The little shops on the pedestrian street were still shuttered and closed. Reading the map that I'd picked up at the hotel reception the night before, I turned left at the palm trees in Piazza Porta Caldari, walked along via Costantinopoli to the church, followed via Margherita d'Austria in a switchback down the slope of the escarpment, and started hiking across the valley, leaving the town behind.

The road through the valley had no shoulders; whenever a speeding car approached, I stepped over the guardrails into wet brush. Fortunately, it was only about a kilometre until the road ascended the hill of San Donato. On the hilltop, through a grove of olive trees to the left, was the lane to the cemetery gate.

As I walked in, a three-wheeled Vespa truck pulled up and two men in blue overalls got out. These were the cemetery groundskeeper and his young apprentice. The groundskeeper, a portly man with a thick moustache and cheerful manner, guessed immediately that I was Canadian. To my great relief, he confirmed that there was an event here this morning; he and his apprentice had come to set things up. To my slight disappointment, however, the event wasn't due to start for another ninety minutes. A chilly wind was blowing in from the ocean, there was nothing on this hilltop but the cemetery, and I had hurried here without picking up a coffee. The two Italians went away to a little building off to the side, and I walked ahead into the grounds of the Moro River Canadian War Cemetery.[1]

The first area that I found myself in was a wide green lawn. At its back centre was a massive rectangular stone on a base of three shallow steps. On the stone were inscribed the words, *THEIR NAME LIVETH FOR EVERMORE*. Behind it, through a row of trees that were leafless now in December, I could glimpse some white grave markers and a tall white cross. A path went from the Stone of Remembrance through the tree line into that space.

When I stepped through the trees, the space opened before me and I was met by a sea of white headstones. All were uniform in shape, size, and colour, and all were perfectly aligned in row after row, with little rose bushes in front of them. As I walked up the middle path towards the stone white cross, I felt the rows of headstones sweep across my peripheral vision. After passing the sixteenth row, I arrived at the cemetery's centre where the twenty-foot-tall cross stood atop a hexagonal base.

Now I noticed that the cross was overlain with a dark metal sword. The hilt was aligned with the cross's three points, with the blade extending downwards. This was the same vaguely medieval style of sword as the one I'd seen in Ted's living room. On the base of the Cross of Sacrifice, there was no inscription. It spoke for itself.

The groundskeeper and apprentice drove up to the Cross in their Vespa truck and began setting up two portable flagpoles. I wandered away, studying the headstones. The top of every stone was inscribed with a maple leaf identifying the buried soldier as a Canadian. Then came the man's military number and rank, followed by his name, his regiment, his age and the date of his death. On most headstones, the space below was inscribed with a cross. A few had the Star of David. On some, the space was blank, no religious symbol at all. Finally, at their base, most of the headstones were inscribed with an epitaph, unique to each man, provided by his next of kin.

Son, while you lie in peaceful sleep your
memory we shall always keep

He died in freedom's cause. He will always be
missed by those who knew him best

Until the day break and the shadows flee away

I walked the cemetery's entire hedge-lined perimeter. The view inland to the west was of the distant snow-capped Maiella Mountains. Over the eastern, seaward edge, I could see the choppy waves below, and the coastal cliffs and gulleys undulating north to Ortona. Then, amid the sound of the wind and the waves, I heard something new. Back at the Cross of Sacrifice, the flags of Canada and Italy had been raised. They were flapping and fluttering, and their metal connectors were clinking against the poles.

I wasn't sure I was having the feelings that I should be having in this place. The cemetery was peaceful, pretty, but also a bit uncanny—a nicely kept green lawn with red roses and one thousand five hundred and sixty-three stone reminders of violent death, each stone bearing a heartbroken thought from back home. Words and bodily remains from my country had long preceded me here. Unlike me, they would never leave. These impressions mingled with my growing, self-conscious anxiety. Was it okay that I was here? Was I going to be the only non-veteran? How was Ted going to react? In the haste of my last-minute decision, I hadn't told him that I was coming. Actually, it wasn't haste. I could have called him. I just hadn't wanted to. It suddenly dawned on me that this was a really strange thing for me to do.

At the Cross now, the two Italians were setting up a pair of speakers. They were friendly. This place was normal to them. Hoping to shake off my malaise, I went over and chatted with them while they worked.

THIS WAS BEFORE I met any of the veterans. It all began with Ted.

At the time, I was finishing my PhD coursework and hadn't yet decided on the topic for my research. Then one day in August 1998, I happened to read a small item in the newspaper about a group of Canadian veterans who were planning to meet their former German enemies.

> Edmonton Journal, 10 August 1998
>
> **Canadian, German Vets May Gather For An Historic Christmas Eve Dinner**
>
> Old army foes from Canada and Germany who fought the Battle of Ortona in Italy in the Second World War could meet for a historic reconciliation dinner.
>
> The 10-day battle in late December 1943 was the most vicious fought by the Canadian army in the entire Italian campaign of the war.
>
> The dinner is planned for this Christmas Eve, on the 55th anniversary of the battle, back in Ortona, an ancient seaport perched on cliffs above the Adriatic Sea on Italy's east coast. . . .

> "It's a reconciliation between old foes," said Edmund Griffiths, chairperson of the Ottawa branch of the Three Rivers Regiment Veterans Association which is trying to organize it.

I had been thinking of doing my fieldwork on something related to war memory. This event certainly looked interesting. The group had approached the Ministry of Veterans Affairs for support, but the ministry had turned them down, so they had started a public fundraising campaign. The point of contact for the campaign was the office of Peter Goldring, Reform member of parliament for Edmonton East and the Official Opposition party's Veterans Affairs Critic. I called the office, explained my interest, and the staff put me in touch with Ted.

Over the phone, Ted's tone was combative and intense. I wasn't sure how much he noticed anything I said about my research—which was fair enough. He addressed me as someone who might be useful to his campaign. The fundraising had just begun, he had limited time to achieve his goal for Christmas, so naturally he was trying to make every conversation count. He gave me a quick run-down of the plan for the Christmas Eve dinner. Thirty Canadian veterans would go to meet thirty of their German counterparts. The Canadian contingent would comprise six veterans from each of the five Canadian army regiments that had fought in Ortona. Ted went into more detail than I could comprehend in that moment regarding his rationale for picking those five regiments. Apparently there was some controversy. Some vets from other regiments were unhappy about being excluded, and they were already complaining to the media, so that was a public relations fire that Ted was now trying to put out—as if he didn't already have enough problems in getting this thing off the ground. He told me the names of some journalists who were supportive. Radio stations in Ottawa and Edmonton had started a friendly competition over who could fundraise the most. Meanwhile, MP Peter Goldring was pressuring the Department of National Defence to provide Ted's group with free transport to Italy on a Royal Canadian Air Force plane. As for Veterans Affairs, those "bureaucratic bean counters" were not helping one bit. They claimed to have no money in their budget. But the real reason for their obstinance, Ted said, was that the current minister was a navy admiral—"he doesn't give a damn about the army." This prejudice was compounded, Ted said, by the same old prejudice against the Italy veterans. The glory was always reserved for the D-Day and Normandy fighters. No one cared to remember the "spaghetti-league troops."

In urgent campaign mode, Ted was in constant calls with newspaper reporters and talk radio hosts. I didn't doubt that his words to me were genuine, but I sensed that what I was hearing from him had already been practiced and honed. His lines were well suited to fuelling the flames of public outrage and lighting fires under powerful asses. I couldn't reciprocate Ted's passionate and punchy attitude, but I did look for ways to affirm him. On the lack of recognition of the Italian Campaign, I told him that he was absolutely right. As a case in point, I noted that despite my interest in Canadian war remembrance, somehow I had never heard of Ortona.

"Are there any monuments in Ortona?" I asked him.

"Just a graveyard," Ted brusquely answered, "where all my friends from public school are buried."

For a moment, I was stunned into silence. And then part of me suspected that my stunned silence had been Ted's intended effect. It was like he'd thrown his bereavement at me, knowing it would catch me by surprise and that I might feel ashamed. Maybe I was misinterpreting—it was hard to tell on the phone—but the whole conversation with Ted had vaguely reminded me of past experiences with aggrieved and entitled types of men who seem to take satisfaction in throwing you off your balance. I wasn't sure how mixed up I wanted to get in Ted's business.

In the weeks that followed, I tracked the progress of the campaign to support the Ortona pilgrimage. Its rhetoric was populist and conservative, consistent with the political leanings of its leading proponents. The opposition Reform Party and the right-wing *Sun* newspaper chain framed the effort to send Ted's group to Ortona as if it was a struggle against the federal Liberal government and liberal elites. "Liberal Grinch Steals Christmas From Canada's Ortona Veterans" was the title of a press release from Goldring's office. "Ordinary Canadians will make it right," declared the fundraising appeals, "Canadian pride will make it happen." The *Ottawa Sun* described the campaign as a "People's War." And "the people" responded. Golf tournaments and country music concerts were organized, with the proceeds going to the Ortona campaign. Donations came in from small businesses, Lions Clubs, city councils, firefighters, and even the Ottawa airport air traffic controllers. *Sun* columnist Earl McRae updated his readers regularly on the progress of the "war," telling "the people" they were "winning" and urging them to keep pushing hard for "victory." At shopping malls around Ottawa, a Patsy Cline impersonator raised $3,200 selling decal stickers with the message, "If you love freedom, thank a vet." It was reported that a little girl donated seven dollars from her allowance.

What was the purpose of this war for Ortona? Why did Ted's group want to go, and why should ordinary Canadians want to send them? Goldring's fundraising appeals provided mixed messages. "After 55 years," one letter explained, "some veterans are simply curious [to meet the Germans]; others wish to bring closure to long-held animosities." The value of celebrating peace at Christmas was put forward: "It is a celebration of our international commonality of a desire for peace. It is a true Christmas story." The tone of the fundraising, however, seemed rather at odds with peace. According to Goldring, the Germans were expecting the Canadians in Ortona. If the Canadians failed to show up, then it would be apparent that Canada wasn't up to the challenge of meeting them, and Canada would therefore be shamed. Goldring hinted that such reputational damage could even affect Canada's international power and security—there was "scrutiny" by "foreign countries," he said, of the Canadian people's commitment to their military. It was important to "show Germans and the world that Canadian soldiers are second to none as tenacious fighters." The fierce fighting in Ortona had proven the strength of Canadians. "Ortona is where Canadians proved their 'mettle' in the face of a crack German army." And now (Goldring suggested) Ted's group of veterans wanted to meet the Germans for Christmas so that their fighting mettle could be affirmed. "Ortona established a respect by the Germans for their Canadian foes that only they can truly describe. That is why many Canadian veterans want to return to Ortona this Christmas."

Was that really why Ted wanted to go? To be affirmed as a great fighter? After our first conversation on the phone, Ted faxed me an information package related to the campaign. This included his original letter to Veterans Affairs in which he'd described his project to the ministry and requested their support. In this letter, Ted repeatedly used the words "reconciliation" and "compassion." It was to be a "dinner of reconciliation" with the Germans. This was "very much in keeping with the compassionate Canadian national character." The fact that the reconciliation would happen during Christmas "lends added significance to the event." In concluding the proposal, Ted once again invoked the idea of Canada as "a kind, compassionate nation."

I wasn't quite sure what point he was making about compassion. Was he suggesting that the government would be showing compassion for

Canadian veterans by supporting his initiative? Or was he suggesting that his initiative was an act of compassion by Canadian veterans towards their former enemies? And given that it was a letter to a Liberal government minister, maybe this was just strategic framing on his part. In any case, the tone and argument of Ted's original request for funding was very different from the rhetoric of Goldring and the Sun media who had picked up Ted's cause—and perhaps had run away with it.

By the end of September, the fundraising campaign had exceeded its target. Victory was declared. The Ortona Christmas Dinner of Reconciliation was on.

IT WAS A COLD, SUNNY morning in October when I arrived at Ted's condo in Ottawa. I had written him a letter, and he had accepted my request.

The door of his unit was open, ready for my arrival. His greeting was formal but not unfriendly, in a certain manner of the Anglo middle class. He was short, a bit plump, with a small nose on his round face, white hair thinning on top. His Oxford dress shirt and trousers looked new and were sharply pressed. But his most striking feature was a prominent goatee, immaculately groomed and bright white.

His apartment was similarly neat and spotless—all the more impressive considering, as he mentioned in passing, that he lived alone as a widower. The place was well furnished in a sort of mid-century modern style. None of this matched the rough image I had formed of Ted from listening to him on the phone. Even his voice seemed different now, much gentler than before. When I gave him the gift of tea and coffee that I'd brought in appreciation for his time, he responded warmly—"You didn't need to do that."

He invited me into the living room where we sat down in opposite sofas, separated by a glass coffee table neatly stacked with books. The conversation went naturally onto the topic of the Ortona trip. "If you'd told me that I'd raise a hundred thousand dollars in less than a month," he said, "I'd have asked you what you'd been smoking." Donations had come in from across Ontario, Quebec, and Alberta. And then an anonymous donor had sent in a whole thirty thousand, putting the campaign over the top. Now there was even a sculpture in the works. It was being created as a gift by a young Ottawa artist to commemorate the Ortona reconciliation. A local trucking company was offering to ship it to Ortona for free. I asked if the Legion had played any role. Ted said that he'd known better than to involve the Legion's leadership—"too much politics . . . we'd still be fundraising"—but local Legion chapters had raised money on their own initiative, especially in Cornwall, despite their financial difficulties.

While Ted was talking, my attention was briefly captured by an object on the wall. *Was that real?* It sure looked like it. But it was so incongruous with the atmosphere in the room that it was hard to believe my eyes. I tried to put the thing out of my mind. And what about British Columbia, I asked Ted. Hadn't there been a Vancouver regiment in Ortona?

Ted frowned.

"The Seaforths," he grumbled. "They think they're special."

At the beginning, when he had shared his idea, the Seaforths had turned him down—not interested. But then, when they'd seen the success of the fundraising and all the public excitement about the trip, not only had they wanted to get back in on it, but those Johnny-come-latelies also wanted to send more members than the other regiments, *plus* their wives, plus even their *bagpipers*. Well, Ted said—his eyes and voice becoming stern—he was *not having it*. The Seaforths were welcome to come, but they would be *equal* to everyone else. The rule was *six men* per regiment. *No* wives. *No* bagpipes. *No one was stealing the show*. As Ted said this, I had a reminder of my first impression of him, the hot-tempered voice that

I'd heard over the phone. I nodded and agreed that his terms for the trip were very fair.[2]

The conversation turned to why I was here. I said I was looking for a focus for my PhD fieldwork. I wanted to study how war is remembered. It was a big topic now, with the recent D-Day commemorations and films like *Saving Private Ryan*—it seemed there was a revival of interest in remembering war. And of course the public enthusiasm for Ted's Ortona project was another sign of that. Anyway, I'd come to Ottawa to get ideas and advice. After meeting Ted, I told him, I was going to the Canadian War Museum to meet its director, Jack Granatstein.

Ted looked impressed at the mention of that name. Canada's most eminent military historian. Ted pointed to the coffee table, noting that he had many of Granatstein's books. He wondered out loud what "direction" Granatstein might send me in. I said I'd be happy to let Ted know—but right now I was interested in getting "direction" from Ted. I wanted to learn about war veterans. What was Ted's advice?

Ted assumed a posture indicating he was about to tell me something important.

"Every man who was in it," he said, "has his own war."

He went on to explain. Men who had been in the same actions during the war would have completely different experiences. You can talk to two men who'd been right beside each other at the time. Ask them now what had happened back then, and they might tell you two completely different things. The historian might not like it, but every man is telling you what was and is true for him.

"That's *his* story. That's *his* war."

I nodded. In my notes, I underlined Ted's emphasis on the possessive.

Ted said he had something to show me. He'd meant to have it out for my visit but it didn't seem to be here on the coffee table. Reproaching himself for his absent-mindedness, he stood up, saying he'd be right back, and left the room.

During his absence, I examined the books on the coffee table. Farley Mowat, *My Father's Son*, with a picture on the cover of Farley as a young man in uniform. I had read most of Mowat's books about the Canadian wilderness, and also his war memoir *And No Birds Sang*, but not this recent one about his relationship with his parents—what he had struggled to tell them, and not tell them, in his letters home during the war. Here next to Mowat was a heavy volume of the *Official History of the Canadian Army in the Second World War*. And here was a book I hadn't heard of—*Ordinary Heroes* by John Gardam. Judging by the cover, this was a collection of stories about Canadian World War II soldiers.

My attention turned from the books to the prominent object on the wall. Mounted on a panel, the sword had a long, straight, gleaming steel blade. Its hilt was in a basic, slightly medieval style. There was an inscription on the panel, but I couldn't quite read it from my seat on the sofa. How, I wondered, could a person be comfortable with this instrument of archaic violence looming over their living room?

"That was a gift from the Toronto Police," Ted said.

He'd returned, carrying a thick binder, and he'd noticed me looking up at the sword. For services to law and policing, he added. I nodded and said it was impressive. So he'd been in the police? No, Ted said, his career had been military and then civil service. After the war, he'd studied at Sandhurst—the British officer training academy—and rose to the rank of major in the Canadian Army. Then he'd left the army and became executive assistant to John Turner during the time that Turner was Justice Minister in Pierre Trudeau's cabinet. So he'd had both a military and a civilian career, and his editor, by the way—he was writing his memoirs, which he had right here in this binder—his editor thought his memoirs should be published in two volumes, one for his life in the military, another for civilian life.

Privately, I was amazed. Ted had worked for John Turner in the Trudeau government. The man Ted worked for had gone on to become Liberal Party leader and also (briefly) the prime minister. Ted must be well connected in Ottawa. And furthermore—another shock in light of my first impressions—*Ted was a liberal?*

Ted was saying that he was pushing back against his editor's idea. Ted wanted his memoir to be all in one volume. I said that I agreed —it's one story, your life story, it shouldn't be broken up.

Ted opened the binder. He emphasized that this was still a draft but he wanted to read me a passage.

In December 1943, Ted was a twenty-one-year-old corporal in the Three Rivers Tank Regiment. On Christmas Day, he was driving his tank down a street in Ortona. He was supporting a group of Seaforth infantrymen. They entered a square. Across from them was an old church and a hospital. Suddenly, the Seaforths outside Ted's tank were dropping. "They all fell down like a bunch of dolls." Germans were shooting them with a heavy machine gun from inside the church. Ted directed the gun of his tank at the church, and fired. The shot blew in the whole church face, burying the Germans inside.

He looked up at me from the binder.

"That's how I spent my Christmas."

Since then, he said, Christmas had never been the same. After the war, every December when the adverts and music and decorations started to appear, he would start feeling depressed. He had hoped that his bad feeling would go away with the passage of time. Instead, every year, it got worse. Christmas was the high point of the Christian year for Ted—yet he dreaded its arrival and couldn't wait for it to pass.

In 1993, the fiftieth anniversary of the battle, he decided he had to go back. He was trying, he said, "to bury the ghosts of Ortona" so that he could enjoy Christmas again. His twelve-year-old grandson came with him so that he wouldn't have to face the past alone. They had found the square in Ortona where he'd destroyed the church. The church had been rebuilt. He and his grandson went inside and sat down. Ted had noticed that in the back half of the church interior there were fifteenth-century frescoes, and he noticed that the front half was twentieth-century modern, built after the damage he'd done. And then Ted had broken down and cried. It was, he told me, "fifty years worth of tears."

It was in a plain voice that Ted recounted all this, but the look on his face was pale and haunted. I regretted all my negative thoughts about him. He'd just revealed himself to be sensitive and vulnerable. I was sure it wasn't easy for him to do.

Ted continued his story. During that visit to the church, he and his grandson had found the priest. Ted wrote a cheque, gave it to the priest, and tried to explain across the language barrier that it was payment "for shooting his church."

Now I felt Ted was recovering some of his swagger. A cheque for shooting the church—it was a sincere gesture; no doubt, but he'd told it with a touch of bravado. He went on to tell me a few more anecdotes, gradually moving the narrative away from his vulnerable Ortona moment. On that same trip, he said, he'd taken his grandson to England, where they had visited Sandhurst. They'd met the college's record keeper who helped them find Ted's old gradebook. His grades weren't very good. But then again, Ted chuckled, neither had been Churchill's. In fact he'd met Winston Churchill at Sandhurst. While Ted was a student there, Churchill had paid a visit, and Ted had an opportunity to chat with the great man. He'd told Churchill it was "hard getting back to books" after the war. Churchill had told Ted not to worry—"Remember how I got out of here!" I didn't get the meaning of Churchill's remark. Ted explained. Churchill had also been a poor student at Sandhurst, but then of course Churchill had gone on to do great things.

It was getting time for me to leave and I had more that I needed to learn. I asked Ted how he'd got the idea for this upcoming trip.

It was the inspiration of his regimental chaplain, Ted answered. The late Padre Wilhelm. After the war, Wilhelm became the archbishop of Kingston, Ontario. Ted became chairman of their regimental association. He and Wilhelm sometimes met and talked about that Christmas in Ortona, remembering the brave Seaforths' dinner and lamenting the absence of peace on that day. One time, during a reunion of the regiment, Wilhelm had said they should go back to Ortona for Christmas—and this time, invite the Germans for dinner. Wilhelm had since died. Ted had often thought about his idea. Now he'd decided to make it happen.[3]

I decided to venture my key question. Tentatively, I asked Ted if it might be alright, as part of my research, if I went to Ortona for Christmas and observed the events.

Ted looked uncomfortable.

The dinner, he said, would be veterans only.

Yes of course, I said. Understandable. I wouldn't want to impose on that.

But Peter Goldring and his family were coming, Ted mused aloud. A lot of media were coming too. The CBC. Team from the *Sun*. The *Citizen*. Some of the events would be public.

So—Ted relaxed a bit, and concluded—there would be things for me to see, he supposed. If I happened to be there. As long as I didn't mind missing the main event.

For the next two months, I had no more contact with Ted. I wasn't sure if I wanted to go to Ortona. It would be a big expense on my limited budget. And what would be the point? I might not get to see very much, and Ted didn't seem to want me there. In addition, I wasn't sure it would be legitimate for me to go "into the field." I was still completing my coursework and wasn't at the stage in my programme where I could request and receive fieldwork approval. I lacked the university's permission to do research with "human subjects." Still, the thought of Ortona appealed to me. I wasted time dithering until it was almost too late.

About two weeks before Christmas, I got the push that I needed. A senior anthropology professor who was also the Chair of my department stopped me in the hallway and asked if I was going on the trip. When I told him my reason for hesitating, he scoffed: *It's a public event! You're not breaking any university rules by showing up. As long as you don't sit people down for formal interviews, you're fine!* As for my worry that I wouldn't learn much, he gave me a little speech about risk-taking and the courageous, improvising spirit of anthropology. After that, I didn't really have a choice. I wasn't going to face that professor after Christmas without a story of how I'd made the trip, or at least how I'd tried.

In the rush to get a passport and book a flight and hotel, I barely had time to think about what I was doing. And then I was landing in rough weather at Roma Fiumicino airport, taking a regional train to an intercity bus terminal, using my rusty high school Italian to find the right bus and get a ticket, and with darkness falling, crossing the Apennine Mountains in the dimly lit coach. At the end of that two hour bus journey, outside the Pescara terminal at night, I found a local bus that took me down the Adriatic coast. Most of what I could see in the window was my own reflection. Finally, at a stop, the driver called me forward. This was Ortona.

It was dark, raining, nobody around. I was in a square with palm trees overlooked by a prominent four-storey building. I didn't know it at the time, but that building had once been the headquarters of the Loyal Edmonton Regiment. From those shuttered windows, Stone and Dougan's men had shot the Germans like jackrabbits and deer. That was where Norman had seen the bodies of Edmonton dead, drained white from loss of blood. I found and walked up the main commercial street, the Corso Vittorio Emanuele, where—another story I didn't know yet—there had been the famous rubble pile that Charlie Rattray had heroically climbed while being strafed by Germans positioned in the municipal building up ahead. Down the pedestrianized street, on both sides, the little grocers, shoe shops, ice cream shops, and cafés were all closed up behind their metal security shutters.

In the small lobby of my hotel, deserted except for me and the lone receptionist, I finally had a chance to ask someone about the veterans. I'd assumed I could get some information from just about anyone in town—maybe the veterans were even staying at my hotel; in a place like this, how many options could there be? But the receptionist knew even less than I did. He said there were no other foreign guests at the hotel; he'd vaguely heard that veterans were coming to town, and that was all. He handed me my key without much else to say—I couldn't tell if he just didn't like talking, or if he thought my Italian was too clumsy to bother with.

So then I was sitting in my hotel room after a whirlwind twenty-four hour trip, feeling brilliantly successful in getting here in the nick of time, but at a loss for what to do next. It was December 21. I knew that events were starting the next day. But *what* was starting, and *where*? Would I have to wander around town in the morning trying to find it by myself? I didn't like my chances. This place had turned out to be bigger than I had thought.

Then I remembered—the People's War. The *Ottawa Sun* had been a big promoter of this event. Surely they would have sent reporters over here to cover it. The time in Ottawa was six hours behind—still business hours there. I connected my laptop to the hotel's internet, looked up the *Sun*, punched their number into the phone beside my bed, and when their receptionist picked up, I asked to speak to the newsroom. They put me on hold. As I waited, I thought about how I was going to explain myself. I'd never called a newsroom about anything, let alone to make an off-the-wall request like this.

A man picked up. I started out by saying that I was a Canadian in Ortona and I wanted to attend the reconciliation but no one here could tell me how to find it so I figured since the *Sun* had . . . and that was more than enough. The man cut me off in a delighted way, as if my call was some kind of godsend. It turned out that he'd been anxiously awaiting a call from Ortona. Yes, he said, the *Sun* had two guys here—or at least they were *supposed* to be here—they hadn't been in touch. So he didn't know much, but he did know there was something happening at a cemetery in the morning. He was expecting a story about it. As I thanked him and said goodbye, he remarked dryly that if I found his colleagues in the morning, maybe I could help them to make a call.

THE FIRST ARRIVALS IN the cemetery were from the CBC. I recognized David Halton; he was a regular correspondent on the TV news. It made sense that they would send him to this event—his father Matthew had covered the battle of Ortona for the CBC. David and his team walked in and began exploring. One of them approached and asked me if I was with the organizers, or was I media. Neither, I answered—just a student here to watch. Having established that I had nothing to offer, they left me alone with the Italians and went about their work, setting up and testing their equipment, conferring in low voices, looking at notes. I envied their clarity of purpose and the coffees they were drinking.

Far away back at the cemetery gate, a few more cars pulled up, followed by a big tour bus. Here was Ted's group of veterans with their entourage. Media and support staff started flowing into the cemetery and congregating around the Cross. Suddenly I felt like I wasn't in Italy anymore. The air was abuzz with English Canadian voices. There was another crew like the CBC with sound and film equipment; there were photographers with impressive cameras and bulging shoulder bags of gear; and there were reporters, some already jotting notes in top-bound spiral notebooks. One of the newsmen I recognized from the mug shot on his byline: the leader of the People's War, the *Ottawa Sun*'s Earl McRae. Peter Goldring was here too; a tall, bearded man, he was accompanied by his wife and teenaged daughters. Finally, a man and woman in Canadian Army uniforms seemed to have managing roles; with the help of the translator who was attached to the group, they were working with the groundskeepers to connect a cassette player to the speakers.

Then voices were saying, "They're ready," "They're starting." Back near the cemetery entrance, around the Stone of Remembrance, the veterans had assembled, all in winter coats and military berets. A few were holding Canadian flags. The cameramen and photographers rushed across the cemetery to get nearer. The rest of us moved to either side of the Cross.

The veterans started their approach. Led by the flag bearers, they proceeded in a column up the path between the headstones. Alongside the column, walking sideways and backwards, the cameramen and photographers were leaning, crouching, snapping pictures, and impressively dodging graves and rose bushes as they went. All talk in the cemetery ceased. The only sounds were of the sea, the breeze in the trees, the flapping and clinking of the flags on the poles, the clicking of the cameras, and the crunching of thirty-odd footsteps coming up the pebble path. When their column reached the central open area, the veterans spread out sideways, forming a line facing the Cross with the flag bearers at the centre. The bearers lowered their flags, and I noticed that one of them was Ted. He looked tense. Actually, so did they all. It was a line of silent, elderly men in winter jackets and trench coats. All wore medals on their chests. Some noticeably shivered and braced themselves in the cold.

A button was pressed on the cassette player.

Nothing happened.

The Canadian soldier who was beside the player crouched down to it and did some fidgeting. The line of veterans remained silent and steadfast facing the Cross.

The button on the player was pressed again.

Nothing happened.

The soldier turned her attention to the speaker cables. The groundskeeper's apprentice leaned in as if to help. The looks on their faces did not inspire confidence. The line of veterans started to stir.

"We can just sing it," said a voice.

Someone else in the line grumbled something about Italians.

More veterans started muttering.

"Sing it."

"Just sing it!"

One unsteady voice began.

"*Ohhh . . . Caa . . . nadaaa . . .*"

Others joined.

"*Our home and native land . . .*"

And then all Canadians—myself and the journalists included—sang the national anthem. The two groundskeepers stood respectfully, the older one sometimes moving his lips to some words.

I was familiar with the ritual from our national Remembrance Day ceremonies. The anthem would normally be followed by a bugler playing the Last Post. However, it seemed that they had given up on the cassette player (and no one had a bugle) so this part of the ceremony was skipped. Ted was looking livid. Everyone continued to stand at attention during a reading of the Act of Remembrance.

They shall grow not old, as we that are left grow old;
Age shall not weary them, nor the years condemn.
At the going down of the sun and in the morning
We will remember them.

Wreaths were brought forward and placed at the foot of the cross. Salutes were performed.

Then, with an air of awkward uncertainty, the ceremony staggered to an end. The stiff line of men relaxed. In a raised voice, Ted declared something about the time available before they had to get back on the bus.

The veterans slowly dispersed, wandering away in solitude or small groups to various parts of the cemetery, pacing the rows, pausing sometimes in front of a headstone. Reporters and photographers followed them around, seeking an occasional word with a veteran while trying to keep a respectful distance. The groundskeepers and I stayed put in our positions near the Cross. The apprentice momentarily fussed with the speaker cables. His master told him to leave it. He looked at me and shrugged.

A veteran came over to us. He was a tall man wearing a long beige trench coat and a shy smile. He wanted to thank the groundskeepers for taking such good care of the cemetery. He offered them each a small Canada lapel pin and asked if he could take their picture. Then he asked me about myself. I briefly explained my purpose. He raised his eyebrows and remarked incredulously, "You came all the way here for this? By yourself? During Christmas?" I said something more about how it was necessary for my PhD. That put him at a momentary loss for words. Then he said, "Well, that is really something," and he left us to go look at more graves.

That was Mel.

Two photographers were talking nearby. The younger man sounded stressed; the middle-aged one was commiserating. I overheard something about the internet. When the young photographer went away to take more pictures, I greeted the one who remained. He was Andrew Stawicki from the *Toronto Star*. Andrew explained to me that he and the other photographers hadn't been able to use the internet. They were staying with the veterans at a big resort hotel down the coast; the hotel was supposed to have internet, but when they dialed in, it didn't work. They had tried a few other places and it was always the same problem. Maybe there just wasn't internet service in this part of Italy. None of them had been able to send pictures back to their editors, and the young guy that Andrew had just been talking to was in trouble. The guy had just been hired at the *Sun*, Andrew said; this was his first big assignment, and his editor had told him that if he went another day without sending pictures then he might as well not come back.

"Well there's definitely internet in Ortona," I said. "Mine worked just fine last night."

The casual manner dropped from Andrew's face; suddenly, he was all attention.

"You have internet?"

He wanted me to take him there right away. I agreed. He hurried across the cemetery to find his teammate, *Toronto Star* columnist Rosie DiManno. The two of them worked out that Rosie would ride on the bus with the veterans back to their hotel, and Andrew and I would drive into town. We jumped into Andrew's rental car, drove down into the gully, back up the other side, and I guided him through town to my hotel. With all of his gear, we trooped through the lobby past the faintly quizzical receptionist and climbed the stairs to my room. Andrew took some gadgets out of his bag, kneeled on the floor, plugged a cable into the jack on the wall, and began tapping some buttons on a device.

We waited. Then Andrew gave a big sigh of relief.

"It works."

Immediately, he offered to pay for my room. In return, I'd let him come here every day to send his pictures back to Toronto. One way or another he was going to book a room in this hotel—but he didn't need to stay in it, so why not just pay for mine? Plus, since he'd be coming and going, he'd give me a lift to all the events in his car. He understood I was a student and was glad to help. It was an added bonus for him that I spoke Italian; it meant he didn't have to rely on Rosie all the time. I wasn't about to turn down that offer—I couldn't believe my luck.

We went back downstairs to change the booking so my room would be billed to the *Star*. The receptionist handled it with his usual economy of words—I figured he found us peculiar, but his expression was unreadable. Then we hurried off in Andrew's car. He wanted to find the *Ottawa Sun* team and tell them about my hotel—they'd want to book a room there too. As he drove, Andrew explained that even when reporters worked for rival newspapers, there should be solidarity among them, especially in the field. Older photographers had helped him when he was starting out; now he wanted to pay it forward to that kid.

In the following days, he also paid it forward to me. He gave me a copy of Ted's detailed thirteen-page plan for the week. He ensured that I got to spend time at the veterans' hotel, where a lot of the action happened at the bar. Unavoidably, I still missed some key events of the reconciliation, but what I did get to witness was largely thanks to him. He was a legitimate observer of the events, and as I tagged along with him, some of that legitimacy rubbed off on me. By the end of the week, I was riding on the bus with the veterans.

1800 - 2000 - CANADIAN EMBASSY RECEPTION AT PALAZZO CORVO FOR CDN AND GER VETS AND INVITEES

2030 - 2200 - DINNER AT HOTEL

2130 - 2300 - BAR HOURS AT GIARDINO HOTEL

At some point later on that first day, I met Ted. My memory of the encounter is vague, and I don't have notes from the time. (Speaking of notes, it's beyond belief to me now that I went all the way there, and then didn't write anything down. That's a symptom of how absurdly punctilious I was about sticking to my university's rules; I worried that if I kept notes, those might turn out to be *field* notes, and then it could be said that I done *fieldwork—unauthorized—with human subjects.*) But the vagueness of my memory of that encounter with Ted is testimony to how anticlimactic it turned out to be. To my great relief, Ted wasn't angry, or at least he didn't show it. Maybe I was with Andrew in the moment when we met. All that I recall is Ted's polite and perfunctory greeting, probably in the hotel bar, some words to the effect that it was nice that I had made it.

And that was it. We didn't speak again for the rest of the trip—not because I avoided him but because he was always busy with other people. He had a lot on his plate. In addition to whatever memories he was working through—whatever had driven him to organize this event in the first place—he was also the event planner and group leader, so he was constantly dealing with logistics, media requests, and all of the little problems and petty conflicts that inevitably arise on a group bus tour.

Of course, some groups on a tour have more conflicts than others. This turned out to be one that had more.

THE PLACE WAS CROWDED with at least fifty Canadians sitting at tables and standing and milling around. In addition to thirty Canadian veterans, there were the Canadian Army support staff, the politician Peter Goldring and his wife and kids, David Halton and the CBC film crew, a crew from the History Channel, and the reporters and photographers from the *Toronto Star*, *Ottawa Citizen*, and *Ottawa Sun*, all waiting for the big moment. From my seat at the bar, it was hard to see the entrance. Amid the general hubbub of so many men talking loudly, suddenly there was a ripple of excitement. Word came through to the back that the Germans were at the door. The reporters and film crews hastened to position themselves strategically. I stayed in my place.

According to Ted's original plan, thirty Canadian veterans of Ortona were going to meet with thirty Germans. As it turned out, however, only six Germans came. They came alone, with no diplomatic or military support staff, and no media. Unlike the big production that was made of it by the Canadians, on the German side it was just six old men, each making a personal trip that he'd paid for himself.

The Germans made their way into the room and started to mingle around the tables. The noise of greetings and laughter became almost deafening. More drinks were ordered. Each of the Germans became a centre of attention for a group of Canadians who converged on him. Media workers hovered to and fro, trying to eavesdrop and capture whatever was going on. Above the sea of heads in the crowd, two furry boom mikes floated around, held aloft by the sound men of the film crews. Andrew was somewhere in the thick of it, doing his job.

One of the Germans was a tall man with a rich mane of white hair and a strong prominent jaw. This was Joseph Klein. He had a confident and highly cultured demeanour and seemed to be the group's unofficial leader. Another was named Willy Fretz. He seemed warm and mild-mannered, in a suit vest, like a modest country gentleman—and always had a camera hanging from a strap around his neck. There was a short man with big glasses—Carl Bayerlein—who had the air of a cold and quirky scientist. Later I learned that Carl had been a demolitions expert in the war; he'd blown up many houses in Ortona, sometimes when Canadians were inside them.[4] Even shorter than Carl was Fritz Illi. Despite his gravel-toned voice and the perpetually stern look on his face, Fritz was chummy and gregarious, ready to put his arm around you while clinking glasses and saying cheers. He had brought a companion, a lady much taller and younger than him, who was clad in an ostentatious fur coat. Gisbert Borucki somehow made me think of the Alps. Quiet but cheerful looking, he had an impressive handlebar moustache and was built like a healthy farmer. Finally there was Hugo Bauer, a big, balding, portly man, very modestly dressed, and looking nervous. From my vantage point at the bar, it was like watching a party from the margins, making out occasional words from all the boisterous talk, and observing the group dynamics. One thing I could observe was that Hugo was becoming lost, either forgotten by the others or choosing to isolate himself.

Next to me at the bar, one of the Canadian veterans was also hanging back, watching things with a wry grin on his resting face that would later become so familiar to me. I learned his name when his comrades started calling for him. "Get Sam!" "Where's Sam?" Some of the Edmonton guys had learned that Hugo, unlike his mates, couldn't speak a word of English. The Edmontons had a solution to that: just as they'd done when they'd caught a prisoner during the war, they called on Sam to come and translate. So Sam left the bar and was led over to Hugo, and then Hugo was surrounded by his own group of Canadians. Poor Hugo still looked nervous—suddenly he was a centre of attention, and it wasn't clear if he liked it. But it wasn't long before Sam's comrades tired of the slow talk of translation, and drifted away; then it was just Sam and Hugo together, now looking deep in conversation.

The next day, December 23, had an odd agenda.

> THE CDN VETS WILL ALSO TRAVEL TO ROME, THOUGH THE VATICAN HAS DECLINED TO GRANT A PAPAL AUDIENCE

As Ted had planned it, all the Canadian veterans and their entourage went to have lunch at the Canadian embassy in Rome. That meant two hours on the highway, traffic in downtown Rome, a formal lunch, then two hours on the highway back. They left early in the morning and didn't return until evening. The Germans were left behind.

What was the point of this? Weren't the Canadians here to meet the Germans? They had just got here the day before. Among themselves, the journalists grumbled that this was bad planning. It stuck them with, as they put it, "no story" for the day. Meeting the Germans was the story. Meeting the ambassador in Rome was literally nothing to write home about. Most of the media chose to stay behind in Ortona, including Andrew and Rosie. With me in tow, they went out driving around the countryside, desperately seeking a story (which they found at Casa Berardi, the site of a battle near Ortona fought by the Royal 22e or "Van Doos" Regiment from Quebec).

I would have preferred to go find the Germans, who were spending the day walking the streets of Ortona. As for the Canadians' perplexing day trip to Rome, later I learned that one of the reasons it was in the schedule was because Ted had put in a request at the Vatican for an audience with the Pope. (The Vatican declined.)

On arrival back at their hotel that evening, Ted's group had to eat a quick dinner before getting back on the bus, this time to go into Ortona for a 9pm orchestral performance inside San Tommaso cathedral. The Germans attended as well. Finally back at their hotel after the concert, hardly anyone was interested in staying up for conversations in the bar. Even I was exhausted, and I hadn't been on the day trip to Rome. This grueling pace of activity would continue for the rest of the week.

December 24 was the day of the main event. Fortunately, Ted's schedule finally allowed for some downtime. Nothing was planned until mid-day when the Germans came for lunch. Here was another unfortunate aspect of the planning—the Germans and Canadians were staying at different hotels which were not within walking distance, so all their interactions were structured and short on time. After lunch, the Germans departed and there was more time to rest before Christmas Eve.

1615 - DEPART HOTEL FOR ORTONA CHURCH S. MARIA DI COSTANTINOPOLI

1700 - 1730 - MULTI-DENOMINATIONAL SERVICE AT ORTONA CHURCH

1800 - 2000 - RECONCILIATION DINNER AT SALESIAN ORDER

2015 - RETURN TO HOTEL

2100? - 2300? - BAR HOURS AT HOTEL? (THIS MAY NOT BE POSSIBLE IN VIEW OF THE FACT IT IS CHRISTMAS EVE!!!)

2330? - DEPART HOTEL FOR MIDNIGHT MASS IN ORTONA (NON-COMPULSORY)

I knew that I wasn't going. As Ted had told me in October, the dinner was veterans-only. Based on that, I had assumed that Ted wanted it to be an intimate gathering.

However, it turned out to be not so intimate after all. The support staff on the trip were attending, as were Peter Goldring, Italian dignitaries, translators, and many of the Canadian media. Many—but not all. Ted had invited the teams from the CBC and the *Sun*, but he told the *Citizen*, the History Channel, and the *Star* teams that they couldn't go. The reason for their exclusion, I heard from Andrew, was that their outlets had not helped with the fundraising for the trip, whereas the *Sun* had helped a lot. But this didn't explain why the CBC was invited. And with so many non-veteran observers already attending, why not allow just a few more? Surely an extra photographer or reporter with a notepad wouldn't be much of an added burden, especially when there was going to be a whole film crew at the event. The big story of the trip, its unique point of interest, was the Christmas dinner shared by former enemies. The excluded media were stuck, unable to cover the climactic moment. My worries about the value of my trip now paled in comparison to what happened to these reporters.

Secretly, I was a bit glad to have company. I sat at the hotel bar on Christmas Eve with this sorry band of the uninvited as they commiserated and brainstormed how to solve their bitter predicament. Tensions were relieved through dark humour. This was a group of people whose job it was to be good with words. They made up nicknames for some of the leading veterans. One was Colonel Sanders, another was The Silver Fox. There was grousing about the CBC. *They think they're better than us. Staying at a different hotel, never joining us at the bar. . . Typical. We do the heavy lifting, find the story, then they swoop in and get the glory. Look how Ted always has time for their documentary. They'll probably win an award.* Some of the reporters gave up and went to bed. A few soldiered on, hoping to get stories about the dinner when the Canadian veterans returned. Those hopes seemed to be dashed when the vets came back exhausted and wanted to go straight to bed. I didn't notice if anyone went out again for the "non-compulsory" midnight mass.

> FRIDAY 25 DECEMBER
>
> (TIMINGS DEPENDENT ON TRAFFIC AND ROAD CONDITIONS BETWEEN CASSINO AND ORTONA)
>
> 0700 - 0800 - BREAKFAST
>
> 0800? - DEPART HOTEL BY BUS FOR MONTE CASSINO (ESTIMATED 2 1/2 HOUR TRIP)

The next day's plan was yet another long road trip with structured, ritualized events. The Canadians and Germans were going on a two-and-a-half-hours drive to the site of another battle, Monte Cassino, where they would perform commemorative ceremonies at their respective war cemeteries. Once again, I thought this was odd timing. Ortona was known as the Christmas battle. One of the reasons that it was memorable and troubling for so many veterans—including Ted, as he had told me—was that they'd fought and killed on this sacred day. Now they were waking up in Ortona on Christmas morning, but instead of marking the significance of being back here on this day, they were leaving for the other side of Italy to commemorate a different battle and doing nothing to acknowledge that it was Christmas.

There were still two more days of events to come after this, but the *Star* team decided they'd had enough. The story was Christmas in Ortona, Andrew explained. Beyond that, there was no more story. So on Christmas morning, Andrew and Rosie departed. Andrew wished me good luck.

I did get some luck in the form of a lift to Cassino with the History Channel crew. We watched as the veterans performed commemorative rituals at the Commonwealth Cassino War Cemetery and the German War Cemetery. Those were much like I had seen on the first day. The ceremonies may have had added significance for the veterans in that they were co-participating and honouring each other's dead; however, I could only guess what this meant to them, because the events were barely over before it was time for them to get back on their bus.

During the two-and-a-half-hour return trip to Ortona in the film crew's van, I was a sympathetic ear to their griping that they had no idea what "story" they were getting, but unlike the lucky *Toronto Star* team, their producer had told them to stay. On arrival at the hotel late that evening, there was a moment of shock when we found that the amenities, including the bar, were closed. We had practically forgotten that it was Christmas Day.

I suggested we try my hotel. Sure enough, the front desk was open, staffed by the same unreadable receptionist as always. Earl McRae and his photographer were there, too. They'd finished sending their story back to Ottawa via the internet of their uninhabited room, and now they were sitting at a table in the small lobby, relaxing with a couple of beers. We all found seats and ordered more from the receptionist. Earl asked if I'd noticed that no matter what time you come here, it's always the same guy. Over drinks, we wondered how that was possible. Maybe the receptionist lived here. But didn't he ever sleep?

SATURDAY 26 DECEMBER

0730 - 0830 - BREAKFAST

0830 - DEPART FOR BATTLEFIELD TOUR, INCLUDES STOP AND WREATH-LAYING AT STERLIN CASTLE

1200 - PRESENTATION OF BRASS PLAQUE TO TOWN OF ORTONA FOR THE MONUMENT TO THE FALLEN ITALIAN CITIZENS AT THE TOWN CEREMONY

The next two days included more travel and structured events. This took the form of a bus tour of local battlefields—in the countryside, though, not in Ortona—with stops for ceremonies and wreath-layings at various sites. Now I got a bit of a breakthrough in terms of my opportunity to spend time among the veterans. The Germans were being invited onto the Canadian bus for the battlefield tour. In the midst of the commotion, with Ted distracted, Mel and Sam smuggled me onto the bus. Even so, the opportunities for casual talking were limited. Much of the time that the bus was moving, we listened to the amplified narrative provided by a local Italian historian, Saverio di Tullio, who was acting as the guide. Saverio was at the front of the bus with a translator repeating his words into a microphone, describing episodes from the war relating to places we were passing through.[5] Here and there, the bus stopped, and we got out for brief ceremonial events.

The tour took us into Ortona to honour the civilian victims of the battle. Many local people had gathered with Mayor Puletti at the Monument to Civilian Victims of War (*Monumento alle Vittime Civili di Guerra*) which stands at the entrance to the cemetery on the northwest edge of town. The large stone monument is in the shape of a triptych, like a giant book standing open, showing seven scenes on painted tiles. The central panel is entirely devoted to an image of the Pietà (Mary holding the dead body of her son Jesus) with ruins of Ortona in the background; on the left and right panels are six more scenes of suffering refugees and animals, and destroyed buildings, including the split dome of San Tommaso and the ruins of Santa Maria delle Grazie in what the Canadians had called Dead Horse Square.[6] During the time they spent in front of this monument, while speeches were given and wreaths were laid, some of the veterans became more tearful than I had seen them at any other moment during the trip. Some told me they were shocked to learn that so many civilians had suffered and been killed. During the battle, they said, they hadn't known about or given much thought to it. On the side of the ceremony, one of the Van Doos broke down crying while telling me that war is terrible and should never happen again.

My other lasting impressions of those days are not so poignant. There were growing tensions among the veterans.

The first point of friction was over Fritz, the short, hawk-eyed German with the tall, fur-clad female companion. Fritz was quite fluent in English and he liked to talk and tell stories, especially to the Canadian media. As time went on, I started to think that maybe he liked it too much—I got a feeling that his stories were a few too many and were a little too good to be true. I wasn't alone in this. Sometimes I overheard Canadian veterans muttering about him. Sam told me that "Fritzie" was claiming to be a millionaire and wanted to get in on his gravel business. Sam didn't trust him.

Apart from questions about his authenticity, Fritz was proving to be rather unpleasant. His lady friend spoke no English, and he never made an effort to include her; sometimes when she tried to join a conversation, he snapped at her in German. "My advice to you, young man," he told me once, with her standing right next to him, oblivious to his words: "never get married." At one point on the bus, under the amplified drone of the battle tour narration, I overheard two Canadian vets talking in the seats behind me. One of them said something about "that poor woman—why bring her along if he was going to treat her that way?" His neighbour growled that he was having a hard time holding back from punching "the little shit."

Fritz also seemed to make his own comrades uncomfortable. My impression of their discomfort was confirmed by a letter that I received from Willy Fretz soon after I got home. At my request, he was providing the addresses of all the Germans—except Fritz. "I do not have any contact to Illi," he wrote. "He seems a bit strange to us."

And there were growing tensions among the Canadians. The grueling schedule with so little free time and so much on the bus was wearing on people's nerves. Around the margins of events, and at the hotel bar in the evenings, there was more and more grumbling about Ted. Various stories circulated about Ted's alleged unfairness. The other vets hadn't been allowed to bring their wives, but Ted had brought his grandson. They had been here for almost a week, but had hardly got to see Ortona. Some of the Seaforths in particular were angry over how Ted had—so they said—treated a small group of their "young guys." Apparently, some soldiers from their regiment who were currently serving as peacekeepers in Bosnia had come over to Ortona for their Christmas break, wanting to meet the veterans and see the events that were meaningful to their regiment's history. According to the aggrieved Seaforth veterans, Ted had been hostile to these young guys and had tried to keep them away.

During the first days, whenever I saw Ted, he had looked extremely anxious. Now, though, after Christmas, he seemed a lot happier. In fact, he seemed happiest now when he was with the Germans, and particularly when he was with Joseph Klein. He and the leader of the Germans appeared to have become fast friends. They sat together at the front of the bus with much smiling and laughter between them. The two certainly had a lot in common. Like Ted, Joseph had chosen to remain in the army after the war. Indeed, Joseph had promptly been recruited by the British, who had sent him to Greece in some capacity as part of their intervention against the communists in the Greek Civil War. Joseph had continued his military career in NATO-allied West Germany. He had an air of authority and appeared fluent in the high diction of military and gentlemanly traditions. He and Ted also had leading roles in their respective regimental veterans' associations, so they probably had much to share and commiserate about the challenges of managing group gatherings—including this current trip.

SUNDAY 27 DECEMBER

TBD - GER VETS DEPART HOTEL AND ORTONA FOR HOME

0730 - 0900 - BREAKFAST

1100 - DEPART HOTEL

1130 - ARRIVE CASA BERARDI. INTRODUCE BERARDI FAMILY. BATTLEFIELD TOUR PORTION. VIEW R 22e R MONUMENT. LAY WREATH? AND CASA BERARDI. PLANT MAPLE TREE. VISIT CALDARE. LAY WREATH.

After the departure of the Germans, the second day of the battlefield tour felt melancholy. Canadian tensions finally broke. Perhaps it had only been the presence of their former enemies that had helped them to hold it together.

Ted was seated in his usual place at the front of the bus, but without his new friend Joseph. I was near the back. Suddenly from up front there was an outburst of angry, snapping voices. The actual words were inaudible at the back owing to the unbroken amplified narrative of our Italian battlefield tour guide. Later, Sam and Mel told me what had happened. Apparently one of the guys seated near Ted had been drunk—already, in the middle of the day. Ted snapped at the guy. The guy threatened to punch Ted. They challenged each other to a fight. Then a third guy seated near the two of them, who was very sensitive, begged them to stop. He got barked at, and started to cry.

Things were really unravelling. Luckily, the reconciliation trip was almost over.

MONDAY 28 DECEMBER

0800 - DEPART ORTONA FOR ROME FIUMICINO AIRPORT

It ended just in time.

On the last morning, after the veterans had departed, Ortona felt like a fairground when the crowds have left. As I stepped out of my hotel with my backpack, I was glad to run into Earl and his photographer—they were on their way in to check out. Earl looked even happier to see me. He was eager to share some news: he'd solved the mystery of the hotel. There were actually two receptionists. The same guy always appeared to be there because they were identical (and equally taciturn) twins.

Apparently there had been a Christmas reconciliation, but my view of it had been limited, and I wasn't sure what to make of the little that I had seen. In brief conversations at the bar and on the margins of events, I had asked some of the veterans about the Christmas dinner and the week in general. There wasn't much depth in the answers that I got—I heard that it was great, that there were good words in the speeches at the dinner, that there was an unveiling of the model of some kind of statue. Perhaps I didn't know how to ask; perhaps it was simply hard for the vets to put words to it. When I arrived home in Toronto, I was eager to see how the Canadian media had done their jobs. What story had they found?

The *Toronto Star* led with a photograph taken by Andrew on the first evening at the hotel bar. The caption said, "Good Health: Frank Johnson, of Dorval, Que., right, shares a drink with his old enemy, Fritz Illi, of Stuttgart." The picture showed Fritz with his arm around Frank as the two of them smiled and touched beer glasses. Rosie's article quoted Fritz:

> 'I am here to remember,' said Illi, now 79 years old, with rheumy eyes a milky shade of green. 'I wanted very much to see the Canadians again. I respect these people. I have absolutely no feeling of hatred for them. You cannot possibly understand because you are young and have had a different life,' he continues. 'Yes, these Canadians were the enemy. But we were all just soldiers, we were fighting for our countries because that is what was demanded of us.'

The article touched on the sensitive politics of German war remembrance and how the German veterans felt like pariahs in their own country.

The German government doesn't wish to have anything to do with these old soldiers, and their ambassador to Italy declined an invitation to participate in the reconciliation dinner.

'In Germany, they build monuments to deserters and call us criminals,' said Joseph Klein, who began the war as a private and finished as a captain. Klein is the owner of two Iron Crosses—the highest award given in Germany for acts of valour in battle. He does not wear his medals. He has not brought them to Italy. 'It is a crime to wear the medals in Germany' . . .

Klein, as official spokesman for the small German delegation in Ortona . . . presented the Canadian vets on Christmas Eve with a large wartime map depicting the Ortona military campaign, one of the few 'antiquities of war' that he was able to secure . . .

Later on, at Christmas mass in a rebuilt Santa Maria di Costantinopoli, [John] Matheson wept unashamed tears after Wilf Gildersleeve once more played 'Silent Night' on the new church organ. 'I was so nervous, I was shaking,' said 81-year old Gildersleeve, from Vancouver. 'Hit a couple of false notes there.' . . .

Klein and [Ted] Griffiths laid down their military berets—one olive green, the other deep red—in a token of peace. Then the mayor of Ortona presented every man with a commemorative medal from the city itself . . .

And the Canadians did, generally speaking, conduct themselves beautifully, as did the Germans. Skirmishes were re-enacted with only oblique reference to those who perished. 'Oh, let's not get into that,' said Frank (The Tank) Johnson, when asked to estimate how many Germans he had killed at Ortona. 'We killed a lot of theirs, they kill [sic] a lot of ours' . . .

> And now these remaining few, aged men, put their arms around one another in a church basement and say: 'Merry Christmas, old friend.'
>
> Fritz Illi drains his glass: 'Pretty soon, we'll all be in the ground. There will be nobody left to remember.'

As I'd witnessed first hand the challenges that the reporters had faced, I was impressed by the rich details in Rosie's account. And then I was fascinated to discover, in the *Toronto Star*'s next and final article about the trip, that Rosie had gone public with some of the tensions of the trip.

> The Canadians have been treated—I'm sorry to say—like schoolboys, who must be closely supervised and firmly handled. Every hour of their visit was precisely planned, often to the discomfort and annoyance of the vets themselves.
>
> It's likely, for example, not a single one of these fine gentlemen has ever spent so much time in church—two masses on Christmas Eve day alone, including a midnight service. And this when they were expected to get up early the next morning for an 8 a.m. excursion across the peninsula to the Canadian war cemetery at Montecassino.
>
> 'Back to church?' sputtered Gwilyn Jones, 78, of the Three Rivers Regiment, sucking on his ever-present pipe. 'The hell I am.'
>
> There has been much sotto voce grumping by some vets during this excursion over an onerous itinerary that has left them little time to wander about Ortona itself, which is what most wanted most to do. Five days into the trip, they had yet to see the town in daylight.

> The vets, who were most content to just sit around a bar yakking with their German counterparts, were reluctant to complain for the record. 'Shhh,' cautioned one old fellow, putting his finger over his mouth. 'Don't want Ted to hear us.' Then he added: 'But I think I'm going to punch somebody in the nose.'

Rosie even took Ted to task for his treatment of the Seaforths. While some *Star* readers may have been surprised by this article's negativity, I knew there was a lot more that Rosie had decided not to share. It amazed me that her editors had allowed her to say this much. Maybe this was payback for how Ted had treated the *Star*. If so, it was skillfully done, focusing on the veterans' own gripes, not those of the reporters. And Rosie's final report was more prescient than she could have known. She and Andrew had left early and never got to see how that threat of a punch would come true.

While the *Star* correspondent had managed to suppress any negativity until after describing the reconciliation, the *Ottawa Citizen*'s reporter didn't show the same restraint. In the very first sentence of his report, Dave Brown questioned the sincerity of the event.

> One had to make a pilgrimage to the overcrowded war cemeteries here to find sincerity in the search for reconciliation between former mortal enemies. What was billed as a reconciliation Christmas Eve dinner between German and Canadian veterans became a media event. If there was sincerity there, it was lost behind the wall of microphones and cameras, as each speaker rose to announce there was no longer animosity between men who spent years killing each other. . . .
>
> The dinner went as planned. But from my perspective, the real

> reconciliation happened Christmas Day at the Commonwealth War Cemetery here [in Cassino], when Joseph Klein stepped forward and stole the show.
>
> A former captain, he was prepared to make a presentation all veterans would understand. He opened a box, and presented to all old soldiers, Canadian and German, a medal. . . .
>
> 'Every one of us here today was a front-line soldier, so we know the horror that is war. Let us all be grateful we survived it, and let us take a moment to remember those who didn't.'

The article went on to note that Ted had made a speech at the Christmas Eve dinner, but declined to tell us what he'd said.

> Although his speech Christmas Eve was carefully planned and presented, it got lost in the media hubbub. But there were few reporters around when Mr. Klein handed out the medals on a beautiful sunny Christmas day here. His speech was a testament to the hopelessness of total war. With each medal went a handshake.

Again I had to wonder, was this payback for Ted? The correspondent downplayed the meaning of Ted's much-celebrated dinner, while laying the blame for the dinner's alleged failure on the "media" (which presumably wasn't meant to include the correspondent himself). This narrative deftly covered the fact that its author hadn't been at the dinner. Ted was even further eclipsed as the article continued, with credit given to Joseph Klein for achieving the true reconciliation, going on at some length about Klein's war experience and illustrious post-war career. In fairness to the *Citizen*'s correspondent, though, this portrayal was partly a reflection of who had been willing to talk to him during the trip (namely, the German leader) and who, by contrast, had not given him the time of day. The *Citizen*'s story concluded with an obligatory happy ending.

> It took 55 years, but they got together like a couple of opposing teams, shared dinner and drinks, and talked the way only old soldiers can. They remembered friends killed, and their own near misses. They met as former enemies and parted as friends. Mission accomplished.

The *Ottawa Sun*'s correspondent Earl McRae was more confident in declaring the success of the dinner. Naturally so—he'd had the privilege of being there. His account was the most vivid, and did the most to emphasize the Christian theme of the day.

> And, now it had come, the hour at last; and beneath the high, arched, sculpted ceiling of the beautifully restored church where the old men who once were young ate Christmas dinner in the midst of war, they file in slowly for what will be the last time in their waning lives, and with them, those who marched under tyranny's banner.
>
> 'I sat just over there to the right,' whispered Pat Searson, 76. 'It's different now. It was all smashed then.' In his hand, he clenched a handkerchief.
>
> They took their places in the pews, and as they did, one of the old Canadian soldiers limped over to the organ where he had last played the organ for his battle-weary brothers-in-arms 55 Christmases ago. . . . Wilf Gildersleeve sang in a sweet tenor voice, and they sang with him, their voices filling the vast canyons of the

church and spilling out into the town, dark and bleak on the night of the Christ child's birth.

'Silent night, holy night,' they sang. 'Stille nacht, heilige nacht,' they sang. . . .

The Germans and Canadians turned and grasped one another's hands, and it was as if they didn't want to let go.

And then it was time for the dinner, and they stood for the national anthems of Italy, Canada, and Germany, and they broke off chunks of bread in solidarity, and they raised glasses of wine in toast, and they removed their berets, which were symbols of war, and laid them down on a table, as a symbol of peace.

Ted Griffiths emotionally thanked all those Canadians whose hard work and donations made the event possible, and MP Peter Goldring, and the media, and then: 'Tonight, we have made history. For the first time in the Canadian Army, a group of veterans has sat down and broken bread with a former enemy. Under God's roof, we are all His children; we are all His brothers. Gentlemen—a toast to those we left behind.'

Peter Goldring lifted the Maple Leaf flag covering the bronze model of Ottawan Rob Surette's sculpture called The Price of Peace depicting a Canadian soldier kneeling over his fallen comrade, the life-size model to be erected next spring in the Ortona town square, and it drew murmurs of approval from the Canadian veterans.

It was at that moment Willie Fretz [sic] decided to make his move. Rising quickly to his feet, he said in a firm voice: 'We are sorry. We are sorry about everyone who lost his life. We are sorry for all the suffering we caused. We are sorry we were your enemy. We are sorry to the people of Ortona. We are sorry for the homes

> we destroyed. It is like a boxing match. But, we lost. We are sorry for what we did. We are sorry it happened. This has been one of the most wonderful nights I have ever had on this, the Holy night. Again—we are sorry.'
>
> Enemies no more, the men of peace rose from their chairs with an exploding ovation for Willie Fretz whose words from the heart in a church he once helped destroy, sealed the Christmas of reconciliation.

AS FOR THE CBC's story about the trip, I got to watch it almost one year later with Sam.

He had it on videotape. The twenty-five minute documentary was called "Return to Ortona: A Battlefield Redemption." He'd already watched it a few times; now he wanted me to watch it with him. He put the tape in the VCR and we sat on his couch with his dog.

There was a scene from the Canadian cemetery on the first morning in Ortona. David Halton was talking with a Seaforth.

> *In the cemetery, looking at headstones, Seaforth Highlanders veteran Bill Worton says it won't be easy for him reconciling with men he once regarded as arrogant Nazis. 'I have mixed feelings, really, you know.'*

"There was a hardcore guy, that Seaforth," Sam interjected. "I talked to him quite a bit. Quite a character."

"What do you mean that he was a hardcore guy?"

"Oh he, just uh, his way. Seeing him you could tell he was really a hard rock character."

"When he saw the Germans?"

"Yeah when he saw the Germans and that."

"Did he say—"

"But he was won over pretty good. Our thoughts changed quite a bit on that you know like, you wondered if you really wanted to meet 'em, eh? That was the thing. Yeah."

"What were you thinking before you met them?"

"Oh, I was just wondering how it would really be. You know. 'Cause, and you wondered how they would be with us, basically. Yeah they were, I guess they wanted to meet, and we come, they come, eh, and come a long ways to meet one another. That's quite a guy there, that. Ted?"

On the television now, Ted was carrying the Canadian flag into the cemetery.

"Griffiths?"

"Griffiths, yeah," Sam said. "Him and that politician didn't get along very well, eh."

"Oh. Goldring?"

"Goldring, yeah."

The documentary had introduced Ted Griffiths as the organizer of the trip. Now it segued to telling the story of the Ortona battle, using old film footage to illustrate the narrative.

> *Griffiths was in one of the first Canadian tanks into Ortona trying to clear the way for the infantry . . . It was a battle for every block, every corner of the town . . .*

"There's a German throwing a potato masher," Sam remarked on the old black-and-white footage. He was watching the television intently. "There's one with a Schmeisser."

"Gee."

"There's tracers going there."

"Who's that?"

A Canadian soldier was shooting through a window.

"That's a Seaforth. He's a sniper. Yeah he's lookin' to see if I got him!"

> *If it wasn't Hell it was the courtyard of Hell. It was a maelstrom of noise . . . the harder both sides fought . . .*

"Were you kinda on your own most of the time?"

"I was pretty well on my own, well, see, with support company, the group we were, if they called us we could be doing anything, carrying ammunition or takin a message, or—"

Sam stopped in mid-sentence, distracted by a scene of action on the TV.

"See there's how they blow the hole in the wall with a beehive, eh, use the beehive."

Now in the documentary, Ted was walking on the street in Ortona in conversation with David Halton. They arrived in the square in front of the church of Santa Maria delle Grazie. Ted was gesturing at the church and telling his story.

> *'The fact it was an old medieval church just didn't enter my mind at the moment.'*

Sam continued talking over Ted's narrative. He was still explaining to me what a beehive was and other techniques that were used in mouse-holing. Then the scene on the television cut from Ted at the church to the dark, circular entrance of the railway tunnel that went beneath Ortona. Sam stopped talking and watched.

> *Many of the Germans spent their Christmas Eve huddled in an Ortona railway tunnel.*

"This is where Bauer was," Sam said.

> *Crowded with wounded and dead, memories of the tunnel that night are draped in trauma.*

The scene cut to Hugo Bauer on a street in Ortona. Hugo was talking to the camera in German, with subtitles showing his words in translation. His voice was strained and slow; he was clearly struggling to get the words out. Even though Sam had watched this documentary many times already, he leaned forward on the sofa now, focusing intently on Hugo's words.

> *'At 2:30 in the morning we had to sing Silent Night. And we had a Christmas candle. And a sack of oranges. That was our Christmas gift, for everybody that was in the tunnel.'*

"Hm," Sam remarked quietly. "Sack of oranges for Christmas."

> *'And that's the kind of Christmas you have to carry around for the rest of your life.'*

Hugo started to sniff and fight back tears.

Sam's eyes remained fixed on the television. "*Weihnacht* means Christmas," he muttered, for no apparent reason.

> *'The people at home can't get me excited about Christmas. On the 23rd and 24th it doesn't work.'*

The pitch of Hugo's voice was rising, his body shaking, his face grief-stricken.

'It's as though I'm dead on those days.'

"Well at first," Sam spoke up, "he never smiled much at anything you know. But at last he was, uh, he seemed to accept things."

"He says it's as though I'm dead on those days."

"Yeah. Well it was hard, 'cause he was down with the, his job was taking care of wounded."

The documentary had moved on to scenes of interviews with other Germans. Sam continued talking about Hugo.

"That was a son of a bitch of a job. Took a pretty good man to handle wounded men, you know. To be a stretcher bearer man. I wouldn't have wanted to."

"Yeah? How come?"

"I don't know. Too tough a job. Too tough, you know, patching guys up and that. And they were, like Buxton got his jaw blown off, when we found him there and we had to bring him in. And that's a son of a bitch to look at a guy like that, that you know, isn't gonna, Christ the jaw is gone he can't talk he can't do nothin'. Think the best we could do was take him to the MO [medical officer] but what could the MO do for, we knew he was gone. I'm standing way in the background there you see."

Sam was pointing to himself on the television. It was showing the first meeting of the Canadians and the Germans.

"Oh yeah," I said, "there you are."

"I'm watchin' the guys meet 'em."

"Who was the first German you talked to?"

"I think it was Joseph Klein."

The documentary showed Hugo alone on the margin of the crowd, holding his beer and looking nervous.

At first, Hugo Bauer, perhaps the most traumatized of the veterans, is isolated by his lack of English.

Then it cut to a scene of Hugo and Sam sitting together. Hugo was listening, face down, while Sam talked to him.

"They're saying that you put him at ease," I said.

"Yeah. Well he was smiling at last. That was, uh, the one thing that was good. But he was just sort of a dour guy when we first met him you know. I guess it was pretty tough for him to accept us."

"You think so?"

"Oh yeah. It had to be."

The documentary had moved on to scenes from Christmas Eve. It showed the Canadians and Germans singing "Silent Night" in the church, then eating dinner and toasting their wine glasses in the dining hall.

"How come?" I asked.

"Well, I guess the memories coming back from, of how bad it was eh? And they caused it on our side and we caused it on the other, eh."

"So do you think maybe he came in as a bit of a hardliner?"

"No, I don't, I don't really think so. I think maybe he was glad, after we come and uh, found out that now we weren't too bad and we found out they weren't too bad, eh."

The documentary showed the veterans getting off the bus for one of the wreath-laying ceremonies on the battlefield tour. Sam and Hugo posed arm-in-arm while a Van Doos veteran took their photograph.

"That's you and Hugo Bauer again!"

"Yeah, Hugo Bauer, yeah."

On television, Sam was alone in front of the monument speaking to the CBC correspondent.

> *'Oh it's really been fantastic. This is something I never, ever dreamt of. Never thought would ever happen, you know. It's uh, some, totally unbelievable.'*

Sam watched himself. When the documentary cut away from his interview, he spoke to me again.

"I didn't really think we'd meet. It's odd."

"What's that?"

"For us to really meet. 'Cause even though we were there, I didn't think we'd meet in such a manner eh? But that turned out good. Yeah. I'm glad it happened too now, yeah. There's that hardcore Seaforth."

The whole contingent of Canadian and German veterans were walking down the main pedestrianized street of Ortona. Bill Worton, who had been depicted at the start of the documentary having reservations about meeting the Germans, was walking now with Joseph Klein, the two of them deep in animated, jovial conversation. There were Christmas lights down the street, and a merry-go-round, and local people were out walking and shopping. The documentary was coming to its conclusion.

> *The tensions have gone now. The reconciliation is almost complete.*

"There's old Hugo!" Sam exclaimed joyfully. "He's—"

Sam didn't complete his thought. On the television, Hugo was grinning and taking a photograph of the merry-go-round.

"Eh," Sam said, watching and smiling. "I hope he comes to Edmonton." Ted's voice came on, speaking over the festive scenes on the street.

'This meeting has sort of been a cleansing of the soul in many ways.'

Sam continued talking over Ted, explaining to me how he had invited Hugo Bauer and Willy Fretz to come to Edmonton.

> *'It's a shedding of some of the ghosts of Ortona. They have forgiven us and we have forgiven them and we've come together in a spirit of friendship.'*

"Yeah it really would be nice," Sam said, wrapping up his story about inviting the Germans. He got up from the couch and stopped the video. "No I'm, I don't, I wanted to show you this . . ."

His voice trailed off as he began searching in one of his souvenir boxes. The sofa was surrounded by these boxes that he'd brought out for us to examine. He exhaled a deep, exasperated sigh.

"I got so much stuff around. I, I got more pictures and that I want to, I'll show, I got a box full I'll show, later on tonight when we're home."

It was almost time for us to go to the restaurant, and he wanted to shave and change into nicer clothes.

I DON'T KNOW IF Sam remembered to show me whatever it was that he'd started to look for. Was it related to meeting the Germans? His hope that Willy and Hugo would come visit Edmonton? If he did share it with me, it wasn't while I was recording, because I can't find it in the transcripts. It's not mentioned in my field notes either, but that's no surprise; Sam and I "worked" and talked so much that when I had a spare moment to myself,

I barely had energy to write. What with all his storytelling, it was hard for me to find out what the meeting with the Germans had meant to him. The few times that I remembered to go back to the topic, he would give a brief answer and then think of something else. On one occasion, as we were going through one of Sam's boxes, we found a newspaper article about the trip that Sam had clipped.

"Oh," Sam said, "it shows—" He read the title aloud. "'Making peace with the past.' Willy Fretz and that other guy."

I took the opportunity to ask what he thought about the trip.

"Do you think that's accurate, making peace with the past, do you think that happened?"

"Ah, well, I'd say it was more of a reconciliation, not making peace with anything."

"What is the difference?"

"Well, with reconciliation, at least you were actually meeting the guys. Making peace with the past, what did that mean, really? Nothing. To me. It meant more to me, just in meeting the guys that were against us, eh? You know it was interesting to meet the fellas, to find out who these guys were, really were."

"Had you ever wondered about that?"

"I've often wondered. What they done, how they done it, you know. But then again we got a lot of them over here after as well eh? In Canada. Here I'm gonna give you this. This was dropped out of a cannon."

Sam went on to tell a story about this German propaganda leaflet. I didn't want to interrupt him. It would have been good to find out why he didn't like the words "making peace with the past" but one story led to another and I didn't manage to return to the subject. In any case, I don't think I was ever going to learn much by asking Sam this kind of question. It just wasn't in his nature to talk about the meanings of things. To the extent that he would tell me how the trip had affected him, it was in his characteristically intellectualizing way of dwelling on the information it had provided him, not the feelings it had evoked. As he put it to me in our brief discussion of that newspaper clipping, the value of meeting the Germans was learning "what they done, how they done it"—filling in more pieces of Sam's mental jigsaw puzzle of the war.

What I should have paid more attention to was the way Sam talked about Hugo. He remembered Hugo a number of times during my visit, on his own initiative, without me asking. What made Hugo so memorable? I think a clue was offered when I wasn't recording, but fortunately I managed to write it in my notes. Sam told this story in the kitchen while heating a can of soup on the stove and making us ham sandwiches for lunch. Later, I wrote:

> Sam enjoyed talking to Hugo Bauer. He said Hugo was a person interested in saving lives. He was helping the wounded, in the tunnel, including some Canadian prisoners wounded, binding their arms, giving water. One Canadian told him to fuck off, didn't want his help.

The clue is in Hugo helping the wounded Canadians—and maybe in Hugo being told to fuck off. That resonates with a moment that I did record. We were on the sofa. Sam was watching the news. He'd told me to keep looking in his box. I interrupted his news-watching with another interesting detail that I found.

"Tells a story here," I said, "that uh, during the battle of Ortona a German sergeant came out under fire to dress the wounds of a Canadian and to give him a shot of morphia."

"Mm-hm," Sam said absent-mindedly, still watching the news on TV.

"Should ask—"

"Someone had seen that then. That'd be a good thing to ask." We'd been talking about things I should ask the other Edmonton guys in my interviews. Sam continued, "Should ask one of the—"

Suddenly Sam turned away from the television and stared at me in amazement.

"By god!" he exclaimed. "I wonder where Bauer was!"

"Could have been him?"

"Could have been Bauer, by god. Could have been Bauer."

What comes to mind when I look at this now is Sam's interminable struggle with "that day" in his memory—his map and his story of the battle at the white house where he and Sergeant Hately had shot the Germans who were running away. When they came upon the body of the German who was still living, though mortally wounded, Sam's sergeant said, *well he don't need no fucking doctor*. And then Sam had considered killing the only German they hadn't shot.

Maybe for Sam there was no making peace with that past. But there was meaning in doing something now for Hugo. The detail about Hugo that seemed to matter most to Sam was how Hugo had cared for the wounded—including his enemies. It was a "son of a bitch" job that Sam admitted he had never wanted.

Willy and Hugo never did make it to Edmonton. I'm not sure why Willy declined the invitation, but by the time the next Christmas came around, Hugo was too ill to travel. Both died shortly after. It's a shame that Sam never got to show them around.

That moment when Sam and I were watching the documentary, and Hugo was talking, and Sam said, "*Weihnacht* means Christmas," I'm sure he knew it wasn't necessary to say the words out loud. There were subtitles. He knew I could read.

Maybe the word *Weihnacht* was special to him and he just wanted a chance to say it.

Or maybe he just didn't want to stop translating for his new friend Hugo Bauer.

CHAPTER 7

The Ghost of That Church

IN THE PAINTING, WE see a narrow street choking with rubble. Broken window shutters hang from balconies and lie strewn upon the ground. Black smoke fills the sky. In the foreground, blending in with blocks of cement and twisted metal, lying on the rubble pile and poised behind a fallen shutter, Canadian soldiers are taking cover with their rifles pointed up the street. At the top of the street, at the centre of the painting, is a church. Its facade has been blown away, exposing its hollow interior. Above its broken dome, however, the bell tower is still intact. Atop the bell tower, barely discernible against the black sky, there is a tiny dot. The viewer would presume it's a cross.

The church is facing the soldiers. The soldiers are facing the church. What is happening between them? Is the church watching over and protecting them—or is it judging them? The soldiers are doing violence under its figurative shadow. Indeed, their violence may even be aimed at it; while they seem to be striving to get to it, it's also in their line of fire. No other possible target is visible in the scene. Perhaps the soldiers are responsible for its prominent wound—its severed facade. What, then, will it mean to the soldiers if they make it to the church?

And what will it mean if they don't?

The painting is *Via Dolorosa, Ortona*. It was painted by Charles Comfort who was with the Canadian army during the battle.[1]

As an official war artist, Comfort was not a front-line soldier, but his role was to witness and document the soldiers' experiences. On December 28, 1943, when the Germans abandoned Ortona and the battle came to an end, Comfort hastened into the city together with his fellow war artist Lawren Harris. Later in his memoir, *Artist at War*, he described that day.

> We parked the Humber in the Piazza Vittoria and picked a careful path along what had been the Corso Vittorio Emanuele. The familiar world had disappeared, and in its place a grotesque and malignant forest of ruins crowded all about us, leaning, tottering crazily, reeking with the malodorous stench of death. We stumbled along in the tenebrous silence, incredulous of what we saw. Here indeed was the imagery of 'purgatory' . . . A gush of rubble filled the roadway, like a tumbling mountain moraine. Above it stood revealed, through tangled skeins of wire, the intimate furnishings of a tiny room, with pictures, washstand, and a tousled bed, dangling in upper space . . . We looked about in bewilderment and exhaustion. One felt a choking claustrophobia in the place. Everywhere was misery, death and destruction.

Normally, on his first visit to a battlefield, Comfort would do some preliminary drawing or painting. In Ortona, however, he was too distressed. "I could not possibly paint, or even sketch, on that first dreadful visit."

What seemed most distressing to Comfort was the sight of the ruined cathedral of San Tommaso. When he returned to Ortona the next day, having gathered the strength to paint, his first subject was that church. In

watercolour, Comfort depicted the details of its ruined facade, the interior of its dome, and tiny human figures standing in the rubble beneath. He gave this watercolour the plainly descriptive title, *Chiesa di San Tomasso* (with a misspelling of the church's name). Later, in *Via Dolorosa, Ortona*—one of his largest oil paintings of the war—he portrayed San Tommaso in less detail, somewhat blurry, more like how the soldiers may have seen it during the battle.

But there is no street named Dolorosa in Ortona. In giving his painting this title, Comfort must have been thinking of the famous Via Dolorosa (the "Way of Sorrow") in Jerusalem, which is the route that Jesus is said to have walked through the city, carrying his cross, as he was led by Roman soldiers to the site of his crucifixion.

The painting's title suggests a sacred meaning. But are the soldiers in the foreground part of the sacred, or are they violating it? It's possible to see it both ways. Surely for most Canadians, the preferred view would be the former, aligning the soldiers with Jesus as they suffer and lose their lives for the greater good of humankind. But objectively, in the same crucifixion analogy, the Canadian soldiers could equally be the Romans who are inflicting the suffering.

What was Comfort's view? Did he want us to see it both ways? He certainly imagined the cathedral as if it had been a sentient victim of violence. At first sight, the ruined building had brought to his mind the thought of an animal butchered by hand.

> The Cathedral of San Tommaso stood half buried in its own masonry, looking as if a mighty cleaver had struck down through the dome and split it in half like a butchered steer. The delicate baroque stucco and plaster work had disintegrated under the blow and spewed into the piazza like so much blood and entrails.[2]

The artist was not alone in his feelings. Long after the battle, the ruined church figured strongly in Canadian veterans' memories. Their ways of remembering were similar to the blurred images and ambivalent meanings of Comfort's painting. Far from the war in time and place, the veterans remembered as old men now in modern condominiums, wearing new clothes, holding cups of tea or coffee in hands that once, in Ortona, had gripped the gun and the knife.

On hearing the Edmonton 49th veterans were returning to Ortona, Mrs Esther Bowen phoned Ed Boyd and told him she had a candle holder her husband, RSM Ranald Bowen, had picked up in the rubble in front of San Tommaso church on Christmas Day, 1943, which she wished to have returned. Ed asked me to see Mrs Bowen, which I did. And I then had a mission to perform.

The carousel made a shutter-and-click, and the next image appeared on the screen. From a cassette player beside the slide projector, Mel's recorded voiceover continued.

At the Edmonton 49th regiment's museum, they show Mrs Bowen a picture of destroyed San Tommaso church as she turns the candle holder over to me for its return.

Another shutter-and-click to the next slide.

No markings were on the six-inch-high holder to indicate the type of enamel or its origin. Its makeup is the front section of a winged horse, possibly Pegasus, with a long tail on which sits a winged cherub holding aloft the cup for the candle.

"It shows up much better in the dark."

We were in Mel's office on the first day of our interviews. He wanted to show me this slide show that he'd made about the trip.

This was a major production on his part. In addition to making slides from his own photographs, he'd also made some from other photos, newspaper clippings, and even images that he'd captured from history books and films. Instead of narrating the show impromptu as he presented it, he'd pre-recorded his voiceover on a cassette tape and was playing it back. This approach had allowed him to mix in music and sound effects from the war. Putting all this together had taken him months. Not long before sharing it with me, he'd given a showing of it in his condo building's community room for his regimental association and other guests.

Creating slide shows was one of Mel's hobbies. He'd got into it as a way of organizing memories of his and Eva's trips to Arizona. Every year, they went by camper van to Tucson where they spent time exploring the land, collecting music, and watching performances by their favourite old-time country-and-western band, the Sons of the Pioneers. He'd started making slide shows about these trips to share with his condo community.

"Do you usually do this sort of thing with your slides, or is this—"

"Yeah."

"—something special?"

"That's what all of that is for, yeah." He gestured at a stack of boxes in the open closet.

"You've put together little programs?"

"Yeah, music and—"

"Really."

"Yeah. Yeah. Well like I said, I started doing that because my wife and I were always arguing about what we were looking at, you know? So I said jeez the best way of doing this I guess is to put it on tape." He smirked. "But even then we argue at times. Because I tend to do things a little faster than I should."

A little faster? That sounded good to me. The story in his slide show had yet to arrive in Italy. An extraordinary amount of time in the lead-up had been devoted to that widow and her San Tommaso candle holder. What about meeting the Germans?

We had a stop to reinforce the breakfast we had on the plane . . . Bill Teleske shows what he thinks of carbonara, and again Sam Lenko is all ears . . . Part of the six-course meal was penne in white sauce . . .

It dawned on me that he was going to document all of his meals.

. . . followed next by spaghetti with tomato sauce . . .

I got another tape ready for my recorder. This was going to be a long show.

It was charming, though. Clearly Mel had made it with his audience, mostly fellow veterans and their families, in mind. There were lots of photos of his fellow travellers from the regiment, including Sam. He'd tried to make the show enjoyable with light-hearted humour and friendly teasing—*This is a kind of strange picture since Joe's glass is empty*—and thoughts about the local ecology—*Some of the food seen in this dish could have come from . . . [click] . . . these trees just around the corner*—along with gentle acknowledgements of the sad and traumatic memories that those on the trip were carrying—*Every vet looking at that signpost [road sign of Ortona] had his own perspective of the hell and the human cost it would exact over the next little days in 1943.* With the Last Post playing on his recording, he showed pictures from the Canadian cemetery, and then the picture of the Italian groundskeepers that he'd taken when he'd come to thank them—*This is Frank, one of the caretakers of the cemetery who do such a fine job of looking after our boys.*

Finally there was the meeting with the Germans.

Thursday 24th of December 1998. Today we were to meet the German vets here in our hotel . . . There was no discernable tension on either side and an atmosphere of congeniality was attained with a couple of beers . . . Here I have my picture taken with two of the First German Parachute Division veterans, Gisbert Borucki, left, and Hugo Bauer, right.

And then an account of the Christmas dinner—the only account of a meal in Mel's show that didn't include a description of the food.

The tables are set up for a reconciliation dinner at Santa Maria di Costantinopoli church where the Seaforths had their Christmas dinner in 1943. A symbolic laying down of berets was held prior to the dinner by both German and Canadian vets. MP Peter Goldring unveiled a replica of the statue which is being sculpted . . . The replica shows the soldier kneeling to assist his wounded comrade. Another symbolic gesture was when a priest gave each vet a piece of bread and a sip of wine followed by the mayor of Ortona who presented each with a medallion showing Ortona's coat of arms on the front and inscripted on the back '1943 - Ortona 24th dicembre - 1998.'

That was the extent of Mel's description of what it was like to meet the Germans. His show went on to document moments from the next days' battlefield tours, with many photos of wreath-layings and explanations of what they were commemorating. This rather dry narrative was finally enlivened when it came to the monument to the fallen civilians in Ortona, which is where Mel finally fulfilled what he called his personal mission. On the screen was a photograph of the candle holder being received by the smiling mayor of Ortona.

Almost passed over was my little mission from Mrs Esther Bowen to pass on the little candle holder her husband had picked up in the rubble of San Tommaso church. It was one of the last presentations but certainly not the least as it created a noticeable stir among the Italian people present. Mayor Puletti seemed delighted with its return.

Then, photos of shops along Ortona's main promenade. *The countdown was on toward our winging our way home. We had one and a half hours of free time in Ortona today, our first of the trip*—a subtle hint here of the frustration with the trip's tightly regimented schedule. Mel showed his comrades shopping for gifts and postcards. In typically modest fashion, he didn't mention his own story, which he'd told me, of purchasing earrings on the Corso for Eva. There were photos of Ortona's streets decorated for Christmas—*The Christmas spirit was alive and well in the Ortona of today, a far cry from the Christmas of 55 years earlier*—and then it was scenes from the bus on the first leg of the journey home—*All roads lead to Rome . . . stop to stretch . . . hilltop villages . . . fruit trees . . . Back home the trip has been given extensive coverage not only in the newspaper but in radio and television.* Finally, wrapping up with thanks for the trip's organizers and sponsors, Mel's narrative concluded with a message to Mrs Bowen.

The little candle holder that has graced her home for fifty-five years has been returned to its proper place.

"Did you know him?"

"I knew of him," Mel said. "Just the name. To see him."

I was trying to figure out why this candle holder had taken pride of place in Mel's show. He'd put it at the beginning and at the end of his story about the trip.

Whatever the reason for its importance, it didn't seem to stem from his relationship with the Bowens. During the war, Ranald Bowen had been a senior officer (regimental sergeant major) in the Loyal Edmontons. Evidently, Mel (a much lower-ranked private) had hardly known Ranald. It didn't sound like he'd known Ranald's wife Esther, either. It was only upon being given his "mission" that he'd learned of the candle holder's existence and how it had come to be in the Bowens' home.

"But apparently Christmas Day in the rubble in front of San Tommaso church he picked up this candle holder. Dusted it off and put it in his pack. Souvenir of the battle I guess. And brought it home. And, anyway when Mrs Bowen found out that there was people going over to Ortona for Christmas dinner, she wanted it sent back. Ranald died about thirteen, fourteen years ago. And she wanted it sent back because she felt that was the proper place for it. And uh, it only stands about six inches high and it's in the form of, almost like Pegasus, you know, the flying, what do you call them?"

"Oh yeah. Horse with wings."

"Yeah. And with a little candle holder on top. And there was still a little piece of candle from 1943 in it. Because they never ever used it as a candle holder, they just had it in, up on a shelf as a memento, you know."

Mel had really taken his mission to heart, saying figuratively that his life depended on it. He'd gone to the Edmonton branch of a national high-end jewelry store to get a suitable box.

"She gave it to me. And then I went to Birks jewelries and I said have you got a box that I can take this candle holder over in, you know, mess it up nicely in there and protect it, because I said I'm going to deliver this thing or it's my life, you know. So anyway, they gave me a nice box for it and so I carried it. I carried it on the plane and I carried it to every ceremony that we had."

He was careful not to name names, but he let me know of his frustrations with the trip's organizers who, he said, kept brushing off his mission. Every time he tried to find an occasion to return the candle holder, he was told that it was not the right time. He suspected that the real reason for this constant deferral was the trip organizers' fear that the candle holder would be an embarrassment, drawing attention to how Canadian soldiers had not always acted honourably. Mel felt this fear was unwarranted; in his view, the story of the candle holder was nothing to be ashamed of.

"'No I can't,' uh, 'No, we, we haven't got time tonight,' and uh, 'No this is not the proper place for it.' Even at the end, it was taken from me and I was told, 'Well I'll just give this to an aide and they can give it to the mayor later.' They didn't want, it was almost as though this was something we stole from the church and, you know. That was the attitude that I got. Rather than, anybody could have picked it up or the next tank that come along could have crushed it in the rubble where it was. So. But anyway I said, 'No.' I said, 'If you think I'm going back to Edmonton and face a ninety-year-old and tell her I didn't make this little presentation to the mayor of Ortona and see that it got back to its rightful place,' I said, 'another think coming.' So I grabbed it."

This struggle happened on the second last day of the trip. There was the wreath-laying ceremony at the monument in Ortona's civilian cemetery; the mayor and many local people were present; Mel felt this was his last chance. He grabbed the Birks box out of the hands that had taken it and he went to the mayor before anyone could stop him.

"I gave it to the mayor and this was in the cemetery, the civilian cemetery right in Ortona. And there was quite a civilian population around. And when I made the presentation there was a bit of a stir in the crowd you know, because it was something that was coming home to them, you know."

"What did you tell them?"

"I told them, I said uh, Regimental Sergeant Major Ranald Bowen picked this up on Christmas Day in the rubble in front of San Tommaso church and he, they feel that uh, this is where, Mrs Bowen feels that this is where it belongs, back in the church."

That was the end of Mel's story of the candle holder—and the end of my thoughts about it. It seemed like a charming story about Mel's sense of duty to his regiment, to his wartime officer, to the officer's widow, and to the people of Ortona. But it didn't tell me anything about what Ortona meant for Mel. There was no apparent connection between the candle holder and Mel's experience of the battle; nor was there a connection to the primary purpose of the trip.

As for that primary purpose—the reconciliation with the Germans—Mel didn't seem to have much to say. Perhaps that was because he hadn't experienced much of an encounter. Considering the ratio of Canadian and German veterans (thirty to six—and one of those six, Hugo, had only been able to talk to Sam) it was understandable if conversations hadn't gone very deep, especially when so much of their time together had been spent in structured, ritual activities. But part of the problem was that I didn't know how to ask. In any case, after this long slide show and my follow-up questions about the candle holder, I really needed to move on to Mel's memories of the battle. In our interviews over the days that followed, as Mel shared more and more of his stories, neither of us returned to the topic of the trip.

When I came home from my fieldwork and started to analyze the interviews, I realized that I really didn't know what, if anything, the trip had done for Mel. It couldn't have been nothing. Ortona meant so much to him, and he had such strong feelings about the moral problem of killing. But then he'd also told me how he'd already made his own personal return trips to Ortona, so maybe this recent one with Ted's group had been less emotional for him.

As for meeting the Germans, maybe for Mel it was sufficiently meaningful that he'd gone to meet them, and he'd been a good participant. There was a personal sacrifice involved, as it meant not spending Christmas at home with his wife. And so he'd demonstrated his commitment to what the trip stood for: recognition of the enemy's humanity, and regret for the violence that was done. Also, as Mel had explained to me, he'd never been sure if he'd actually killed or wounded anyone; it was just the thought of what he might have done that troubled him.

In a way, then, there was symmetry in Mel's experience of reconciliation as a mainly performative gesture which didn't leave him with detailed memories of connecting with his former enemies. If that was the case, that wasn't necessarily less meaningful to Mel, but I could imagine it was the sort of meaning that could be hard to express; and so maybe this was why he'd talked so much more about the candle holder, and the food, and other apparently trivial details in his slide show. These details were simply what was available to him for telling his story about the trip.

That was my guess at the time. There was more that I didn't know, more that I wished I had asked—but that was true for all of my interviews. Anyway, the focus of my research had moved well beyond the trip. By the time I wrote my dissertation, the trip with the reconciliation dinner was just a bit of background to how I met the veterans, briefly summarized; I had given up trying to interpret it.

But recently—just a few days ago, as I write this now—I was looking at Charles Comfort's painting. I'd seen *Via Dolorosa* before but hadn't paid it close attention. It was only now that I noticed that there are soldiers in the foreground. They're holding rifles behind a rubble pile and facing up the street. Mel's words came back to me.

"And I can remember, uh, lying. Here. Lying on a pile of rubble, way back this way, and firing up into here, into the bell tower."

In the painting, I saw Mel. He was shooting at the church. And I remembered the candle holder.

Of course. The candle holder belonged to San Tommaso—and San Tommaso meant a lot to Mel.

Any church would have given the candle holder meaning, simply by virtue of what churches symbolize: peace, moral community, innocence, redemption. But San Tommaso is not just any church. It is Ortona's cathedral—the tallest building in town and its most recognizable landmark. Its dome serves as the visual emblem of Ortona, the first feature to appear on the skyline when you approach from a distance. In Mel's account of his first return to Ortona after the war, with Eva in 1985, he told me how they'd pulled over before reaching the town and got out of the car to look.

"Outskirts of town, just coming into it, you know. The wife and I had rented a car in Amsterdam, of course we drove all the way to Rome and then across over to, and we sat across the valley from, I could still see San Tommaso church, the church from across the valley."

The church was the first thing he noticed when he returned. He didn't just look at Ortona; he looked at San Tommaso. Then he and Eva entered the town.

"I didn't recognize anything in town to begin with. Then we got walkin' around later on and then I recognized that one, that one wall, that one that I was thinking of, you know."

That was the wall he'd pointed out to me in the old photograph. ("One of those guys could be me.") He saw nothing else in town that was memorable—except for San Tommaso.

"But there was very little else. San Tommaso church had been rebuilt."

"Was the tower still the same?"

"No. No. Huge dome on it now, you know."

"That tower you were shooting at, that had the bell in it, was that still there?"

"Oh no. No. Maybe the tower is somewhere, I don't know. Because that was still on the church when it was left standing. But it seems to me that they have taken most of it down, you know."

Mel's memory of San Tommaso seemed a bit mistaken. Now, looking back, it occurs to me that this was one of the reasons that I underestimated the church's significance to Mel. Previously, when telling me his story of lying on the rubble pile and shooting at a bell tower, he'd pointed to a picture in the book we were both looking at. He'd said his target was San Tommaso, but the building in the picture wasn't the church; it was the municipal building. The municipal building had a small clock tower. Mel was pointing at that.

"'Cause I thought Jesus that's a good place for a sniper to be, you know. But I guess everybody else thought so too. And I think there was a bell up there, but I'm not sure whether I was ringing it or not. You couldn't hear. Because, you know, there was firing going on all around you, and coming from the other direction too. So, how are you going to know if there's a bell being rung?"

He thought there was a bell up there. So he wasn't sure? In the photograph, it was clearly a clock tower. And then later, when he told me about his return to Ortona with Eva and described looking at San Tommaso, his comment on the dome's apparent newness also made me question the reliability of his memory. The dome was indeed partly new, but it was a faithful restoration of the one that was half destroyed during the war. Essentially, the same dome had been there at the time of the battle. It was a remarkable feature of the church, remembered by other veterans, featured in wartime photographs, and depicted in Charles Comfort's paintings. That led me to wonder whether Mel had actually been shooting at the municipal building and had later come to think of it as the church.[3]

However, even when I had the impression that Mel's memory was mistaken, I still should have seen the importance of his *belief* that he'd shot the church. It's a memory that he mentioned to me on numerous occasions. And now I notice the important place it has in his poem about Ortona.

Back then as you lay on a huge rubble pile

This moment stands out as the most personal of the poem. It's even a bit uncanny. Up until this point, the poem has been devoid of a first-person perspective. But then, in the two stanzas about San Tommaso, the poet shifts, speaking directly to a "friend" who was there.

Back then as you lay on a huge rubble pile
With your rifle loaded and cocked,
Your sights on the dome of Ortonas church
Overlooking the length of the block

San Tomasso the church, was a sniper up there?
Who could see every move that was made
Better not take any chances my friend
And so the tower was sprayed.

I think of Mel as he was writing the poem. What made him want to speak to himself, as a friend, about that moment? What had happened to him when he was shooting at San Tommaso? And not just shooting *at* it; he felt like he'd *shot* it. Because he saw it as a threat—*was a sniper up there?*

For the most part, he'd told me, all his shooting in Ortona had been at windows.

"Windows."

"Other windows."

"Yeah. Well, there's nobody standing there to take a shot at."

This was why he wasn't sure if he'd ever shot anyone.

The church of San Tommaso was the one other target that he knew (or thought he knew) that he'd hit. He wasn't sure if he'd rung its bell, but he knew he was hitting the church. And unlike windows, this target had a sort of personhood. Figuratively, it had a face. It had a history. It had a name.

The candle holder had belonged to it—and had been taken from it. It's fair to say that Mel felt he'd been part of the ruination of the church, having harmed it with his rifle. In helping to return its candle holder, he was undoing some of the harm. And while Mel didn't know if he'd taken anyone's life in Ortona, and I don't know if he was religious in this way, I wonder if his thoughts for San Tommaso were also thoughts for the souls he might have harmed with his rifle—including his own.

In coming back to write about the Ortona reconciliation trip, I've come to discern more of what it meant for Sam and for Mel.

But what about Ted? What did it mean for him?

This is hard to admit. Back when I was starting to do interviews with veterans, it would have made sense to begin with Ted. After all, he was the reason I'd first heard of Ortona. He was the first to talk to me about it. And he was a leader among veterans—chairman of his regimental association, prominent in the remembrance of Ortona. Following the CBC documentary on the Christmas dinner of reconciliation, Ted had gained even more prominence in Canadian war remembrance. Yet, I chose to start with veterans from other regiments. Eventually, I told myself, I would ask Ted for an interview. But not yet.

I could list practical reasons for that decision, but really what it came down to was fear. I didn't want to include Ted in my research too early, for fear that he would try to control it—just as he'd been so controlling on that trip. At the outset of my fieldwork, I couldn't know where my questions and interpretations might lead, but I suspected that whatever I did, Ted would have a problem with it. If he were involved, I would always worry about his approval, not wanting to end up in his crosshairs. Ortona was deeply important to him, and I'd seen his sensitivity and quickness to anger. He was well-connected, and I believed that, if he chose, he could make my life difficult. As a PhD student trying to do my first major project while navigating the politics of academia, I didn't need that added pressure. Just the thought of interviewing Ted was stressful. And so, I decided to defer it. This made sense, I reasoned: first, I'd focus on gathering as much data as I could, and later, when I felt more confident and secure, I'd get back to Ted.

Later never came. I returned from western Canada with more than enough data. I'd done too much. Behind schedule, short of money, beginning to feel the immensity of the task that was still ahead of me, the last thing that I wanted was another interview, let alone an interview with such a challenging participant.

So I gave up all thought of contacting him. However, from time to time, the thought of him returned to haunt me. Whenever I imagined the prospect of finishing my PhD and sharing my work, I anticipated that he would somehow pop up to criticize and shame me, aggrieved by the fact that (in his eyes) I had snubbed him. He might use his moral authority as a leading veteran to publicly find faults with my work. Part of me suspected that my fears were unreasonable, but still I preferred not to face them.

And then it became a moot point. By the time I completed my PhD, I was fed up with Ortona and the whole topic of war. I wasn't going to share my work anyway. There was no need to think any more, let alone worry, about Ted.

Now I'm back. But in the time that I've been gone, Ted—like all the others—has passed away.

When I looked him up and learned of his passing, I also learned that he'd published his memoirs. From an online search, I found there was a copy of it in the library of my old university.

> Griffiths, E. R. M.
> Dare to be True: An Odyssey of Hope and Challenge.
> Subjects, Canada, Canadian Army; Civil Service—Canada; World War, 1939-1945.
> Available, Scott Stacks, call number FC 601 G73 A5 2000.

All in one volume. I remembered him telling me that his editor suggested two, separating the war from the civilian story. Ted wanted it in one—it was one life. Looks like he got it that way.

Available.

And so, on a hot summer day, twenty-four years after my last sight of him in Ortona, I returned to my old library for my long-delayed meeting with Ted.

HE'S BOOKENDED HIS LIFE story with the battle of Ortona. The prologue to the memoir is a scene from the start of the battle. The penultimate chapter is the reconciliation dinner. *Chapter 9—Ortona Revisted: Through a Political Minefield to Reconciliation*. I decide to read this chapter first.

From the trip, I remember him being high-strung and short-tempered. Now I can see he had some good reasons. His story about revisiting Ortona is as much about the torments he suffered from his "allies" as it is about reconciling with his enemies. Already in this chapter's second paragraph, he's introducing the main source of his aggravations.

> There is only one issue which remains prominent and constant in the mind of any politician, and that is to do whatever is needed to get re-elected. At this late stage in my life I should have exercised more caution, but my latent distrust of our elected representatives was overcome by one whose fawning approach seduced my common sense. Presenting himself as the avatar of concern for war veterans, he was literally to become an albatross before I was able to persuade his party leader to get him off my back.

He's talking about Peter Goldring. It turns out it was Goldring's idea to launch a public fundraising campaign after Ted was turned down by Veterans Affairs. Ted credits Goldring with kickstarting the campaign and getting the attention of key media players. But then Ted got the "inkling" that Goldring was "trying to turn our trip from a veterans pilgrimage of reconciliation into a quasi-political voyage where he would gain political mileage."

Ted's not holding back here in laying down all of his beefs with Goldring. At a pre-departure reception, Ted writes, Goldring made a speech that went long over his allotted time. Goldring handed out framed wartime photographs with Goldring's name printed in the captions. Goldring sent letters of thanks to all the donors on behalf of Ted's regimental association—without the association's approval. Matters became worse during the trip. According to Ted, when the group was having lunch at the embassy in Rome, "Goldring rather childishly began complaining the Ambassador didn't invite Goldring's wife and two daughters." Goldring then made himself a "fly in the ointment" during the Christmas Eve dinner in Ortona.

> When he saw the Canadian Ambassador and the Mayor seated with me at the head table, he belaboured John Gardam [Ted's assistant]

> to the point where Gardam finally slotted him at the end of the head table to keep him quiet . . . Goldring seemed totally insensitive to the fact that this was a time for veterans, not politicians. At this time he was taking much of the joy out of the trip.

In short, Goldring "continued to plague us to the end."

Ted also describes problems with Rob Surette, the young sculptor who created the *Price of Peace* monument. Surette had initially offered to donate a statue to commemorate the trip. After agreeing to work with the sculptor, Ted then learned the statue would only be free if it was done in cement; if he wanted bronze, he would have to pay. After settling the price for bronze, Surette informed Ted he had no experience working in that medium and would need additional funds for his training and equipment. "Our 'free' statue was beginning to get expensive, and this was just the start of the job." When Ted rejected Surette's idea to send a model of the statue to Italy, Surette—encouraged by Goldring, no less—went ahead and sent it anyway. Ted got stuck with the cost of shipping and insurance, plus the hassle of clearing it with Italian customs who had impounded it as a work of art.

So the unveiling of the model statue at the Christmas Eve dinner had not been Ted's idea at all. Indeed, its presence at the dinner was an unwelcome reminder of how others were imposing on his trip.

Another torment was the Seaforths. I had got a hint of this already—Ted had told me how the regiment wanted to send more members on the trip than were allowed, including its bagpipe band. He had told them no; all regiments on the trip had to be equal. Now here in his memoir, he writes that the Seaforths nevertheless sent an additional group to Ortona, in advance of Ted's group, and without informing Ted. "We found the group front and centre when we arrived—fully expecting to participate in all our activities." It's not clear from Ted's account, but it sounds like this was a group of Seaforth reservists and band members, not World War II veterans. "I am not a person of infinite patience," Ted writes, very truthfully, "so I told the leader of the group that if he and his associates were not out of town by the next morning, I would arrange for the local police chief to escort them out." Ted mentions nothing more about it, so I assume that he succeeded in making the group go away. Where they went, I can't imagine, but there was certainly no sign of them on the trip.

It's no wonder to me now that Ted was so irascible in Ortona. It's a lot easier to sympathize with him. He was trying to create a dignified and spiritual experience, and (in his view at least, keeping in mind this is only his side of the story) he was getting constant interference from selfish interlopers, one of whom he was maddeningly beholden to. Mind you, Ted's manner of writing sometimes hints at his own self-importance and a propensity for escalating his conflicts. For example, had he really ordered the uninvited Seaforth contingent to leave Ortona? Certainly he was within his rights to exclude them from private events, but it was ridiculous to think he had authority to banish anyone from the town. Probably that was just bluster on Ted's part, but it suggests that Goldring wasn't the only one with the tendency to engage in what Ted described as "braggadocio."

What about the purpose of the trip—the reconciliation? Oddly, the time shared with the Germans is given only two pages in the chapter, and Ted's account of it is surprisingly short on detail. On the first meeting between the Canadians and the Germans, Ted writes:

> Both parties recognized each other for what they were in 1943—soldiers fighting for their country. Without a hint of resentment or recrimination, the Canadians took the Germans as friends, and

> within a few minutes all were seated together drinking vino and swapping war stories.

There's brief mention of the visit to the cemeteries at Cassino, and the Ortona battlefield tour—"interesting in that, for the first time, we could see the battle from both sides." Then the Christmas Eve dinner—"it was to be a memorable, emotional, enjoyable evening . . . even though the Italian ladies who cooked the meal boiled the turkeys." Ted continues:

> Prior to being seated for the meal, the local priest, assisted by the Mayor of Ortona, passed bread and wine to all veterans in both parties. Speeches were purposely kept short, and tears flowed freely. When we rose from the table we felt a closeness—something beyond a mere physical closeness—almost a communion of minds and souls. It was a blending together of human beings who had faced each other as foes, and now with age and the greater understanding that goes with it, recognized that forgiveness and reconciliation is the only true path to follow.

That would seem to be the most meaningful moment of the trip for Ted—and yet, that's all he says about it. In the next paragraph, he's right back on the topic of the chapter's main antagonist: "Sadly, the only fly in the ointment, once again, was Peter Goldring . . ." There's no more mention of the Germans. The remaining pages describe Ted's efforts to get the statue—made in honour of the reconciliation—permanently placed.

Ted's description of the reconciliation is strikingly impersonal. He's not even in his own narrative—there's no "I" in the story. For the duration of the time spent with the Germans, he shifts out of the first person; only when that time is done, and he returns to the subject of Goldring, does the first-person voice reappear. The Canadian media reports provide much richer accounts of the encounters in the hotel bar, the church, the cemeteries, and the Christmas Eve dinner. In Ted's account, the Germans don't even have names. Yet I remember how much he was enjoying his time on the bus, talking and laughing with Joseph Klein. What had they shared? What had it meant to him?

And what about the ghosts that Ted had wanted to bury? What was it like for him to be back in Ortona for another Christmas Day? He hasn't mentioned any of this. I wish that I could go back in time with the courage to interview him and the clarity of mind to ask.

But maybe the lack of detail is actually a clue to what, for him, reconciliation meant. What he does describe is the ritual of bread and wine—an imitation of the Christian ritual of communion. He uses the phrase "communion of minds and souls" and this seems to be his way of underlining the achievement of the trip's objective. Maybe his account is short on interpersonal details because the interpersonal wasn't really the point; whatever he got to know about the Germans as people, that wasn't nearly as important as the shared ritual—which would mean that Ted really believed in the ritual's transformative power. Such belief in the real power of communion is shared by many devout Christians.

And now it occurs to me that, up to this point, I've never really taken seriously Ted's apparent religious beliefs. When he talked about ghosts and souls, I always assumed it was figurative, but perhaps he literally believed in them. At the conclusion of the CBC documentary about the return to Ortona, we hear him saying, "This meeting has sort of been a cleansing of the soul in many ways. It's a shedding of some of the ghosts of Ortona."

Cleansing of the soul. At the very end of his memoir, in the last paragraph where he concludes his life story, Ted makes clear his literal belief in God, in heaven, and—by implication—in his soul.

> On my going I want no tears, only the understanding I tried to do my duty as God gave me the vision to see that duty. If I am to be faulted the responsibility is mine alone, and I must atone for it . . . When I depart I will go with a lifetime of memory and love. Love of family, love of the inestimable joy of grandchildren's laughter, love of friends, love of country and, waiting for me, the transcendent love of God.

He was a devout Christian.

And this makes me wonder. Perhaps the primary objective of the return to Ortona, for Ted, was not to reconcile with the Germans; it was to reconcile with his God. In that scenario, the ritualized encounter with the Germans was undoubtedly important, but it served as the means to a more transcendent end. And so, where others on the trip had complained about the overly regimented schedule, this regimentation had perfectly suited Ted's purpose. For Ted, the quality of personal time on the trip was secondary; it was the *performance* of the trip—sharing time and ritual with the Germans—that mattered. By bringing Germans and Canadians together in mutual celebration of Christmas, Ted had done "my duty as God gave me the vision to see that duty." That duty—what God expected from him—had been passed on to him by his revered regimental padre Joseph Wilhelm who had suggested the reconciliation dinner long ago. In coming to accept and finally perform his religious duty, Ted had made things right with his soul.

But what had happened to his soul that it needed to be cleansed? Thus far, all that I've known about Ted's actions in the battle is that he destroyed a church. Was that the ghost? If so, then Ted had already made peace with it on a personal trip in 1993. He'd told me how he'd sat inside the church, observed its restoration, cried "fifty years of tears," and—it would seem—atoned for the damage he'd done. He'd met the priest, apologized, and made a donation to the church. He'd done all of that, but it had not cleansed his soul. He'd done all of that, but it had not buried the ghost.

What was missing?

I turn the pages of the book, searching for an answer.

> Christmas Day, 1943, is a day I've never been able to forget, and over the years the season has been hard for me to bear, notwithstanding the joys in later years of family and grandchildren. Even as I write tears fill my eyes as I remember how the day began. In 'Dead Horse Square' the Seaforth company I was supporting had lost a number of men when the enemy blew up a school they had just taken on the south side of the square, and they were under heavy enemy fire as they attempted to recover any bodies from the rubble. In addition, the Germans were in Santa Maria delle Grazie Church on the north side of the square, and the huge doors were opened wide to permit their machine-gunners an unrestricted field of fire. This was the church where the relief troop yesterday destroyed the sniper post in the bell tower. The accurate heavy machine gun fire from the church impeded further infantry movement until I ordered my gunner to open fire. In seconds we blew in the front of the church which had stood for hundreds of years, then the infantry went in to do the nasty work in taking out any Germans left alive.
>
> As if this weren't enough, the enemy was barricaded in the hospital next to the church, and when the infantry moved on the Germans again opened up with a withering crossfire of

> machine guns from the ground floor of the hospital, and from some buildings on the south side of the square. Needless to say the hospital was destroyed, too, before the infantry went in with fixed bayonets to take the paratroops out by hand . . .
>
> Christmas Day has never regained its allure and solemnity for me since December, 1943, for every Christmas morning I still see Seaforth bodies scattered across that damned square. Even today I find it very difficult to fully describe the actions of this terrible day, and many of the events that occurred are never far from mind.

I remember him telling me how, when they entered the square, the Seaforths around his tank had dropped "like a bunch of dolls." He had returned fire with his tank cannon, blowing apart the face of the church. Here, he's written that story in more detail, noting that it was "nasty" work the infantry had to do in finishing off the Germans in the church—and in the hospital beside it. It's the vision of "that damned square," he says, that comes back to him every Christmas.

This was Ted's main story of Ortona. He'd told a version of it to me. He'd told it also to David Halton when he was interviewed for the CBC documentary in Ortona while standing in front of the church.

> Narrator: On Christmas morning, Griffiths was in his tank moving into the Piazza San Francesco . . . German snipers in the church there are about to mow down several Seaforth Highlanders.
>
> Ted: And it wasn't until we moved up here that uh, the uh, machine guns opened up, from the church.
>
> Narrator: Griffiths didn't hesitate. He blew the church, seen here a few days later, into pieces.

> Ted: The fact it was an old medieval church just didn't enter my mind at the moment. And bear in mind the business of the day was killing. The fact that it was Christmas, uh, just didn't enter my mind at that time. But uh, when you survive a battle and you begin to think back at what transpired, this is when all the ghosts arrive. And it is the ghosts of Ortona, it is the ghost of that church that uh, keep coming back to haunt you.

He'd told this story to me and the CBC in less detail than in his book, but in essence it's the same. The key elements are the bodies of dead Seaforths and "the ghost of that church." In the more detailed version here in his memoir, the most notable addition is the infantry's follow-up attack. Ted describes this as "nasty"—perhaps because there's a hint here of the use of bayonets, and perhaps because the remaining Germans were wounded or helpless in the rubble. Still, the focal point is the church. In his memoir, as in his stories to me and the CBC, Ted emphasizes these events of Christmas Day. It's the climactic moment in his account of the battle, the recurring memory that haunts him.

After that, in his memoir, he describes no further actions in Ortona on his part. His story of the battle ends on a sad and disturbing note.

> This mad dance of death finally drew to its conclusion on the morning of the 28th when patrols reported the enemy had withdrawn from the town . . . The battle over, we were left with the battered, empty shell of a centuries-old medieval town, and the increasingly pungent odor of death. Bodies, sprawled in grotesque shapes, cluttered the doorways and rooms of many houses, while others had begun to rot under the rubble.

Then, quoting Churchill, he abruptly changes tone, lifting the mood.

> Recalling the visual evidence that exposed the ferocity of the fighting brings to mind the prescient words of Winston Churchill in 1897 during the Malakand Campaign in India, when he said, 'The keener the competition, the greater the honour of success. In sport, in courage, and in the sight of heaven, all men meet on equal terms.'

It's as if he's reached for this metaphorical high diction as a means of comfort and distraction from the gruesome details he's just told.

I turn back a few pages more to read his story of the battle from the start.

> The Canadian Army history, in a matter-of-fact manner, describes Ortona as a medieval leftover from the days of Venetian dominance in the Adriatic and says, 'the Old Town with its tall, narrow houses and dark, cramped streets, merged into the more modern section which had grown up on the flat tableland to the south.'

He's quoting from the official history of the Canadian Army. That was the heavy hardcover book I had first seen on his coffee table. The tank he commanded was in A Squadron.

> The Seaforths and 'A' Squadron were in the area of the Old Town and the narrow streets certainly impeded tank movement. The historian's tale tells nothing of the old woman who ventured out of her house only to be shot by a German sniper. Her body slumped down against the front wall of her house and there was no way to

avoid her as we went by. Gradually her legs were ground into the cobbled street and by the second day only her torso was left. There she remained like a silent sentinel as we wound our way past her day after day for the next week . . .

We continued to support the Seaforths up each narrow street, gradually refining our tactics as we learned new lessons of fighting in built-up areas. Throughout the 22nd and 23rd the Seaforths suffered continuous mortar, machine-gun and anti-tank fire . . .

The [German] snipers were so accurate, and persistent, that tank commanders were forced to close the turret hatch, or 'button-up', thereby cutting down one's vision, and creating an almost claustrophobic atmosphere within the turret. The smell of three unwashed bodies of the commander, gunner and wireless operator, added to the smoke and odor from the turret machine gun and the 75mm cannon, made life less than pleasant . . .

The 24th, the day before Christmas, was more of the same. Inching our way forward, house by house, we slowly moved through the dust and smoke in the narrow, confined street. The Germans tenaciously held on to each house, making us pay dearly, before they pulled back into the next building. The stench of death was everywhere. It permeated your clothes, and clung to the hair in your nostrils, so you were never free of it . . . The enemy tactic of forcing us to attack each house meant that our tank guns were firing constantly, and the turret floor was cluttered with empty 75mm shell casings. Machine gun barrels grew so hot from sustained firing that we often experienced 'cook-offs', when the round in the chamber exploded due to the heat of the barrel . . .

By now the infantry had cleared the last houses on the street, and were breaking out into a small piazza which became known as 'Dead Horse Square' because a dead horse, or mule, was lying in the middle of it . . . Leaving the scene we returned to the ammunition point, stocked up, and returned to the squadron harbour area. After a quick wash, we were told to move on foot to the Church of Santa Maria di Costantinopoli for a Christmas dinner with the Seaforths . . .

We ate with the Seaforths in a partly-destroyed church, the Santa Maria di Constantinopoli, on Christmas Eve. The unit ate in relays, company after company, and it was a most welcome break, even if only for a few minutes. A Seaforth officer, Lieut. W. Gildersleeve, played the church organ and a carol was sung before we returned to the killing . . .

Had I known what the next hour would bring I may have been tempted to remain in church and ask for a second helping of dinner. After we finished eating the squadron commander told me to get up and see the Seaforth company and platoon commanders I would be supporting in the morning. Making my way through the narrow, pitch-black street I grew increasingly nervous for I didn't encounter a soul, nor could I detect the presence of any infanteers. It was quiet as a tomb, something quite unusual instead of the normal crash of gunfire. Uncertain, I stopped at a corner where I tried to orient myself. Suddenly, in the silence, I became aware of approaching footsteps. Not knowing who it was, and unsure where I was, I didn't want to make any noise by using my pistol if I were forced to, so I quickly removed a commando knife I carried in the sleeve of my tunic. The faint glimmer of a silverized belt buckle as the person rounded the corner told me he was German. Lunging forward I drove the knife in deeply just above the belt buckle then swiftly drew it upwards effectively gutting

> him before he could utter a sound. Realizing I was in German territory I turned to retrace my steps and eventually made contact with the Seaforths without further incident. Over the next day or two I saw the German body of Christmas Eve still slumped against the wall, and one day I stopped to go through his pockets where I found his field service book only to discover he hadn't yet reached his 17th birthday. Given the brutality of the day I thought nothing more of the incident but, with passage of time, it has increasingly haunted me—and continues to do so to this day. Time has taught me how easy it is to kill, but how hard to forget.

IT'S PROFOUNDLY DIFFICULT TO live with such traumatic memories. The associated details and feelings can be frightening and debilitating to remember, and yet they are too powerful to completely repress. An effort to avoid these memories or completely erase them from our minds can limit our ability to tell a coherent and satisfying story of our life—which makes it difficult to feel real and authentic in the world. The emotional strain of incomplete repression, avoidance, and broken sense of self, harms our ability to relate well with others.

One of the ways that the mind tries to remedy this is by finding a workable and less threatening substitute for the traumatic memory. This substitute would be an experience that is somehow connected or adjacent to the traumatic event but is more benign and comfortable to recall. The substitute's proximity allows some of the feelings about the event to be displaced onto it, thereby giving those feelings a manageable outlet; at the same time, the substitute provides distance, thus sparing us from having to confront the worst details of the event. All of this facilitates the telling of a story from that time in our life which makes sufficient sense to ourselves and others without breaking our mental and emotional composure.

In psychoanalytic terms, these protective strategies have been described as "screen memories" as they take the place of, and shield the self from, the original traumatic experience. In Freud's definition, the screen memory "owes its value as a memory not to its intrinsic content, but to the relation obtaining between this content and some other, which has been suppressed." The paradigmatic cases of this phenomenon include memories of childhood objects and events which seem relatively trivial to an outside observer, yet the narrator invests them with extraordinary significance. Further analysis then reveals that the emotion invested in these "screen memories" really derives from another experience which has been buried. For example, a recurring childhood memory of a broken teapot might be a screen for experiences of domestic violence which were too painful to register or recall. None of this means to suggest that the traumatic memories are completely forgotten and don't come to mind; what the screen does is facilitate their avoidance, backgrounding them and removing them from the stories we tell about ourselves.

Ted's main story about Ortona was the story of a church.[4] When he talked to me and the media about his experience of the battle, he emphasized his act of destroying a church on Christmas Day. His story wasn't only about the church; he mentioned the deaths of his Seaforth comrades and hinted at the deaths of German machine gunners. But the church was the focal point; it was what haunted him. On his first return trip to Ortona, with his grandson, it was to the church that he returned, remembered, and grieved. "It is the ghost of that church," he told the CBC in Ortona, that "keep[s] coming back to haunt you."

Meanwhile, Ted was carrying another memory of destruction. He had killed a young German soldier on Christmas Eve. This had never been his main story of Ortona. Even in the memoir, he didn't give it as much prominence as the church. And yet, one would think that killing a man by your own hand would be a far more impactful experience than shooting a building—even if that building has sacred value. Certainly, Ted knew that he had also killed Germans in the church; but in the case of the church, he'd done that killing at a distance and couldn't see the result. In killing the German on Christmas Eve, he must have actually felt the young man's body, seen the blood on his knife, and possibly had to wash it from his hand. That's not an easy observation for me to write; I can only imagine how much harder it was to experience and then recall. Furthermore, during the next few days, even in midst of the battle, Ted made a point of returning to the body, to see the young man's face, to search his pockets and find his service book. He got to imagine the German as a real person with a life story—a story that he had violently ended.

Did that church really matter more to Ted than "the German body of Christmas Eve" (as he called it)? Prior to publishing his memoir, he'd frequently spoken of ghosts in connection with the church. In his memoir, however, his only mention of being haunted is tied to the young German he killed with his knife. It is the troubling memory of this act of killing, he writes, that has worsened for him with the passage of time: "it has increasingly haunted me—and continues to do so to this day."

I think Ted's story of the church was a screen for his memory of the Christmas Eve German. There are signs that when Ted was talking about the church, he was channeling—while still keeping at a safe distance—his thoughts and feelings about that other, more personal act of destruction.

One of those signs is the way Ted spoke about his thoughts. When he told his story to the CBC, he emphasized his lack of thought at the time. "The fact it was an old medieval church just didn't enter my mind at the moment . . . the fact that it was Christmas just didn't enter my mind." He made the point again in another moment of the interview: "The enemy was the enemy. We fought him, we killed him, uh, without, you know, any thought. You know we just uh, we're killing Germans. Period." This implies that Ted felt troubled by his sense that during the battle he'd become a thoughtless killer. In the interview, he was trying to convey that troubled feeling while still distancing himself from the act; in speaking about killing Germans, he used the collective pronoun *we* rather than *I*. And yet it's notable that he didn't use a collective pronoun for the Germans; he said, "we killed *him*"—not *them*—as if the enemy he had in mind was a single person.

The unspoken idea behind that statement could be: "I killed him without any thought." And that unspoken idea of thoughtless personal killing is effectively what Ted described later in his memoir—when writing about the German of Christmas Eve. "Given the brutality of the day I thought nothing more of the incident." He goes on to say how the thought (and probably feeling) that was absent at the time became a recurring presence later in life: "it has increasingly haunted me . . . Time has taught me how easy it is to kill, but how hard to forget." He had talked the same way about the church: "But uh, when you survive a battle and you begin to think back at what transpired this is when all the ghosts arrive. And it is the ghosts of Ortona, it is the ghost of that church that uh, keep coming back to haunt you." In both cases, there's a story of initial absence of thought followed by recurring, ghostly presence.

In Ted's speech and writing about the church and the Christmas Eve German, there is also a common concern with their age. His grief and guilt feeling for destroying the church was connected with its antiquity; he appears to have mentioned this every time he told its story.

> The fact it was an old medieval church just didn't enter my mind . . .

> In seconds we blew in the front of the church which had stood for hundreds of years . . .

He was similarly fixated on the youth of the Christmas Eve German. "I found his field service book only to discover he hadn't yet reached his 17th birthday." The church affected him because it was so old; the German affected him because he was so young. In both cases, through the common signifier of age, Ted expressed his feeling of wrongful destruction.

Later in the memoir, Ted describes his first return trip, the one he'd told me about in my first meeting with him, when he'd gone to Ortona with his grandson. The focus of that trip was the church of Santa Maria delle Grazie.

> The church I partly destroyed on that dreadful Christmas morning so long ago had been restored, but the exterior had none of the beauty and appeal it possessed before the battle. As we sat in it on Christmas Eve I noticed the front half of the church had escaped battle damage and the area around the altar was original 16th century, whereas the back portion was stark 20th century modern. The beauty of the medieval frescoes and the artisanship of the original workers struck me with such force that fifty years of pent-up emotion suddenly spewed forth with such intensity that my grandson wondered if I was well. I cried like I've never cried before, but when the wave of intense emotion had spent itself I sensed a feeling of inner peace that was unique and surprising. I still don't know why—sitting on the spot where I had killed so many people—I felt such emotion.

Here again he finds meaning in the church's age—and now experiences it as a composite of young and old. Its surviving beauty becomes a trigger for his pent-up grief. He says he was mindful of being in a place where fifty years ago, on Christmas Day, he had killed "so many." Evidently, he had timed his visit quite deliberately to coincide with that date.

But there's a meaningful discrepancy: he didn't visit the church on Christmas Day. He went the evening before—"we sat in it on Christmas Eve." In his words, Ted was recalling an event of Christmas Day, but in his actions he was marking an event of the previous night. And it was on that night before Christmas that he'd killed the not-yet-seventeen-year-old German.

Ted was dwelling on the church in order to suppress an even more troubling memory. However, it doesn't seem quite right to think of the church merely as a screen. In that analytic concept, the screen is a trivial object that only matters because of the feelings that are displaced onto it. But Ted was a devout Christian; for him, the church was intrinsically meaningful. (And even if he hadn't been especially religious, it's likely that he still would have experienced it as a powerful cultural symbol.) There's no reason to think that Ted's feelings about the church were inauthentic.

Rather than deflect from something deeper, the church—and its destruction—may have become the very symbol through which Ted grasped the meaning of what he had done. His memoir traces a symbolic thread between two churches, connecting his most troubling experiences. First, he had dinner and celebrated Christmas in the church of Santa Maria di Costantinopoli. Then he left its shelter, lost his way in the dark streets, and killed what he later called "the German body of Christmas Eve." The next day, he destroyed another church: Santa Maria delle Grazie. In his story, he looks back with foreboding and regret on the moment when he stepped out of the first church: "Had I known what the next hour would bring I may have been tempted to remain in church." There is a symbolic logic whereby Ted lost his place in "the church" not merely as a building but as the whole moral structure within which he understood and measured his life. He lost his place in that structure on Christmas Eve; the enormity of that loss was driven home the next day when he quite literally blew the structure to pieces.

That being so, it could still be true that Ted found his story about the church more comfortable to remember and tell. Certainly for most people the details of shooting a church are less viscerally disturbing than gutting a sixteen-year-old with a knife. Not only might the church story have been more comfortable for Ted to recall to himself; it would also have been more comfortable for him to share with others. A story of destroying a church manages to convey the image of oneself as a perpetrator of violence, and share the guilt that one feels about it, without going into gruesome details that might alienate the audience. When a person is already traumatized and seeking comfort, the last thing they typically want when sharing their story is to experience themselves as a cause of fear and revulsion in others.[5]

And so, for a number of reasons, Ted's remembrance of Ortona gravitated to the church as a symbol that conveyed the metaphysical meaning of his acts of violence while avoiding the raw, vivid details. But then it seems that returning to that church and atoning inside it wasn't enough to settle the issue. That was in 1993. Five years later, in 1998, the ghosts were still haunting Ted. He hadn't—as he put it in the CBC documentary—"cleansed his soul." What had he missed?

In his memoir, as he describes his first return to the church, there is a narrative shift. That shift might represent a new understanding of himself and his experience that actually came to him while sitting there. It's a shift in the object of his emotional attention. At first, he's describing the church's beauty; when he's done grieving over that, he then reflects on how he's in a place where he'd killed "so many." And the following thought comes to him:

> When I think of the joys and pleasures of the past fifty years which I have taken for granted, I cannot escape the fact that I took away the delights and rewards of life to many other human beings—but, to put it bluntly, if I hadn't killed them, they would have killed me. This is the horrid aspect of war that one must wrestle with after the bugles stop blowing.

It's a complicated emotion. He was justified in killing the enemy soldiers. According to the laws of war he did nothing wrong. Still, though, he recognizes the humanity of those he killed, and regrets taking their lives. Perhaps this was the thought that, until now, he'd been unwilling to have (as he'd often emphasized his past thoughtlessness about killing.) It's as if, by visiting the church, the symbol of his trauma, Ted was then able to open his thoughts and feelings to the enemy soldiers he had killed.

I can imagine that Ted would have preferred to be understood in Christian rather than psychoanalytic terms. The two approaches aren't necessarily in contradiction. For my part, while I'm now an atheist, I grew up in the Christian tradition, and there is an interpretation of what happened to Ted in Santa Maria delle Grazie that comes naturally to my mind. He wrote that he didn't understand why he'd felt compelled to return to that church, and didn't understand why he'd had such thoughts and feelings while he was in it. I think one could say, in Christian terms, that God was calling Ted back to that church. And when Ted was there, God spoke to him, implicitly, through the "still small voice" that comes from within.[6] The insight that came to Ted was that the church, as a building, was restored. The church was fine. It had been fine for a long time. For all these years, Ted had been grieving for it, but the church—the house of God—didn't need his compassion. God didn't need his compassion. What God needed was for Ted to be compassionate to his fellow men. The insight waiting for Ted in the church was that it was time for him to acknowledge and commemorate his fellow men whose lives he had ended.

Five years later, on the pilgrimage that Ted organized, the place for the Christmas dinner was the dining hall belonging to the Salesians of Don Bosco.[7] When Ted gave his speech, however, he spoke somewhat inaccurately as if they were inside a church—he said they were "under God's roof." In terms of Ted's faith, this could be a true statement; the church is supposed to be a community much more than a mere physical edifice. In what for Ted must have been a key moment of the reconciliation, he said at the dinner: "Under God's roof, we are all His children; we are all His brothers." It strikes me as a performative utterance that doesn't merely describe a reality; it intends to create one. In declaring brotherhood with the Germans, Ted restored that brotherhood; and in restoring it, he restored the roof of the church—and brought himself back under it.

Perhaps it was the act of performing the Christmas reconciliation that gave Ted the courage to move beyond the safer narrative of destroying the church, and to acknowledge, at last, the more painful memory of the German on Christmas Eve. The title of his memoir, *Dare to be True*, suggests the difficulty of that effort; sharing such memories was a real risk. War stories are vivid and enduring; but Ted had a whole life that he hoped to be remembered for. He wouldn't have wanted *killing* to be the first thing that people associated with his name. And yet, that's the risk he took in choosing to honour the humanity of his enemy and in choosing to tell the truth about his memory of war.

However, there was one detail in his memory that must have troubled him, yet he didn't acknowledge it. That was his memory of the Christmas dinner in Ortona—the original dinner in the church with the Seaforths in 1943. Ted said he was there. He said it was Christmas Eve.

> After a quick wash, we were told to move on foot to the Church of Santa Maria di Constantinopoli for a Christmas dinner with the Seaforths. Thank goodness those behind the line whose job it was to look after troop welfare were determined to see that we had a hot Christmas dinner and the Seaforth diary on the 24th noted, that despite the intensity of the battle, troops collected chinaware and cutlery from houses for the table. We ate with the Seaforths in a partly-destroyed church, the Santa Maria di Constantinopoli, on Christmas Eve. The unit ate in relays, company after company. . . .

It's an important part of Ted's story. Shortly after the gift of that dinner, he suffered the traumatic encounter with the "German body of Christmas Eve." The next day, Christmas Day, was his experience destroying the church.

But the dinner wasn't on Christmas Eve. It was on Christmas Day.

While writing his memoir, Ted must have noticed the discrepancy. It's clear that he was consulting the official history of the Canadian Army and the War Diary of the Seaforths; he quotes from both these sources in his narrative. Both make it clear that the Seaforths' dinner was on Christmas Day. This is also clear in the diary of the Seaforths' chaplain, Padre Durnford; in reports from war correspondents at the time; and in other sources, including the personal narratives of Seaforth veterans and the commemorative traditions of their regiment.

When Ted organized the reconciliation dinner with the Germans in Ortona, he scheduled the church service in Santa Maria di Constantinopoli and the subsequent dinner in the Salesian hall so that they took place on Christmas Eve. At the time, I felt there was a discrepancy, but I didn't hear anyone else questioning it, and I was new to the story of the battle, so I figured that I must be wrong. Later, as it became obvious that all the sources dated the dinner on the 25th, I still figured that Ted's decision to commemorate it on the 24th was driven by circumstances beyond his control, some sort of compromise he'd had to make—maybe the local parishioners didn't want to give up their church on Christmas Day; maybe on that holy day the Salesians and their staff didn't want to be disturbed. After reading Ted's memoir, however, it's clear that he really believed the dinner was on Christmas Eve. He'd scheduled the reconciliation dinner in alignment with his memory—which was at odds with the historical record and the memories of the Seaforths. I wonder now if some of the tensions between Ted and the Seaforths on that trip were related to that discrepancy.

The fact that Ted had mixed up the dates should not be taken as a weakness of his mind. It seems to be a universal human tendency that we retrospectively displace some of our experiences onto other times and locations. This temporal and spatial displacement is a way of keeping things in memory, and it's often motivated by the meanings that those times and places hold for us.[8] This can also happen simply because at the time of the original experience we were already confused or mistaken. While he was in the battle, sleep-deprived, under extreme stress, and possibly in shock, Ted might have been confused as to what day it was. He wouldn't have been the only one. For example, Bill had no memory of his regiment's famous dinner and was mistaken in thinking his captivity happened on Christmas Day.

So what actually happened? One possibility is that everything unfolded in the sequence as Ted told it, but his sequence was off by a day. In this scenario, Ted ate Christmas dinner with the Seaforths on the 25th; then he went out, ran into, and killed the young German; then the next day, the 26th, he destroyed the church of Santa Maria delle Grazie—so destroying that church wasn't actually how Ted "spent my Christmas Day."[9] His confusion of the dates may have been unconsciously motivated: the act of killing the German was too horrible to associate with Christmas, so he had convinced himself that everything had happened earlier by a day.

Another possibility is that Ted had the dates right but was wrong about his presence at the dinner. It could still be true that, on Christmas Eve, he ate dinner in Santa Maria di Costantinopoli; but this was not the famous dinner the Seaforths had the next day. The dinner that Ted did have in the church might still have felt remarkable. Later, when he heard about the famous dinner, maybe he assumed it was all the same.

Yet another possibility is that the sequence of events got mixed up in Ted's memory. Perhaps all of his traumatic experiences actually happened on Christmas Day: first, the destruction of Santa Maria delle Grazie; then dinner in Santa Maria di Constantinopoli; then getting lost in the dark streets and killing the young German.

There are surely more possibilities. Every scenario would raise the question as to what might have motivated Ted, probably unconsciously, to remember these events as he did. There would be reasons why it made sense or was emotionally important to him to pattern his narrative this way. The reasons would shed more light into the meanings of the events for Ted.

As much as that would be valuable to learn, it would have been hard to ask him. There's nothing shameful about mixing up dates and places; we all do it; it's natural. But such "mistakes" are often stigmatized, sometimes with an added element of ageism. Furthermore, people generally don't like having it pointed out that their memories are mistaken, especially when those memories deeply matter to them. I was careful about this in all of my interviews. With Ted in particular, I wouldn't have wanted to be that messenger.

However, if I had somehow found a way to share this with him, I would have wanted him to know that his mind had done similar work as the war artist whom he admired. Indeed, the way that memories take shape in our minds has more in common with the interpretive brushwork of painting than the apparent objectivity of photography. In Charles Comfort's *Via Dolorosa*, there's more than one discrepancy from the physical reality of Ortona. It's not just that there is no street named Dolorosa. It's also that there is no street (nor was there in 1943) that offers such a view of San Tommaso. Comfort painted a scene of street fighting which no one could have actually seen at the time. He did that in order to create a meaning—or rather, to raise questions about meaning. That was his job as a war artist: not to record exactly what happened, but to convey the soldiers' experiences. The stories of Ted and Mel suggest that, for at least some of the soldiers, Comfort had grasped very well what it would feel like to look back on Ortona.[10]

And actually maybe it would not have been so hard to share this with Ted. After all, this was the advice that he gave me at the very beginning of my research. When I first met him on that cold October day, I asked him what I should know about war veterans. He told me that, even when they had been right beside each other at the time, every man had a different war.

"That's *his* story," Ted told me.

"That's *his* war."

CHAPTER 8

Something Left Behind

I THINK THE FIRST POEM I ever learned by heart was "In Flanders Fields." It was a school assignment. I would have been about eleven or twelve.

Our teacher gave us lessons in how to memorize a text. We practiced reading the poem aloud in class and were told how to rehearse it at home. At first, the poem felt like an intimidating long discourse, archaic and vaguely disturbing. But within days, its words came as naturally to me as riding my bike or tying my shoes.

The climax was our group recitation on Remembrance Day, when our entire class stood together and spoke the poem aloud. Even now, when I encounter it, I feel again that strange transcendent sensation of our twenty young voices becoming one.

In Flanders fields the poppies blow
Between the crosses, row on row,
    That mark our place; and in the sky
    The larks, still bravely singing, fly
Scarce heard amid the guns below.

We are the Dead. Short days ago
We lived, felt dawn, saw sunset glow,
Loved and were loved, and now we lie,
In Flanders fields.

Take up our quarrel with the foe:
To you from failing hands we throw
The torch; be yours to hold it high.
If ye break faith with us who die
We shall not sleep, though poppies grow
In Flanders fields.

We also learned the story and the meaning of the poem. It was written during World War I by a Canadian soldier, John McRae, as he observed the crosses on the graves of his fallen comrades. We were told how McRae had been afraid that, in the future, those dead would be forgotten. They had "given their lives"—"made the supreme sacrifice"—to defend our country and our freedoms. Canadian soldiers continued to risk their lives for the same values to this day. And this was why every year on November 11, Remembrance Day, we recited the poem and we wore red plastic poppies, showing we "kept the faith"—we honoured the sacrifice. The meaning of the tradition had grown beyond the Great War that had given rise to it, so that now the tradition encompassed World War II and Korea and all subsequent actions of our soldiers.

In school, we performed some of the other rituals of Remembrance Day. At eleven in the morning—symbolically marking the end of the Great War—we stood solemnly during a playing of the Last Post (a mournful bugle call for a military funeral) followed by a minute of silence. We knew, during that call and the ensuing resonant silence, that we were having this experience at the same moment as virtually everyone across our nation (or so we imagined—the simultaneity was actually limited to our time zone). It was a powerful feeling of togetherness with an unknown multitude of fellow Canadians.

In its complete form, the ritual of Remembrance Day is performed at war monuments. These monuments exist in almost every city and town; they typically honour soldiers who died in military service for Canada. As with other core features of the tradition, these monuments are mostly legacies of the First World War but they have come to stand in for subsequent wars, especially the Second. The paradigmatic ritual is the National Remembrance Day Ceremony in Ottawa which is televised by the national public broadcaster (the CBC). The ritual has the tone and aesthetic form of a memorial service. The central actors are the war veterans led by the Royal Canadian Legion. While members of the public attend and observe, the veterans march in procession to the National War Memorial at the front of which is the Tomb of the Unknown Soldier. The veterans are met at the monument by representatives of the People of Canada, the Mothers of Canada, the Government and Parliament of Canada, Veterans Affairs Canada, the Canadian Armed Forces, and the Youth of Canada. The national anthem, Last Post, and two minutes of silence are performed. Then comes what is arguably the ritual's most powerful moment. In the Act of Remembrance, the assembled recite in unison their commitment to the war dead.

They shall grow not old, as we that are left grow old;
Age shall not weary them, nor the years condemn.
At the going down of the sun and in the morning
We will remember them.

It's commonly said that the practices associated with Remembrance Day serve to remind and teach Canadians—and especially Canadian youth—about the essential meaning of war. The tradition fosters an attitude whereby war is a tragedy (though perhaps a tragic necessity). The implied reason that war is a tragedy is that soldiers of Canada had to (and continue to) suffer and die. The suffering of surviving war veterans is publicly observed in the rituals at the monuments. The ritual logic suggests that what veterans suffer, and what they feel duty-bound to remember, is the loss of their friends, their comrades, their fallen "brothers in arms." That's the message of "In Flanders Fields." That's the message of the Act of Remembrance. That, in essence, is what Canadians tell themselves it is to remember war.

In his photograph at the monument, I've always felt that he doesn't look like the bright, spirited man that I met. In his Legion uniform, his pose stiff and solemn, his jaw firm, his chest burdened with medals—next to that dark stone statue, it's the image of a grave old man.

But now I'm noticing how his arm is resting on the statue with his hand on the dying soldier. That detail has always been there, but until now I had never given it a thought. It reminds me that he told me once about his desire to touch the monument. And now I think this photo he gave me truly captures the warmth of his heart.

It was a frigid evening in late November when I went to interview Maurice. The streets all over Edmonton were packed hard in snow. In his suburban neighbourhood, some of the houses and their front lawn trees were already decorated for Christmas, brightening the darkness with multicoloured lights.

He greeted me enthusiastically at the door of his modern bungalow. As I removed my boots, I noticed his war medals in a frame on the wall.

His wife came to say hello, asked if I'd like some tea or coffee, then went to the kitchen while Maurice and I took a few steps down to the carpeted living room. The decor was contemporary. We sat on sectional sofas beside a bookshelf with a glass coffee table between us. His wife brought us tea in stoneware mugs and left us alone there to talk.

I observed the books on the shelf. Many were on topics of local history and nature. Maurice told me that he and his wife enjoyed hiking in the wilderness and volunteering with a team at the university doing archaeological digs in Jasper. In order to stay fit for all of this, he worked out at the gym three times a week. He was seventy-four years old, nearly bald, a bit lanky, but he did indeed look robust and had a strong grip. In his big metal-framed glasses, black turtleneck shirt, jogging pants, and black cloth Chinese slippers, it was easy to imagine him doing karate—or French philosophy. However, in the way that he talked, with a shine in his eyes and lilt in his voice telling stories of his youth, he had the air of the simple country boy that he remembered he once had been.

"I was raised at Grassland, about 120 kilometres northeast of here."

That was a tiny hamlet within the northern boreal forest. When he joined the army, he had just turned seventeen.

"What were you thinking about when you signed up?"

"Well, I was patriotic I guess. For one thing. And for another thing, uh, we were a poor family. Sixteen kids. And there wasn't too much to eat."

He talked fondly of his parents. In going off to war, he was following in the steps of his father.

"My dad was in the First World War, in the artillery. And, you know we, well he didn't talk about it very much but, you know I felt I should at least do my part. I felt like I was doing the right thing."

"Did it still feel like that when you were in Italy?"

"Uh, yes and no. You know, when I was in Italy during battles and that, man, you know I felt like a little kid that had got lost. I really did, you know. And 'cause I was just a kid. Like I said, I was raised at Grassland, I had no idea what the big world was like at all you know just, like a hillbilly you might say, really. And uh. Yeah. Yeah, yeah, I still felt patriotic but I was still scared, scared, man, just, you can't believe how scared you can get and still, your heart'll still beat."

"What's it like, how do you deal with that kind of fear?"

"I don't know. Really don't know, because many many many times you know I felt that, that I was so afraid that my heart would just explode. That's the way I felt. But what can you do? There's nowhere you can go. And, the thing doesn't change from day to day to day to day from night to night just, you're just scared to death, I mean really to the point you think that you should just die from fright. And really there's no way that I or anybody else could explain it to somebody that didn't experience it and have them feel exactly the way it is. It's just not, not possible. 'Cause you wouldn't believe that you could get that, be that afraid and still not die of a heart attack."

"And is that what Ortona was like?"

"Oh yeah for sure. The only, we've had a lot of real hard battles you know, but they last hours and it's over and you get some relief. But in Ortona it was like that for seven days and seven nights. It didn't stop. Not at all. I don't even remember sleeping. And when we went into a house, you couldn't go down the street because you just wouldn't get two steps, the German was behind the next pile of rubble with machine guns and whatnot and you just didn't have a hope in hell. So we started blowin' holes into a house and then go from room to room, upstair, downstair, and that's how we took Ortona."

Maurice had recently been back. In October 1999, just over a month before I met him, he'd been part of a pilgrimage to Canadian war graves in Italy organized by Veterans Affairs. He showed me the album he'd put together of his photos from that trip. This was when I first saw the picture of him at the monument.

"Yeah that's in Ortona," he said when we turned to that page in the album. "I had the privilege of unveiling that monument."

It was the highlight of his trip. As we sat together looking at the photo, he described the monument to me, touching his finger on the details.

"This, I don't know if this fellow is wounded, or dead, and this guy is bent over him uh, attending to his wounds or, whatever has taken place. And like I say the uh, the uniforms, the gas cape that we always wore, or carried with us, and uh, the Bren gun pouches on the front . . . and the gaiters and uh, the boots and everything is actual equipment that has been bronzed over. It looks life-sized."

"And what do you think of the monument?"

"Oh I thought it was, I thought it was great. Yeah. 'Cause it depicts what really happened you know. And what it's all about."

"Is that what you like about it?"

"Yes. Yeah. Of course to somebody who wasn't there or doesn't know anything about it may not feel the same, eh. But we know because we were there and we know what happened."

The recent pilgrimage was just the latest of many trips to Italy that Maurice had made since the war. Sometimes he'd gone with his family, sometimes with groups organized by Veterans Affairs. He'd always gone especially to see Ortona. Over the years, he'd observed the gradual changes to the town.

"They've opened up a lot of shops on main street. The old town doesn't look like an old town anymore. Which is good to see. You know, you like to see it starting to go and come alive again."

"Do you feel like you've got some kind of a special relationship to Ortona?"

"Oh for sure, yeah. Uh—"

He paused in thought for a moment.

"As a matter of fact I've always felt, and I've been to Italy I think a total of six times, five or six times, and I've always felt that uh, I left something behind. And I, I have no reason to think that, but I've always wanted to go back. But after this trip I feel that I don't have to go back anymore. You know like it's just put a real good closure on it and, and, and, for whatever reason, and I couldn't really answer that, you know, the reason for that, but uh, I don't know I feel, comfortable now, sort of thing. Strange, but that's the way it is."

Later, he gave me a copy of the photo plus an article he'd written for *The Forty-Niner*. In the article, he stated: "I personally was most emotional at the unveiling of the Price of Peace monument in Ortona. I was honored to help perform this duty." His article concluded with the same feeling of closure that he had shared with me—and the same feeling of mystery about what he had lost and then found.

"The Pilgrimage makes me feel that everything is complete now. I do not feel that I have to return to find whatever it was that was left behind."

TED WAS ON THAT same pilgrimage as Maurice, and played an important role. The *Price of Peace* monument that was unveiled in Ortona and was cherished by Maurice would not have existed without Ted. It was a legacy of the 1998 Christmas Dinner of Reconciliation. A small-scale model of it had been displayed at that Christmas Eve dinner. In the months that followed, Ted had worked hard at making sure the full-sized monument got completed and installed in a public Ortona square. While he had some frustrations with the monument's creator, in the end he was delighted with the finished work. He describes it in his memoir:

> The monument entitled 'The Price of Peace' is the most moving piece of military sculpture one will ever see. It tears at the heart-strings, especially among old soldiers who understand the agony of the battlefield. The statue is mounted on a marble base—over a pile of rubble from houses destroyed during the Ortona battle of Christmas 1943, meant to illustrate the terrible price paid by the local population as the battle raged around them—and below is a facade of stones from the Moro River angled down to the street to remind one of the awful price Canadians paid to gain a foothold across the river.

The ceremony to unveil the monument was attended by citizens and dignitaries of Ortona, the Canadian Ambassador to Italy, and members of the Canadian Forces stationed in Bosnia and Kosovo. Ted gave a speech on behalf of the veterans.

> I was honoured to deliver the veteran's [sic] response before the unveiling took place. With great emotion, I managed to say:
>
> 'Today we witness completion of the second, and last, phase of a movement which had its origin with the wartime Padre of the Three Rivers Regiment—the late Archbishop Joseph L. Wilhelm—who was awarded the Military Cross for rescuing German and Canadian wounded under fire in Sicily. The Padre was not only a theologian; he was a man's man beloved by the troops as he shared their fears, their terrors and their hardships. He is a man of fond

memory by all who knew him. Sadly, he did not live to witness the movement of reconciliation which arose from his sense of compassion and forgiveness.

'The first phase of reconciliation, which took place here in Ortona last Christmas was a success as German and Canadian veterans of the 1943 battle met in friendship and forgiveness. Now we witness this statue which is meant as a tribute to those who forever will remain at Ortona.

'The statue, appropriately named 'The Price of Peace' is the creation of a young man, Robert Surette, who never experienced the horrors, or the brother-hood, of the battlefield. Yet he managed to capture much of the humanity and compassion that one finds there. It is on the battlefield where one finds the average man performing exceptional feats and deeds; it is on the battlefield where one witnesses—all too often—the ultimate sacrifice when one gives his life trying to save his brother. The sculptor has managed to seize within this statue much of the compassion and humanity of which I speak and, as I look at it, I recall the immortal words of Shakespeare in Henry V—

We few, we happy few, we band of brothers:
For he to-day who sheds his blood with me
Shall be my brother.

'Father Wilhelm would be proud of this permanent memorial to our brothers who remain here in rest—at the site of their last battle.'

A group of 14 veterans of the Ortona battle slowly moved forward, and jointly unveiled the statue. As they did so, church bells

> across Ortona burst forth in a paean of praise and thanksgiving which rose to the heavens, while bringing tears to the eyes of many present.

Ted concludes the Ortona chapter of his memoir with news about the monument that he later received from a local historian and artist.

> A recent message from Saverio Di Tullio says the statue has had a profound effect on the town and surrounding area. He claims the statue has made Ortona much richer and more interesting than it was before. Local citizens have taken to placing fresh flowers at the base of the statue daily, and more visitors arrive as news of the statue spreads. It seems Father Wilhelm's message of forgiveness is spreading.

Ted doesn't mention it, and I don't know how much he knew, but in fact there were some political issues in Ortona with the acceptance and placement of the statue. These issues related to how the Ortonesi wanted to remember their own history and the Canadians. Also, I could imagine some quite understandable and non-political reasons for objecting to the statue or for wanting it in a less conspicuous place. The memorial to civilian victims of the war, which commemorates the deceased family members of the Ortonesi themselves, was on the edge of town at the civilian cemetery. Why should a monument to foreign soldiers be more central than the one for the town's own people? Furthermore, the Canadian statue is a vivid portrayal of violent death. It's one thing to choose to visit a monument like that for a single occasion, such as on a pilgrimage from Canada. It's different if you have to see it every day from the window of your home or as you go about your business.

In his memoir, Ted describes how he managed to get the monument into one of his preferred locations—in Piazza Plebiscito, the next major square after the municipal building, behind San Tommaso cathedral.

> The months following our trip of reconciliation was taken up with the problem of the statue and, in Ortona, finding a suitable site for it. Before leaving Ortona we left a list of three suggested sites with the mayor, but it seems none met approval, so for a period we were left in limbo. At one point I was forced to ask Jack Granatstein, Director-General of the Canadian War Museum, if he would accept the statue should we not reach agreement with local authorities in Ortona.
>
> At this point I leaked details of our problem to Elio Coppola, Editor of L'Ora di Ottawa, the local Italian newspaper. His story got the local Italian community agitated as they wanted the statue to go to Italy, not to stay in Canada. The uproar brought the Ambassador of Italy into the act, and by the time he finished with local officials in Ortona, we secured the most appropriate site in town.

It's a story of powerful political actors pressuring Ortona's elected leaders into giving Canadians what Canadians wanted. "By the time he finished with local officials . . ." And yet, from the inscription on the monument, it seems it's meant to be understood as a gift.

> A deliberate, low-key plaque only says, 'From The People of Canada'.

"I TEND TO GET pretty emotional sometimes, and I'm surprised that I haven't tonight."

Maurice was telling me why he rarely talked about the war.

"And I think that this is probably a reason a lot of veterans don't want to talk about the war, for the simple fact that they're maybe afraid that they might break down. You know a man doesn't, some men don't feel that they should cry. And I don't feel that way but it's still, I'm sure that's why a lot of soldiers, ex soldiers don't talk about their experiences."

"Do you think going, did going through the war change your feeling about what it meant to be a man, sort of tough or—"

"Uh. I suppose. Yeah. 'Cause you, you, you feel that you're really growing up. Ha! And especially when you're not! You're just a kid and you don't know very much about life. At all. At least I sure didn't, because uh, you know being brought up out in the sticks and never being away from home before and, you know it's like stepping into a whole new world. I mean everything you've got to learn, from scratch sort of thing. And uh, sometimes you make some awful stupid mistakes and say a lot of stupid things that you wouldn't do otherwise."

Maurice was reminded again of his sense of his lowly background.

"To start with, I had no education. I had grade six."

"Wow."

"After I got married I got correspondence, I got my grade ten. But it's not the same as learning it in school I guess. But I, I was pretty ignorant. You know, again you know I say when I learned a lot, I had to learn it the hard way. And through a lot of embarrassment. And as a matter of fact, one guy, I don't remember who it was but he kept telling me, he said 'Whitey, you're as ignorant as hog shit.'"

"Where was that?"

Maurice didn't seem to notice my question.

"He was right. It hurt my feelings when he said that but it was true you know, I was pretty ignorant."

As we were talking now there was a distant sound of rhythmic cracking. Maurice's wife was chopping vegetables on a cutting board in the kitchen.

"What was it like to come back? Come back to Alberta or to Canada?"

"Hm. Well, really, I uh, maybe I was surprised that I even got back. You know I uh, it was nice to come back, and I guess I wanted to see my mother, more than anything. You know that was most important to me was seeing my mother."

He returned to the topic of struggling not to cry. Funny stories were easier to tell, he said. Even during combat, sometimes things would happen that they were able to laugh about later.

"That's one of the things that helps you to cope I guess. With the bad situations. I know quite a few times, I can't remember any incidents but you know you'd, when you'd get back in a rest area or something, you get talking about it you know, and you'd have some really good laughs about different situations. That kinda helped you out too, yeah."

"Did you have any laughs in Ortona?"

"No."

His answer was quick and sharp. His mood had turned grim.

"No. No. No."

He paused in thought.

"None at all. No."

From the kitchen, I heard an oven door open and close.

Later in the interview, Maurice mentioned another source of comfort during the war—the kindness of older Italian women. They had reminded him of his mother. While this was comforting, it was also a source of grief when he saw them suffering or dying.

"Yeah what really used to get me too is if I'd see some civilians killed."

"Really."

"Yeah. Especially the women and the kids. Man that used to get me. Because you know I would automatically think, you know what, if that was our country, that could be my mother, you know. Yeah. Even though the Italians were your enemy at one time, you know I still, I had a lot of respect for them because I think they gave me a lot of comfort."

"Really."

"Oh yeah."

"They helped you out? In what way?"

"Well whenever they could, you know, the women which was my mother's age would come up to you, you know, and give you a big hug and a kiss on the cheek and say 'Ohhh,' you know 'you're a *bambino*, you shouldn't be in the war, you're still a baby,' sort of thing you know. And that gave me a lot of, motherly comfort I think, you know. And I respected them for that."

He felt this connection whenever he returned to Italy. It was felt in his recent trip to unveil the monument in Ortona.

"I still uh think of them the same way when I go back, the older women that would be my age or mother's age, you know. Well there's not too many of them my mother's age left any more but I still have the same feeling for the women that are my age. I kind of still look at 'em as, well, the motherly type. They helped me out a lot, I think."

Showing me photos he'd taken during the ceremony at the monument, he pointed out the local children who had participated. He struggled to finish his words.

"These kids were readin', little, poems, about the war, and why we shouldn't have wars."

THE THEME OF THE Christmas reconciliation dinner in Ortona was the healing of animosity and embrace of shared humanity among former enemy soldiers. The memories that needed healing among Canadian and German veterans were their acts of killing or trying to kill one another. Those were the memories that Ted had set out to reconcile.

The sculptor of the *Price of Peace* was inspired to create the monument in support of Ted's project. The work on the monument started during what the *Ottawa Sun* had called "the People's War"—the public fundraising campaign across Canada. The model of the sculpture was displayed during the Christmas dinner in Ortona. From Ted's memoir, it's clear that he regarded it as a legacy of the Ortona reconciliation.

But the monument conveys nothing about reconciliation. It depicts a dying Canadian soldier who is being comforted by a fellow Canadian. It's an entirely Canadian scene evoking a spirit of brotherhood and self-sacrifice among compatriots. Given that the monument is meant to realistically depict a scene from the Ortona battle, it follows logically that the Canadian is lying there dying because he's been hit by a German shell or bullet. The only way in which the Germans have a place in the monument is in that act of killing a Canadian. The *Price of Peace* monument freezes that moment of Canadian "sacrifice"—caused by German violence—permanently in stone.

In that respect, the monument aligns with the conventions of Canadian war remembrance. It honours the sacrifice of Canadian soldiers and evokes the pain of veterans who lost friends in battle. This is what the tradition teaches Canadians to associate with veterans. Ted's project of Christmas reconciliation went further, confronting veterans' own troubled memories of killing. The *Price of Peace* sculpture, though intended to support Ted's project, ignores everything that made it unconventional. The monument recasts Ortona into a familiar commemorative mold.

In the years following its installation, the *Price of Peace*—along with Ortona—became yet another stage for rehearsing the standard tropes. Prior to 1998, the battle of Ortona was mostly unknown in Canada. Now, thanks in part to Ted's efforts, it was on the war remembrance map. This growing interest in Ortona took place in the context of new conflicts in which Canadian soldiers were engaged. In March 1999, Canadian forces participated in the NATO war against Serbia. Then from 2001 until 2014, Canada joined the US-led coalition fighting the Taliban in Afghanistan. More than forty thousand Canadians served in the Afghan war; 158 were killed; it was the Canadian Army's largest combat operation since the Korean War.

In 2004, the Canadian government designated Ortona as "an event of national historic significance." A plaque marking this designation was added to the *Price of Peace* monument. It was unveiled by Canada's governor general during a pilgrimage of Canadian veterans organized by Veterans Affairs. Speaking at the monument, Adrienne Clarkson said:

> The price of peace is staggering. Historically, as it did here in Ortona, it has required blood, the extinction of horrifying numbers of human beings. . . . It is the price, however, that Canadians in the Second World War, and the Italian people that they helped to liberate, were willing to pay.

In these words, Clarkson was expanding on the monument's title—*The Price of Peace*. The name itself suggests that peace is achieved through the very act the monument depicts: the soldier's violent death. It's a small step from that notion to the circular logic that war is necessary for peace. That same argument was echoed by Peter Goldring in a Remembrance Day speech to the House of Commons in 2011. Referring to the monument in Ortona, Goldring said:

> In Ortona's Piazza del Plebiscito is a poignant memorial of two soldiers, one lying dead and one bent over in grief, created by Ottawa artist Robert Surette. Entitled 'The Price of Peace', it speaks of the supreme toll in the 'Stalingrad of Italy', the battle for Ortona, and for all who have faced their soul in the finality of the theatre of war [. . .] The price of peace is paid in war. We ought never to forget those that serve, those who truly pay the price of peace.

In this discourse, Ortona was being remembered in a way that upheld the necessity of war.

As for Ted, he did not seem to notice the discrepancy between his reconciliation mission and the monument it left behind. Perhaps it was too much for him to consider that he might be in conflict with traditional war remembrance. At the monument's unveiling, he spoke as if the tradition and his mission were one. He referred back to the Christmas reconciliation of former enemies—

> The first phase of reconciliation, which took place here in Ortona last Christmas was a success as German and Canadian veterans of the 1943 battle met in friendship and forgiveness.

He described the monument as a continuation and legacy of that mission—

> Today we witness completion of the second, and last, phase of a movement.

And he framed its meaning within the conventional terms of the soldier's self-sacrifice.

> It is on the battlefield where one finds the average man performing exceptional feats and deeds; it is on the battlefield where one witnesses—all too often—the ultimate sacrifice when one gives his life trying to save his brother.

For much of his life, Ted had been haunted by his memories of killing in Ortona. In the end, however, he chose to affirm the greater virtues of war. At the conclusion of his life story—the second last page of his memoir—he wrote:

> Underneath the brutality of war one often finds many examples of the innate goodness of the human spirit, the self-sacrifice to help others and the indomitable desire to achieve something better. It is amidst the horrors and compassion of the battlefield where the human spirit rises to its greatest height. It is on the battlefield where one finds true brotherhood and sacrifice.

Perhaps Ted emphasized war's redemptive qualities as a means to make peace with his memories. It's an understandable personal response to a deeply painful past. But does this emphasis on war's positivity not risk glorifying it, and does it not awaken in others a desire to experience it for themselves? If we're told that war is where we find the greatest heights of the human spirit, then how can each new generation not, even if quietly, yearn for it?

"I THINK WHAT I really liked best about this trip," Maurice told me, "was we had, I believe it was four people from the youth group, two boys and two girls from different parts of Canada, seventeen to nineteen years old, and we had I believe it was six cadets and they were also in the same age group, eh? And uh, it was good to see those kids there, 'cause I, when I was there, I was their age, eh?"

I nodded. Maurice continued.

"I was eighteen when Ortona was taken. And they really got to feel how we feel about it. They cried right along with the rest of us you know, at the cemeteries. And it's strange that, you'd think grown people shouldn't cry but uh, you feel just like a little kid. Lost, you know? And it's just a very strange feeling but you have to cry. It's—"

His voice began faltering, fighting back tears.

"You know?"

"Hm," I said. "When you get to, uh—"

"Yeah, when you go into the cemetery, especially—"

"Yeah."

"—if, for example, uh, one of the guys. What was his name now? Wychopen. You either knew 'em by a nickname, a first name, or the last name. And I always knew him as Wychopen. And uh, for some reason, you know, the guy gets wounded or gets sick and goes out, and you don't see him again. And you assume that he's gone home or whatever. And all of a sudden go into these cemeteries and then you find his name on a, on a tombstone, eh?[1] And boy, that, that really shocks you. Because you, you know, you've forgotten about the guy, and, and you feel guilty that you forgot about him, and, and uh, so it's uh—"

"Gee."

"And you'd run across this on almost every cemetery, even guys you don't know. Uh, they, you know it's a soldier that hasn't been identified, and it's uh, known to God only. And that's troubling too, you know, very emotional. And you just have to let the tears flow."

In the course of talking about the challenge of remembering, Maurice had recovered his composure. I thought of another question.

"What do you think about the ceremonies that they have in the cemeteries?"

"Oh I think they're great but I think they have to get more young people involved. To go there you know and uh, like you know take two or three hundred of 'em."

"Hm."

"Yeah really because I mean your generation now coming up are the ones that's gonna have to try and prevent this sort of thing, you know. And if we don't do anything about it, or if nothin' is done about it, I mean they're, they're not going to have that feeling of such a horrible thing as war."

Youth engagement has long been a feature of Canadian war remembrance. In the years after I interviewed Maurice, it was intensified and enhanced. Veterans Affairs adopted a "new pilgrimage model" for the trips to overseas war graves; in the new model, the travelling veterans would always be accompanied by young people. Both the Legion and Veterans Affairs produced substantial guides for school teachers, encouraging and facilitating the incorporation of "remembrance" themes into the curriculum during the weeks leading up to Remembrance Day (which was now the high point of an official Remembrance Week). Nationwide poster and essay contests for students were judged by panels of Legion members with the winning entries displayed in the Canadian War Museum. Roles for youth were added to the official Service of

Remembrance. Non-governmental organizations came on the scene with mandates to promote war remembrance through new technologies and methods of experiential learning.[2]

In 2008, a massive youth pilgrimage to Ortona took place. The "Remembering Ortona Tour" involved approximately one thousand two hundred students from high schools across the country. It was organized by a leading war remembrance NGO specializing in educational battlefield tours for Canadian youth. One of the goals was to create young remembrance leaders; participants were selected based on their commitment to share what they would learn on the tour with their schools and communities back home.

The number of participants in the Remembering Ortona Tour was deliberately set to equal or closely approximate the 1,375 Canadian soldiers buried in the Moro River Canadian War Cemetery. Each youth was matched with a dead soldier and was given the task of learning about him. In addition, each youth was partnered with a Canadian soldier presently serving in Afghanistan. In an activity called "Hands Across a Generation" every participant created a square of fabric inscribed with information about themselves and "their soldier" buried in Ortona; they were sent a similar piece of fabric from their partnered Canadian soldier in Afghanistan; and all of these 2,400 pieces of cloth were stitched together into a huge banner representing the continuity of past and present military service and sacrifice.[3]

On a late November day, more than one thousand two hundred young people along with their teachers and tour organizers flooded into the Moro River Canadian War Cemetery. The youths were all dressed in matching uniforms—red windbreakers over khaki shirts bearing their dead soldier's name stitched onto their chest. The pilgrims marched into the cemetery in a procession, carrying flags up to the Cross of Sacrifice.

They conducted a memorial service that included wreath-layings, a sermon from a Canadian Army chaplain, speeches by some of the youth, and a musical performance. Every youth stood before the headstone of their appointed soldier, mirroring the dead, as if risen or reincarnated. In unison, the assembled multitude knelt and placed a poppy on their graves.

One of the teachers told a journalist, "Once again we have a generation of Canadian youth standing on the ground near the Moro River, facing the hill of Ortona. Once again Canada is represented by its youth from across the country . . . They have travelled here to show that Canada's youth do remember the sacrifices of the men buried here. They do remember the soldiers who gave their lives."

In the final rite of the ceremony, the pilgrims departed the cemetery in a long procession carrying the massive Hands Across a Generation fabric banner. They descended the hill of San Donato, crossed the gulley on the road that was closed to traffic, and climbed the switchback street, via Margherita d'Austria, up into the town. As they marched, it began to rain. One of the organizers described the rain as "a symbolic cleansing, a rebirth of memory. I found it most fitting, not too harsh but a stark reminder for the students as they followed in the footsteps of their soldier."

Some of the youths on the tour were imaginatively prepared to fight the Ortona battle. Before the trip, they had been given mock combat training. At a Canadian Forces facility near Ottawa, high schoolers attended an overnight "living experience" camp designed to educate them on tactics used by the Canadian Army in Ortona. The learning modules included "the challenges of fighting in built-up areas, house clearing and the deadly business of unarmed combat." An online slideshow from one participating school showed students and teachers smiling as they handled World War II-era rifles and machine guns.

"WHAT WAS IT EXACTLY that you were doing in Ortona?"

"Well I had, like you say I had a series of jobs, just busting, blowin' holes through the wall to wall, or backing somebody up if he had to dart across the street or from one alley to the other, you know, somebody's gotta be there to start firing down at, even at nothing. I mean you fire, you don't necessarily have to see something, you just start shootin' down the street sort of thing, or wherever they're shooting from in hopes that you can keep their head down while somebody makes their move."

Maurice had raised the issue that I'd heard about from other veterans—how rare it was to see the enemy he was shooting at.

"Could you see them at all when you were fighting in the streets?"

"Uh, yeah sometimes you'd see 'em uh, you know, doing like us, jumping from pillar to post, sort of thing. And uh. And of course it happens quite a, so fast sometimes that you don't even have the chance to shoot at that particular guy. Generally when you are shooting you're just shooting at where you, where a machine gun is firing from, out of a window or over a pile of rubble or something, you know. Very seldom you actually see the guy that you're shootin' at."

"That must be another difference, because in war movies it always seems that they're aiming at somebody."

"You don't actually see people that you're shootin' at. You're shooting at smoke comin' from the machine gun or, you know that that's where they're firing from and you just shoot."

"Could you tell if you ever got anybody?"

"Oh well yeah you could either hear them or, or all of a sudden it would, no noise. And so yeah you'd know that they're, you'd got them."

"Hm."

"Either that or they pulled out but if you find, when you advanced you'd find them laying there so you'd knew you got 'em."

"That must have been a strange feeling."

"Yeah, um."

Maurice paused.

"It was him or you. You know. The only thing that really, really got me is on Christmas Day in Ortona. I was out, right up in the eve of a house and I had a couple a bricks knocked out, and I was out watching out there all day. That's where I had my Christmas dinner was up in the perch there. And uh, a German took cover, ran out and uh, and then, so I got my rifle ready and another guy come out and I shot him. You know. And uh, you know, and then it, it started to bother me, you know. Shootin' a guy on Christmas Day. Yeah, so that was a terrible thing, I, I don't like, still don't like that. It bothers me."

"Really."

"Yeah. So, that's, really that's the only guy I can say I shot. And I think you could uh, ninety-nine percent of the soldiers can't say that yeah I shot ten guys, I shot, you know, that's a bunch of crap . . . 'Cause ninety-nine times out of a hundred you're just shootin at, uh, well once in a while you'll see 'em running across, you know, trying to get out of there, but generally you're shootin' at smoke from a machine gun, or movement in the grass or whatever."

"But I guess you got a good, that was the one guy. Where was that, was that in a street, or—"

"It was in, over, they were in a square, just a little square. That square's no longer there. Because I found that, last time I was in Ortona, I found that house. But the square was all filled up with other houses. I didn't go into the house but I walked around back and then this uh, it was all built up."

"You went back to look for the house?"

"Yeah."

"That was something that you set out to do?"

"Yeah. Yeah. I'd tried five years ago and I couldn't find it. But this time I found it."

Early in the interview, when we first started talking about Ortona, Maurice had told me that he'd always felt that he'd left something behind, and that the most recent trip had somehow settled that.

"I've been to Italy I think a total of six times, five or six times, and I've always felt that I left something behind. And I have no reason to think that, but I've always wanted to go back. But after this trip I feel that I don't have to go back anymore. You know like it's just put a real good closure on it and, and, and, for whatever reason, and I couldn't really answer that, you know, the reason for that, but uh, I don't know I feel, comfortable now, sort of thing. Strange, but that's the way it is."

In the course of telling me this, he downgraded his feelings, emphasizing the groundlessness and irresolvable mystery of both the loss and the newfound comfort: "I have no reason to think that . . . for whatever reason . . . I couldn't really answer that . . . Strange . . ." It was as if he was pre-empting my inevitable inquiry, telling me that there was no point in asking him why; he wouldn't be able to answer.

In the article he wrote for his regimental magazine, he shared the same feelings of loss and comfort and mystery: "The Pilgrimage makes me feel that everything is complete now. I do not feel that I have to return to find whatever it was that was left behind."

Late in the interview, Maurice told me about something he had found in Ortona. It was the place where he'd shot the German—the site where something had "got" him: "The only thing that really, really got me . . . that was a terrible thing, I, I don't like, still don't like that. It bothers me." He'd searched for this place on previous trips without managing to find it. This time, finally he did. "This time I found it." It was the one thing on the recent pilgrimage that he told me he had found.

Shooting the German was clearly one of Maurice's most powerful memories of Ortona. Yet it seems that, for most of the interview, amid all the other details that he told me about the battle, he hadn't considered that story worth telling. I only got to hear it by chance. He had emphasized how rare it was to see the enemy he was shooting at. I had asked directly if he ever knew he'd shot someone. Even then, he'd continued speaking in general terms about the conditions of knowing. It was only when I shared my own belief that it must be a "strange" feeling that Maurice opened up and told me the story that troubled him.

Had he been hiding it from himself? Trying to convince himself it didn't matter? In searching for that place every time he went back to Ortona, Maurice had behaved as if it were deeply important. Yet at the same time, he seemed to have buried his own knowledge of what he was looking for, and why—to the point of becoming a mystery to himself.

To what end? Could it be related to his fear of crying? Maurice frequently mentioned that fear. He'd also mentioned his surprise that he hadn't cried more while talking to me. Perhaps that realization of his newfound composure had given him the courage to open up and share the story. However, that doesn't explain why Maurice had professed to be mystified even in his piece for his regimental magazine. If the story had already been available to him and he'd been willing to share it, he could have done so in writing, where there's no risk of anyone seeing you cry.

Another possible reason for burying this memory is that Maurice feared being judged for the fact that he cared. Tears or no tears, he had been affected by shooting the German; this had troubled him enough that he'd gone back repeatedly to find the place. Indeed, Maurice's return to the place of the shooting could be regarded as an "act of remembrance." He was showing his commitment to remember the life he might have taken on that day so long ago. But how would Maurice's comrades and fellow Canadians react if they knew of his commitment to this memory? He might have feared criticism; and maybe he criticized himself. For most of his life after the war, he probably felt very alone with these feelings. Certainly nobody else in his culture seemed to be remembering war in this way.

During the interview, Maurice told me that he no longer felt the need to go back. However, years later, I learned that he had returned again. While writing my dissertation, I came across an article in which Maurice was mentioned as having taken part in a November 2004 Veterans Affairs pilgrimage to Italy. As was now the rule, the veterans on the pilgrimage were accompanied by young people. At one point during the trip, the reporter for *Legion Magazine* found Maurice seated in the hotel lobby in Ortona telling some of the youths a story:

> 'I have a sad story to tell you. If tears start to come, forgive me.' Former lance-corporal Maurice White, 79, of Edmonton, is talking with several Canadian teenagers. . . . 'On Christmas Day they brought our lunch to us—beef, mashed potatoes, gravy and a bottle of beer—and my outpost was up in the attic of a house. I'd knocked two bricks out and I sat there all day on a rafter, looking out this hole. Some Germans came out, and I actually shot one of them on Christmas Day.'
>
> White holds back tears. . . . 'I thought, 'What the hell did I do that for?' It damn near makes me cry every time I talk about it, but it's important to know that we do have feelings and (the Germans) were people, too.' The teenagers listen silently.

Maurice had opened up about the story. And then I found that he had told it again at another pilgrimage some years after that. In each telling, he revealed more details.

> 'I shot a German on Christmas Day. At the time, it didn't bother me. But ever since, you know, I thought, 'Why did I do that?' It was Christmas. But you don't have a choice, you either shoot somebody or they shoot you. When I shot him, he fell, and two German soldiers came out and grabbed him and I didn't shoot back. I thank God that I didn't because that would have been even worse to handle.'

Suddenly it struck me. The scene that Maurice remembered—the place and event that he kept returning to—was a mirror image of the *Price of Peace* monument. In both the monument and Maurice's memory there was a mortally wounded soldier being attended by his comrades. In Maurice's memory, however, the suffering soldiers in the scene were his enemies, and he was responsible for their sacrifice.

When Maurice wanted to grieve for lost comrades, there were places he could go—the Moro River Canadian War Cemetery, the *Price of Peace* monument—and public rituals to validate his feelings, with youth accompaniment for support. But when Maurice wanted to grieve for the lives he might have taken, he had to find the place for himself, and he felt he had to go alone. On what might have been his last pilgrimage to Ortona, however, he had figuratively taken some of the youths along with him to the place where he'd shot the German. He had conjured another monument in the mind's eye of his listeners. That other monument speaks to a different cost of war.

We can go to Ortona, walk deep into the narrow streets, and in a square behind San Tommaso cathedral, we'll find the monument to Canadian sacrifice. It's a life-sized, realistic depiction. We can reach out and touch the stone soldiers, and leave flowers for them there. In Maurice's memory, somewhere deep in Ortona, there was another monument to loss. Maurice had managed to find it. For the rest of us, however, it will never be found. No one can go there to remember. It was known only to Maurice. With his passing, it is gone.

IT WAS LATE WHEN I left. I walked down the snow-packed sidewalk to the end of the street and waited for the bus. It was dark. Nothing was stirring. I stared at the Christmas lights on the houses, listened to the sound of my own breathing, felt the pinch of cold in my nose, and watched the clouds I made with my breath.

It's hard to understand why I stood there passively for such a long time. After half an hour or so, you'd think I'd have started to question. It's as if I'd forgotten that I was waiting for anything. Perhaps I was deep in thought. Perhaps I was too tired to think. Whatever state of mind I was in, it was interrupted by the distant sight of Maurice.

He came tramping up the sidewalk towards me. Despite the frigid cold and the snow, he was wearing only his black cloth slippers on his sockless feet, no hat on his head, no coat over his black turtleneck. He'd suddenly remembered that the bus didn't run at this hour and he'd come out to make sure I wasn't still waiting. I don't know what surprised me more—his appearance, or the fact that I was still there.

Sometimes when I'm hiking in the woods, I think of Maurice. I remember how he told me that he was never afraid of getting lost.

"You know, I was raised in the bush. And I can find my way anywhere."

"Really."

"Yeah. I have a good sense of direction and a keen sense of observing things so I'll know where they're at. As a matter of fact I can go on a trail even yet, that I've never been on before, and I could go back ten years later and go on that same trail. Just by remembering a stump or a knoll or, you know, any object."

And sometimes when I see a deer, I remember asking him:

"Did that come in handy during Ortona?"

"It come in handy anywhere during the war. 'Cause you can see something without even looking at it. Like you might be looking here and there's some movement over here and you'll pick it up. Your eye will automatically pick it up. Whereas the people that didn't have the experience that I had hunting, and I credit this to hunting, uh, would not see that movement. Even today, like we go on hikes out in the country, and have ten or fifteen people, if there's a moose or a deer or anything, I'll see it, first, way before, the others won't even see it. And you know they keep saying well how do you do it, how can you see that stuff. And I say well I guess my eyes are just trained to do that, so I can just do that unconsciously. Anyhow that, that I believe helped me through the war."

And I wonder what it meant to him.

"I think that was probably taught to me by my father. I used to do a lot of hunting with my father when I was a kid. And it's just a way of survival I guess, you learn to do that to survive. And it just stays with you all your life."

CHAPTER 9

A Story He Didn't Know

"THE FRONT WAS DEATHLY QUIET."

At the time, Alon Johnson was the twenty-three-year-old Scout Officer of the Loyal Edmonton Regiment. Every morning during the battle, with two or three of his men, he patrolled the front lines and reported back to battalion headquarters. Now, in his Victoria home, he was telling me about his patrol on the early morning of December 28, 1943. It was a story he'd also told in his regiment's journal, giving it the title, "The Last Patrol in Ortona."

> The forward localities of all the companies were very forward indeed—in most cases only a wall or at most an alley away from the German paratroop defenders. Offensive progress had been slow for the previous several days, so the positions were largely familiar to me. As I came through a battered building near a well-known and very dangerous doorway, I heard something unusual . . .

"Now this is 55 years ago. I don't want to—, but it seems to me there was a sentry at the door, because it looked out into an alley, and the alley had been swept with German fire. It was suicide to step out there. I think the sentry was probably as much to keep anybody from stepping out as he was from getting anybody to creep in."

Through this perilous doorway, Alon could hear an unusual sound—"off in the distance, yelling and shouting, or uh, I don't suppose yelling and shouting but excited babble, let's put it that way."

> The significance of this babble seemed to escape the tired company rifleman guarding the doorway, but to me it suggested a sudden and radical change in the situation. Important enough to risk being shot at by showing myself in the doorway. Nothing happened, so I stepped into the street.

"I stepped out in the alley. Nobody killed me. So away I went."

"The sentry didn't try to stop you?"

"Nope. He didn't give a damn. 'Fucking officer.'"

"Right. So you stepped out alone into the alley and nothing happened, and then what?"

"I took my two men and we covered each other. We advanced in bounds, as we're supposed do in the infantry."

"In bounds, what's—"

"Well, one man ready to fire in case of hostile activity, or maybe two men ready to fire while one moves. The bedrock of infantry tactics is fire and movement, and we were prepared for fire and movement."

> Immediately the scouts and I moved forward through rubble and battered buildings, taking what cover we could as we searched

> for the source of the ever-louder sound of chatter. Within a short distance, probably less than fifty meters, we saw and were seen by a civilian who recognized us as non-German soldiers, and made that peculiar Italian gesture which we would normally interpret as 'go back' or 'take cover', but which means really for us to 'come on'. Suspecting a trap, we took cover, and momentarily prepared to return fire if necessary.

The noise grew louder. More civilians appeared.

"By the time where I could, where it was no longer just a babble in the distance but distinguishable voices and excited people talking, I had a pretty goddam good idea what was, what was on."

> . . . shortly we were in the middle of an increasing crowd of Italian civilians, as more and more people emerged from the cellars where they had sheltered during the days of battle in the streets of Ortona.

"Was it strange to see civilians suddenly?"

"I was surprised. I was surprised. I didn't realize, there seemed to be no civilians in our part of town. I was really surprised to see all those civilians."

"What did they look like?"

"I don't know. Just civilians. Yeah. Civilians are a, are an impediment." Alon smirked. Then he corrected himself. "In this case they were a big help. I shouldn't knock them."

> I well remember one man who spoke some English. He was very helpful to us, pointing out the location of the former German

> headquarters, and he then cautioned me that the enemy may have mined it. Then he spoiled the good impression by saying, 'I can't understand what took you so long. There weren't many Germans here.' I was tempted to return the insult, but held my tongue with the thought that I might need this man more than he needed me.

"And I met a fellow who could talk English, who offered me the well-known insult, I think it's recorded a few times, it's uh, 'I don't understand what took you so long, there weren't many Germans here.' And then there was a young fellow, eighteen years old or so, just a kid, and he guided me up to the castle."

> . . . the old castle of Ortona which stood prominently on the north-easternmost headland and atop a cliff overlooking the Adriatic Sea . . . When we got there we found it unoccupied. We were not fired on at any point, so it was more than obvious that the enemy had not only vacated Ortona but had withdrawn from some distance without leaving as much as a rearguard.

At the same moment that Alon and his men were following the kid to the castle, just a few hundred yards away, Matthew Halton was walking into the Edmonton regiment's headquarters. In a broadcast to his CBC radio audience, Halton described the scene:

> This is Matthew Halton of the CBC speaking from Italy. At eight o'clock this morning I was bumping over the tank ruts into the outskirts of Ortona. There was a strange silence, and I surmised something. I got into the command post of a western Canadian regiment in the heart of the town. Only a few machine guns were clattering, only an occasional enemy shell was falling, and bearded

> men who hadn't had their boots off for thirty days were laughing. A colonel grinned when I came in. I said, 'Don't tell me,' and he replied, 'Yes, I think we've got Ortona. There's a patrol going through the fort now and if they find no Germans there, the thing is over. We'll know any minute.' Not two minutes later, the radio buzzed and Corporal Bill Polhill of Edmonton took the message from the signaller at the front not four hundred yards away. Then he took off his earphones and turned to the colonel. 'Sir, the Jerries have gone, or else they're all dead.' Ortona was ours.

In Halton's story of the battle's end, the Italian civilians aren't mentioned. That absence is understandable. Halton heard the news as it was relayed to the colonel by Corporal Polhill, and Polhill heard it over his radio set from the signaller with Lieutenant Alon Johnson, and there was no reason for Alon or the signaller to relay the role that was played by civilians. The sounds of Italian voices had inspired Alon to step out through the doorway; an Italian had waved at Alon and his men to come forward; an Italian kid had led them to the castle. But none of that was important for Canadian commanders to know, nor was it decisive in how the battle ended. Even if there had been no Italians in that corner of Ortona, the Canadians still would have learned that the Germans had retreated and that "Ortona was ours."

In his attitude to Italian civilians, Alon was resolutely practical. Beyond the tactical military framing of civilians as utilities or impediments, Alon wasn't terribly interested in learning more about them. This attitude had persisted after the war. He told me about his return trip to Ortona, when he had found the street to the castle and retraced the steps of his last patrol. On his way back from the castle, he'd been greeted by some local men. They asked him if he was Canadian. Alon told them that he was, and not only that, he was a veteran and he had been "primo soldato al castello," the first soldier to the castle. The men became excited and told Alon that the "kid" who had guided him on that day was right there inside a nearby bar. They wanted to take Alon to meet the guy. Alon declined.

His response to the invitation and his way of recalling it struck me as cold. His tone was almost contemptuous of the excitement the Italians felt for him. But his emotional reserve wasn't limited to Italians. Alon seemed to have a cold relationship to all of his war memories. When I asked him how he had felt at the end of the battle, he replied: "It was all a part of the day's work. That's about all." I sensed that he didn't like being asked about feelings. But perhaps the same characteristics that made him a bit of a disappointing storyteller had also made him effective during the war, a sort of indifference that might amount to courage, such as when he stepped through that "well-known and very dangerous doorway" and led the last patrol in Ortona.

As for the Italian man who had waved to Alon's patrol, that man had also stepped through a very dangerous doorway at his end of the heretofore machine-gun-swept street. He knew that the Germans were gone, but he might not have realized just how much risk he was taking when he stepped into view of the Canadian patrol. Alon and his men were moving up in bounds, "two men ready to fire while one moves." They weren't accustomed to seeing civilians in the street. Civilians were not the intended targets of the Canadians, but many were killed in Ortona by Canadian fire.

THE OFFICIAL CIVILIAN DEATH toll in Ortona for the entire period of the war is 1,314. The count begins in September 1943 when the Germans occupied Ortona and ends in June 1944 when the Adriatic front moved northward after the Allies had captured Rome.[1] Most civilian deaths occurred from November 1943 to January 1944 when the fighting around Ortona was fierce. People of Ortona (the *Ortonesi*) were killed in the town and in the nearby countryside, struck dead by artillery and tank fire, shot in the crossfire of rifles and machine guns, and buried in exploded buildings. Some who were frail or sick undoubtedly died from hunger, thirst, or stress. In addition to those killed, many more were wounded. Among the survivors, some were left with lifelong disabilities and psychological traumas.

Civilians were not supposed to be in Ortona by the time of the Canadian attack. On November 2, the Germans ordered everyone out of the town, giving residents only three hours to evacuate. The Germans were preparing their defensive positions; for them, the Ortonesi were not only an "impediment," they were also potential spies. Even the hospital—located in Piazza San Francesco, which was to become, for the Seaforths, "Dead Horse Square"—was ordered to evacuate its gravely ill patients. Some Ortonesi had family or friends in the countryside who could take them in. Others crowded into rural building cellars, hillside caves, and their own makeshift shelters.

By early December, tired of the cold and discomfort, some refugees began returning to the town. They kept a low profile and either escaped notice or were tolerated by the Germans. On December 5, the Canadians began shelling Ortona, killing and injuring several townspeople. That prompted some to flee down the escarpment and hide in the railway tunnel. Others fled back into the countryside.

But the countryside was about to become a hellscape. On December 18, a few kilometres west of Ortona, the Canadians launched one of the heaviest artillery bombardments that had ever been conducted by the Eighth Army. Code-named "Morning Glory" and "Orange Blossom," this was a creeping barrage in support of two infantry attacks that aimed to break through the German defences.

> Precisely at 0800 hours, the massed artillery fired as one. 'The barrage opened,' read an after-action report, 'with a deafening roar . . .' In front of the 48th Highlanders, the ground erupted in geysers of earth quickly obscured by a thick fog of smoke. . . . Everybody was partially deafened by the explosions, so verbal orders were useless. The two lead companies waded through mud, trying to keep up with the advancing artillery as it followed its schedule of a 100-yard lift every five minutes. Although described as open ground, the battlefield was a bewildering mess of shattered orchards and demolished vineyards. Wire for supporting the vines tried to tangle the men's feet and legs as they stumbled through the mud. Smoke lay so thick that visibility was cut to 200 yards . . . Dead and dying Germans lay everywhere. Few of the machine guns were manned. The Canadians rolled grenades onto the guns and, in compliance with their orders, kept going. Every wine cellar or deep hole in the ground had a grenade tossed into it.

Panicked Ortonesi—some of whom had been hiding in wine cellars and holes in the ground—fled the countryside once more, heading for what they thought would be relative safety in the town. Many ended up in the hospital. Others went to a small church in the cemetery, and into homes—often not their own—around town. The Germans made some effort to keep them out but were busy with preparing their defences. However, the Germans dealt harshly with anyone they found and suspected of supporting the Allies. When they encountered a man who was carrying a bag of British sweaters, they shot him on the spot.[2]

On December 20, the Loyal Edmonton Regiment launched the Canadian ground attack on Ortona. This was the attack that Mel remembered, in which he advanced through an orchard and saw Buck Holder get shot dead right next to him. The Edmontons were supported by an artillery barrage. When Ortonesi in a nearby villa tried to flee from the barrage, ten of them were struck and killed among the olive trees.

Meanwhile, inside the town, the Germans were blowing up buildings to create rubble piles for their "killing zones" and to eliminate easy reference points for Canadian gunners. They forced Ortona men to carry TNT to the Cathedral of San Tommaso so that the adjacent signal and lookout tower could be destroyed. When the tower fell, it struck the cathedral, bringing down half the dome. The Germans banged on doors of buildings they were about to destroy in order to warn any civilians who might be hiding in them. Sometimes, out of fear, the Ortonesi didn't respond. One building near the cemetery was blown up by the Germans with thirty-four people inside. Ortonesi hiding in the cemetery attempted a rescue but had to call it off because the Canadians began shelling the area.

The next day, the Edmontons' attack was protected by artillery fire on their left flank; those bombs killed five members of an Ortona family, sparing only the thirteen-year-old son and a baby. When the Seaforths made their attack on Santa Maria di Costantinopoli, some of the protective artillery fire called in by Captain Harley struck a house on via Costantinopoli, blowing the head off a nine-year-old boy, Tommaso Vena, and also killing his six-year-old sister, Silvana. Down below the escarpment, the civilians who were hiding in the railway tunnel were forced out by the Germans, who wanted the tunnel for a headquarters and a safe place for their wounded. When the civilians ran out, seeking new hiding places around the port, their movements were spotted by the

Canadians and they were mistaken for Germans. Canadian artillery guns fired on them, killing three.

Inside the hospital on Piazza San Francesco, more than a hundred Ortonesi were sheltering under the care of the nursing sisters. The Germans had set up machine gun positions in buildings adjacent to the hospital, including the terrace of the public bath house and in the church of Santa Maria delle Grazie. When the Seaforth infantrymen and Three Rivers tanks arrived, the Germans opened fire and the Canadians responded. One of the shells fired by a Canadian tank struck the woodhouse next to the public bath. Twelve Ortonesi hiding there were killed. A frightened horse ran into the square. Prior to the battle, the Germans had taken it from its owner, a drayman named Alfredo Ciampoli. Alfredo was among the people in the hospital. When he saw his distressed horse in the square, he went out to rescue it. The Germans shot and killed Alfredo and his horse.

By December 27, many civilians in Ortona hadn't eaten for days. Clean water was in short supply. In the hospital, one of the nuns talked to the Germans and convinced them to hold a brief ceasefire to allow the civilians to escape. It's also remembered that a Canadian soldier discovered the presence of civilians in the hospital and informed his officers. It isn't clear from any reports how the ceasefire was coordinated. It wasn't mentioned by any of the veterans whom I interviewed and there's no record of it in the Seaforths' War Diary. In the diary of the Three Rivers Regiment, it's briefly mentioned, but it's unclear if it was expected by them.

> Comic relief was provided by the hospital doors opening, at 1100 hours, and over 100 civilians streamed out. They had remained underground and unharmed during the three days the Squadron had continually shelled the building.

But fighting was still happening in the streets around Dead Horse Square. Some of the Ortonesi who escaped from the hospital unwittingly got caught in the crossfire as they went down the streets.

The end of the battle was not an end to civilian casualties. From their new defensive lines to the north, the Germans periodically shelled Ortona and the countryside, targeting Allied positions, sometimes hitting civilians. Ortonesi were also killed while returning to their homes and farmland as they stumbled upon and triggered boobytraps, mines, and unexploded bombs.

In 1959, the Italian government awarded a Gold Medal for Civilian Valour to the people of Ortona for demonstrating "the highest spirit of human solidarity" amid their suffering during the war. In 1965, a Monument to Civilian Victims of War was erected in the square in front of the restored San Tommaso cathedral. Later, it was moved to the cemetery. The parish priest of Ortona, Don Antonio Politi, compiled an incomplete list of Ortonesi killed in the war which he included in his memoir *I Giorni del Martirio* ("The Days of Martyrdom"). Don Antonio organized the names by the date of their death, and noted their ages at the time. In his list, from December 20 to 28, 1943, there are 188 dead. The ages of the men, women, and children range from four months to ninety-one years.

"I FIRED FOUR THOUSAND and fifty rounds of ten-pound bombs in Ortona, but you can say like, in Ortona, I never killed a soul."

When Jack said this, he was of course being ironic about his experiential distance from killing, but even so, the souls he had in mind probably did not include civilians. In that moment, the conversation with Gus, Rollie, Jack, and Bill was on the topic of how rarely they had seen Germans. Their impressions of civilians during the battle were even foggier.

"Do you remember when you were going house to house, what it was like inside the houses?"

"It was just rooms," Gus answered, "that's all they were, furniture and rooms."

"Did you ever meet any Italians during the battle?"

"Not during. Well, early on in the battle, yes, there were a few civilians there. But uh, you didn't carry any conversations because they were trying to get out of there, trying to find cover. But uh, I didn't really meet any Italians. They didn't want to be involved where there was fighting. Some may have been hiding out in the cellars, we really don't know."

Later in the conversation, Gus remembered a detail.

"You talk about what happened to the civilians, we were in a house there, in Ortona, and it had a great big oak table. And this young woman come in, she would have been about twenty-three, come right into the, where the battle, practically where the battle was goin' on, so that she could inspect this table and make sure that we were treating it properly."

It was a light-hearted story told in the same spirit as other stories about harmless, slapstick moments of the war. Everyone chuckled.

Maurice, on the other hand, had a more vivid memory of civilian suffering.

"When we first entered Ortona, the first building I think we come to was quite a large building that I remember, long, single story building but it was quite a long building and uh, we thought we'd heard some noise in there and we pounded on the door and then, we didn't hear anything, and we hollered to open the door and nothing happened so we shot, shot the lock off. And of course then we heard screamin' and hollerin' in there and there was twenty-one civilians, from little babies to old people, eh?"

"That many people."

"Yeah. And stink. Oh my god it stunk in there. And they said they hadn't been out, hadn't seen daylight for two weeks."

"How come?"

"Well, we were shelling, and they [the Germans] were shelling, uh, so they were just in where they felt it was safe. Especially when the attack come they just, weren't going to come out. And uh, I think we fed them, gave them what food we had with us, and I think there was a couple of them who needed some medical attention and the first aid man gave 'em medical attention. And then we were gone, you know, on. Otherwise, during the battle, I don't remember seeing, very few civilians . . . I don't know where they were at, but they were around somewhere."

June Thomas, who was a Seaforth Captain and was commanding at the front line at Dead Horse Square, only had a vague memory of civilians.

"Do you remember seeing any Italians during the battle?"

"Very, very few. They were hiding down in the cellars."

"I heard a story that at one point during the fighting in the square there was a ceasefire between the Canadians and the Germans to allow the Italians to come out of the hospital."

"I don't recall that. It could have happened."

Dave Fairweather recalled seeing some old Italian women during the battle.

"They were just sitting in a, in a, or cowering in one of the houses that we went through on the way up. And I don't know why they were there, no idea why they—, I understand there was quite a few caves outside that the Italian population had gone to."

Mel and Ted didn't seem to be aware of any civilians during the battle. And among all the veterans whom I interviewed, with the exception of Bill, I didn't detect any sign that they had considered the possibility that their rifles and grenades may have harmed civilians. When Mel asked himself, "Whose life did I end?" he was referring to Germans. He hadn't seen any Italians, and of course he wasn't thinking of them as targets.

Indeed, at the time of the interviews, I wasn't thinking about this possibility, either. When I asked Bill, "Did you ever go into a house and find some Italians?" I was expecting that, if he'd found any, they would have been alive. His answer confused me, as did his sudden dejected manner. He replied slowly, looking down at the table.

"Yeah, sometimes, yeah, I know, most Italians killed too because . . . I mean what you done, you threw a grenade through a window if you could first, you know. . . . But you didn't know. You didn't know who was in there, actually, you know? Usually there was Germans in there but, uh. Yeah . . ."

Puzzled, I could only say, "Hm."

Bill took a deep breath, sighed, and stood up.

"I'm going to get a drink of water."

Bill didn't say what he had seen, but clearly he'd been affected by it. And even if I had clued in to what he was hinting at, I don't think I would have asked him to clarify. We'd just been through his story of his captivity with the Germans. Partly for his sake and partly for my own, I wouldn't have wanted to open up yet another wound. I let him get his drink and come back to a change of topic.

I wonder if his remorse was one of the reasons he took nothing from the town.

"Did you get any souvenirs from Ortona?"

"No, I didn't get anything. I wasn't even interested."

"Why not?"

"Well I don't know, I didn't think it was the thing to do, you know or, I didn't want any souvenirs."

"You didn't think it was the thing to do?"

"No."

"Like, you didn't think it was a good thing?"

"War souvenirs, you mean?"

"Yeah."

"No I didn't think so, no I didn't think so, no."

"'Cause a lot of guys took stuff from the houses."

"I know."

At the battle's conclusion, according to Major (later Colonel) Jim Stone, Canadian soldiers went on a looting rampage.

> I think before leaving Ortona I should mention the, our enemy the Germans. They were the troops of the German First Paratroop Division, without doubt the equal of any troops I think who were actually fighting in the field . . . To me they were the most determined and disciplined, well-trained people I came, either fought with or against, and I was against them that time. In the town itself there were notices in German which said plundering and looting is punishable by death. And that was why in all the Italian houses and places like that their trinkets and things were intact. But as soon as our troops got in there, lacking that discipline, everything was plundered and, and taken, that everything was possibly be grabbed. And uh, somebody had found some silver behind a wall in this hotel place we first got into, and from then on every wall in the town about was knocked down to see if there was anything was behind it. One man found twenty golden sovereigns that some Italian ice cream vendor had saved from his time in England and brought back. The number of parcels that went out of that town, uh, being sent back to England or to Canada, of household linen and all kinds of stuff, that was, it was absolutely straight looting that was going on. And it was

> taking from people who couldn't afford to lose it, it was the kind of the, the poorer people who were living in these places that were, lost the stuff.
>
> (Interviewer: At that time they were the enemy though still were they not, and that's uh—)
>
> The Italians? No, no, the Italians were out of the war by then.
>
> (Interviewer: They had surrendered by then had they?)
>
> Oh yeah but even then you don't, you're not supposed to plunder.

In his criticism of his fellow Canadians, Stone might even have been thinking about some of the high-ranking officers. In the Seaforth archives, I found this allegation of an act that was similar to what Stone described.

> *A. Staples, Letter to Reginald Roy, August 10th, 1967*
>
> Sid Thompson [sic] liberated an ermine jacket from behind a false wall just before returning to England for a staff course and we understand he put it to good use in London.

"DO YOU THINK THAT the Canadians behaved well after the battle?"

I was with Denis at his kitchen table in Vancouver.

"Depends on what you call *well* I guess. If they got enough vino they got drunk. You know. I don't know that they raped anybody but if there was a willing participant there was some of that going on. No, we were not angels. We had, you know, we, when we landed in Sicily, Italy was part of the Axis, it was part of the enemy. And whereas there was a lot of fraternization, there was also a lot of, of uh, you might call it looting, you know. . . . No we didn't, we were no saints. But soldiers aren't. You get hardened, you get inured, you don't, you know, you look after number one. I don't think guys were necessarily cruel, but they weren't considerate either."

Denis reminded me that Italy had been an ally of Nazi Germany. Italian troops had supported the Germans against the British Eighth Army in North Africa. During the landing in Sicily, while most Italian soldiers quickly surrendered, a few did put up a fight that caused some Canadian casualties. Many Canadian soldiers probably shared the sentiment that Sam expressed to the old Italian man who accosted him on the road outside Ortona.

"And then he asked me, he says uh, do you guys know what you're doing over here? And I says yeah, if it wasn't for you bastards and Mussolini, and you'd have been on the right side, we wouldn't have been here."

Hence the Canadians' sarcastic use of the word *liberation*. They never said that they "liberated" Italian people or places. What they did frequently "liberate" was Italian property, including eggs, pigs, wine, and ermine jackets. They weren't interested in liberating Italians and they knew that wasn't really their mission. To put it bluntly, as Major-General Vokes had done, their mission in Italy was to kill Germans. Once Italy was taken out of the war, the strategic objective of the Allied invasion was to draw the Germans in, grind the Germans down, and thereby weaken the Germans on other fronts—especially in France for the planned Normandy invasion.

While it was both politically and militarily expedient to minimize damage to Italy, ordinary Allied soldiers might have felt that Italians didn't have much right to complain. Certainly, the Canadians experienced many warm welcomes in the southern Italian communities that they passed through, but problems of trust were understandable. At least a few Italians within the recently "liberated" territories still retained their fascist beliefs and loyalties. Mussolini spoke to them by radio from his new Nazi-aligned republic in the north. Indeed, about a week after the Ortona battle, the Canadians learned from their interrogations of German prisoners that the Germans had some informers among the Italians who were "helping" the Canadians. An intelligence report advised: "The tragic consequences for ourselves of this kind of treachery by Italians need not be pointed out. All ranks will be reminded that Italians, though at times friendly, are not to be trusted."

Denis's anger finally peaked a few months after Ortona when one of his close comrades was killed. That was Pop Warner, Denis's fellow signaller who had famously passed out from exhaustion at his radio in the house at Dead Horse Square. On May 23, 1944, Joseph Victor "Pop" Warner was killed in the Liri Valley battle with the Germans.

"I had to be part of the burial detail. We brought Pop or what was left of him back, buried him with his headphones still on."

"Still on."

"Yeah. Yeah. And it was an eerie sort of place, it was kind of a, olive grove, or orange grove, or something. And a mist, about four feet off the ground. Mist. Fireflies."

Denis sucked his breath in sharply through his teeth and exhaled.

"*Ffffff!* It was, I say it was really quite a sight."

Later in the interview, when he was talking about becoming hardened, he mentioned that he had been cruel to "refugees, for instance" and he added this detail about Pop's burial.

"We had a couple of Italians to help us dig the graves, and uh, I was kind of emotionally upset because we'd lost a couple of guys in the circumstances, and they started complainin' and whining about, oh we're hungry, and we're tired. And that's when I pulled my Tommy gun and I said dig, you son of a bitch. Dig. And I would have shot 'em. You know."

Denis wasn't proud of this moment. And when it came to the topic of civilian suffering in Ortona, it was Denis, among all the veterans, who expressed in words the strongest feeling of responsibility and shame. This was regarding a notorious scene from the battle. It was clearly much talked about among the Canadian soldiers at the time, as Bill recalled being told.

"One poor old lady," Bill said when I asked him about civilians. "They had to go out for water you know, she was laying half on the street and half out, and I didn't see this but they said the tanks were running over her feet, mind you. Nobody pulled her out."

Some had seen how it happened.

> Clifford Wood: I remember one corner building . . . an old woman had been killed and she was sitting there and the tanks were running back and forth across her . . .
>
> Don Harley: Before she was killed she was mad . . . she was in the middle of that square, wandering about with her hair down, yelling and screaming, and then she was shot.

Denis called it a "very vivid memory" of Ortona.

"In front of that church in the rubble, there was—oh how quite to describe it. You know the way older Italian women are all dressed in black."

"Yeah. Yeah."

"Well, this woman had obviously been killed from something or other, shellfire, hit by a truck or blown up by a booby trap I don't know but it was, she was on the road and she had been run over until she was just flat like roadkill. I've never forgotten that my whole life. Terrible thing, you know."

"I guess there were a lot of—"

"Oh of course. Sure there were. Sure there were. But uh, you get inured, you get a little callous. I mean that obviously affected me because it still does, to think that that a human life was so little valued that it would become roadkill in effect, like a, like a raccoon that's been run over on a highway several times, you know. That was somebody's mother, or sister, or wife."

Along with other veterans who remembered it, Denis located the woman's body in Dead Horse Square. But he remembered it specifically lying in front of the church, and he added this detail about it: "the dome of the church had been half blown away." He was mistakenly picturing the body in front of the ruined San Tommaso cathedral.[3]

Denis was factually wrong; but for the people he was remembering, he was symbolically right. San Tommaso was their protector, and the ruined cathedral embodied their suffering. That's why Ortona's Monument to Civilian Victims of War was originally placed in the square in front of it. Denis didn't know this, but his way of remembering the civilian dead was in tune with the people of Ortona.

"I've written only what I saw for myself."

Adriano di Luzio had kept a diary during the war. At that time, in 1943, he was a high school secretary in Ortona. Fifty-five years later, he'd adapted the diary into a memoir and published it.

In March 2000, when I met him and his wife Luisa, they were both pensioners—a sweet and diminutive couple. When I entered their building just off the Corso they were waiting for me outside their flat at the top of the stairs. On the landing, I was startled by Adriano giving me an immediate hug and kiss on my cheek. It was the first time we'd met, but he'd greeted me as if I were a long and dearly missed family member or friend.

We sat in their living room and talked.

Me: And how did you get the idea to write a book like this?

Adriano: Because I saw that the others were doing so little . . . whereas I, I took notes, I took.

Luisa: At the time.

Adriano: At the time. And immediately, well, in the spring of '44, so immediately after.

Luisa: You have them. Show them to him.

Adriano: Do you want to see the notes that I took?

Me: Oh, yes, yes, it would be fascinating.

(Adriano gets up from his chair and crosses the room)

Luisa: Oh I know, it was a tragedy. Oh a tragedy.

Me: How old were you?

Luisa: Eleven, eleven, eleven and a half. *(To Adriano)* Show him the diary.

Adriano: (*returning to his chair)* This I kept with me all the time. Here it is. Here.

Me: How old were you?

Adriano: I was twenty-three.

Me: Twenty-three, and you kept a diary from the beginning.

Luisa: Twenty-two.

Adriano: Eh?

Luisa: Twenty-two.

Adriano: Twenty-two years. Eh. This begins, uh, so . . .

For almost three months during my fieldwork, from March to May 2000, I lived in Ortona. I went with the aim of learning more about the battle, including how it was remembered by the townspeople.

My home there was the guest residence of the Salesians of Don Bosco, an order of Catholic priests whose mission is the care and education of young people, especially the disadvantaged. The Salesian residence was recommended to me by local people soon after my arrival, and coincidentally it turned out to be a place that was very resonant with my research. The Salesians had been invited to Ortona after the war in order to provide services for the town's physically and emotionally wounded children. Their compound was across the street from Santa Maria di Costantinopoli. In fact, they had been the hosts of Ted's Christmas Eve reconciliation dinner. My meals were served in the same dining hall; as the only guest for the duration of my stay, I ate alone in that hall among twenty or so empty tables. The cooks, cleaners, and servers were a small team of local women. It was they who had, according to Ted, boiled the Christmas turkeys.

The area by the cliffs next to the church, where Don Harley and his men had once fiercely battled the Germans, was now the location of the Salesian-run youth social centre. There was an indoor space with ping pong tables and an outdoor court for basketball and other games. It was well used; I regularly saw children and teens playing and hanging out there. Many of their grandparents hung out there too. My guest room's window overlooked the church. A few times during my stay, I saw wedding parties posing for photographs at the doors. At night, I could hear trains passing on the tracks below the cliffs, and the sounds of the Adriatic Sea.

It wasn't hard to find people who were willing to talk about the war. I had already met a few members of Ortona's wartime generation when I'd been here for the Christmas reconciliation. Some Ortonesi had come out to the public events of that week in hopes of meeting the Canadian veterans. Owing to the language barrier and the veterans' rigorous schedule, the Ortonesi's chances to interact with them had been limited. As a Canadian who was somewhat associated with the old soldiers, I think in some ways I was treated as a stand-in.

Among those who took me instantly under their wing were Tommaso Sorino and Angelo Tenisci. The two men had been friends since childhood. In December 1943, they were both sixteen; now they were seventy-three-year-old pensioners—and very different characters. Tommaso was portly with a round face, dark hair, thick moustache, and big eyeglasses that made windows on his face. He looked a bit like a sympathetic video game hero, especially because he always wore the same style and colour of clothes, including a navy blue sweater and a navy coppola cap. An enthusiastic storyteller, to my knowledge Tommaso had no official public role, but he still acted like an authority, and had an uncanny knack for appearing in the photos of every event he attended. Angelo was the opposite: soft-spoken, not the least bit brash or edgy; you would hardly notice him in a crowd. He was pale and a bit pear shaped, wearing baggy pants and jackets that somewhat matched his slightly baggy face, but his eyes were bright, and in his quiet way he had subtle warmth and wit.

Both men were regulars at the clubhouse of the *marinai*. The word means *sailors* but officially the clubhouse belonged to the Ortona branch of Italy's National Association of Navy Veterans (*Associazione Nazionale Marinai d'Italia*) which includes those who served in the wartime merchant marine. This house of the *marinai* was centrally located, steps away from the municipal building with a view of the main square (the former Piazza Municipio, now called Piazza Della Repubblica).

But the place didn't have much of a military vibe; it was easy to forget that I was among any kind of veterans. I don't think I ever met anyone there who had served in a war, and peacetime military service was nothing remarkable to most Italian men; everyone in Tommaso and Angelo's generation had been required to do it (and it was still mandatory for young men, although now it could be done as community service if you were a conscientious objector). Most in Ortona had done their service in the

Italian Navy—but it didn't seem to have left them with many stories they wanted to tell.

What they did like talking about was Ortona's connections to the sea. Many of the *marinai*—including Tommaso and Angelo—took great pride in belonging to fishing families of Terravecchia ("Old Town") even when they themselves hadn't done much fishing in their lives. Angelo, for example, had been a floor waxer. Nicola had been a coal miner. Others had spent parts of their lives working overseas as labourers. On the whole, the *marinai* clubhouse struck me as a hangout for like-minded male pensioners, a place where they would go to smoke, read the newspaper, and socialize while sitting at tables among bric-a-brac with a nautical theme.

Some of my contacts for interviews came from the *marinai.* Some came from looking up local historians and getting their referrals. Some came from the women who worked for the Salesian priests. And some came about just by the fact that I was unavoidably conspicuous. I stood out with my accent and red hair, and this wasn't a place that got many foreign visitors. Ortona was no longer the thriving resort town that it had been in its pre-war days.

Another valuable connection that I made at the Salesian compound was somebody who didn't want to be there. This was a local guy in his mid-twenties who was tasked with minding the reception. With his long hair, bandana, and the way he was always reading the radical leftist *il manifesto* newspaper while sitting at the compound's entrance gate, Daniele (name changed) was almost more out place than I was. Indeed, I learned that he'd been desperate to get away from Ortona, and for a while he'd succeeded; he'd worked hard at improving his English and had managed to get into university in Ireland. But something had gone wrong with his deferral of military service; in the middle of his studies he'd been forced to come back to Italy and do it. Considering the type of guy he was—intellectual, vegetarian, environmentally conscious—it wasn't surprising that he'd declared himself a conscientious objector. In an ironic twist of fate, he'd been assigned to do community service back in his home town at the society of Catholic priests.

Through Daniele, I learned about another side of Ortona. He described it as a dead-end place for young people. Good jobs were scarce, and (in his opinion) it was spiritually dangerous to stay. He'd noticed that most of his generation who hadn't gone away were narrow-minded and wasted their time doing drugs. However, he still had a few friends in town. Sometimes I was invited out with them. Luca (name changed) was quirky and passionate about music with a bit of a romantic bent; he got me to translate the lyrics to some of his favourite Dylan and Hendrix songs. Piero (name changed) was a heavy-metal looking dude with more of a business mindset; he was planning to open his own restaurant. In their teens, these guys had played Dungeons and Dragons; now on occasional Saturdays they played Risk. One thing they didn't do together was talk about politics. Luca was firmly uninterested, Daniele told me; even worse, he lamented, Piero was a fascist. I was startled when he said that so casually about his friend, as if "fascist" was a normal, albeit regrettable, thing to be. I wasn't sure if he meant it literally—I didn't ask. But it couldn't be ruled out—especially in Ortona.

The meaning of fascism was being hotly debated in Italy at the time. The major trigger for this debate was the rise of a new political party connected to Italy's postwar neo-fascist Movimento Sociale Italiano (Italian Social Movement). The MSI had been founded in 1946 by unrepentant Mussolini loyalists. Some of its leading members had served in the government and the army of the Italian Social Republic (also known as the Salò Republic), the Nazi-aligned regime headed by Mussolini in German-occupied Italy. In 1995, the MSI disbanded and reconstituted itself as the Alleanza Nazionale (National Alliance). The AN disavowed racism, antisemitism, and totalitarianism; however, it also argued for the good intentions of the old fascists and for the contemporary value of many of their ideas. Notably, one of the party's high-profile members was Mussolini's granddaughter Alessandra. Some supporters described the AN as the "evolution" of fascism; the party leader called himself a "post-fascist." This balancing act was symbolized by the AN's logo which placed the tri-colour flame of the old neo-fascist MSI within a friendly blue circle that was prominently inscribed with the new party name. That logo was a familiar sight around Ortona, as Mayor Puletti and many of the councillors were party members.[4]

In some respects, Ted's project of reconciliation had played right into the AN's "post-fascist" agenda. Tommaso and Angelo told me that Mayor Puletti had used the occasion of the reconciliation to say that Italians should follow the example of these Canadian veterans and put the past conflict over fascism to rest. For the *marinai,* it was scandalous to suggest that the Canadians were morally equivalent to the Germans and that the same respect should be given to Italian fascists. Tommaso told me how his father had been fired from his job at the state railway (*Ferrovie Statale*) after refusing to join the Fascist Party. ("I don't put filth in my pocket," his father had said, referring to the party membership card.)[5] On the other hand, the monumental legacy of Ted's project—the *Price of Peace* statue—posed a dilemma for the AN-dominated town council for the same reason that it delighted the *marinai:* the statue was a one-sided celebration of the Canadians who were a symbol to many in Ortona of the fight against fascism. The *marinai* told me that the council had at first tried to reject the "gift" of the monument, and when that wasn't possible, the council had tried to place it on the town's periphery. Thanks in large part to the outside pressure that Ted had mobilized, the council had relented and given the statue a relatively central place.

Some of the *marinai* would have liked it to be even more central—and a bit more alive. The tragic mood of the statue didn't fit with Nicola Bottega's preferred memory of the Canadian soldiers.

"They felt, well, also glorious to have saved us, no? Also proud."

"Yes?"

"To say, fuck, we've done a good job, eh?"

There was no doubt that the *marinai* were politically conscious. But they were also vulnerable to criticism that they were just reflexively against change. Younger Ortonesi were talking about bringing a shopping centre to town as one way to improve the local economy. The *marinai* were adamantly opposed. They feared the shopping centre would be a Trojan Horse for the dreaded lifestyle of Italy's largest city, Milan. In Milan, they told me, people ate sandwiches at their work cubicles without taking a break for lunch, and grandparents had nothing to do. In Ortona, by contrast, you could set your clock according to when you saw Angelo heading up or down the Corso. Every weekday, he and his wife picked up their grandkids at school, brought them home for lunch, took them back to school, and then picked them up again when school was done. Later that evening, you'd see the whole family together on the Corso for *la Passeggiata* when the street filled with people taking a stroll after dinner, getting a gelato, greeting one another, and milling about in conversations. Above all, there was the veneration of San Tommaso, patron saint of Ortona. The traditional feast day of Saint Thomas in the Latin calendar was December 21, but he was uniquely celebrated in Ortona with the *Festa del Perdono* every May.

The Ortonesi had been following these traditions for centuries. After World War II, it had also become somewhat traditional in Ortona to venerate the Canadian soldier. I started to understand why many in Ortona's wartime generation felt that way—and why the feeling wasn't universally shared.

One day, Tommaso and Angelo took me on an improvised historical walking tour. Starting from the clubhouse of the *marinai,* we headed into the narrow streets of Terravecchia.

"There were a lot of dead, there were a lot," Tommaso said.

"Every family has, certainly, one or two people dead," Angelo added.

"Civilian, and also military," Tommaso continued. "For example, there was, in the piazza near the association [the *marinai* clubhouse], really, there was, you know those little beds for small babies? The cradle, the one that goes like this?" He made a rocking motion.

"Yes?"

"And there was a German placed inside it, and there were the Canadians passing by, who were moving down the line, no? Every one of them, as he passed, went like this"—Tommaso made a sideways blow with his fist—"and it went *darum, darum. Darum, darum.*"

"Really!"

"Yes. Across from the *marinai* [clubhouse] I remember it well. Them going by, with all their rifles, and this guys goes, boom! And it goes, *darum, darum. Darum, darum.* He didn't have any shoes."

"Didn't have shoes?"

"The German, no, because, uh. Eh! Even I swiped the shoes off a German. A dead German, no?"

Tommaso and Angelo had grown up in this ancient neighbourhood of fishing families. They told me stories of how they used to play here as kids. We stopped in front of San Tommaso cathedral and they pointed to where the signal tower had stood before the Germans blew it down (taking the dome of San Tommaso with it). Sometimes the navy sailors who were stationed in the tower would let the boys come up. The boys got to have a few drags of the sailors' cigarettes and enjoy the view through their binoculars. "You could see the sea, you could see the countryside, you could see everything." Continuing our walk, the men pointed out an area by the Orientale where the public gardens with exotic animals had been. As boys, they had tried to play with the monkeys, and had stolen fruit from the trees. During the war, one by one, all the animals disappeared. "People were hungry." Walking deeper into Terravecchia, we passed a house that they told me had been a brothel before the war. The neighbourhood boys used to try to peek inside. Continuing up the street towards the castle, we passed some of the places where their families had sheltered during the battle.

"And how does it feel to do these streets again?" I asked.

"Now, doing them, I feel more cheerful," Tommaso replied. "Because I'm telling the story. Tomorrow, for example, you'll tell it to another, and another tomorrow. It doesn't get forgotten."

"Hm."

"And for what the Canadians did, etcetera. Who lost their lives in order to save us, basically."

Adriano: 8 September. Fifteen. Eighty first air raid alarm. Here in Ortona. Radio London announces that the Italian government has signed an unconditional surrender. 10 September.

Me: Oh, you listened to—

Adriano: The radio.

Me: The radio from, from England?

Adriano: Eh.

Me: That was, maybe, a bit dangerous, no? If someone hears.

Adriano: Quietly, quietly, we listened. And this, I say it here. Quietly, quietly. Radio London. Look at this, eh? *(He points to the diary page on his lap.)* Looting at the port of Ortona. Tuesday the

> fourteenth, Germans machine gunning and throwing hand grenades have killed seven people, numerous wounded at the station. Because there was a riot.

For days prior to that German attack, there had been chaotic scenes at Ortona's train station and harbour. Italian soldiers who no longer wanted to fight were arriving and departing in haste, ditching their weapons and uniforms in fear of German reprisals following Italy's surrender to the Allies. Nine-year-old Tonino Catena watched it happen from his home on the Orientale overlooking the harbour. "The soldiers who found themselves in Ortona threw their weapons under the Orientale. Everything, the bayonets, all their things, they threw it all down there. So then, my brothers and I, we went to collect this stuff. And each of us took the bayonet that he liked the most."

"As toys?"

"To play. To play Zorro."

The boys hid their bayonets under their mattresses, as they knew their parents wouldn't approve.

The railway yards were crowded with abandoned military supply trains. Encouraged by Allied radio broadcasts, Ortonesi raided the trains and carried home food and clothing. The Germans had not yet occupied Ortona, but when a lone Italian soldier attacked a passing German convoy, killing two, the soldiers in the convoy went on a rampage. In addition to the seven civilians they killed in the harbour, the Germans shot more at random in the countryside as they continued on their way.

On September 24, the German 16th Panzer Division arrived in Ortona and took over its administration. Their task was to create defensive lines to halt the Allied advance. For this, they needed Italian labour. At first, they tried to enlist labour voluntarily and offered payment in return. However, they also threatened to execute anyone who had weapons and failed to hand them over. German fears of armed resistance were realized just over a week later when there was an uprising in Lanciano, fifteen kilometres south of Ortona. It took the Germans three days to defeat the Lanciano resistance, killing twenty-two. Fear and tension between occupiers and civilians increased further as the Germans began demolishing Ortona's harbour and all of its ships in order to deny that strategic resource to the Allies. Ortona's sea-faring men were forced to do the work of destroying their livelihoods. As the men engaged in passive resistance, the Germans began forcing them to work at gunpoint. The German 65th Infantry Division arrived, adding to the number of troops in town. Relations between Germans and Ortonesi became more acrimonious.

"AND THEN, WHAT WAS life in Ortona like under the Germans, when the German soldiers were here?"

At a kitchen table overlooking a garden patio, I interviewed Rosilda Giambuzzi, Tecla Garzarelli, and Rosilda's daughter, Viviana. Rosilda was nineteen years old in 1943. Tecla was twenty.

Tecla: Eh, imagine. It was the end of the world, because you couldn't come or go, everyone inside their houses, because they, as soon as they saw anyone, they took them. You could hardly go out.

Rosilda: But Tecla, now you're exaggerating.

(They argue briefly in local dialect that I don't understand.)

Rosilda: *(now speaking in Standard Italian)* Yes, we were on Costantinopoli, near the church of the Madonna. That's called Costantinopoli.

Me: Ah, the Church of Santa Maria. Okay.

Rosilda: And our property had an enclosure, it had an enclosure. And there was a girl who came running, running, she was the daughter of, of [?], she came, Oddio! Mamma! The screams, the screams that she made! Who knows what they had in mind, those soldiers, to run after her. So, Papa—

Viviana: But these were Germans, these ones?

Rosilda: Germans, they were. And Papa had made a hiding place, under, and they came and said hey, tell me what's under there! Only then, the Germans—

Tecla: Eh, when there were Germans in Ortona, you could hardly go out.

Rosilda: Eh, it was something.

Tecla: Everyone, everyone down in their hiding places, everyone.

Me: Because, because the Germans had said to—?

Tecla: In Ortona you couldn't even walk because it was all destroyed.

Viviana: But do you remember that they were bad, the Germans?

Tecla: Eh, bad.

Rosilda: But no, Tecla, to me they never . . .

Pressed for time and facing more passive resistance from the Ortonesi, the Germans began rounding up men and forcing them to work. They came for Tonino Catena's father.

"They were speaking German. I was a child. I understood '*raus*' [out]. That is, I understood, I knew, I heard that word, *raus, raus!* However, I didn't know the meaning. My brother, the second oldest, his name was Giovanni, he went under the mattress, took the bayonet, and he wanted to kill the German. And he ran after him. It was only my mother, by force, with her crying, her pleading, who managed to stop him . . . Twelve years old, so he was, and he wanted to kill this German. And he ran as far as San Tommaso, not bad, from, then, from where I lived up to San Tommaso."

"Your brother ran behind this German?"

"Yes. Eh, and my mother who was running behind him! Then this happened, that before arriving right in the middle of Piazza San Tommaso, my mother succeeded in stopping him. Because the Germans were taking all the prisoners into the church of San Tommaso."

"Inside the church?"

"Inside the church. It was a collection place. All the people swept up, all the men swept up, they could hardly put them, now there are sports grounds, but rather, they put them in the church. 'You stay here where we can see you well.' Because they needed the men to go to dig the trenches on the Sangro [River]."

> Adriano: The second [of] November the Germans order to leave the city. Everyone, that we had to go toward Pescara on foot. Everyone . . . Now, look at this. *(He points to a page of his diary.)* The second November, it begins with pencil. There's no more pen.

"I absolutely did not want to go toward Pescara."

Tommaso explained to me why his family chose to hide in Terravecchia, risking the wrath of the Germans.

"I wanted to stay here in my hometown (*mio paese*).[6] Because if we went up there, we'd always be in the middle of war, in the middle of war, in the middle of war. Whereas here, with the passing, the entrance of the Canadians, the Germans uh, were at Pescara, and we were free."

Tommaso's answer also explains why many of the Ortonesi who did flee into the countryside nevertheless stayed as close as possible to the front instead of going further north. They wanted the war to pass them; they figured it would come to them anyways; it was better to endure it closer to home.

"I CAN ONLY TELL you from the point of view of a five year old child."

When I interviewed Professor Antonio Falcone, he was a distinguished Ortona citizen: a former teacher and principal at the *liceo classico*, former city councillor, expert in Byzantine history, and founder of the local historical and archaeological association (*Associazione Archeologica Frentana*) whose name harkens back to the town's ancient Frentani roots.[7] In November 1943, the future professor was a small boy "who doesn't have reason, who doesn't have rationality." Antonio's family had been part of the Ortonesi exodus to the countryside. He remembered one time he was playing in the fields and suddenly there were planes (which he now knew must have been British) flying overhead. Anti-aircraft guns started shooting at them. He was excited to watch, and then angry when his parents forced him to get down into a trench.

"When I remember, it's like watching a movie, except that I know it was real."

One night a German soldier entered their house. It was cold out and the soldier wanted to warm up. He sat by the fire and put his machine gun down to rub his hands. Antonio noticed the look of pain in the German's face, probably (he now reasoned) from being cold. He didn't know why this man was dangerous, but he understood that there was danger because his grandmother held him tight and held his mouth. Years later, he learned that his uncle was an antifascist and that an escaped Italian soldier was also sheltering in their house.

Adriano: The seventh [of] December. Seven December, Tuesday 43. By now one can no longer go outside the house. The front is getting nearer. The Moro, the Moro River, eh? Has been crossed, but there is no precise news. We didn't have any precise news, because by then the radio, no one, uh—

Me: Oh, no one had—

Luisa: No one had it, nor lights.

Adriano: One couldn't cook.

Luisa: One could hardly even cook.

Canadian artillery was bombing the countryside, aiming at German defenses and supply lines.

Adriano: 13 December. We're going forward, eh? More terrible days. Intense fire on barricades. One no longer eats. The nights are passed sitting in a chair. Waiting for, waiting from one moment to the next for the arrival of the English.

Luisa: Always for the English. And instead thanks to the Canadians.

Adriano: But this hell, but this hell never ends. Hell, no? Never ends. Hours and days go by. 14 December, still bombardments, one can no longer stand—

Luisa: One couldn't stand it.

Nicola Bottega, one of the regulars at the *marinai* clubhouse, told me of his father's struggle to protect his family.

"My father with seven children, in open country, the shells were arriving continuously. From the Canadians, continuously! So he said, it's better to go home, more sheltered, than to stay here in the open air. We had made, I don't know, a shelter underground, but it wasn't a house. We went back to Ortona."

Adriano: The Canadians or English, I don't know. We didn't even know, but we thought. I don't know, have unleashed another storm of steel . . . It was close to us, the line, we hear one explosion after another around the house which shakes to its foundations. But it doesn't get hit. It seems protected by a mysterious hand. We start to pray again, entrusting to the spirit of God and to San Tommaso. While the children scream.

Luisa: From fear.

Adriano: Oh, something.

Luisa: Eh, it can't be described. I say, it can't be described.

Adriano: Hide, the children, hiding their faces in their mothers' breasts. It is a truly agonizing scene. Maybe this agony lasted three hours, but it seemed an eternity. At the end, our nervous system is really tested. We have reached a point of total exasperation. With the last shots fired, decisively and without reflecting on the great danger that we will face, on impulse, we put our sacks and bundles on our backs, and we exit, almost all of us going directly for Ortona.

Me: And you went right away to Terravecchia?

Adriano: No, no, right away to Terravecchia, no . . . Together with a group of families we went to the city hospital. But we were turned away by a nurse who told us it wasn't possible to enter, because there were already many hundreds of refugees inside . . . And then we hid, a crowd, by the bakery in the old part of the city. At the beginning of the old part. Which on one side faces the basilica of San Tommaso.

Luisa: On the square.

Adriano: On the square. And there we put blankets on the floor to sleep.

Nine-year-old Tonino Catena was now sheltering in the church of Ortona's cemetery. With his father taken away by the Germans, his twenty-three-year-old Uncle Guido was helping care for him, along with his mother and siblings. At the start of the war, Guido Grilli had been called up to serve in the navy. He was a hero to young Tonino. He'd survived the sinking of his ship by British warplanes, and after the armistice he'd made his way home.

When the front of the war arrived in Ortona, Guido had led his family to a villa near the cemetery where many others were taking shelter. When Germans found them and chased them out, the group of refugees crowded into the cemetery church. On December 20, as the cemetery came under Canadian artillery fire, some decided to go back to the villa, believing it would be safer. Guido advised against it and kept his family with the group that remained. The next day, after knocking first, the Germans blew up the villa, burying thirty-four people inside. Only one person made it out and called for help. Guido was one of three men in the church who answered the call, risking their lives by going outside and attempting a rescue. However, the Canadian bombardment was severe and unrelenting, and the rescuers had to give up and run back to the church without managing to free any survivors.

Guido kept a diary through these days. Tonino shared it with me. On December 23, Guido wrote:

> There were still three people alive, one of them a child who knew me. I comforted him and from under the rubble he begged for my help . . . There was nothing I could do because of the bombs and

because we were only three people. It would have been a huge job. We had to leave them to die. Poor Dodò. . . . I haven't slept at all. I spent the night crying . . . The bombardment continues here, also the crackling of machine guns but of the English you don't even see a shadow.

Luisa: In that bombardment, that's when I was wounded.

Me: Oh yes?

Luisa: The twenty-first of December.

Adriano: Ah, this, this morning, in the first hours of the morning, the, the day of San Tommaso, it was dedicated the Feast of San Tommaso eh?

Luisa: Eh, it was dedicated, I remember it perfectly!

Adriano: A mine exploded, it was a terrible moment. After that, there appeared before our eyes the terrible vision of the basilica in ruins. I was there in front of it. Now, when that mine brought down the whole church, that happened right where we were, it all entered inside, the noise. And I wrote two lines on it. *(He finds a page in his memoir and reads from it.)* 'The sky is just white and the enormous mass of the basilica can be clearly seen, torn in half. The dome with its stucco and coffered gilding looks like a giant pomegranate cut in half. Twenty-first of December! The day dedicated to the Feast of San Tommaso . . . I couldn't help but say a curse on the Germans.' *(He looks up from his book.)* I, for many years, I had a recurring dream.

Me: Yes?

Adriano: That recur. I was always dreaming of that moment. I had them for many years. Recurring dreams.

Me: Why do you think—?

Adriano: Recurring dreams. You understand, no?

Me: Uh huh.

Adriano: I had them for many years. I was always seeing it again. Because it was a terrifying spectacle. Then, you have to imagine all the stones with the dust that entered, because we were right there on Piazza San Tommaso, inside that.

Luisa: Facing the church.

Adriano: And there, then, on the rubble of San Tommaso, of the church, there was the machine gun nest. Of the Germans.

Luisa: Because that one went like uh, eh, and could see those who were coming from down there and—

Adriano: And they were shooting constantly towards where the post office is today. You know where the post office is, today?

Me: Mm hm.

Adriano: From there, they were shooting towards the post office, to prevent the advance of—

Luisa: The Canadians.

Adriano: The Canadians.

On the same feast day of San Tommaso, eleven-year-old Luisa di Luzio was wounded in the eye. Her family's house on via delle Speranze had been destroyed and they'd taken shelter with other families next door.

Me: How did it happen? You were at a window?

Luisa: No no no no no no. It was, a shell fragment made a trajectory that rebounded and came to me. And a good thing it didn't go straight at me.

Me: Oh, maybe it slowed down.

Luisa: Eh, eh, this rebound.

Me: And what, what, you were wounded, your parents helped you? What happened?

Luisa: Yes, it was crowded with people.

Me: But there was nothing could be done, or someone did something?

Luisa: Eh, we put something on it. Then when the Canadians arrived, they treated it.

"The bombs were coming down like crazy."

Angelo Tenisci's family had returned to Ortona from the countryside but hadn't made it to their house because bombs had started falling all around them.

"And so we were forced to stop there, at that door, that first one that we found, the first house that we found."

They sheltered there with three other families. They broke interior walls to make it easier to manoeuvre and avoid going near the windows. Their little compound surrounded a courtyard with a cistern.

"And this German came to get water. He came to get water, we were always inside the court, inside the houses, no? And meanwhile, eh, he came to get water, we asked him, where is the front? And he, this one here, said twenty metres, forty metres away. That it was, on the street . . . And so this one here, he had a machine gun on top of a pile of earth, a pile of uh . . . Eh, he, this one here came quite a few times, I knew him because he came to get water."

Angelo's friend Giordano Angelone was with him in that house. Giordano also remembered a German who came to them for water.

"He came banging on the door . . . A young German. He came banging, he wanted a bit of water. I gave it to him. We gave it to him . . . He gave his thanks in some way, and we didn't see him again. Then they saw him. Dead bodies. They saw him, he had fallen, he was wounded, further up the street. You see that immediately after, following this bombardment, this youth left an impression on us because he was very young. He was sixteen, eighteen years old. . . . That left an impression on me . . . Because that one there, he was, he too was afraid, him. When he came to ask for water, he asked as if he wanted something more. We didn't understand, but maybe he wanted to be, who knows, he wanted uh, he wanted to be given shelter inside. What do I know? He wanted water, and we gave him water. But he was frightened, the thing that left an impression on me, because, a youth, truly frightened, frightened of the war."

"And you felt afraid too."

"Yes, yes, yes. Of course."

On the southern outskirts of Ortona, fifteen-year-old Anna (name changed) was hiding in caves among the orchards that the Loyal Edmonton Regiment was advancing through.

"You could see the flames, the fires, and so, we saw this in the countryside. And, nothing, these Canadians weren't arriving. Thus, we were really worried, unhappy. Such that, the twenty-first of December, word circulated that, Oh! Canadians have arrived, entered, there's no more shooting! We came out of these caves, and we met one of these Canadians, a certain, little boys really. Shy, very, uh, polite, they were even afraid to greet us."

"Really?"

"Yes! Very uh, maybe they felt embarrassed because, look how they arranged a fine disaster, both the Germans and the Canadians."

Anna wasn't alone in holding the Canadians partly or even equally responsible for the disaster that was befalling Ortona and its people. Uncle Guido wrote in his diary on Christmas Day:

> Ortona has become a pile of rubble; Germans and English are crumbling it. Now it seems they have it in for the cemetery. You can see they want to bring the church down to the ground. Wrath and terror reign everywhere. We are at the end of our tether, it's not possible to go out for anything because they're constantly shooting. It's the end of the world and the worst is that you don't see the end of it.

"I witnessed many unpleasant things."

When I interviewed Stefano Durante, he was an accomplished sculptor; among other things, he had contributed to the restoration of San Tommaso cathedral. On Christmas Day in 1943, Stefano was a boy among the hundred or so refugees inside Ortona's hospital. He saw what happened to the horse and its owner.

"On the piazza we saw a horse that was wandering about . . . This horse was taken by the Germans to do their business. Except that this horse freed itself, and wandered around in the piazza. In the midst of us was the owner of this horse, whose name was Alfredo Ciampoli. He started to shout, to call the horse in a loud voice. And then, what happened? From the windows of the hospital the Germans machine-gunned the horse and the owner."

"Why?"

"Eh, *boh* (dunno)."

"Why? They weren't doing anything."

"Eh, *boh*."

Stefano's manner suggested it was pointless to ask. He continued:

"One evening the Germans came and lined up all the girls. The prettiest. And they took them away. Outside. And the girls returned after a few hours. However, no one knows what happened. And then, the day before Christmas a tank placed itself in front of the hospital. There was some, some, let's say, some shelling. And inside a room, there were twelve people. They all died." A German soldier called on Stefano to help move the survivors, but little could be done to comfort them. "We didn't have anything to eat. We didn't even have anything to drink . . . We even had lice."

It was Christmas Day when he first saw Canadian soldiers. Two of them entered the hospital to "liberate us." People started to cheer: "Viva the English!" This drew the attention of the Germans, including an Italian fascist soldier who was fighting alongside them.[8] "They shot down the corridor, and a Canadian died, while a civilian was gravely wounded. The Canadian died of, of, he died, in fact then we put him on a cot, no? A little bed. And I saw that blood was coming out, below. Then, we covered him with a sheet."

The other Canadian had escaped being hit by the German fire. Stefano didn't remember what happened to him, but the hospital's doctor, Carlo Bernabeo, wrote in his memoir:

> The situation of the surviving Canadian was very dangerous. He had to be saved. He was stripped in a hurry, a bed was prepared for him in the place where the wounded lay, and he was bundled up to make him look like one of them.[9]

The Germans came and demanded to know where the other Canadians were hiding. Nobody answered. The Germans took two civilian men hostage and threatened to shoot them, but when the men were left unattended for a moment, they managed to escape. Later that night, the hidden Canadian also managed to get away undetected.

> In leaving, he promised to make his superiors aware of the tragic situation of the civilians . . . The Canadian kept his promise. The morning of the 26th, contrary to usual, silence reigned in the piazza: no cannon fire . . . The tanks were in their usual position, but instead of shooting, they were making signals. The people were invited to leave their refuge and go towards them. A few minutes passed, then a mass of people were seen running out of the hospital. Old people, women, infants, wounded, nursing sisters had found within themselves a miraculous energy. Faces pale and emaciated by hunger, eyes dilated by martyrdom, faces blackened by smoke and dirt, tattered clothes that showed bloodied flesh, heads bandaged in white, ran across the 200 metres jumping over every obstacle.[10]

Around this time, in the house on via delle Speranze just a few blocks away, Luisa learned that her father had been killed.

> Luisa: He couldn't be found. Is Pasquale here, is Pasquale over there?
> Adriano: No one found him, because he'd gone upstairs . . .
> Luisa: Three days later. The Canadians arrived. Three days later. Because the twenty-first, and the evening of the twenty-fourth, they took that house. . . . Then when they arrived on the evening of the twenty-fourth, in that house, eh, they went up, to a balcony, to see what the situation was. And they found my father there, dead . . .
> Me: But for what reason did someone shoot—?

Adriano: Maybe he [the shooter] thought, who knows, maybe this could be an Englishman, could be a Canadian, could be a spy, I don't know.

Luisa: I don't know. In time of war—

Adriano: In time of war.

Luisa: One becomes worse than an animal.

Adriano: I, when they did the reconditioning of the, uh, of the bones, I was there. That, that hole in the head was still there, on the skeleton.

It wasn't clear to me how Luisa and Adriano could know that it was a German who shot her father. Could it not equally have been a Canadian who mistook him for a German or shot instinctively at him when he moved near a window? Telling a similar story, Rosilda and Tecla revealed how hard it was to know anyone's responsibility.

Tecla: My uncle died. The poor man, he went outside to do something.

Rosilda: Which one?

(They exchange some words that I don't understand.)

Tecla: *(to me)* The brother of my mother. And so, they hit him, they machine gunned him. And after a little while, he died.

Viviana: Madonna! This—

Me: Who, who machine gunned him?

Rosilda: Who? The Germans?

Me: The Canadians?

Tecla: The Canadians.

Rosilda: Canadians.

Tecla: Yes.

Me: They machine-gunned him?

Tecla: Eh, they machine-gunned him.

Me: Why?

Tecla: Well, if it was Canadians, Germans, who knows.

Viviana: *(to me)* No, she doesn't know.

Tecla: No. How are you going to know? But then, they were gunning down everyone. If they saw someone, they machine-gunned, there you go. And so, you couldn't go out at all. Those poor souls that had to go outside, it was for something they had to do.

"I knew him because he came to get water."

Angelo Tenisci was telling me the story of the young German soldier.

"However, a shot from a machine gun got him in the head. So the Germans put him on a door and they took him to us. Where we were."

"On a door, that is, they took a door like a bed?"

"Well yes, the doors were all broken, they were all open, they took a door because, uh—"

"He, he was still alive?"

"Yes, yes, yes, he was alive. . . . I talked, we talked to him quite a bit, also Giordano and the others . . . He, but he only complained, he only said 'oh, oh, oh, oh.' We say, 'oh', but we didn't know what he was saying. He only said 'ah, ah, ah,' eh. Because, he knew how he was."

"Hm."

"Now let's say it, eh? When someone is wounded, someone is uh, in that condition, what could you say . . ."

At this point, without any change in Angelo's demeanour, the coherence of his narrative started breaking down.

"I just told him, yes, you're alright, you're doing well, you're alright, it's nothing. But still . . . When the Canadians came, when they came, we called the Canadians. The first two Canadians that we saw, we called them and uh, and uh, and uh, and we told them that, the German, that a soldier was with us. So, another Canadian came, with the red cross, and they took him and carried him away. And they took him, I don't know if he's dead, if he's alive, because they got him in the head . . . However, after two days, after two days, two Germans came. Two Germans, to the courtyard. From the courtyard, they came, and they wanted to retrieve, the uh Cana—, the German. The soldier. They wanted to know where the German was. And we said uh, eh, they went away, the Canadians took him. Meanwhile, so, they, they went away. They went away, because, this one, he was always going through the courtyard. And they threw some bombs, some hand grenades. That, there, Angelone was wounded."

He was referring to his friend Giordano. Shortly after the Germans who'd come for their wounded comrade had gone away, a blast struck the compound, badly wounding Giordano in his eye. When the battle was over, the Canadians sent Giordano to an Allied hospital further south where he was given surgery and an implant. For the rest of his life, he'd had what he described to me as "basically a glass eye."

"We were drawing water," Giordano told me. "Me and a friend of mine who came to help. Then a bomb exploded . . . and a fragment wounded my right eye. And I was taken inside . . ."

"It was a German soldier who threw the bomb?"

"We think so, but we're not sure, understand? No, we're not sure . . . We think, we thought, because we hardly saw anything. We think so . . . This happened the twenty-fourth of December, is when this thing happened. After two days, there were Germans on our, the Germans were there, on the street where we were. Then, at a certain point the Canadians arrived. And the Germans went away. The first treatment I got, from the Canadians. During the night, the Germans came back again . . . Eh, it was, because here, the front, one night was, *Oh!* The day later, *liberated!* And then, *Oh!* [Control of the house kept changing hands] For two or three times . . . One of these Germans came close to me, and he saw the bandage that the Canadians had made. It was a particular brown colour, the gauze. He said, 'Ah! Canadian! Canadian!' That one pointed his pistol here, to say that—"

"He pointed his pistol?"

"He pointed it here."

"He was angry?"

"Angry because I had been treated by a Canadian. Who knows. Even he was just a boy. Eh. I was frightened. My mother said, 'What do you want?' He didn't want anything. He didn't want to do anything. He was just angry because he saw the bandage, understand? And then, during the night, the Canadians came back again . . ."

Adriano: I didn't include it here [in the book]. Once, when we were at that bakery, there, in Terravecchia, where we were until the twenty-sixth, there entered one of those who were at that machine gun at San Tommaso. He entered because, this one here, he almost didn't have any shoes left. They were worn out. You could see that they were really in dire straits. He pointed the barrel of his machine gun at my stomach.

Luisa: Why didn't you write that?

Adriano: I don't know why I didn't write it.

Me: He pointed his—

Adriano: At me, yes, at me. But like this.

Me: Why?

Luisa: He wanted his shoes.

Adriano: He wanted my shoes. He saw that his, that my shoes didn't fit him, and he went away. That, I don't know why I left it out. Eh, many things left.

Luisa: Eh, who knows how many things.

In his book, Adriano described what he saw in those days when he looked outside from the bakery:

> Meanwhile the Germans on the rubble of San Tommaso continue to shoot and the Canadians, just a few tens of metres from them, behind the rubble of Corso Matteotti . . . From the windows of the top floor you can see the piazza below; what a macabre spectacle! Rubble, rubble, countless bullet casings scattered everywhere, hidden German soldiers shooting machine guns. In front of us is the Corso cinema with its doors wide open and in the small lobby you can clearly see the movie posters waving in the wind. . . . I will never forget that. Maybe because it's like an image of something still living in a dead square, in a dead city in front of the dead.

Meanwhile, the cemetery had been under constant bombardment for days. Inside the church, babies were crying in hunger, children were covered in lice, and there was an unbearable stench from the growing pile of waste in the corner by the altar where it had been agreed that everyone should do their business. Suddenly a woman screamed that her husband, who had been sleeping while seated next to her, was dead. She jumped up and his body toppled over. Scared by the dead body, Tonino and his siblings ran to the opposite side of the church. Writing in his diary, Guido vented his anger and fear.

> Here it's always the same story: they're here, they're near and sadly we never see them.
>
> It is literally sickening. So many English who are scared of four Germans and they don't know how to do anything but fire bombs from morning until night.
>
> This continuous bombardment is intolerable; if Ortona were Stalingrad, it wouldn't be the same.
>
> To think that they only needed thirty-eight days to take Sicily, in Ortona already twenty-five days have passed and they still don't manage to occupy it.
>
> Just yesterday there's been a good twenty hours of bombardment.

In Terravecchia, as the Canadians advanced, the Germans began chasing any Ortonesi they found on their side of the line away from the front and towards the castle. In my walking tour with Tommaso and Angelo, we retraced the route that Tommaso's family took when the Germans forced them to move.

"What did the Germans say when they came to the house?"

"They knocked on the door, he spoke in German, uh. Then he made it understood. 'Pescara! Pescara!' He didn't speak Italian, no? That I have to go to Pescara, Pescara, Pescara. Understood? So, and we uh, *beh*, alright."

"Did you have time to take anything?"

"A few little things. From here, when we ran away from here, we had uh, we were boiling some beans in this thing. We ran away, my mother carried this pot with the beans that was still going *blub-blub-blub-blub*."

"Yes? On the street?"

"Eh, it's a shame to throw away, no?"

The Germans led the family to a house very close to their headquarters.

"And the last German headquarters was here, on this corner. Now I'll show you."

"And you saw it?"

"Yes. There was a radio and everyone inside."

"But this was dangerous, then, because if the Germans see that you are—"

"No, there were, there was, the officer, it seems, the way he behaved, that he couldn't really be a German. He must be an Austrian. Understand? Austrian. However, dressed like a German, he was with the Germans, no? Because he was kind, he wasn't bad, he wasn't really, understand?"

"Why? What did he do?"

"He wasn't bad. He entered. He didn't want the door to be closed. That one there. He entered, at night, he entered gently. Over there, there's another window that looks onto the castle on the other side. So he went to the window, looked if he could see any movement, anything. And he turned around and closed the door. This one time, he went to get a mattress, he brought it and put it on the floor for the children. My little sisters who slept on the floor, no? There wasn't anything. This one, there were all these acts of kindness, I understood that this one here is for sure an Austrian."

Adriano's family were also chased from the bakery at San Tommaso to a house by the castle.

Me: When you arrived at the end, at Vicolo San Domenico, first there were German soldiers who were more aggressive, more—

Adriano: Yes, aggressive.

Me: But then, you wrote, at—

Adriano: At a certain moment.

Me: At a certain moment.

Adriano: They gave us over to another patrol that seemed to us more humane. We thought maybe they aren't Germans. Maybe they're Polish.

Luisa: Austrian.

Adriano: Aus—, Austrian.

Me: Yes, I wanted to ask about this.

Adriano: They told us, see, here you'll be safe . . . They started to talk. They gave chocolate to the children. They seemed, and we said, but these are Austrians. Because Austrians, you know uh. It's another race. Needless to say. They're just better natured. And he started to, since there was one of us who had been to work in Germany and knew a bit of German, so this fellow told us [translating for the 'Austrian'], he says do you hear the noise of those guns? This, now, he says, we will make another, a great offensive and we'll chase the English. We'll chase them all the way to Sicily. And we said, Madonna!

Luisa: Eh!

Me: He was so—

Luisa: Enthusiastic.

Me: So sure of himself! But at the same time he wasn't aggressive?

Adriano: No, no, these weren't aggressive. Not these last ones that we had. No no no no.

Me: It's interesting because also Signor Sorino remembers the German officer in that alleyway and also he told me that he seemed perhaps to be an Austrian.

Adriano: You see!

Luisa: Ah, you see!

Adriano: How it connects!

During the night of the twenty-seventh, it became strangely quiet around the castle. Adriano wrote in his memoir:

> In the air it feels that we're on the eve of something. Eve of liberation or of death, I don't know. But death doesn't frighten us, by now we're indifferent, dying tomorrow has no meaning . . . Bit by bit the silence returns, terrible, anguished silence. Every little sound in the street makes your heart skip a beat. There's no more shooting, there's only silence. But in the middle of the night we hear many footsteps of German soldiers passing in front of our door, noises of metal tools, a commotion that is not easy to identify. One of these soldiers gives a hard kick on our door. We all wince, almost stop breathing. What's happening or is about to happen? Then we no longer hear anything, no noise, absolute silence. Anxious hours pass in that night that never finishes. For us will there be another day?

When the dawn came, it was still quiet.

In the cemetery, Uncle Guido didn't want to believe it. He took the risk of climbing up to look out through a hole in the roof.

> I didn't believe it so I wanted to make sure so I climbed up to the ceiling of the church and I saw: a soldier with a saucepan and khaki uniform. It's them.
>
> When I came down they [the refugees in the church] were all hanging on my every word. I didn't know what to say because a lump of tears was tightening in my throat. I hugged my mother tightly.
>
> Everyone understood and rushed out waving handkerchiefs and

> rags at the CANADIANS who were coming to liberate us while I finally let out the tears that had been in my throat for days.

After putting Canadians in all caps, Guido wrote no more about them.

It was probably hard for him to reconcile his feelings. In his own words, the Canadians had "liberated" him.

But, like the "English," they had also recently been his enemies—part of the same Allied force that had nearly killed him twice: first when they sank his ship, and again when they came to his hometown and turned it (needlessly, in Guido's view) into a little Stalingrad.

The next thing Guido wrote in his diary was that he finally got to smoke a cigarette. Notably, he didn't mention that he got it from a Canadian. That detail comes from his nephew Tonino's memoir, written about fifty years later.

> How different they are from Germans! They also look around warily, but they don't kick or shout orders, and their weapons are levelled but not at us.
>
> Some of them get a pat on the back, some of us get a cigarette.
>
> 'You English?' asks Grampa Rocco.
>
> 'No, Canadian' is the answer, while they point to a badge that is sewn on the sleeves of their jackets.

When Tonino gave me a copy of his memoir, he signed the title page: "To Ian Cosh, and for him and all Canadians with gratitude and appreciation."

> Me: What did you write for the twenty-eighth?
>
> Adriano: The twenty-eighth?
>
> Me: That day.

Adriano: *(reading from his book)* We wake up. The Germans are gone. Later, the Canadian patrols arrive. They were Canadian. One helps—*(suddenly he stands up from his chair, shaking and sobbing)*

Me: Yes, it remains a moment.

Luisa: They are terrible moments. People don't believe it.

Adriano: *(gradually composing himself)* Because, in that, in that moment, we were saved. Because if it goes on any longer, they would have wiped everything out with the artillery. They would have retreated, the troops, to bomb the last part of Ortona.[11] And we would all have died, the twenty-eighth December. And then I describe the twenty-eighth December, as I saw it, how I—*(still standing, he picks up his book)*

Me: And you, you saw from the window? How—

Adriano: When they arrived?

Me: Because you were in a house full of people?

Adriano: No, a house, the ground floor, I, the ground floor, no? Because then, there were others who, you couldn't hear a thing, and now, facing the door next to us, who's there?

Luisa: The Germans.

Adriano: The Germans. But instead, on that morning, there was no one. And so they went towards the Orientale, that part by the sea, there. Went there, oh, they said, they came back, the Canadians are on the Orientale! How are they coming? Here, they're arriving. And here we went in front of the door to see how they were arriving. In front of the door.

Me: And when they arrived, was it quiet?

Adriano: Yes, silence.

Luisa: Indeed, they showed you that finger.

Adriano: Yes, because there was someone who started to applaud, to this one. But he made this—*(puts his index finger to his lips)*—to be quiet, because they were afraid that there were still Germans up at the castle. So, right in front of us, for a little while, with the rifles. When they, then the signaller arrived. The signaller announced that, uh—

Luisa: That Ortona was taken.

Adriano: *(sitting down and reading from his book)* But here they come, a patrol in single file coming down the steps of Vicolo San Domenico advancing slowly along the wall until reaching our door in sight of the castle. Some refugees begin to applaud but are silenced for fear that the Germans might still be in the vicinity. The Canadians themselves wave their hands to keep quiet. Still in single file, they stop now in front of us holding rifles in their arms, they smile at us, we look at them, we almost want to touch them—*(he breaks down in tears and stops reading)*

In his memoir, Tonino described how he and the other refugees left the cemetery church:

> The Canadians make us exit through a window at the back of the building under which they have placed a chair to make it easier for old people to exit . . .
>
> What we thought was the sound made by the waves against the rocks down by the sea, is nothing other than the quiet hum of the engines of a column of tanks stationed along the road . . . Soldiers emerge from the open hatches with radio headphones on their ears and look at us with a look full of compassion.

> Unknown hands emerge from the portholes and offer us chocolate bars, biscuits, cigarettes and a few packets of bandages for dressings.

Guido wrote:

> Along the streets of Ortona it's a massacre, everywhere there are dead Canadians, dead Germans still with weapons in their hands; civilian dead with bundles of rags in their shriveled arms.

THE ORTONESI HAD VIVID memories of the end of the battle. The Canadian veterans whom I interviewed barely remembered the end.

"How did you feel when the battle was over?"

Bill thought for a moment.

"Well, of course I had to feel better all right."

Bill's answer seemed like no more than a guess. Denis made it clear that he was only guessing.

"Do you remember what happened when the battle was finished and how you heard the news?"

"No I don't. Not specifically. No. I guess we did. I guess we did. We knew the town was taken. So it was a case of uh, counting up the losses, and consolidating, and finding out what uh, the equipment you needed . . ."

As David said, "We were so frazzled at the end of the battle, from overtiredness." And the immediate "rest" period for the Canadians was taken up with gathering, transporting, and burying the dead—their own, the civilians, and the Germans. Jack remembered this detail about the work.

"When we were getting the bodies all ready, you took a fifteen hundred weight. And we're putting the guys on, and they kept slippin' off. So some young farm kid said, 'You know when I was putting bundles on the rack,' he said, 'we put three that way and three this way and three that way.' And we did this. And here the guys are standing back patting themselves on the back and sayin' oh we did a really good—you know? These are bodies you're working with. That's how you can become, you know? That uh, they're congratulating themselves on how do you stack bodies on the car, that they won't fall off, you know?"

In addition to whatever state the Canadians' minds were in after seven days of continuous fighting and little sleep, this work on the dead might explain why the veterans had so little to say about the end. More detail on the battle's immediate aftermath is found in testimonies from soldiers who arrived in Ortona with fresh eyes and minds.

A. Staples, letter to Reginald Roy, August 10th, 1967

> I arrived in Ortona, as a reinforcement to the Seaforths from the Canadian Scottish, just as the Germans were pulling out and my two most vivid memories are being scared silly by my first taste of shelling and appalled by the civilian dead and the devastation of this once beautiful city . . . Thinking back over those days I can still remember the overwhelming sense of sadness at the short burial service a day or two after the battle. The service was held on a small level patch of ground high above the Adriatic and the lament fading slowly over the water emphasized the finality of it all.

Charles Monroe Johnson, Action With the Seaforths

It was the last day of 1943 when we marched into Ortona . . . After putting my junk in the old room where we were to sleep, I went out with Fein to find mattresses . . .

We stepped over the body of a male Italian whose body had been flattened like a pancake by the track of a heavy tank. Just inside the main hospital door, which had been strongly sandbagged, lay two Jerries, one with his head blown off, the other minus an arm and shoulder. Evidently one of our tanks had beaten the bazooka-men to the draw. Drawn snugly against the wall of the hospital was a German Panther tank, a gaping hole in its turret . . . One German must have foreseen the end, for his blasted body was sprawled half out of the turret opening. Blood had dripped and frozen in his matted blond hair. I walked down an inside corridor, we saw more Jerry bodies in the enclosed garden . . .

Entering a large, dim room we managed to see two mattresses among the mass of junk . . . Fein and I picked up two mattresses, put our backs to them, and began to drag them into the corridor . . . Fein, who had preceded me, dropped his mattress in the hallway and shouted, 'What've you got there?' 'What do you think it is?' I sarcastically retorted . . . 'No, look on the mattress.' Looking, I saw a gnarled old woman, whose bare legs showed gangrenous sores. A shiver ran up my spine. I began spitting. 'Let's get out of here. I'll find a mattress somewhere else.'

As soon as they learned the battle was over, the family of five-year-old Professor Falcone came back into Ortona from the countryside. He remembered seeing an eyeball stuck to a wall. He couldn't even say if it had frightened him; as he'd told me earlier, it all felt strangely unreal, like scenes from a film. But he did know for sure that he was hungry. He saw two Canadian soldiers eating. One of them noticed him watching them. That one reached into his jacket pocket, removed something, and gave it to the boy. Professor Falcone didn't know at the time what it was, but now he figured it must have been chocolate.

Nicola Del Ciotto told a similar story.

"By the side of the house, there was a Sherman, a tank, a tank that had cut down all of our houses that were before it, reduced them all to pieces. Eh, war is war. And I was a little boy. There was a soldier who, the first thing he does on seeing me, he says 'Hello boy,' and he gives me some kind of a brick, shaped like this. And, what, I look to my mother, 'Ma?' Little boy, eh. 'Ma, that man there gave me this, what is it?' And my mother says 'Eat! Eat! It's good!' It was a chocolate bar. . . . And it left me, it left me perplexed. But these, being used to seeing that other kind of warrior [the Germans], these [Canadians] were people who, you say, how do they fight, really? So relaxed. They were playing cards, in a normal way . . . They fought the war, but they weren't warriors. They fought war because they had to do it . . . There wasn't that cruelty."

Viviana: And you never talked to the Canadians?

Rosilda: No, no, no. However, Papa talked a bit, you know.

Viviana: You kept yourselves hidden.

Rosilda: Eh, hidden.

Me: Because you were also afraid of the Canadians?

Rosilda: Eh, the Canadians, yes, but there was never any, uh—

Tecla: But the Canadians, it's not that they ever did, uh, almost nothing really.

Rosilda: Yes. They had fun, they—

Tecla: They took liberties, certainly. However—

Viviana: What did they do?

Rosilda: What, what, there were Canadians, and also a few girls, who then, I didn't see any more, I don't know.

Viviana: They had fun.

Rosilda: Eh, there was the, the—

Tecla: Eh, there was—

Rosilda: There was—

Tecla: However out of hunger, in order to eat—

Viviana: But still they wanted to do it, it's not that—

Rosilda: No, no, polite enough, they were polite, it's not that, it's not that that happened to us.

Viviana: Who knows. They were polite.

Rosilda: Yes, yes, yes. No. That's war . . .

Viviana: But they stole a lot.

Tecla: Eh.

Rosilda: Eh, I know.

(Rosilda and Tecla discuss something in dialect.)

Tecla: *(switching back to Standard Italian)* A suitcase of gold.

Viviana: Who had a suitcase of gold?

Tecla: Eh, a case full of gold!

Viviana: But who took it, soldiers?

Tecla: Eh, they stole it. What do I know?

Rosilda: They say, they say.

Tecla: The people who were in Ortona say that they stole a lot. Of things, you understand? Because, no one saw, no one heard, uh—

Viviana: But, this, we don't know, was it the soldiers, or—

Tecla: Eh, we don't know if it was the soldiers or the civilians.

Viviana: Or the Ortonesi who had remained here.

Tecla: There were also civilians.

Rosilda: Eh. The soldier, who knows, maybe he was looking for money.

At the Salesian compound, I got two opposing points of view on the Canadians' behaviour after battle. One was from an older priest. One day, while we were chatting on a bench outside the youth centre, he told me that the Canadians were worse than the Germans. He hadn't experienced it; his opinion came from his uncle, who had said he had to beat Canadian soldiers away to protect his daughters. According to him, the Germans never threatened any women or stole anything.

That priest's story echoed many remarks that I heard from Ortonesi about Canadians getting drunk and unruly. Once, while chatting with Maria, the lead cook in the Salesian kitchen, I brought up the topic.

"I've heard that sometimes the Canadians got drunk and made trouble."

Maria was chopping rapini on the cutting board. She paused to look up at me and shrugged with her hands.

"The Canadians were men. They did things men do."

She went back to chopping.

"The Germans were evil. There's no comparison."

Me: When you walk in the streets of Ortona—

Luisa: Eh, I remember.

Me: Do you still see—

Luisa: For example, I remember here, there was the German who shot Papa. I remember. I see it again. Every time I pass that spot I say an Ave for the martyrs.

Even among the Ortonesi who regarded the Canadians as liberators and the Germans as cruel and evil, there were many who nevertheless had paid their respects to both Canadian and German dead. Stefano Durante told me: "The cemetery of Ortona kept a zone all for the Germans. There was a cemetery for the Germans. However—"

"Oh really! I've never heard this."

"Yes. Then, they came, they came to take them back. Ten years later . . . But the zone, it was called the German zone, but they came to take them back, the bones, and they took them back to Germany."[12]

"And before that, how was the behaviour of the Ortonesi towards this German cemetery?"

"I saw that the Ortonesi certainly uh, the Ortonesi aren't mean. They hardly speak the language, but they aren't mean-spirited. I saw that also, on the second of November, the Day of the Dead, on a few Germans there were some flowers."

I asked Angelo about this. He was strongly antifascist. Didn't it bother him when those Germans were buried in the people's cemetery?

"*Beh,* no, it was, well, they were dead, those, you could hardly say, you are a German, you are a Canadian, I am an Italian, no. The dead are dead, what can you say? You say peace to, to his soul. You say peace to his soul. What can you say? The dead are dead."

"I remember that mamma used to put flowers," Tonino told me. "My mother had one or, that is, two or three sons, how is it, uh, adopted sons. Canadians. She used to go and put flowers every, every, before this permanent custodian [of the Moro River Canadian War Cemetery] came, no? And she would go there, and—"

"How come?"

"It was an act of gratitude."

"These were Canadians that your mother knew before?"

"No, no."

"How did she choose these three Canadians?"

"Without choosing. By chance. Two or three, I don't remember very well now. She would go every week, she would take some flowers. And then she'd go also to the cemetery of Ortona, and where out of pity someone would put a flower there too, on the Germans."

"On the Germans?"

"Yes, yes."

"Your mother did that?"

"Eh, I think so, my mother, yes. I think that it was done, that it was done also by other women, because, for the dead there's no uh, you have to respect the dead, regardless. I don't think there was resentment against these poor souls."

The dead were dead. But Nicola Bottega insisted that their deaths had very different meanings.

"Here in Ortona there's a cemetery. You've seen it, no? More than 1,500 boys." He was referring to the Moro River Canadian War Cemetery. "There are some, eighteen, nineteen years old. And they died, for what? Did they not die for us? For what?"

"I don't know what to say."

"Eh, for us! No, no, no, for us, those boys died to save us!"

In his study, Professor Falcone described his lifelong positive image of Canadians. He had a theory as to how it had been etched in his mind.

"I have always had a very positive memory of the Canadians. Because they helped. Imagine you're living through so much suffering and destruction. Then it ends—and who do you see? It's a Canadian. People remember who helps."

Whenever he visited the Canadian cemetery, he pondered how fate had brought those men to this place. For him, this was home. But what was it to them?

"And now you are here," he said. "The ancient Greeks might have said you have *come back*. They were fascinated with the idea of The Return."

His philosophical attitude gave me the courage to share a thought that had been growing in my mind throughout my time in the town. I hadn't voiced it to anyone else—not wanting to stir controversy or cause hurt feelings.

"When I talk with a Canadian veteran," I said, in my uncertain Italian, the singular coming to me more easily in that moment, "I don't have the impression that he was thinking of liberating anyone. He barely even remembers seeing civilians in Ortona. I don't think he would recognize himself in the way he is remembered here."

The professor listened intently. He nodded when I was done, and a slight smile crossed his face.

"The Canadian," he said, "was the protagonist of a story he didn't know."

(Anonymously published in La Ronda Ortonese, January 1947.)

This is a gray morning, December 28, 1943.

But even through the thick blanket of clouds, a few timid rays of sunshine filter through, occasionally gilding the whitened piles of rubble. During the night, the Germans committed their last act of barbarity, destroying many houses with TNT; then they silently leave. They retreat.

The area is free of the Teutonic soldiery but not yet reached by the British 8th Army. There is a mixture of relief and fear in the air, on this cold December morning. Relief for the end of the nightmare and fear that they will return. Disparate conversations criss-cross each other, in the heavy air of the mill, under whose sturdy vaults hundreds of people from all social classes find refuge . . .

'They are coming . . . they are not coming . . . the Germans are coming back . . .!' These phrases can be heard . . .

The now familiar voice of the cannon is not heard; every now and then, carried by the wind, the chatter of some machine guns can be heard in the distance.

This silence heightens the anxiety of waiting and keeps the minds disoriented.

Some young people get tired of waiting and decide to go to Ortona in search of news. They set off . . . and a few minutes later we see them returning in the company of three soldiers with strange helmets, elegant in their khaki uniforms, with a look in their eyes that has nothing in common with the look that flashes from the cold and ferocious pupils of the descendants of the Goths.

A moment of amazed silence . . . then a frenetic explosion of joy; waving of handkerchiefs, rushing of men, women, children, old people, out of their dens, smelly, out, into the open air that fills the lungs, hugs, tears . . .; the sun shines in everyone's eyes, the most beautiful sun, the sun of freedom.

A little girl, daughter of a farmer who had been in America, approaches the Canadian corporal who commands the patrol and says to him, enunciating the syllables well: 'You are welcome, liberator!'

The corporal smiles, gives the little girl a caress and a candy while a tear appears in his eye.

I would give a little of my life to relive this moment, even in a dream.

Diary 28 - 12 - 43

IT WAS ONE OF my last days in Ortona. In the central square, a political rally was underway. Elections were coming soon to determine the regional governments across Italy. In front of the municipal building, the Alleanza Nazionale had set up a stage with towering speakers and a sea of party flags. Mayor Puletti was addressing the crowd. As I walked down the Corso toward the rally, Angelo was coming up the street, on his way to pick up his grandkids as usual. As we passed, he gestured over his shoulder. "Everyone here is tired of this guy."

Inside the *marinai* clubhouse, Tommaso was waiting for me. He had laid out all of the war souvenirs they kept in storage, spreading them across two long tables. There were black-and-white photographs of Ortona in ruins, twisted shards of bombs, German and Canadian helmets, and stacks of old newspapers and books. We sat down, and he began telling me stories. "In this photo here, you see the body that soldier is looking at? That was one of the prostitutes. Remember on our walk, I showed you . . ."

Nicola Bottega stood in the open doorway, smoking a cigarette and watching the rally. The speeches kept growing louder, as if the organizers were cranking up the volume. To keep telling me his stories, Tommaso had to raise his voice more and more.

Finally, Tommaso thumped the table with his fist.

"*O!* Who's yelling out there!?"

Nicola turned around. With a grim look, he waved his cigarette hand at the souvenirs.

"The ones who caused all this misery."

Me: Do you think an experience like this, that it has changed your character?

Luisa: I think so. I think so.

Me: That's different from the others who haven't had this experience?

Luisa: No, no, it's different. It's a thing that everyone carries, a baggage, that everyone carries inside. But since no one understands it, everyone closes up, and never talks about it. The experience, when it's so tragic, you don't talk.

Adriano: I'm always saying, also my wife, saying, when we see them, you know those security shutters of the stores, those of metal?

Me: Oh, yes, yes.

Adriano: This, they came out from, blown away, by the movement of air, just by the movement. And I say to my wife, is it possible that this metal was moved, blown out by the—, and nothing would happen inside of us? You understand?

Me: I understand.

Luisa: But not only that, but psychologically it's something that everyone carries inside.

Me: But you think, you said earlier that the others don't understand and so you close—

Luisa: Eh. They can't. It isn't that they don't want to understand. They don't manage . . . They are deep wounds. Especially for a child, it remains, because it's not that you were so young that you didn't understand. You understood, but you weren't old enough to be able to move on. And so you remained there. Do you understand?

CHAPTER 10

Dulce et Decorum Est

. . . he gave us a talk, and he said uh, the more Germans you k—, you kill, he said, the quicker you're gonna get home.

WHY GIVE THEM THIS TALK?

Major-General Chris Vokes may have given it more than once. The only documented occasion I've found, however, was on the ship, on the eve of the Sicily landing. Padre Durnford wrote in his diary that Vokes delivered a speech "intensely blood-thirsty in its sentiment." It concluded with the words, "good luck—and good scalping."

The tone made the padre uncomfortable. "For such men as myself the speech was welcomed only for its brevity." Yet he acknowledged that "from a military point of view" it was "a much needed injection." In other words, the padre believed the men needed encouragement to kill.[1]

In his books *On Killing* and *On Combat*, former US military psychologist Dave Grossman examines how soldiers experience and make sense of lawful acts of killing. Grossman argues that humans have an innate resistance to taking another person's life even when their own is in danger.

> [T]here is within most men an intense resistance to killing their fellow man. A resistance so strong that, in many circumstances, soldiers on the battlefield will die before they can overcome it.

Military training is designed to overcome that resistance. Since World War II, Western militaries have become more and more successful at doing so. The result, according to Grossman, is the growing number of veterans who have needed treatment for post-traumatic stress disorder (PTSD) from psychologists like himself.

Grossman's work is widely used and respected in military and law enforcement circles, including the Royal Canadian Mounted Police and the Canadian Armed Forces—but not without controversy. Canadian military historian Robert Engen has pointed out serious weaknesses with the research behind Grossman's claim about innate resistance.[2] That claim is largely based on the allegedly low firing rates among US infantrymen during World War II, as observed by US Army historian S.L.A. Marshall. From after-combat interviews with infantrymen, Marshall concluded that only fifteen to twenty percent of the riflemen were actually using their weapons to fire at the enemy. There seemed to be an implicit understanding among the men that some had it in them to shoot, and most of them did not. "Those who would not fire did not run or hide (in many cases they were willing to risk great danger to rescue comrades, get ammunition, or run messages), but they simply would not fire their weapons at the enemy." Marshall postulated that what was preventing most of these men from firing at the enemy was their attachment to civilian norms against killing. Interpreting Marshall's work, Grossman suggests that it's simply not in our nature to kill one another.

As Engen points out, that's a sweeping claim to make based on a small sample of men from a single country at a singular moment in history.

Furthermore, the evidence that's been used to support that claim—the apparently low firing rates of American World War II riflemen—is contradicted by the behaviour of Canadian soldiers in the 1943–44 Italian Campaign. In a thorough study of after-battle reports that were written by Canadian officers in Italy, Engen finds no mention of low firing rates; on the contrary, there was widespread concern among officers that their men were shooting *too much*. "Canadian soldiers normally fired their small arms in great volume, and often to excess." Far from wanting their men to shoot more, officers in Italy wanted them to shoot *less*. This was not only because the men were wasting ammunition, but also because their habits of shooting too soon and too often were making them less effective in battle. Accordingly, a May 1944 Canadian Army Training Memorandum instructed riflemen to "make sure of it—wait—wait and again wait even if you are frantically excited—WAIT!" Engen concludes that unless Canadians are intrinsically more violent than Americans, then Marshall and Grossman's claims cannot even be true for American soldiers in World War II, let alone for human nature.

Perhaps Marshall and Grossman overstated the divide among World War II soldiers between those who would shoot at the enemy and those who would not. Still, that doesn't mean such differences didn't exist. This may be what some of the Edmonton veterans were referring to when they described a comrade to me as a "real killer." As Gus said of Charlie: "He wasn't afraid to go around that corner there and *pop-pop-pop-pop*, you know? He was a fighting man . . . he was there to do away with Germans and so he did." The fact that Gus and Rollie used that label for Charlie suggests they saw him as different from themselves. And in the way they spoke about Charlie—and about Norman Letendre—I sensed a trace of gratitude toward those men for helping the others to get home.

An important reason for gratitude was the belief that those who killed were taking on a heavy burden. Mel said that the "hero" of the Italian Campaign had become an alcoholic because he had killed "twenty some Germans at the same time." Rollie thought Norman Letendre had got drunk and sexually assaulted a woman under the strain of combat: "the pressure must have been pretty terrible because he killed a number of snipers." Even if their diagnoses were off, it's clear they saw killing—even within the accepted rules of war—as something that came at a personal cost.

Mel and Rollie were not alone in that belief. Setting aside Dave Grossman's arguments on rates of fire and innate resistance, there is another important aspect to Grossman's work: his argument on the psychological costs of lawful killing. Based on testimonies from American and British veterans of twentieth-century wars, and his own clinical experience as a military psychologist, Grossman describes the typical soldier's reaction following an act of killing, and he outlines a set of variables that influence whether or not it becomes a lasting trauma.

Immediately following the act, Grossman writes, there is typically an "exhilaration stage in which there might be joy and elation" due to the satisfaction of hitting your target and "knowing that you are alive." Then there is typically "a backlash of remorse and nausea. Many soldiers vomit after their first kill." Whether or not the soldier suffers a lasting psychological injury from this experience depends on variables of the soldier's physical and emotional distance from the person killed.

Physical distance can range from point-blank encounters to actions carried out from so far away that the person isn't even visible as a human figure. The latter is the case with most air-to-air combat and aerial bombardment. Grossman quotes a US Air Force Colonel:

> In the air environment, it's very clinical, very clean, and it's not so personalized. You see an aircraft; you see a target on the

> ground—you're not eyeball to eyeball with the sweat and the emotions of combat, and so it doesn't become emotional for you and so personalized. And I think it is easier to do in that sense—you're not so affected.

Grossman adds that this can also be true for artillery. On that point, I remember Jack:

> I fired four thousand and fifty rounds of ten-pound bombs in Ortona, but you can say like, in Ortona, I never killed a soul.

At mid-range, Grossman writes, "the soldier can see and engage the enemy with rifle fire while still unable to perceive the extent of the wounds inflicted or the sounds and facial expressions of the victim when he is hit. In fact, at this range, the soldier can still deny that it was he who killed the enemy." There is the potential here for what Grossman calls "group absolution"—the feeling that it's not the individual but the group that's responsible. Nevertheless, despite these opportunities for denial, there may still be a legacy of guilt and remorse—if only because the soldier knows that he initially felt elation at seeing the enemy get killed. Here I remember Mel:

> So did you get him or did, did the guy next to you, or somebody at a window further down get him. So. But. And you always wonder about that too, you know. Whose, whose life did I end.

And Sam:

> Hately and I were both firing, I wouldn't say who got him but, one guy I'll bet he jumped as high as this ceiling. Screaming, eh?

When it comes to killing at close range, "the screams and cries of the enemy can be heard, adding greatly to the extent of the trauma experienced by the killer." However, the key factor influencing the likelihood and severity of trauma, Grossman adds, is "the undeniable certainty of responsibility"—as such, this may also apply to sniping, even though sniping is typically done from a greater distance. The guilt feeling that follows is "often so strong as to result in physical revulsion and vomiting."

> When I shot him, he fell, and two German soldiers came out and grabbed him and I didn't shoot back. I thank God that I didn't because that would have been even worse to handle.—Maurice

> But when I get home I never want to see a rifle again.—Norman Letendre

> And of course London pulled the trigger and shot the German officer right in the heart, right dead centre you know . . . So he just keeled over and died.—Bill

"At close range the resistance to killing an opponent is tremendous. When one looks an opponent in the eye, and knows that he is young or old, scared or angry, it is not possible to deny that the individual about to be killed is much like oneself."

> Poor bloody Italian. He was an old man, standing there. Jesus. But you know, I had the rifle cocked, safety off, ready, and, and, it would have been, if he'd have had good clothes on, and boots on, he'd have been dead. There's no two ways about it.—Sam

> . . . maybe 15 feet away. I was standing there with a Tommy gun. . . . I pulled the trigger, and nothing happened. And had he looked, had he looked toward me, I was dead.—Mel

> So anyway the little German guy had his, his uh, Schmeisser pointed right at my chest you know? And I don't know why he didn't pull the trigger. But he didn't.—Bill

Even harder is to kill an enemy soldier with a bayonet or knife. This comes with "enormous potential for psychological trauma." In the trench warfare of World War I, Grossman observes, bayonets were rarely used to kill even when their use would have been more expedient; at close range, even with bayonets attached, soldiers tended to turn their rifles around and use the butt to strike their enemy instead. Most knife kills are from behind. Soldiers are instinctively aware that killing from behind is "less traumatic than a kill from the front, since the face and all its messages and contortions are not seen. But what is felt are the bucking and shuddering of the victim's body and the warm sticky blood gushing out, and what is heard is the final breath hissing out." Grossman is only aware of one personal narrative of a knife kill, from an American World War II infantryman. "He had many personal kills that he was willing to discuss, but it was his one kill with a knife that caused him to have nightmares long after the war was over."

> Lunging forward I drove the knife in deeply just above the belt buckle then swiftly drew it upwards . . . Given the brutality of the day I thought nothing more of the incident but, with passage of time, it has increasingly haunted me—and continues to do so to this day.—Ted

Regardless of the distance of the kill, "[i]f a soldier goes up and looks at his kill—a common occurrence when the tactical situation permits—the trauma grows even worse, since some of the psychological buffer created by a mid range kill disappears upon seeing the victim at close range." Furthermore, some veterans told Grossman that they remained "haunted by photographs" they found while searching the bodies of those they had killed. "What those photographs represented was a crack in the veil of denial that makes war possible."

> Over the next day or two I saw the German body of Christmas Eve still slumped against the wall, and one day I stopped to go through his pockets where I found his field service book only to discover he hadn't yet reached his 17th birthday.—Ted

> Anyway, somebody rifled his pockets. They usually did, you know. And they found a picture of his wife and a little girl.—Bill

However, the key factor in Grossman's typology is the soldier's ability to maintain emotional distance. The physical distance from killing is really just a variable that makes it easier or harder to control one's emotions. There are other methods of emotional protection. This includes "group absolution" whereby you experience your actions not as your own but as those of your group. The enemy can also be distanced from you in racial, cultural, or moral terms. Language of war helps to produce and maintain distance and dehumanization. "Most soldiers do not 'kill,' instead the enemy was knocked over, wasted, greased, taken out, and mopped up. . . . The enemy's humanity is denied, and he becomes a strange beast called a Kraut, Jap, Reb, Yank . . ."

> And then we had fun shooting them, like they were a bunch of deer when they started to move away.—Jim Stone

> . . . and they'd rush across, these paratroopers, and one of my men got this fellow completely through the neck, and it was like shooting ducks.—Clifford Wood

> We used to say when we were down the line, 'Going up to meet the hated Hun,' but uh, I don't think that meant anything, you know. I don't think we hated them, no.—Bill

In his later book, *On Combat*, Grossman adds another variable that contributes to the possibility of trauma from killing: the soldier's age. Following his first book, *On Killing*, Grossman was contacted by some war veterans who told him that they had not struggled with guilt or remorse. He observes that these men had typically been older at the time of their experience, whereas his sources for *On Killing* were mostly reporting on experiences from when they were aged eighteen to twenty. He speculates that with maturity there is more ability to comprehend and rationalize one's actions within a moral or political framework.

> I was twenty-one years old and, I didn't know what the hell was botherin' me.—Mel

> You're just a kid and you don't. You don't know very much about life. At all. At least I sure didn't.—Maurice

Given all this, one can imagine that Ortona was a psychologically challenging environment—far beyond the norm—where it was difficult for the Canadians to maintain their protective emotional distance.

First, there was the broader context of the war in Italy. Certainly, some Canadians in Italy did manage to feel significant moral distance from the Germans. Bill told me of the "German hater" in his company. In his study of Canadian Army records, historian Robert Engen observes that "hatred and animosity toward the enemy, though not universal, appear to have been noticeable among the combat troops in 1943, and cycles of excessive, reciprocal violence are hinted at within the sources." But there were circumstances in Italy that made it hard to distance the enemy. Whether such assumptions were valid or not, the Germans were imagined to be culturally (if not also racially) similar to the majority white and Christian Canadian soldiers. Furthermore, in Italy, both sides were fighting away from home—the Canadians especially so. For them to believe they were defending their homes required a stretch of the imagination. Most weren't even convinced that they were liberating Italians. Indeed, sometimes they seem to have felt more respect and sympathy for their German enemies than for the civilian population.

The Canadians and Germans even shared a song: "Lili Marleen," a German ballad about a soldier bidding farewell to his sweetheart before heading off to the front. It was first broadcast on German army radio, but its popularity crossed enemy lines. Allied military authorities eventually embraced it too, commissioning English versions by Marlene Dietrich and Vera Lynn. Canadian soldiers went a step further, making up their own lyrics (see Chapter 2).

Mel told me about "the most stirring rendition" he ever heard—immediately after landing in southern France, as the 1st Canadian Infantry Division was leaving Italy.

"Got off the boat there. And, we're goin' along in trucks, and here's two, three thousand [German] POW's marching along singing 'Lili Marleen' and that just made the hair stand on the back of your neck you know."

Mel probably didn't realize that by then, in 1945, "Lili Marleen" had been banned in Germany—Goebbels deemed it bad for morale. Ironically, it was in captivity now that the Germans were free to sing it.

"They were coming from a work camp someplace, you know."

"Gee."

"And on the way back to their own, uh, billets under guard of course, you know."

"Yeah."

"But all singing in unison 'Lili Marleen,' you know. Beautiful."

"Why do you think that made this—"

"Oh just—"

"—this deep impression on you?"

"Well, just the fact that uh, that, that was one of the World War II songs that hit not only the German side but the British side too. Because the Britishes were all singin' it, you know? Such a beautiful number. You know? So even us Canadians were singing it, you know?"

"Yeah?"

"The words that we could remember, you know!"

In short, in the context of the Italian Campaign, it was hard for young men like Mel, Bill, and Maurice to feel distant from the Germans. And then in Ortona, one can imagine it became even harder. Throughout the week-long urban battle, there was close physical proximity—always at mid-range, if not closer. Often, Canadians and Germans were in the same building. In addition, they were surrounded by reminders of domesticity, the normal life of home. They were under the towers of churches. And above all, it was Christmastime. Even for the Canadians who weren't deeply religious, the season was significant to most of them at least in a secular sense; it was a reminder of "peace on earth, goodwill toward men"—and the Canadians knew it was sacred for the Germans, too.

BUT THE CANADIANS IN Italy weren't just fighting Germans. They were fighting Nazi Germany. The Third Reich was aggressively pursuing its racist ideology through conquest and genocidal violence.

In Canada, it's almost universally believed that the war against Nazi Germany was a just cause. One of Canada's leading historians, Jack Granatstein, has described World War II as "genuinely a struggle for survival against a monstrous evil, a just war, the last good war." In the words of Tim Cook, Chief Historian at the Canadian War Museum, it was "a necessary war against evil" and the Canadians who participated "should be remembered as the ordinary men and women who found the courage to do fighting things, pushing themselves beyond their limits, aware that to lose or even draw with the Nazis would leave the world a much darker place."

In that light, it's puzzling that the veterans I interviewed rarely mentioned the ideology they fought and defeated. In Sam's case, I think the only time I heard him use the word "Nazi" was when he complained about his old Alberta German school principal who punished him for bringing a chipmunk to class. The most substantive comments on the subject came from Denis. When I asked him, "What was your feeling about the Germans back then?" he inhaled and exhaled sharply through his teeth just as he'd done when remembering the mist and fireflies around Pop Warner's grave.

"*Phew.* Well . . ." He paused in thought for a moment.

"No, I guess no particular personal feelings. I mean I think we separated it from what we knew of Nazism and the pogroms against the Jews and that kind of thing. We were aware of that, and we were aware of the Gestapo, and we were aware of those kind of things, but I guess we had a lot of respect for the Germans as fighters. I mean they were never a pushover, they were never easy, until the end of the war, the last week or two."

Denis named the ideology and alluded to the atrocities but made a point of "separating" it from his thoughts about individual German soldiers. Maurice expressed a similar idea more plainly: "They're people like you and I. Just because they had an idiot for a leader, you can't condemn them."

The German soldiers did, indeed, have an "idiot" for a leader. But what if they believed in that idiot's ideology? And even if they didn't, it can still be argued that their refusal to be "pushovers" (as Denis put it) was not admirable; on the contrary, their strong fighting spirit prolonged the war and gave the Nazi regime more time to carry out its atrocities.

According to Grossman, a soldier's strongest psychological defence against the trauma of killing is moral distance—the conviction that one is fighting for a just cause against an enemy engaged in evil. Most, if not all, of the veterans I spoke with were aware that this framing was available to them. They could have drawn on it to justify their actions. But for some reason, it wasn't working. It wasn't helping them put their troubled memories to rest—and strikingly, many didn't even seem inclined to invoke it.

Maybe it wasn't working because of how they remembered themselves at the time. In their enlistment stories, they rarely mentioned humanitarian or political motives. Most spoke of feeling a duty to fight for their country. Some joined because their friends were going; others wanted to earn their fathers' respect. A few admitted that desperate poverty had also been a factor.

Their fight, of course, turned out to serve a much greater cause. But they weren't taking credit for this—perhaps because they knew that greater moral purpose hadn't been theirs at the time. Maurice described himself as "just a kid" who didn't know much about life. He probably imagined that the enemy he shot on Christmas Day had been a kid much like himself.

It wasn't only the veterans who rarely mentioned the "just cause" of the war. In my conversations with them, I rarely mentioned it myself. I had a gut feeling that if I raised it—"What about the Nazis?"—this might shut them down or change the way they talked to me. My priority was to give them space to tell their stories their own way, and I didn't want them to worry about upsetting my feelings or beliefs.

I learned this lesson during the Christmas Reconciliation. When the group was at the monument to the civilian victims of the battle, there was a Van Doos veteran standing next to me who started to cry. Through his tears, he told me that until now he'd never given much thought to the civilians' suffering. Now he felt terrible. He went on to tell me that the whole war had been wrong and should never have been fought. My reply to him went something like, "But you had to do it. You had to stop the Nazis." My aim was to console him. He did indeed stop crying, and he acknowledged that I was "right"—but this left me with a bad feeling. He had wanted to condemn war. Rather than consider his point, I had interrupted and corrected him. For whose benefit had I done that, his or mine? I resolved not to do it again.[3]

I DID HAVE SOME misgivings about the Christmas Reconciliation. Many—possibly most—of the Germans who fought in Ortona were teenagers or very young men. At one point during the battle, the Seaforth war diarist noted that the average age of the prisoners they were capturing was just nineteen.[4] However, those young Germans were not conscripts forced into Hitler's army. The German First Parachute Division was an elite unit of volunteers.

Granted, some of those paratroopers may not have volunteered out of ideological conviction, but rather because they saw the writing on the wall—figuring they'd be conscripted anyway, and volunteering might offer better options. That was Willy Fretz's story. As for whatever amount of Nazi ideology they may have believed at the time, perhaps, as teenagers and young men, they could be forgiven; they could be seen as Maurice saw himself: kids who hadn't yet had much chance to learn about the world.

But the Germans who came to the Christmas Reconciliation were not those kids anymore. They were former volunteers who had survived the war and had gone on to live for more than five decades in a democratic state. They could be accountable for what they believed—including how they now viewed their wartime service, in light of everything they'd had a chance to learn.

Did it matter what those beliefs were?

For many of the Canadians on the trip, including Ted, the answer seemed to be no. Or maybe it's more accurate to say they weren't interested in finding out. Ted emphasized what the two groups had in common: the Germans had fought for their country just as the Canadians had fought for theirs.

Even the fact that these Germans had been volunteers was reframed as a virtue—another point of similarity.

Walking on the Corso side by side with Joseph Klein, Seaforth veteran Bill Worton told the CBC's David Halton he'd had mixed feelings about the Germans at the start of the trip. "But I don't now, because when you meet these gentlemen you realize . . . that they're some of the finest people in the world, because they had an esprit de corps in the paratroopers like the Canadian army had"—and here he leaned in closer to Halton, pointing his finger for emphasis—"because we were a *volunteer army*."

They were bonding through martial values—and the scapegoating of politicians. "Soldiers don't make war," Joseph Klein told Canadian reporters, "Politicians make it. That is the point." Was Joseph's point that Hitler was solely to blame for Germany's crimes? Surely Hitler couldn't have made much war without the cooperation of a lot of Germans—including Joseph, who had volunteered to fight. Further on the topic of politics and martial values, Joseph lamented to the Canadian veterans and reporters that it was a crime in Germany to wear his World War II service medals—he spoke of this as if it were a grave injustice. The Canadians listened sympathetically. On learning that the Germans were not allowed to wear their medals, Canadian veteran John Matheson decided that for the duration of the trip he would not wear his own.

Then there was Willy Fretz's speech at the Christmas Eve dinner. When Willy stood up and said, "We are sorry," the *Ottawa Sun* proclaimed it as the key moment of reconciliation. "We are sorry for all the suffering we caused. We are sorry we were your enemy. We are sorry to the people of Ortona." On one hand, having observed Willy throughout the week in Ortona, I didn't doubt the sincerity of his remorse. On the other hand, I couldn't help noticing its possible limits. Was he sorry for all of Germany's actions—or only for those that had harmed Canadians? Was his regret about having been an enemy, or simply about having been an enemy of *us*? After all, even Hitler had claimed to regret being an enemy of the British; he had wanted them to be partners in his fight against communists and "inferior races." Finally, Willy concluded his Christmas Eve speech with the words, "It was just like in a boxing ring. We lost." It was the kind of thing a gracious competitor says in defeat—the implication being that, of course, he would have preferred to win.

About a year and a half after the Christmas Reconciliation, I came to learn more about Willy's beliefs. During my stay in Ortona, I wrote to him asking if I could meet him in Germany. He replied that he'd soon be Italy on his annual trip to visit the German war cemetery near Cassino, and suggested we might as well meet there. So on a hot day in May, I took the train across the peninsula and joined him in Sant'Elia, two kilometres from the vast cemetery on the hill.

We sat on the patio of his hotel restaurant with an expansive view across the valley. Of course, being German, he wanted to sit directly under the sun. Drinking a cold lager, with his shirt partly unbuttoned and the sleeves rolled up his forearms, Willy looked a little tougher than he had in Ortona at Christmas.

"Everyone was fearful," he said, "and those who died seemed to know it beforehand."

"What did you do on Christmas Day?" I asked him.

"I was alert, yeah? We had to be alert because uh, the troops were attacking. Our Christmas, uh. Rainy. Cold. Holes. We got some supply, yes, but there was no, not much to sing about the Christmas spirit, because there was the fighting going on as usual."

"Did you know that it was Christmas?"

"We knew that it was Christmas but we weren't together, we couldn't do anything, we couldn't sit underneath a Christmas tree or anything like that. The only thing is those nights when the sky was clear, yeah, and you could see the stars. Might be that the contact to Germany, that somebody is watching from the family or from the friends, your friends. They had, I had a special star, for contact. And so I was watching, and thoughts were going."

"Where were you?"

"I was in a foxhole, yeah? When you made a noise, yeah, it would have been deathly. They would say, Oh! *Bang!* There was, I only know, yeah, I didn't like cake, yeah, and everybody got a little cake for Christmas, eh, one from the company, one from the regiment, and one from the division, yeah. And I changed it into brandy."

As I'd been hearing a lot on this topic from the people in Ortona, I asked him:

"Did the German soldiers drink a lot?"

"A lot?"

"Because I hear that the Canadians—people in Ortona tell me that the Canadians were always drinking wine."

"We were drinking wine, yeah, but uh, we weren't drunk, yeah, we had it just to give a little bit power. So I don't have to say what they told me?" He was referring to conversations he'd had with people in Ortona about what it was like after the Germans had left. "I asked, I don't know was it, who was it, from the old people, I said after we went back, yeah, to Pescara and the front line, Ortona must have been quite good now, uh, when there no troops were no more. 'What? Was terrible! Six months drunken British soldiers!'"

Then he told me something surprising. He had intervened in Ortona on behalf of the *Price of Peace* statue. He'd heard about the town council's resistance, so he'd written to Mayor Puletti, telling the mayor that as a German veteran, he wanted the statue in Ortona, too.

"It's interesting that you cared about the monument, because—"

"I'm—"

"—in a way it's a Canadian monument."

"Uh, that doesn't matter. That monument is such realistic monument, that shows, the hardness of the battle, yeah? And, for me, a monument honouring the dead soldiers is for me universal, not only for the one side, it's for all sides, when it shows the stupidness how people are being killed."

And then he went on to confirm what I had suspected about his Christmas Eve apology. He had never wanted to fight the British or

Canadians. That fight should never have happened. When he had volunteered, his only desire was to fight Bolsheviks. "And to see now in Germany, now they are in power." He was referring to the coalition of Social Democrats and Greens that was governing Germany at the time. "What a worthless sacrifice."

He consoled himself with his belief that the German Army had behaved honourably. Whenever he was in Italy, he was always comfortable identifying himself as a German World War II veteran. He could go "anywhere the German Army was" and meet people "with esteem." Coming to Italy was "medicine for the souls of us full of dirt of our government today."

So his conscience in Italy was clean; the only "dirt" that he felt was the fault of his present-day government.

Did Willy know nothing about German war crimes in Italy? The most infamous was the Ardeatine Caves massacre. On March 24, 1944, German forces killed 355 Italian prisoners in retribution for a partisan bomb attack on fascist policemen in Rome. Beginning in June 1944 and for the duration of their occupation of Italy, German forces were under orders from their Commander-in-Chief, Field Marshal Albert Kesselring, to shoot civilians and burn villages whenever they were attacked by partisans. When partisans killed three German soldiers in the Tuscan village of Civitella, the local German Army units reacted by killing 204 men, women, and children in Civitella and nearby villages, burning many alive in their houses. The British military court that convicted Kesselring of war crimes found that his orders resulted in "over twenty instances of indiscriminate killing of Italians by German troops." More than ten thousand civilians, including women and children, were killed. According to a report by the British War Crimes Section, "a large number of the atrocities in Italy was committed by the Hermann Goering Parachute Panzer Division. Notable offenders also were l Parachute Division . . ."[5]

In the "Atlas of Nazi and Fascist Atrocities in Italy" (a project of Italian historians with support from the German government) there is a list of forty-seven incidents of violent crimes against civilians that were committed by the 1st Parachute Division. The worst was in Pietransieri, a mountain village in the Upper Sangro Valley approximately 60 kilometres southwest of Ortona, on November 21, 1943—one month before the Ortona battle. The Pietransieri massacre happened as part of the paratroopers' scorched earth tactics that aimed at slowing the Allied advance and depriving them of resources. In the Upper Sangro, the paratroopers were holding the mountainous section of the German winter defensive line against the attacking Canadian West Nova Scotia and Royal 22e (Van Doos) Regiments. They stymied the Canadian advance by burning villages across the valley, sometimes evacuating the villagers northwards, sometimes forcing them south towards the Canadians, creating columns of refugees that blocked the roads. When a paratroop unit came upon a group of Pietransieri villagers who had resisted the evacuation order and gone back to their homes, the paratroopers penned them into farm buildings and machine-gunned them, killing over a hundred men, women, and children.[6]

Willy didn't join the paratroopers until early December 1943 (he transferred from another volunteer German Army unit) and was in the division's 3rd Regiment which had not been in the Upper Sangro. Nor was he in the same unit that killed twenty civilians in Francavilla al Mare, ten kilometres north of Ortona, on December 30, 1943, after a local farmer fatally stabbed a drunk paratrooper who was chasing the farmer's daughter. I have no evidence that Willy's unit of the 3rd Regiment ever committed any war crimes in Italy. But it's hard to believe that he never heard so much as a rumour about such incidents, and he surely must have been aware of his army's brutal anti-partisan warfare tactics that were ordered by his Commander in Chief.[7]

As for the roundups and deportations of Italian Jews, Willy and his comrades *might* have been unaware of it at the time, but those like him who survived the war certainly had plenty of opportunity to learn about it later. The deportations to death camps were carried out by the German SS with assistance from fascist Italian armed forces starting in October 1943. The longer that Willy and his paratroop comrades fought "honourably" to hold the German defensive lines, the more time they gained for those arrests and deportations. At the time of the Ortona battle, the twenty-four-year-old Jewish Italian chemist Primo Levi had just been captured by police in Aosta. In January 1944, while the 1st Canadian Division was recuperating from its losses in Ortona, Levi was taken to a concentration camp in Fossoli; the next month, along with 650 other Jews in the camp, he was deported to Auschwitz. Of those from Fossoli, he was one of twenty-four who survived. In *The Drowned and the Saved*, his last book before his death, Levi wrote:

> And yet there are those who faced by the crime of others or their own, turn their backs so as not to see it and not feel touched by it: this is what the majority of Germans did during the twelve Hitlerian years, deluding themselves that not seeing was a way of not knowing, and that not knowing relieved them of their share of complicity or connivance.

Rings of water had pooled on the table around the bottoms of our empty beer bottles. Soon, I'd have to leave to catch my train.

Before we parted, Willy shared one more story. He was remembering a sergeant in his unit. One time, this sergeant had "tried to make love to another trooper." The sergeant wasn't officially punished, but not long after, the unit got rid of him: they sent him on an impossible mission behind enemy lines, alone.

"He never came back."

A grim smirk crossed Willy's face. I read it as dark humour—a feeling I didn't share—and didn't press him further.

But maybe it wasn't humour. Maybe Willy's smirk was covering for something else. *Everyone was fearful, and those who died seemed to know it beforehand.* Maybe he was thinking about this sergeant when he looked across the valley. And maybe when he looked at the statue in Ortona, this sergeant was also in his thoughts.

Even though I'd been able to meet Willy in Cassino, I still opted to make a brief trip to Germany. I didn't have time and money to go all over the country, but two of the veterans from the Reconciliation trip—Fritz and Hugo—lived quite close to one another in the south, just over the Alps.

Willy had not given me Fritz's address, but I had it anyway—the ever-gregarious Fritz had given it to me (and I think to everyone) at Christmas. For the interview with Hugo, I lined up a translator. Unfortunately, a few days before our meeting, Hugo cancelled, saying he was ill.

Fritz, on the other hand, was still eagerly awaiting me. As he spoke English fairly well—in fact, he was more fluent than Willy—I went to meet him alone.

We sat at the kitchen table in his Stuttgart flat. His partner was there too; even though she could understand little or nothing of what we said, she sat with us the whole time. I already had a bad impression of Fritz from the way he had treated this woman in Ortona. I hoped that I wouldn't see more of that unpleasantness. I wasn't expecting to like him, but as a researcher, I figured I could set those feelings aside in order to get one more German paratrooper's perspective.[8]

The conversation started off not too badly. He told me that by the time he was in Ortona, he'd come to the conclusion that the Nazi leaders were lying and that Germany was going to lose the war. I wondered how, in those circumstances, he'd managed to stay motivated to fight.

"But I'm asking myself, how, if, you were fighting in Italy, and at that time, at that time you were already thinking that Germany is losing the war, you're thinking about the Nazi party telling all these stories, how did, how then did you keep fighting, how did you keep your uh, your—"

"Yeah, I understand what you're, what you want to say."

"Because it's very depressing."

"We get the order. You're gonna stay here till the end. And if you don't get, if you don't take the order, they're going to shoot you or they hang you up in the next tree. We have a lot of discipli—, you know what I, how do you say in English—"

"Discipline, yeah."

"Discipline, you know. The German, you're gonna stay here. You are German officer, captain, you fight for your country. Discipline, you know. The Italian takes a mandolin and an ice cream, and singing *amore amore*, and take off your hands [surrender], but not the Germans. They gonna stand, till to the end."

"Do you think that was the right choice?"

"Not the right, but, I grow up in this system, you know? I was ten years old . . . and Hitler was coming when the government, uh, the whole education, you know? The whole system. You can't get out from the system. You get a hell of a lot punishment. That's the Germans, you know. It's good and the other side is stupid, I know."

"Did you have—"

"It's a good education, but on the other side is . . . when I go back on my life I would say, why I have been so stupid and fight for that fucking people six years? The best would be in the first days I take off my hands and, live an American and be happy okay. But you are in the system you know? You can't break out . . . I feel till today very very sorry that, uh, Germans was fighting against the British or against the American, you know. But I think the Germans and the British is a people, not nearly the same but a very good relationship you know? White people and uh, German race you know? British race and the German race, it's not a big difference. I mean, against, the Russia that's another people, it's another race you know? But the uh, the British, I feel in, in, in England like at home, you know?"

"You've been to England?"

"And a very good relationship between the Germans, between the Germans and the British, you know? Or the Canadian, it's about the same. All the Canadian was coming four hundred or two hundred years from Europe, you know. Where you come from, Europe?"

"Uh, Scot—, Scotland."

"Scotland, see. You see. The Germans and the British together, we run over the whole world in two years, five times we run around the world . . . It's the same people like myself, you know. It's another thing when I would fight against the Chinese or Japanese it was the, the coloured people you know? But—"

"But this is different."

"Yeah, you understand what I try to explain you . . . The German government treat us like criminals, you know. The German, I can't carry my decorations. That's forbidden you know? You know the story."

"Do you think that some of the Germans—"

"Cause we gonna start the war, and you know the right to justice. This one who is going to start the fight, he is guilty. And, you know as the Germans has done against the Jews, and the Jews, the mightiest people of the world, you know? They're controlling the whole world with, you know that story?"

"Hm. Yeah. So . . ."

By this point, only half of me was still there. The other half was thinking about how to cut this short and get out. I should have known that I might need an exit plan, but foolishly, I hadn't come prepared with one.

While I was trying to pull my thoughts together he launched into a long story about the Battle of Monte Cassino. It ended with him in a foxhole, giving comfort to a dying New Zealander—another sorry tale of having to fight the white British.

At that, he broke down into a fit of uncontrolled sobbing. His partner got up from her chair and went over to console him. I thanked god she was there, because I didn't want to be any more involved.

It took a painfully long time for him to regain his composure. Finally, when he did, that was my chance to wrap up and be gone.

This was not someone Canadians should be having a beer with, saying let's let bygones be bygones and isn't it a shame that we ever fought.

To put it in some perspective, the German veterans who came to the Christmas Reconciliation were undoubtedly a unique group. There might have been other First Parachute veterans who more strongly acknowledged and repented of their country's crimes, and who renounced the whole ideology, not just the "tragedy" of fighting the white British. But the ones who had those attitudes might not have wanted to come to the Reconciliation. They might not have wanted the attention. They might not have felt they deserved the invitation. They might not even have known about it. The invitation was sent to the First Parachute veterans association. Those who felt no pride in their wartime service may have long since cut ties with it.

I'm sure that the majority if not all of the Canadians on the Reconciliation trip would have been deeply troubled to learn about Fritz's beliefs—and maybe troubled by some of Willy's, too. I think Ted would have been mortified. In his memoir, Ted proudly writes that his mentor Joseph Wilhelm, the Catholic padre of the Three Rivers Regiment, was highly respected by all of his Jewish comrades. Ted also writes that in the days shortly after the Battle of Ortona, the Canadians in Italy started hearing news of the Nazi death camps.

> [T]he war against the evils of Hitler had long passed the political stage. With tales slowly seeping out of German-occupied Europe of concentration, or death, camps beginning to exert a profound influence on politician and soldier alike, our war was gradually assuming the cloak of a great crusade.

Ted was hardly indifferent to Nazi ideology. Indeed, unlike some Canadian soldiers, Ted was already politically motivated to fight Nazism from the war's very start. His sense of moral difference from his enemy became even stronger as the war continued. In his words, it became a crusade.

But that moral conviction was not enough to protect him from the psychological cost of killing. Ted started to learn of the Nazi death camps shortly after he'd killed the young German on Christmas Eve. The news didn't help him. Five decades later, he was back in Ortona trying to bury the young German's ghost. His need for resolution was so deep that he let his guard down and "reconciled" with German veterans who, despite half a century to reflect and learn, were still downplaying the crimes of the regime they had served.

It wasn't unusual for a Canadian soldier with strong moral convictions against Nazi Germany to be deeply shaken by the violence of the war. Ted wasn't alone in this—and perhaps he knew it from reading Farley Mowat, whose memoir *And No Birds Sang*, traces that very trajectory. Mowat's story begins on the second day of September 1939 with his father coming home and telling him that Canada was about to mobilize.

> My father's news excited me tremendously for I had long been inflamed by his fulminations against the Russophobe French, British and U.S. politicians and industrialists who had connived at the growth and spread of fascism, concealing their real admiration for it beneath the public explanation that it was the only trustworthy 'bulwark against communism.' I shared my father's conviction that these men had betrayed democracy and I took the debacle of Munich and the sell-out of Czechoslovakia as proof of this. I believed that every healthy young man in the freedom-espousing countries was duty bound to take up arms against the Fascist plague and, in particular, the singularly bestial German brand.

The story ends on Christmas Day in 1943 with Mowat suffering a nervous breakdown in the fighting west of Ortona. The immediate cause of his breakdown appears to have been the death of his friend, Major Alex Campbell, but Mowat describes himself already in a state of delirium in the preceding days. During the attack by his Hastings and Prince Edward Regiment on December 23, in a fit of terror under bombardment, he dove into a ruined stone hut and came face to face with a German paratrooper. The young man was sitting on the ground with a severed arm.

> Dark gore was still gouting between his fingers and spreading in a black pool about his outthrust legs. Most dreadful was a great gash in his side from which protuded a glistening dark mass which must have been his liver. Above this wreckage, his eyes were large and luminous in a young man's face, pallid to the point of translucency.
>
> 'Vasser . . . please giff . . . vasser.'

Mowat only had rum in his water bottle.

> Oh, hell, I thought, he's going anyway. What harm!
>
> I held the water bottle to his lips and he swallowed in deep, spasmodic gulps until I took it back and drank from it myself. And so . . . and so the two of us got drunk together. And in a little while he died.

Then Mowat found a Canadian tank and got a lift back to headquarters. "I remember sliding off the front of the Sherman, and then my legs collapsing under me, then there was nothing." When he woke the next day, he was sent out again. "Presumably there was shellfire, but I do not recall it . . . I walked in the silence within myself, hearing nothing but an echo of the great wind."[9]

The moral of Mowat's story is not only that war is horrific. He intended his book to be a condemnation of all wars, including this one that he'd fought against Nazism. The book's epigraph is the concluding lines of "Dulce et Decorum Est" by the British World War I poet, Wilfred Owen.

> *My friend, you would not tell with such high zest*
> *To children ardent for some desperate glory,*

The old Lie: Dulce et decorum est
Pro patria mori

The Latin words are taken from the ancient Roman poet Horace and translate as, "It is sweet and fitting to die for one's country."

For the American edition of *And No Birds Sang*, Mowat added what he called "An Anti-Epilogue" in which he explained his purpose in writing it:

> Let it be said then that I wrote this book in the absolute conviction that there never has been, nor ever can be, a 'good' or worthwhile war. Mine was one of the better ones (as such calamities are measured), but still, a bloody awful thing it was. So awful that through three decades I kept the deeper agonies of it wrapped in the cotton-wool of protective forgetfulness, and would have been well content to leave them buried forever . . . but could not, because the Old Lie—temporarily discredited by the Vietnam debacle—is once more gaining credence; a whisper which soon may become another strident shout urging us on to mayhem.[10]

While acknowledging that World War II was one of the "better" ones, Mowat nevertheless questioned its worth and condemned it along with all wars. Despite his hatred of Nazi ideology and his knowledge of its crimes, he struggled to reconcile his personal role in the violence that was done to stop it.

Not all of the veterans I met shared Mowat's political convictions. Those who did—like Ted—had similarly found that such convictions wouldn't protect them from trauma.

In his own way, Bill gave voice to this moral complexity. When he told me about the Reconciliation, he offered a noteworthy reason for why it hadn't appealed to him.

"Some of our boys went back, you know, and met some of the Germans that had fought in Ortona you know. Um, Bill Worton. You probably interviewed him?"

"I talked to him, yeah."

"Yeah, and uh, a few more, yeah."

"Yeah. Gildersleeve."

"Gildersleeve, yeah, yeah. Yeah. I couldn't have, I wouldn't have went myself, you know because, I don't know it seems to me, it was a stupid war anyway, you know. And, and uh, they were all volunteers too, they weren't conscripts that First Paratrooper Division you know."

For Bill, it was absolutely not a point in their favour that the First Parachutists were volunteers; on the contrary, it was a strike against them. And yet, at the same time, Bill recalled that when he'd been their prisoner, those volunteers had treated him well; he recalled how the surrendering German officer had been shot in the heart by a Canadian; he recalled how the "little German" had pushed the muzzle of his Schmeisser against Bill's chest—but then, for some reason, hadn't pulled the trigger. That experience probably had a lot to do with why Bill called it a stupid war. The same moral confusion was apparent in his answer to my question, near the end of the interview, about the war's worth.

"I guess the Germans had to be defeated I suppose. Yeah. I don't know who was wrong and who was right in that war but, all wars are the same aren't they? Uh, I don't think they need to happen at all, you know. Wars, you know. I don't think so."

Most Canadians would condemn any suggestion that both sides in World War II were equally right or wrong. But I don't think Bill's comment was meant as a literal moral comparison. He wasn't indifferent to Nazi ideology or to the argument that it had to be defeated. I think, like Farley Mowat, he simply couldn't accept that *goodness* should be the war's last word.

TED'S WAY OF COPING with his trauma was to organize the Christmas Reconciliation. I had misgivings about the politics of his project—misgivings that were, unfortunately, confirmed by later meetings with two of the German participants. But it's important to recognize that Ted was trying to solve a painful problem that had been darkening his life for decades—and he was alone in doing so. His society wasn't exactly coming to him with solutions. In fact, his society barely acknowledged that there was a problem to be solved.

At the time of my research, many of the veterans in this book probably would have been diagnosed with PTSD if they'd seen a psychologist. Some of their symptoms were self-reported (e.g., Ted's haunting; Mel's stomach ailment and "constant flip-book" of pictures in his mind) and other symptoms could be observed (e.g., Bill's moments of narrative incoherence.)

However, these men might well have been misunderstood and found themselves frustrated by the dominant clinical approach. Until recently, therapeutic treatments have assumed that soldiers' traumas are caused by fear. Consider the following definitions of psychic trauma: it's caused by "terror and helplessness," a violation of "our taken-for-granted senses of security, predictability, trust, and optimism," a "fundamental rift or breakdown of psychological functioning (memory, behaviour, emotion) which occurs as a result of an unbearably intense experience that is life threatening to the self or others." All of this posits a breakdown in mental function resulting from an experience of extreme fear and threat to one's life.

The veterans whom I interviewed might *also* have suffered from fear-based trauma. But what I saw them struggling with was not a reaction to fear—it was a reaction to causing death and suffering to others.

Since the time of my fieldwork, a new clinical approach is now in use to address this oversight. The concept of "moral injury" was introduced by psychologists working with American veterans of wars in Afghanistan and Iraq to address the moral dimensions of soldiers' traumas. Writing in 2009, Brett Litz and his colleagues at Boston's Veterans Affairs National Center for PTSD defined a "morally injurious experience" as "[p]erpetrating, failing to prevent, [or] bearing witness to acts that transgress deeply held moral beliefs and expectations." The symptoms might be the same as those of conventional PTSD, but in the case of moral injury the symptoms arise from emotions of guilt and shame.

Therapists are advised to accept and take those emotions seriously; it's important not to "undermine the patient's need to feel remorseful." The steps for treatment begin with "psychological- and emotional-processing of the memory of the moral transgression" followed by "forgiveness-promoting experiences." Regarding the latter, the authors add, "In simple terms, this is couched as *making amends*." Finally, social connection or "being accepted by a group" is important to healing as it "helps construct meaning and purpose that transcends the self."

Dutch anthropologist Tine Molendijk has critically expanded the way we think about moral injury. Molendijk teaches at the Netherlands Defence Academy and has studied trauma among Dutch veterans of the UN peacekeeping mission in Bosnia and the NATO mission in Afghanistan. As an alternative to the clinical notion of injury, she suggests that we also think in existential terms. When individuals experience profound moral distress and disorientation, this can result in feeling that they have lost their coherent sense of self and their place in the world.

> A moral injury may entail questions and insights about the self and the world that go beyond and deeper than the event. A veteran's experience may have shattered his trust in people's ability to do right; moreover, it may have shattered his very moral

> frame of reference with which he used to make judgments about questions of wrong and right. He may struggle not only with moral questions such as 'Am I/are others good or bad?' but also with such ethical questions as 'What is good and bad?'

This "shattered moral frame" can lead to feeling alienated from yourself and your society. In part, this alienation stems from the inability to construct a coherent story about what happened. Such narrative difficulties are typical of all traumas. In her interviews with Dutch veterans, however, Molendijk found that much of the "profound confusion and disorientation" in their narratives was rooted in a persistent internal conflict, as they grappled with incompatible moral interpretations of their actions.

> The stories of Bob and other veterans conveyed all sorts of ethical questions. How to do right when forced to choose between two evils? What do right and wrong mean in the battle for survival? What is goodness when it only confirms the evilness of a situation? Was I a good soldier, and is being a good soldier really good? Do my guilt and other worries make me a good or a bad soldier, and a good or a bad human being? What do good and bad even mean?

The unsettled, self-contradictory nature of these narratives may actually be very appropriate representations of the situations that the soldiers were involved in—situations of genuine "irresolvable moral conflict" in which "it makes sense to feel guilty and not guilty at the same time." Sometimes, as a result, the soldiers came to "feel that their belief in right and wrong failed *them*."

In Molendijk's descriptions of veterans' narratives, I see Sam's obsessive work on mapping his battle; the ambivalent stories told by Mel, Gus, and

Rollie about "real killers" and Norman Letendre; Bill's confusion about who was right and wrong; Ted's arguments with himself that he was not guilty but still needed to atone; and Maurice's feeling that he had left some unknown thing behind. All of them were struggling with deep moral disorientation. In a way, that disorientation *was* their wound.

As for what helps veterans to recover from moral injury, Molendijk offers an anthropological perspective that goes beyond the usual focus on individuals and medical institutions. She observes:

> [M]any societies used to have rituals for returning soldiers which acknowledged the moral complexity of military intervention and involved both the returned soldier and society . . . [T]he Christian community of the first millennium generally assumed that warriors returning from battle would or should feel guilty and ashamed for all the wartime killing they had done . . . It was believed that although the evil in which warriors had participated might have been necessary, it was still evil. So, rather than dismissing guilt and shame as 'insignificant or irrelevant', returning warriors were encouraged to seek resolution . . . through rituals of purification, expiation, and reconciliation.

She further notes that similar traditions have existed in other cultures, including those of Indigenous North America. These traditions share in common "an understanding of military action as something that may be morally polluting" and a process of "purification and reintegration" of the returning soldier that involves "active engagement by the wider community."

Importantly, what is absent from these traditions is the celebration of the returning soldier as a hero. In Molendijk's view, there is wisdom in that absence. Most of the Dutch veterans whom she interviewed "did not see much value in being applauded as heroes" and in some cases "it made them feel extremely uncomfortable and aggravated their guilt." Nor was it helpful to glorify their suffering. The latter is a tendency when veterans are viewed too much through the frame of PTSD. While the intention behind that is sympathetic, it "portrays veterans as victims of war, and as with heroization, victimization leaves veterans with no space to feel remorse." Instead, Molendijk recommends a social response that respects the moral complexity of what veterans have experienced.

Finally, Molendijk found that "in the absence of existing meaningful rituals," the veterans she met had "invented their own symbolic acts." Many of them had returned more than once to Srebrenica, the place of their disastrously failed UN peacekeeping mission.[11] Sometimes bringing family members and friends, the veterans participated in marches for peace and other activities through which they expressed remorse and created new, positive relationships with the local community. Other veterans had attempted to share their stories with the public at home, seeking not only understanding for themselves but also a new sense of purpose in educating the public about war.

Here, I think of Ted's public ritual of reconciliation; Maurice's private act of returning to where he shot the German; and Maurice's decision to keep going on pilgrimages in order to talk to Canadian youth.

And I think of why the veterans talked to me.

He's the guy who wants to know about Ortona.

I worry sometimes that, in being that guy, I opened wounds that I didn't know how to console. I knew very little about therapy at the time. But I hope that my basic instinct to listen without judgement offered some help to the men who spoke to me.

What some of them seemed to want most of all was not help for themselves, but reassurance that their story might help others. One of the first things Mel told me was, "I don't think any veteran wants the schoolkids today to glamorise war or anything. It's a terrible thing. Nobody should have to go through it." And when Norman was telling me about the much-celebrated Seaforths Christmas dinner in Ortona, he concluded: "I hope those things never happen again." He looked frightened when he said it. While the memory still haunted him, he surely knew it was unlikely to happen again to him. What troubled him was the thought that it would happen again to anyone.

When I read about treatments for moral injury, my feelings are mixed. Of course it's a good thing. If we need to have soldiers, then we should absolutely be ready to help them cope with the consequences of what we ask them to do. Ideally, we wouldn't only find ways to cure the psychological costs. In the first place, we would try to prevent those costs from being incurred.

One way of prevention is to avoid the use of violence. Another is to immunize ourselves from the harmful consequences of its use. We can pursue both approaches without contradiction. But if we become too effective at the second approach, will we stop feeling the need for the first?

This might already be what's happening. We seem easily convinced of our own goodness and the depravity of our enemies. By prioritizing the use of long-distance bombing, and promising "no boots on the ground," we protect our soldiers not only from physical but also from psychological harm. And our technological ability to distance ourselves from killing continues to advance. In the not-too-distant future, much of our violence may be carried out by devices and drones—intelligent weapons that do not feel.

Will that be the end of moral injury?

That depends, I suppose, on the moral.

Since the last time I saw it, the *Price of Peace* monument has had inscriptions added to its base. There's a plaque to commemorate the 48th Highlanders of Canada who fought the Germans in the countryside west of Ortona. There's a plaque to commemorate members of the First Nations of Canada who served and died in the Italian Campaign. There's a plaque to commemorate two Ortona women, Maria and Francesca La Sorda, who tended the statue until their deaths, ensuring it was always adorned with fresh flowers. There's a plaque created by the government of Canada to identify the Battle of Ortona as a National Historic Event. That might not be the end of it. By the time you're reading this, there could be more.

The square in which the statue stands has been renamed. What was previously Piazza Plebiscito is now Piazza degli Eroi Canadesi, or Canadian Heroes Square.

The municipality has also greatly enhanced the space.[12] They removed the car parking to create a large pedestrian area with benches on a mix of cobblestone and grass. The stone is laid out in the shape of a giant maple leaf. Near the leaf's base, at the centre of the plaza, there's a floor fountain with six jets of water that rise to just under an average person's height. In evenings, the jets engage in a play of colour, alternating between red and white for Canada, blue for Ortona, and red, white, and green for Italy. On a grey stone stela, there are words in Italian, English, and French:

CANADA AND ITALY

War brought us together and peace made us friends

They've made the square much brighter and more uplifting. The solemnity of *The Price of Peace* is respected, but now the statue anchors one corner of an architecturally interesting and positive space. There are symbols of life, two cultures, and the ocean. It's good to see some beauty added to Ortona after it lost so much to the war.

If you find yourself in Ortona, standing in this place, and thinking about *The Price of Peace*, consider also having a thought for the ghosts. There is no trace of them in Canadian Heroes Square—and maybe it's better that way. But if they hadn't mattered to some Canadian soldiers, there would be no statue here.

And when you're ready to move on from the square, please don't forget the civilian monument. It's on via del Cimitero less than five hundred metres away.

CHAPTER 11

In Another Life

"I DON'T KNOW WHETHER I've been much help."

Immediately, I wanted to reassure him. "But it's the thoughts that you have that are interesting," I replied.

Not my best answer. I would have liked to leave Norman with better words than that.

"I find it difficult to uh, to really put my thoughts out," he said. "Put them into words."

His box was on the sofa beside him. The lid was closed. He was staring at it. I waited, sensing that he had more to say.

He looked from the box to me.

"Like another world."

MY BOX IS STILL open on my living room floor. I've grown accustomed to it here. Soon, though, I'll put the lid back on and take it back down to storage. I'll return it to its usual place on the shelf, but with a difference now. I won't feel like I'm hiding from it anymore.

For years, at the back of my mind, I had the idea that this box should be a book. It was a nagging idea, not a welcome one; a perfectly fine idea, but not for me. In principle, I wasn't against it. I just didn't want to be the author.

And so I lived with the feeling that I was shirking some kind of duty. I used to think of ways to argue back. This idea that there should be a book—where did it even come from? No one had asked for one. No promise had been made and broken. On the contrary, I'd kept my promise: I'd finished the dissertation. That was a book-length public document, available online to anyone who cared to read it. True, I hadn't told anyone about it—not even the veterans I'd interviewed. But by the time I'd finished, most of them were dead, and in all the years following our interviews, not one had reached out. They knew how to find me if they wanted to. The reasonable conclusion was they had got on with their lives and weren't thinking much about me one way or another. If I continued to dwell on my supposed debt to them, that would be a symptom of my needs, not theirs.

As for the Ortonesi, I had a more valid reason to feel I'd let them down. None of their stories had made it into my dissertation. But that hadn't been intentional. A dissertation can't be a mixed bag of stories; as an academic work, it needs a thesis; things that don't support the thesis, don't belong. I would have preferred to include their stories, but when the thesis took shape—when I'd finally unlocked the way forward—there simply hadn't been a place in it for them.

Anyway, how much was fair to expect of me? At least I'd done something rather than nothing, and that something hadn't been easy. With the same time and effort (or god knows, maybe less) I could have gone to medical school and become a "real" doctor instead.

Those were the arguments that I repeatedly made to myself. And it was all beside the point. The point was, none of that would have stopped me from writing a book from the box, if only the topic in the box hadn't been killing. I did want to write a book; I just didn't want to write one about *that.* I was sick of the topic and didn't want it in my life. My aversion stemmed from more than just the time I'd have to spend living with it while writing; what really made me recoil was the thought of how the finished book would tie me to it forever, binding it to my name. Maybe I would only get to publish one book in my life. And that book would be this? Why do that to myself?

Meanwhile, from time to time, I had to go down to the storage locker. And every time, there would be the box. I just wanted to get these balcony chairs out for the summer, or store these pots for my plants, but the damned box wouldn't let me do it in peace. It always summoned the same gnawing feeling inside me; not exactly guilt, more like an existential dread. Naturally, I started to hate it for that. Sometimes I imagined taking it outside and tossing it into the dumpster. *There you go. Problem solved.* Then I'd feel bad for the thought—which of course only added to my resentment.

I won't try to explain how it happened; I'm not sure I fully understand it myself. Whatever the reason, it's enough to say that one day I grabbed the box, carried it upstairs, dropped it on the living room floor where it couldn't be missed, and sat down, finally, to write.

I still didn't want to be the author. Of course my name would have to be on the book—no way of getting around that—but I reckoned there must be ways of writing that would give up at least some of my ownership. Maybe I could craft it like one of those observational documentary films, the kind that have no voice-over and provide no explanations. Following that model, I could take snippets of stories and texts, create a sort of collage, hand it over to the reader, and let them decide what to make of it, having said nothing about it myself. For a little while, I tried it that way. For a variety of reasons, it didn't work. I had to accept that I needed to put more of myself in the book.

But that didn't mean I was out of options. There was another way I could distance myself from the topic—my narrative voice. The narrator doesn't always have to explain, clarify, or stay in control. There are literary forms that intentionally leave things unsaid, ambiguous, or opaque. In fiction, especially, it's common wisdom that it's better to show than to tell. That approach is less typical in research-based non-fiction, but if I could get away with it, then why not. And come to think of it, the veterans themselves had often been elusive and indirect in their storytelling. I could say their style had influenced mine—and maybe that was even true.

At the most basic, sentence level of writing, I wanted to reduce my need to name or state the topic. The literary approach certainly facilitated this, but it wouldn't be quite right to say it made it easier. On the contrary, it was a lot of extra work. That's generally the case with avoidant behaviour—it can take a lot of effort, especially if you're trying to pass it off as natural.

A moment arrived when the strain became too much. I was writing a passage and reached a point in a sentence where the obvious and easiest word choice was the dreaded one. I was on the verge of typing it when I stopped. *Is it really necessary? Maybe there's a way around.*

A sudden wave of frustration took hold of me. How many times in my life had I started and stopped and agonized over that basic four-letter word? It's just a word! How had I become so freaking phobic!? I had accepted my condition as normal—but it was not.

I remembered Norman.

The more Germans you k–

And I thought, *I'm doing what he did.*

I'm like him.

Of course, I wasn't doing exactly what he did, and I wasn't just like him. Norman's aversion to the word came from a much deeper place.

I don't know if he told me by choice or if it was by mistake. It started with me asking him about the street fighting in Ortona. He was looking a bit nervous, as usual, but still welcoming my questions. His answers came in quick, softly-spoken phrases with frequent pauses in between.

"It was just like house clearing," he said. "And, you had to make sure there was . . . no Germans around. Of course. And uh . . . luckily I guess, we didn't run into any. So uh . . . some of the other outfits had . . . a hard time. You could only really take in what's going on immediately around you. You know, what, if you saw the overall picture it would be . . . really frightening. Anyway there was a lot of sniping, that sort of thing. And uh—"

His mention of sniping sparked my curiosity.

"Could you tell when some, like, can you tell when somebody's shooting at you?"

That change of tense in the middle of my question served a purpose, even if I wasn't fully aware of it. In switching from the past (*could you tell*) to the simple present (*can*) I was giving Norman more options. The past tense would have sent him back and called for a more personal story, whereas the simple present was relatively more open to answering in general terms. At first, Norman took up the terms that I'd offered.

"Oh yeah, yeah. Usually. You can hear it."

He could have left it at that. But then he recalled a personal experience. When he decided to share it, did he know from the start where it was taking him? Or did he not see the destination until it was too late to change his course?

"Uh . . . Let's see now, at uh . . . Agira, which was before Ortona . . . I think I saw the bullet, I don't know, go by me. And . . . that was quite an experience. And uh . . . I . . . I saw the fellow who had fired the shot.

And I just . . . I just waited. And uh . . . then he showed himself, and I was able to uh . . . shoot him. That time. But that was the only time that I—"

He stopped short and paused for a moment.

"—I know that I shot someone."

I CAN'T BE SURE what the "Safe Conduct" leaflet meant to Norman. I never thought to ask him. After handing it to me, he had seemed to change the topic from the leaflet to his general's words. Briefly, I was confused; then I moved on to my questions about Ortona. I gave the leaflet back to him and he returned it to his box.

When I think of the leaflet now, I remember some lines by the World War II veteran and literary critic Samuel Hynes. Hynes used some of the same words as Norman to describe his war experience: "a kind of exile from one's own real life, a dislocation of the familiar that the mind preserves as life in another world." After observing that his war memories felt like "another world," Hynes asked himself why in his attic there were "two tattered pilot's logbooks, an air-wing shoulder patch, and a yellowed plastic container that once held survival gear and now is full of old photographs." He answered, "I keep them, I suppose, for their reality."

Sometimes, when we hold on to certain objects, what we're trying to hold is some aspect of ourselves. The memento reassures us not only that the past was real, but that we were real in that moment. And sometimes, we pick something up precisely because we sense we'll need it later for that purpose. We know there's the risk of losing touch with who we are now; one day, the person we are now might become distant or unreal; we keep the object, hoping it will protect us from that loss.

I can imagine many reasons why, when he came upon it, the "Safe Conduct" leaflet would have captured Norman's interest. Here was an object made by his own side in the war that was intended to be picked up and read by his enemy. Not only that, the leaflet was intended to convert his enemy into—if not necessarily a friend, then at least a harmless fellow person. The leaflet promised the German that he wouldn't be harmed if he surrendered. Holding it in his hands, Norman could imagine being the German. He could also imagine the scenario of the German coming to him with this leaflet. The leaflet, in short, was a little story of a nonviolent meeting. Norman might have believed that, in the real world, this was impossible; but even as a fantasy, the leaflet could be held onto as a statement of principle. The statement was: we only harm or kill when it's necessary—it's not what we want to do.

Was there a connection between the leaflet and his general's words?

"Anyway, his, he gave us a talk, and he said uh, the more Germans you k—, you *kill*, he said, the quicker you're gonna get home . . . So that was the, his, his approach."

"That was pretty harsh."

"Yeah, that's hard. Yeah. But, I guess it was a fact."

Norman didn't believe that he could argue with the facts. But he had kept the leaflet.

It wasn't clear if he'd ever killed. Maybe he couldn't be sure of it himself. Later in the interview, when he told me he'd shot someone, I tried asking him more about it.

"But that was the only time that I . . . I know that I shot someone."

"I guess it's not often that you can actually see—"

"No—"

"—the—"

"No. No usually it's uh . . . So, uh . . . Anyway this uh . . ."

He picked up a book that was beside him on the couch.

"This uh. . . . Here's a book here that uh . . . my son got this book for me. He got, he found it through the internet."

He was referring me now to a book.[1] I took that as a signal. I wasn't going to ask him any more about his story.

"But anyway," he continued, "it mentions a lot of the fellows."

Fellows. That got my attention. Not while I was there, but later, when I read the transcript. By *fellows*, he was obviously referring to men in his regiment. But this was the second time he'd used the word. Barely a minute earlier, he'd used it for his enemy.

I saw the fellow who had fired the shot . . . then he showed himself . . .

Maybe for him it was just a habit of speech to call every man a fellow. Even so, from what little I knew of Norman, I think it was more to him than that.

NORMAN HADN'T WANTED TO speak about killing any more than I had wanted to write about it. I imagined that, like me, he was sick and tired of that topic in his life.

The same was probably true for all the men in this book. And when I thought about how much I had wished not to be the author—and these stories weren't even mine—well then, I had to wonder: what must it have been like for the men who truly owned them? If I had feared that writing this book might bind me to the topic forever, wouldn't they have felt the same? In fact, unlike me, maybe they already felt bound—their fate was already sealed. Even so, they surely didn't want their lives to be known only by this one chapter.

I started digging deeper into my material, looking for ways I could show these men as whole people, not just narrators of violent stories. At first, I worried it wouldn't be possible. I didn't think I'd learned enough about them. But I began noticing that, even when I didn't know the full context, I'd collected lots of small details that hinted at more in their lives. Sometimes those hints were in the ways they'd arranged to meet me—like Sam inviting me over when his wife would be away at bingo, and Gus asking his daughter to host the gathering with me and his friends. Other hints came from things they told me on the side of the interviews, like Mel describing his sign museum and his trips to Arizona with Eva. And there were glimpses in what I had quietly observed and jotted down, like Norman's birdfeeder, and Bill's dogs, and the way Bill's son had greeted me and pointed out the deer.

As I pored over my field notes and re-entered the world of the recorded interviews, looking for ways to portray these men as more fully dimensional, I began to notice more substantive elements too—things related to the stories' meanings and interpretations that I'd previously overlooked or misunderstood. New questions began to surface. And to my surprise—despite my original wish to get this work over with quickly—I found myself willing to do more research. Each step I took made me more open to the next. I made the effort to look up Norman Letendre—now that it was a simple online query, it was hard to justify not doing it. From there, it wasn't such a leap to go to the library and learn more about Ted. Then I spotted something in Bill's story that I'd completely missed, something clearly important to him. I was moved to reach deeper into the box and bring out the stories of the Ortonesi.

Somewhere on the way—I don't remember how—it suddenly came to me that I had got something else incredibly wrong. I saw it now with such clarity that I couldn't fathom how I'd ever missed it. These stories were not really about killing. They were about compassion and caring deeply for life. If compassion hadn't been there as an instinct, a goal, or a measure, the stories would have been completely different. The wounds, the confusions, the buried feelings, the attempted reconciliations—none of it would have made sense.

Compassion. I was stunned. The word had been right in front of me on the page. Ted had used it a lot. I'd often written it on the page myself. I simply hadn't connected it up. I'd been identifying the trees, but never rethinking the forest. I'd been mistaken about my topic all along.

WHEN MEL'S POEM ABOUT Ortona unexpectedly came out of the box, another poem came out with it.

The first, I could remember him sharing with me. I could remember us talking about it as doggerel, and laughing when Eva told me to look it up.

This second poem, however, I didn't recognize at all. I had no memory of receiving it. Not that there's any question of who gave it to me—even if he hadn't put his name at the end, it's the same lined paper with the same all-caps printing by hand. I'm sure he told me something about it. I just didn't retain what he said.

And if I never took the time to read it, that's because—well, I simply couldn't. The poem wasn't about war. I needed to focus, get my job done, and put all this stuff away.

I can read it now.

"Wishful Thoughts"

In another life and another world,
Were my choices free and justly heard,
I would love to live in a western clime,
Not a fancy city nor a small town fine.

Let me live on a range where horizons seem,
As far away as the deepest dream,
And hear the wind moaning through the pines,
And the coyote cry his lonesome whine.

Let me know the smell of fresh clean air,
With a hint of woodsmoke somewhere near,
Let me see a valley where cattle graze,
And dark clouds sail on rainy days.

In the distance mountains, with peaks of snow,
That feed the lakes and streams below,
Let me hear the song of the meadow lark,
And watch the deer as they feed at dark.

Let me see each season of a wondrous land,
From spring's awakening to Jack Frost's hand,
The blue of crocus as it comes alive,
On hills where they and the cactus thrive.

Let me hear the sound of the Canada goose,
As I watch from a grove of woodland spruce,
And smell the pungence of new mown hay,
From a fresh cut field across the way.

In these wistful thoughts, let me see a stream,
As it wends its way in the sunlight's gleam,
Through meadow verdant and valley wide,
Alive with trout and with depth to hide.

And in the fall when the frost has come,
The vivid colors that nature's spun,
Then a carpet of snow of the purest white,
On a wonderland to behold at night.

They're thoughts that come to a wanting mind,
When most of your life has been left behind,
A secret desire to begin again,
Spinning wishful webs, but done in vain.

He is surely blessed who has lived this dream,
At one with nature to me it seems,
But we each have purpose to exist as meant,
In this great land that was heaven sent.

Mel McPhee, 1996

Charles Comfort.

Notes

This book uses a dual endnote system. When the only purpose is to provide the source reference, that's done through a phrase-cued endnote (a short phrase from the text followed by the source, without any number in the main text). Numbered endnotes are used when there is more to say—commentary, context, or clarification.

CHAPTER ONE

Ortona is an ancient town My sources for the following historical overview of Ortona (the town) include Basti, *Ortona Ricorda*; di Tullio, *1943*; Pacaccio, *Tommaso*; and di Paolo, "Curare le Ferite di Guerra"; for Italy's fascist period and how it was experienced in Ortona: Bosworth, *Mussolini's Italy*; Catena, *Mi Ricordo*; for the war in Italy: Beevor, *The Second World War*; Nicholson, *Official History*; Morgan, *The Fall of Mussolini*; Ginsborg, *A History of Contemporary Italy*; and for the experience of the war in Ortona: di Tullio, *1943*; Catena, *Mi Ricordo*; and di Luzio, *Ortona Guerra e Dopoguerra*.

An epic thing is happening Halton, quoted in Zuehlke, *Ortona*, 346-7.

December 25 is Christmas in Ortona "The Spirit of Giving," *The Globe and Mail*, December 24, 1943, p.6. City of Edmonton Archives (War of '39, Loyal Edmonton Regiment Collection).

A military commentator said "Canadians Dig Last Nazis Out With Bayonets," *Toronto Daily Star*, December 24, 1943, p.1. City of Edmonton Archives (War of '39, Loyal Edmonton Regiment Collection).

These prairie farmers are the men Gregory Clark, "Tells How Edmonton Men Attempted 'Sound Attack' in Ortona Battle," *Edmonton Journal*, January 17, 1944. City of Edmonton Archives (War of '39, Loyal Edmonton Regiment Collection).

Rifles, Bren guns Zuehlke, *Ortona,* 254.

The process of clearing Ibid., 285-6.

1 My approach was based on the ethnographic research tradition of social and cultural anthropology. The main objective in ethnographic research is to get to know your research "subjects" (nowadays typically called "participants") on their own terms, as they see themselves, as they interpret and experience their world. This entails meeting people as much as possible in places where they "already are"—their homes, communities, anywhere that's natural for them (as opposed to bringing them into labs, focus groups, or dedicated interview-recording rooms).

Among anthropologists, the word "ethnography" also refers to the written work that results from and describes the research. (In fact, that's the original meaning of the word, as the suffix *-graphy* suggests.) It's common for ethnographic writing to be narrative and semi-autobiographical. Indeed, it's unusual if it isn't. That's largely due to the distinctive fieldwork method of participant-observation whereby the fieldworker immerses him- or herself (to varying degrees, depending on topic and circumstances) in the social world and activities of the people being studied. As the fieldworker's identity and personality unavoidably affect the research, it's important for that to be documented and considered in the written report. Furthermore, in this research method, a great deal is learned through the friction of differences (cultural and otherwise) between fieldworker and participants, and from their mutual attempts to understand one another. Accordingly, these "ethnographic encounters" are often described in rich narrative detail, wherein the fieldworker is naturally one of the characters.

All of which is to say that the present book is an ethnography of memories of the Battle of Ortona—it's a narrative account based on ethnographic research that includes my own experience of doing and remembering it. It's a bit more novelistic than most academic ethnographies, especially in my use of delayed decoding (i.e., not explaining everything to the reader up-front) and in the moments where I've left something for the reader to wonder about, offering no explanation of my own. These "show, don't tell" stylistic features are rare in academic writing, I think generally for two reasons. First, academic writers know that their colleagues have to read a lot for work and need to get on with their own; it's understood that such readers are going to appreciate a book whose points are clear and easy to find. Second, academic writers have a career interest in demonstrating their mastery of a topic; this drives them to write more assertively and to leave nothing that could be explained, unexplained. That said, among social scientists, anthropologists are the most open to experimentation in writing, especially when it comes to ways of sharing the vicissitudes of fieldwork and the provisional nature of knowledge.

The standard guide to anthropological research methods (the textbook that I, along with most anthropologists, learned from in grad school) is Bernard, *Research Methods in Anthropology*. Recent discussions and examples of experimentation in ethnographic writing can be found in Pandian and McLean, *Crumpled Paper Boat*. Feminist anthropologists have been at the forefront of experiments in writing; see for example Ruth Behar's groundbreaking book, *The Vulnerable Observer*. Behar's work on life history and memoir is especially pertinent to my own, and I benefitted from attending one of her writing workshops.

2 In scholarly terms, I was doing a type of life story research. Broadly speaking, life story research is concerned with how individuals experience and narrate their lives, and how those narratives reveal individuals' understandings of themselves and their relationships to others. Varieties of life story research can be more or less concerned with establishing "what really happened" (and are often called life *history* when that matters) and can be more or less focused either on the self that is being narrated or on the narrative's stylistic features. In all cases, what distinguishes life story from other types of ethnographic research is the greater attention on individuals rather than groups (although when it's done by anthropologists, the individuals are still studied with attention to their cultural context). Scholars in many disciplines, including oral history, sociolinguistics, and psychology, are effectively doing life story research even when they don't call it by that name. For a cross-disciplinary sample of influences on my work, see: Peacock and Holland, "The Narrated Self"; Watson and Watson-Franke, *Interpreting Life Histories*; Tonkin, *Narrating Our Pasts*; Thomson, *Anzac Memories* and "Anzac Memories: Putting Popular Memory Theory into Practice"; Portelli, *The Death of Luigi Trastulli* and *The Battle of Valle Giulia*; Linde, *Life Stories*; Ochs and Capps, *Living Narrative*; and McLeod, *Narrative and Psychotherapy*.

Alongside life story research, there's also scholarship on "social memory" where the attention is on how narratives about the past are constructed, shared, and contested within social groups, and how that's important to group identities (e.g., nations, social classes, villages, etc.). An example that's close to my own topic is Cook's *The Fight for History* which documents how dominant meanings of World War II have changed over time in Canada. At the time of my research, the key text on social memory was Fentress and Wickham's aptly titled book, *Social Memory*.

Of course, individual memories and narratives are affected by social discourses, and vice versa. How to interpret and represent that interconnectedness is a thorny issue. What I found most helpful here was the work of the Popular Memory Group, "Popular Memory: Theory, Politics, Method"; oral historians Thomson and Portelli, cited above; and the "cultural models" approach developed by cognitive anthropologists (starting with Holland and Quinn, *Cultural Models in Language and Thought*). However, I never really got around to doing a rigorous study of *social* memories of the Ortona battle. There just wasn't much of it to study at the time. If I had been serious about it, though, I'm sure I could have found it at the community level in Edmonton, Vancouver, and of course, in Ortona itself. To some extent, I looked for it; but I got caught up in the challenge of collecting and interpreting individual and archived narratives. My dissertation did get into the question of how Ortona veterans' personal narratives related to social discourses, but the social context that I ended up examining was the national tradition of war remembrance, not the social memory of the battle per se. Most of that analysis is absent from the present book, but you'll find a bit of it in the later chapters.

My work also drew on psychoanalytic approaches to ethnography—but that didn't happen until years after my fieldwork. The value of that approach is explained later in this chapter.

3 The challenge I've just described is associated with the method called "unstructured interviewing." In this method, you have an agenda of the topics and perhaps some of the details that you want to cover, and you might have some of the actual questions sketched out, but you don't follow that agenda rigidly and you definitely don't read your questions out as if you're following a script. The aim is to make the interview as conversational as possible; you want to free the participant from any preconceptions they might have about how they "should" be talking, and encourage them to go wherever their thoughts might take them. Of course, I still took the lead when I introduced a topic and when I prompted participants to clarify or expand on their answers, but I was open to them changing topics, making apparent digressions, repeating themselves, and "talking back" against my agenda. In ethnographic research, this is a common approach to interviewing. It puts a lot of cognitive load on the fieldworker, and it's time consuming, not only while you're doing it but also later when you have to make sense of it. The payoff is in the depth of insight and unexpected discoveries that you get. Other methods are faster, more amenable to large-scale projects, and require less training and practice; they're well suited for some types of research, but they tend to skim the surface and can easily miss what the researcher didn't already expect to find.

4 Norman was referring to the Allied propaganda shells that were packed with leaflets and fired into enemy territory from regular guns. The shells would explode harmlessly in mid-air or on impact with the ground, scattering the leaflets. For more about the Allied safe conduct leaflets, see Friedman, "The Allied 'Passierschein' Safe Conduct Passes of WWII."

5 *Saracen* was a generic term for Muslims in medieval and early modern Europe. It has pejorative connotations and was used especially by Christians to describe their Muslim opponents during the Crusades.

6 In October 1935, Italy invaded Ethiopia (then known as Abyssinia). The League of Nations (predecessor to the United Nations) condemned Italy's aggression and imposed economic sanctions. However, the sanctions were limited in scope (notably excluding oil) because Britain and France did not want to risk war with Italy and still hoped to entice it away from its deepening alliance with Nazi Germany. In May 1936, Italy completed its conquest of Ethiopia. (Taylor, *The Origins of the Second World War*, 87–97.)

7 Across Italy and its occupied territories, some Italian troops fought the Germans for days—and were then slaughtered upon surrender; some joined the local partisans; some joined the Germans; most just tried to go home.

Anglo-American narratives have often portrayed Italian soldiers in World War II as cowardly or comically inept. Italians have sometimes embraced this stereotype (e.g., Gabriele Salvatores' film *Mediterraneo*). This obscures the complexity of the Italian military's collapse, and the realities of its war crimes in North Africa, Ethiopia, and the Balkans. For more nuanced English-language accounts of this period, see Morgan, *The Fall of Mussolini,* and Holland, *The Savage Storm.*

8 The Germans created a network of overlapping defensive lines stretching roughly from Gaeta on the west coast (about 100km south of Rome) to Ortona on the east. They used a variety of names for different segments, including Victor, Barbara, Bernhardt, and Gustav. The classification of Ortona's position within this network varies; some Canadian historians (e.g., Zuehlke) place it on the Bernhardt Line, others (e.g., Windsor and Geroux) on the Gustav. The confusion is partly due to the fact—as noted in the British official history of the Italian Campaign—that the Germans "continually altered the titles of their lines or parts of them," resulting in a "bewildering" situation for later historians (Molony et al., *The Mediterranean and Middle East*, 429). Collectively, this network of defenses from Gaeta to Ortona was known to the Allies as the Winter Line.

9 The Canadian Army in World War II was structured similarly to the British. The 1st Canadian Infantry Division included a divisional headquarters; artillery regiments; engineering, signals, medical, and other support units; and three infantry brigades. In each brigade there were three regiments. In each regiment, there were four rifle companies, labelled A, B, C, and D. Companies were subdivided into platoons and sections. At full strength in the field, there were typically 800–1,000 men in a regiment, 100–150 in a company, 30–40 in a platoon, and 8–12 in a section. Brigades were commanded by a brigadier, regiments were typically commanded by a lieutenant-colonel supported by a major, companies by a captain, platoons by a lieutenant supported by a sergeant, and sections by a corporal.

Strictly speaking, the regiments were "battalions"—that's the term for the operational or fighting unit of a regiment. But that distinction didn't seem relevant to the veterans whom I interviewed; they mostly used the term "regiment" and for the sake of clarity that's what I've consistently used in this book. As with the British Army, the Canadian Army's regiments were (and still are) geographically based, each with its own traditions and institutional memory. From the start of the invasion of Italy until the Battle of Ortona, the Canadian regiments remained "extremely regionally homogenous" (Engen, *Strangers in Arms*, 43). In other words, nearly all of the soldiers in the Loyal Edmonton and Seaforth regiments fighting in Ortona were from Alberta and British Columbia. However, following their casualties in Ortona and then for the duration of the war, the regiments lost their regional homogeneity as new recruits from across Canada were assigned to wherever they were most needed.

10 The myth of the Fallschirmjäger was documented in a 2021–22 exhibit at the Military History Museum in Dresden, curated by Dr. Magnus Pahl, titled "Hitler's Elite Troops? The Myth of the Fallschirmjäger." Pahl is the scientific director of the Centre for Military History and Social Sciences of the Bundeswehr in Potsdam, Germany. A summary of the exhibit is available online at https://www.bundeswehr.de/de/organisation/zentrum-innere-fuehrung/unsere-angebote/if-zeitschrift-fuer-innere-fuehrung/hitlers-elitetruppe-mythos-fallschirmjaeger-5092942. See also Sven-Felix Kellerhof, "So kampften Hitlers 'Grune Teufel' Wirklich," *Welt*, June 7, 2021 https://www.welt.de/geschichte/zweiter-weltkrieg/article231637959/Fallschirmjaeger-So-kaempften-Hitlers-Gruene-Teufel.html.

Early in the fighting at Ortona, Canadian intelligence officers noted that the paratroopers were "the toughest [German troops] we have had to face yet." Based on interrogations of fifty captured paratroopers, the Canadian divisional intelligence report on December 22 made a distinction between "the good type" and "the better."

"The first were those young men who in their keenness and eagerness for an adventurous military career, volunteered to join this hazardous branch of the GAF [German Armed Forces] but who have not been in the service long enough to be instilled with that fanatic discipline and sense of security. A few months with a parachute training Bn [battalion], in FRANCE, training which did not even incl [include] jumping, and they were rushed off to the front. The reality of war must have been a rather sudden revelation to them, and they were quite willing and prepared to impart their limited knowledge."

"The latter type were the older veterans who had been to SICILY, CRETE, and who, at some time or other, had seen service on the RUSSIAN front. Those men knew what the score was and their discipline, morale, and security are excellent. It is no wonder that they are the 'picked tps [troops]' and sent to whichever sector of the front needs strengthening. It is also interesting to note the condescending way in which the parachutists talk about the inf [German infantry], 'they always mess things up, and we, the parachutists have to straighten them out again.'"

("1 Cdn Intelligence Summary No. 30 (22 Dec 1943)" in Appendix D, "Operations of 1 Cdn Inf Div and 1 Cdn Armed Bde in Italy, 25 Nov 43 – 4 Jan 44." Canadian Military Headquarters Report No. 165. Directorate of History and Heritage, Department of National Defence.)

On the mix of experienced and "green" paratroops in Ortona, see also the testimony of paratroop veteran Fritz Illi in Zuehlke, *Ortona*, 197-9 and 223.

11 Canadian and German casualties for the urban battle of Ortona are documented in Nicholson, *Official History*, 333-8, and Geroux, "The Urban Battle of Ortona," 63–4. The data on psychological casualties is reported in Copp and McAndrew, *Battle Exhaustion*, 56. Civilian deaths in Ortona were counted by the parish priest Don Antonio Politi and listed by name in his 1948 publication, *I Giorni del Martirio: Ortona 1943*. The entire 1st Canadian Division was engaged in battle during the month of December in the countryside around Ortona as well as in the town itself. This was the most intense and prolonged period of combat for the Canadian army since the start of the war, and by the end of December a total of 2,339 Canadian soldiers were killed, wounded, or missing (Nicholson, *Official History*, 338). Ortona civilians were also killed during fighting in the countryside and during the months that followed the end of the fighting when they stumbled upon unexploded bombs, mines, and booby traps. A total of 1,314 Ortona civilians were killed during the ten-month period that the front of the war passed through the region (Zuehlke, *Ortona*, 375. This was the official count cited by the Italian government in 1959 when it awarded a Gold Medal for Civilian Valour to the people of Ortona in recognition of their solidarity through suffering during the war.) Data on Ortona's physical damage is in Serafini, *Danni di Guerra*, 35.

The only published book-length study of the battle is Mark Zuehlke's *Ortona: Canada's Epic WWII Battle*. Zuehlke's book focuses on the soldiers' experiences and covers the actions of the entire 1st Canadian Division in December 1943. Jayson Geroux's MA thesis "The Urban Battle of Ortona" is also a richly detailed book-length study that pays special attention to Canadian and German tactics; in addition, Geroux provides a thorough historiography of the battle. Most recently, in their book chapter "Urban Anchor on the Gustav Line," Windsor and Geroux emphasize that the urban battle should be understood in the context of the simultaneous efforts by other Canadian regiments and their Eighth Army allies, the 19th Indian Brigade, to capture Villa Grande, a village four kilometres west of Ortona. The urban battle has received most of the attention from historians and the Canadian public, but the fighting in the countryside and Villa Grande was equally important in forcing the German 1st Parachute Division to abandon Ortona. In fact, during the last week of December, Canadian losses (killed and wounded) were higher in the countryside than they were in the town.

The attention of academic military historians has focused mainly on questions of whether the town should have been attacked and what was gained as a result. The strongest critic of Major-General Vokes' decisions at Ortona is Greenhous ("Would It Not Have Been Better to Bypass Ortona Completely?") who argues that the whole urban battle was unnecessary. That was also the opinion of Major Jim Stone who led the Edmonton troops in Ortona and later said, "It should never have been fought" (quoted in Dancocks, *The D-Day Dodgers*, 190). Critics regard Vokes as having blundered into Ortona; he had only recently been promoted to the divisional command and was arguably lacking in confidence and imagination. Vokes is most strongly defended by Case ("Trial By Fire") who argues that none of the Allied commanders in Italy had expected the Germans to fight an urban battle, and Vokes was under tremendous pressure from his superior, General Bernard Montgomery. Furthermore, once the urban battle had started, it was hard to stop; after the media (including the CBC's Matthew Halton) had compared Ortona to Stalingrad, it became a "prestige battle" that neither the Canadians nor the Germans wanted to appear to lose; the Canadian public was invested in victory, and Hitler ordered his generals to defend Ortona at all costs. In fact, four or five days into the battle, Vokes asked Brigadier Bert Hoffmeister who was commanding the regiments in Ortona if he wanted to stop; concerned about the effect that would have on his men's morale, Hoffmeister replied, "absolutely not."

As for the battle's outcome, there is consensus that the town of Ortona provided the Allies with little strategic value, as the Germans had destroyed the port; and the costs in taking it crippled the 1st Canadian Division for months. On the other hand, by fighting in Ortona, the Canadians became experts in urban warfare and shared their lessons learned with other Allied forces. The value of attacking Ortona also has to be considered in light of the objectives of the Allied campaign in Italy, which were less about gaining ground and more about diverting and destroying German resources in order to weaken Germany on the war's other, more important fronts.

In that respect, when Vokes told his men (as remembered by Norman) that their objective was to kill Germans, it could be argued that he was sharing the blunt but basic truth of the Italian Campaign. In addition to sources cited above, see Bercuson, *Maple Leaf Against the Axis*, 172-7; Brown, "The Rock of Accomplishment"; Cook, *The Necessary War*, 405-17; Copp, *No Price Too High*, 132-7; Dancocks, *The D-Day Dodgers*; Gooderson, "Assimilating Urban Battle Experience"; and Granatstein, *The Generals*, 191.

There are many accounts of Ortona civilians' experiences of the battle published in Italian (e.g., Giannetti et al., *La Battaglia di Ortona*; Iubatti, *Testimonianze*). The most complete English-language account is di Tullio's graphic history, *1943: The Road to Ortona*. Zuehlke's *Ortona* includes some civilian narratives. Cavasin's MA thesis, "Hai Visto i Canadesi?" focuses on Ortonesi-Canadian relations during the four months after the battle when Ortona was a rest area for the 1st Canadian Division.

Little has been published on the German experience of Ortona, but see Bayerlein, "Parachute Engineers in Combat" which is a brief memoir by a paratrooper translated into English; and Holland, *The Savage Storm*, quoting passages from another paratrooper's memoir that originally appeared in di Marco, *Assolutamente Resistere!*

While the Eighth Army's advance stalled at Ortona in December 1943, the US Fifth Army on Italy's west coast was similarly bogged down in the battles for the Mignano Gap, about 15km southeast of Cassino. Apart from the Anzio landing in January 1944, both fronts settled down into a period of static winter warfare. At the end of April 1944, the 1st Canadian Division left Ortona—replaced by the 10th Indian Division—and moved across the Apennines to the west coast, joining other Eighth Army units (including the Polish II Corps) in preparation for a spring offensive toward Rome. That joint offensive by the Fifth and Eighth Armies began on May 11, culminating in the final Battle of Monte Cassino. (In Canada, this is more often referred to as the Battle of the Liri Valley.) The Allies finally captured Rome on June 4, 1944.

12 This sign has been quoted in a number of Canadian books and articles about Ortona. The source seems to be the memoir of C.P. Stacey who was the Historical Officer at Canadian Military Headquarters during World War II. Stacey was based in London, but visited Ortona shortly after the battle. His memoir *A Date With History* was published in 1983. However, in the City of Edmonton Archives (War of '39, Loyal Edmonton Regiment Collection) I found a clipped newspaper article that quotes the sign as follows: "You are now entering a west Canadian town." Whoever clipped the article didn't note the newspaper name, but it's by Doug How, titled "Ortona Like West Canadian Town As Edmonton Troops 'Take Over,'" and date-stamped May 9, 1944. Stacey himself would probably want us to trust the contemporary report more than his memoir. But his version is more satisfying, and reporters do make mistakes, so maybe we'll continue to say that Stacey got it right.

13 Mowat's Hastings and Prince Edward Regiment fought in the countryside south and west of Ortona, not in the urban battle that was the focus of my fieldwork. His breakdown is further discussed in Chapter 10.

In one of his later books, Mowat described his homecoming: "War's end found me in western Europe, where I remained until the end of 1945, serving as a kind of glorified garbage man, charged with collecting samples of the weaponry that had obliterated some thirty or forty million human beings. By the time I returned to Canada I desperately wished to escape from what had been, and seemed likely to remain, a world run by maniacs. So I fled north to spend much of 1947 on the tundra plains of Keewatin, northwest of Churchill. There I lived and travelled with a young Métis, who introduced me to the barrenland caribou, arctic wolves, and a little-known and dwindling tribe of inland-dwelling Inuit" (*Aftermath*, ix-x). For more detail about his homecoming, see his memoir *Otherwise*.

14 On the surge of interest in World War II commemoration during the 1990s, see Cook, *The Fight for History*, and Chapter 2 of my PhD dissertation (Cosh, "Killing Matters"). My fieldwork was supported by a SSHRC Doctoral Fellowship, IODE War Memorial Doctoral Scholarship, Mariano A. Elia Chair Graduate Student Scholarship, and the York University Faculty of Graduate Studies Fieldwork Costs Fund.

15 The news report was about the effort by Edmund (Ted) Griffiths to organize a Christmas "reconciliation dinner" with the Germans in 1998. This event will be described in Chapter 6.

16 The foundational text in this tradition is Bronislaw Malinowski's *Argonauts of the Western Pacific*. Malinowski is widely credited as the founder of the immersive fieldwork tradition of participant-observation which later became synonymous with the ethnographic method. Malinowski's fieldwork is also a foundational story of anthropologists being diverted by circumstances and making do. He had set out to conduct research in Australia, but World War I broke out while he was crossing the ocean; on arrival in Australia, as a citizen of Austria-Hungary, he was effectively an enemy alien. As an alternative to internment, he was allowed to stay in relative freedom in the Australian territory of New Guinea. Stranded on the island of Kiriwina for the duration of the war, he came up with the idea that living with "the natives" and participating in their customs could be a way of continuing his research.

Malinowski's story also exemplifies anthropology's implication in European colonialism. Much work has since been done in anthropology to critically examine the discipline's colonial origins while continuing to refine and reflect on the foundational method. Key models for me in terms of dealing with contingencies and existential dilemmas of fieldwork were Weiner, *The Trobrianders of Papua New Guinea*; Kondo, *Crafting Selves*; and Rabinow, *Reflections on Fieldwork in Morocco*. Roger Keesing was my undergraduate professor at McGill University who told our class many stories about the vicissitudes of fieldwork, including how he'd steered away from the Solomon island he'd originally prepared to study, either to get away from an intrusive fellow anthropologist or a missionary who threatened his plans—I can't remember which. (He told stories of being bothered by both.) Notably, Keesing was a strong advocate for decolonizing the discipline.

17 Mark Zuehlke's *Ortona* went on to be a national best-seller. *Ortona* was Zuehlke's first book of military history; since then, he's gone on to write thirteen more about

Canadian World War II battles. In 2014 he won the Governor General's History Award for Popular Media, and in 2024 he was appointed to the Order of Canada for his significant contributions to raising public awareness of Canada's military role in World War II.

18 A note on my approach to transcribing the interviews: Along with most anthropologists, I understand transcription as a "value-laden and disputed process" (Finnegan, *Oral Traditions*, 198). Spoken discourse is not as linear and well-organized as the written word; it's full of pauses, filler words, false starts, repairs, and hedges. When speech is transformed into text, the writer or editor usually "cleans it up" into standard written forms. In that process, much of what gets removed is the speaker's active work of composing their narrative. One of the reasons that oral interviews are valuable to researchers is that, unlike written responses, oral discourse is more revealing of people's not-always-successful efforts to express and suppress their thoughts and feelings; that is, we get to observe their struggles with *composure* in both the narrative and emotional sense of the word (Thomson, *Anzac Memories*, 8). Another reason for not tidying up the original spoken discourse is to provide the reader with a certain kind of experience, one that places them in the moment of the interview and keeps them aware of the text's provisional and "ragged at the edges" origins (Samuel, "Perils of the Transcript"). Of course, all transcription is a transformation of speech, and too much effort at preserving the original can get in the way of the reader's immersion. I've tried to strike a balance, preserving the twists and turns of the spoken discourse while quietly removing many of the false starts and fillers, except in places where those appear to be meaningful. Following the practice of many oral historians, I've punctuated the speech in ways that are often ungrammatical but serve to convey the speaker's pace and rhythm, and I've included speakers' erroneous nonwords and malapropisms, adding clarifications in square brackets or a note where necessary. For more on transcription methods in oral history and anthropology, see Portelli, *The Battle of Valle Giulia*, 15-22, and Finnegan, *Oral Traditions*, 194-8.

19 The reader might find it odd that I had set out to study memories of a battle without any knowledge of psychology and only passing familiarity with anthropological work on emotion. It certainly looks strange to me now, too. There are two reasons why it didn't seem that way at the outset. First of all, it's rare that anthropologists interpret phenomena at the individual, psychological level; indeed, historically, and especially in the British tradition in which I was mostly trained, there's been a firm disciplinary line drawn against psychology; if you ventured into it, you'd get a sense from your peers and professors that you're going out of bounds. American cultural anthropology has been relatively more open to it, with small but well established subdisciplines of psychological and cognitive anthropology; however, those simply weren't on my radar as a graduate student in Canada. (On the marginality of psychological anthropology, see Ewing, "Is Psychoanalysis Relevant for Anthropology?" and Strauss and Quinn, *A Cognitive Theory of Cultural Meaning*.) Secondly, at the outset of my project, I was thinking in terms of *social* memory. That's something you can study at a group level using pretty conventional ethnographic methods. (Indeed, some scholars

argue that "social memory" is a misleading term, as the group dynamic of so-called "remembering" is really very different from the individual faculty of memory.) Of course, I did plan to interview veterans (and Ortona civilians) but I wasn't expecting to go so deep into the individual narratives.

What I stumbled into doing in my fieldwork, I later learned is an actual method that has a name: it's the "person-centered ethnography" of psychological anthropology, a type of life story research that goes into greater psychological depth, drawing on insights from the clinical practice of psychoanalysis to examine the expression and suppression of thoughts and emotion in the open-ended interview setting (Ewing, "Clinical Psychoanalysis as an Ethnographic Tool"; LeVine, *Culture, Behavior, and Personality*; Levy and Hollan, "Person-Centered Interviewing and Observation"; Hollan, "Developments in Person-Centered Ethnography"). I found more tools for narrative analysis in related work by psychological and linguistic anthropologists (e.g., Ewing, "Revealing and Concealing"; Ochs, "Narrative Lessons"; Besnier, "Language and Affect") including studies of trauma (e.g., BenEzer, "Trauma Signals in Life Stories"; Kirmayer, "Landscapes of Memory") and eventually (for this present book—the concept only came to my attention after I completed my dissertation) moral injury (Litz et al., "Moral Injury and Moral Repair"; Molendijk, *Moral Injury and Soldiers in Conflict*).

CHAPTER TWO

I think it was at Vinchiaturo Edgar J. Bailey, "With the 'Eddies' in Italy," *The Forty-Niner* 85 (1982), 56-8.

1 The Canadians landed on beaches near Pachino, Sicily. The landing crafts carrying Sam and Jim's Loyal Edmonton Regiment struck a sandbar approximately 100 metres from the beach. Many veterans, including Farley Mowat in his memoir, recalled stepping off the crafts and falling into six to eight feet of water. Against more determined opponents, this might have ended in disaster, but the Italian soldiers in the Canadian landing area had little interest in fighting. (Bercuson, *Maple Leaf Against the Axis*, 155-6.)

2 On intellectualizing responses to trauma see BenEzer, "Trauma Signals in Life Stories"; Hollway and Jefferson, "The Free Association Interview Method"; and Vaillant, "Ego Mechanisms of Defence." Vaillant defines intellectualization as "thinking about instinctual wishes in formal, bland terms that leaves the associated affect unconscious. . . . Intellectualization includes paying undue attention to the inanimate in order to avoid intimacy with people, or paying attention to external reality to avoid recognition of inner feelings, or paying attention to irrelevant detail to avoid perceiving the whole" (246-7).

3 The Bren was a light machine gun used by British and Commonwealth troops in WWII. Fitted with a bipod, it was suitable for shooting from a prone position.

4 Sam was intending to publish this story in *The Forty-Niner*, the journal of the Loyal

Edmonton Regiment. However, it does not appear that he ever did. (The regiment perpetuates the First World War 49th Battalion, hence the journal's title.)

5 In the terms of linguistics and conversation analysis, a "false start" is when a speaker begins an utterance and then stops before it's completed. A false start is often followed by a "correction" or "repair" in which the speaker rephrases and finishes what they had begun to say. Katherine Pratt Ewing, an anthropologist trained in clinical psychoanalysis, defines repairs as "corrections that involve a syntactical reorganization of the utterance in midsentence." False starts and repairs sometimes indicate a speaker's deeper emotional struggle with how to compose and share their story. "For instance, repairs may occur when the speaker suddenly realizes that the hearer may 'take it the wrong way,' or that the initial structure commits the speaker to a sentence that will reveal information that is best left unsaid" (Ewing, "Revealing and Concealing," 100.)

6 "Lili Marleen" (also spelled "Lili Marlene" and "Lili Marlen," among others) was a German romantic song about a soldier saying goodbye to his girlfriend as he's about to go away on service. He wonders if she'll wait for him, if he'll survive the war. First recorded in 1939 by Lale Andersen, it was popular among German soldiers and was frequently played on German forces radio broadcasts (Evans, *The Third Reich at War*, 575-6). As Norman mentioned to me (see Chapter 1) the Canadians and other Allied soldiers sometimes listened to the German broadcasts. They learned the tune and made up their own English lyrics. The best known Canadian version is "The D-Day Dodgers."

The Edmontons had their own satirical take on the song which poked fun at expectations of bravery and comradeship. See "When I Am L.O.B.," *The Forty-Niner* 107 (2007), 32-3.

7 War Diaries were kept by all regiments (battalions) and many other units of the Canadian Army. The Diary was "the essential tool for tracking events; it was to supply authentic material for the history of the unit 'with regards to operations, training, equipment, and organization'… commanding officers were told [by the army's Historical Section] that they and their men might be forgotten by future historians if they ignored this task" (Cook, *Clio's Warriors*, 97). The diarist was typically a staff officer in the unit.

8 Sam had purchased the official history of his regiment in hopes that it would help him make sense of his memory. He would not have found it any help. There are only three brief lines about the October 3 event in the book: "On October 3rd a patrol led by Lieut. W. Hutton bumped into a demolition party which took refuge in a cemetery. In the fracas one German was killed, one wounded and a sergeant taken prisoner. Edmontons losses were one killed and one wounded" (Stevens, *A City Goes to War*, 256). The official history of the Canadian Army in World War II reports that two days later (October 5) the Edmontons suffered no casualties while taking German prisoners during a raid in Baselice (Nicholson, *Official History*, 240). Regarding Guardiaregia, where Gus located his version of the story, the Canadian army official history reports that it was "taken without resistance on 18 October" (ibid., 257). However, the

Loyal Edmonton official history suggests that there was combat in Guardiaregia in which some Germans were killed: "On October 21st the Edmonton detachment at Guardiaregia was relieved. In its only contact with the enemy it had accounted for 13 Germans, of whom 6 were taken prisoner" (Stevens, *A City Goes to War*, 260).

9 By "blockard" Sam probably meant *blackguard* (normally pronounced as *blaggard* and sometimes written that way, too). It's an old English word for a person (usually a man) who is dishonest and unprincipled.

10 Sam was correct: the Edmontons were on the *Durban Castle* and there was a storm on the eve of the landing. "A southwesterly gale whipped up and although it subsided by nightfall, a heavy swell was running" (Stevens, *A City Goes to War*, 232).

CHAPTER THREE

These prairie farmers are the men Gregory Clark, "Tells How Edmonton Men Attempted 'Sound Attack' in Ortona Battle," *Edmonton Journal*, January 17, 1944. City of Edmonton Archives (War of '39, Loyal Edmonton Regiment Collection).

I said to Dougan James Riley Stone: My Army Recollections (reel 1, side 2). Interview by William Thackray, May 13, 20, and June 3, 10 and 17, 1980. University of Victoria Canadian Military Oral History Collection, Reginald H. Roy Collection.

They had a system John Dougan: My Army Recollections (reel 1, side 1). Interview by Tim Torrie, July 27, 1987. University of Victoria Canadian Military Oral History Collection, Reginald H. Roy Collection.

Then we moved up Interview by Dr. R.L. McDougall with Don Harley and Clifford Wood, Toronto, June 7, 1961, p.9. Seaforth Highlanders of Canada Archives. Box 998.135.118.

It says here uh Stevens, *A City Goes to War*, 279.

Here's his army enlistment form Second World War Service File of Norman Joseph Letendre. Library and Archives Canada. Second World War Service Files – War Dead, 1939 to 1947. RG24, vol.26365.

1 In Canada today, the preferred term is *Indigenous* or *Aboriginal*. *Native* is not necessarily offensive but may sound a bit old-fashioned. The white veterans whom I was interviewing were in the habit of using the term "Indian" which is offensive to most Indigenous people; however, in fairness to those white veterans, they might have been confused by the fact that some of their Indigenous comrades had seemed to identify themselves as "Indians" (even if that might not have been what those comrades really preferred). For example, at the time that I was doing my fieldwork (1999-2000) there was an Edmonton branch of what was then called the Alberta Indian War Veterans Society, and some of the Indigenous veterans of the Loyal Edmonton Regiment were members. I attended one of their meetings at the Native Seniors Centre (now the Edmonton Aboriginal Seniors Centre) in hopes that the executive members could put me in touch with Indigenous veterans of the Ortona battle. Unfortunately, while they knew of many World War II veterans, they couldn't think of any who were local and had

fought in Ortona. Overall, my method for finding research participants relied mostly on the social networks of veterans who belonged to their regimental associations, starting with those who had attended the 1998 Reconciliation Dinner in Ortona (see Chapter 6). The fact that these social networks didn't include any Indigenous veterans speaks to the segregation in Canadian society. Despite my efforts, I was unable to make my fieldwork more inclusive, which remains a regret.

2 "During the course of the day, when 11 Platoon of B Company and its flank comrades of A Company came under heavy fire Sergt. J.E.W. Dick crossed an alley, shinned up an outside waterpipe and pinpointed the positions of the enemy. He was spotted and made his way back to his platoon under fire; fetching two sections who also used the waterpipe to clamber to a point of vantage they silenced both machine guns and snipers." (Stevens, *A City Goes to War*, 277.)

3 Measuring forty-eight feet wide by eight feet high, the *Battle of Ortona* mural was created in 1945 by Ottawa artist Gerald Trottier on commission from 26 Central Ordnance Depot, a Canadian Army supply unit. In 1961, it was donated to the Loyal Edmonton Regiment and installed in the Prince of Wales Armouries, which later became the Prince of Wales Armouries Heritage Centre. (Loyal Edmonton Regiment Military Museum, "About the Battle of Ortona Painting.")

4 "On approaching the Piazza Municipale, D Company was halted by intense fire, for the entrance to the square was covered by no less than five machine guns, three in a building on the left side of the street. Pte. C.G. Rattray with two comrades crawled over a rubble pile; disdaining snipers and grenade throwers, they reached the entrance to the building which housed the machine guns. Leaving his comrades to clear the ground floor, Rattray continued to the upper storeys and single-handed captured five paratroopers, three machine-guns, four rifles and three pistols." (Stevens, *A City Goes to War*, 274-5.)

5 Rollie was referring to the Castello Aragonese. During the time that the 1st Canadian Division stayed in Ortona as a rest area (January–May 1944) the castle was used as a military prison (see Galloway, *A Regiment at War*, 130). When I was in Ortona, some residents (Tommaso and Angelo—see Chapter 9) told me they recalled watching the imprisoned Canadians being made to carry rocks from the base of the escarpment up the winding path to the castle.

6 Private Garrett Holder was killed in action on December 20, 1943.

7 *Battle exhaustion* was a deliberately vague diagnostic category used by the Canadian Army during World War II to describe a wide range of war-related neuroses, replacing the earlier term, *shell shock*. The rebranding was motivated partly by advances in psychiatric understanding, and partly by concerns about how soldiers interpreted the labels, which could affect their attitudes to recovery and their ability to return to combat. As military and medical historian Adam Montgomery explains, the term *exhaustion* carried no stigma and "allowed a soldier honourable escape from the battlefield while also suggesting that his condition was transient instead of permanent, since 'exhaustion' implied a state of weariness reversible by rest" (*The Invisible Injured*, 65-66).

Only one psychiatrist was attached to the Canadian division in Italy. While the preferred approach to battle exhaustion was early intervention close to the front, during the Ortona battle the divisional psychiatrist, Major A.M. Doyle, reported he could not "keep up with the deluge" and had to evacuate all but the "most hopeful" cases further south to a British field hospital (ibid., 66.).

Many Canadian Army officers remained skeptical of the legitimacy of psychological injuries. Furthermore, after the war, veterans who were unable to work due to such conditions were often denied pensions by the Department of Veterans Affairs. The department—relying on its own psychiatric consultants—often ruled that long-term conditions were pre-existing, and therefore not attributable to war service, or argued that the possibility of financial compensation might be unconsciously prolonging the veterans' symptoms (ibid., 70-71). These factors, combined with the broader social stigma of mental illness, probably explain Mel's ambiguity when he spoke to me about his breakdown and how he was treated for it. He strongly preferred to attribute his condition to a stomach ulcer. Sensing his unease, I was reluctant to press him for more details.

Tellingly, however, Mel became passionate when recounting the story of how US General George Patton, during the Sicily Campaign, had abused two soldiers receiving treatment in a field hospital for combat stress. Patton had slapped the men and shamed them as cowards, prompting General Eisenhower to order him to apologize (Atkinson, *The Day of Battle*, 147-49, 170-71). For Mel, that punishment wasn't nearly enough: "He should have been fired."

8 Associazione Archeologica Frentana, *Ottobre 1943—Giugno 1944. Nove mesi di martirio. Immagini.* Ortona: Soc. Coop. Iniziativa Cristiana—Libreria Europa, 1993. This book is a collection of photos of the battle and its aftermath that the editors retrieved from archives of the Imperial War Museum (UK), Library and Archives Canada, Bundesarchiv-Militararchiv (Freiburg, Germany), and archives of the city of Ortona and its regional capital, Chieti. Copies of this book were given to all of the Canadian and German veterans who participated in the 1998 Christmas dinner of reconciliation (see Chapter 6). I also had a copy and sometimes used it as a prompt during my interviews with veterans (including Bill—Chapter 5).

9 German MP 40 machine gun. The Canadians called it a "Schmeisser" after the name of its designer Hugo Schmeisser.

10 The PIAT (Projector, Infantry, Anti-Tank) was a British-manufactured anti-tank weapon used by British and Commonwealth armies in WWII.

11 "Tommy gun" is a nickname for the US-manufactured Thompson submachine gun that was widely used by Allied troops in WWII.

12 As Thomas King pointed out in his Massey Lectures (*The Truth About Stories*), while Indigenous people of North America encompass a wide range of social groups and identities, "the Indian" is an imaginative construct of white colonial culture. The colonial symbolic discourse of the Indian has sometimes been hostile towards Indigenous people, and sometimes romanticized them, but at all times it's been an oppressive barrier that works against their full acceptance as equals. Mel's romantic image of the

Indian may have been influenced by Grey Owl, who was very popular across Canada in Mel's youth. Grey Owl was really a white Englishman (Archibald Belaney) pretending to be Indigenous. Belaney promoted wilderness conservation through his Indian "Grey Owl" persona which drew upon and further entrenched white Canadian (as well as British and American) stereotypes of Indigenous North Americans as "creatures of the wilderness who possessed innate knowledge of wild ways" (Francis, *The Imaginary Indian*, 178). This is not to say that Mel was necessarily mistaken if he imagined that hunting was somehow spiritually important to Norman; it may well have been so. But the fact that Mel placed so much emphasis on Norman's "Indianness" suggests that Mel was thinking of him in strongly symbolic terms. Norman's story may also have fascinated Mel because it fulfilled the colonial wish for an "Indian who was a friend to the White man, who was strong, brave, honest, and noble" (King, *The Truth About Stories*, 105). Finally, the fact that Norman "lost himself" in the war and didn't make it home is resonant with the tragic image of "Indians" as noble savages unable to survive the forces of modernity.

CHAPTER FOUR

This chapter quotes extensively from the War Diary, Seaforth Highlanders of Canada. Library and Archives Canada. RG 24, vol.15256 (1943/12 to 1944/07). All other documentary sources quoted in this chapter were found in the Seaforth Highlanders of Canada Archives, Box 998.135.118.

1 This description of the room is drawn entirely from my memory; I didn't think to describe it in my fieldnotes at the time. My mind has probably warped and woven the room's elements in ways that are meaningful to me but are not how it really was. Maybe it wasn't an attic, but it felt that way; maybe the stag head was in an adjoining room, but I felt it watching me the whole time. I'm as certain of these things as the veterans were certain of their stories—and as likely as them to be mistaken.

2 The interviewer was Robert L. McDougall, who was a former Seaforth and World War II veteran. After the war, McDougall became an English literature professor and founded the Institute of Canadian Studies at Carleton University. In 1960, he was asked to write the official history of the Seaforth Highlanders. He gave up the project in 1963 after the death of his wife. The work was handed over to Reginald Roy, a history professor at the University of Victoria who had served in the war with the Cape Breton Highlanders. Later in his life, McDougall returned to the material he had collected for the regimental history and published it as the book, *A Narrative of War* (which includes the story of how his work on the official history was cut short).

3 Zuehlke relates this story in his book *Ortona* based on his interview with Ernest "June" Thomas and his correspondence with the tank commander's family: "Thomas ran over to the tank and pointed the target out to its commander. 'As much as I hate blasting the tower of that church,' Thomas said, 'I want you to get him out of there.' The 'A' Squadron

tank commander was Gord Turnbull. Turnbull said, 'It's Christmas Eve and that's God's house.' Thomas insisted and Turnbull knew the officer was right" (Zuehlke, *Ortona*, 311). Another detailed account of the incident, told by Thomas, is quoted in Geroux, "The Urban Battle of Ortona," 112-3.

4 Many veterans spoke ironically about their appropriations or thefts of Italian property as if these were acts of "liberating" the goods. This might have been motivated by the ambivalence that some of them felt towards Italians, mindful that the people who were welcoming them as "liberators" had only recently been their enemies, and so their sentiments might be insincere. Alternatively, it might have derived from the Canadians' ironic awareness that their mission in Italy was not really to liberate the country but rather just to take it from the Germans. In Wilf's use of the word, however, I didn't detect any ironic intention. I think the word had become so commonly used by the Canadians that the original sarcastic thought behind it was sometimes forgotten. The varied and ambiguous meanings of "liberation" are further discussed in Chapter 9.

5 Denis was referring to the birth of Jesus by recalling the Bible words from Isaiah (9:6) which are also heard in the rousing twelfth-movement chorus of Handel's *Messiah* that is performed every Christmas: "For unto us a child is born, unto us a son is given: and the government shall be upon his shoulder: and his name shall be called Wonderful, Counsellor, The mighty God, The everlasting Father, The Prince of Peace."

CHAPTER FIVE

This chapter quotes a number of passages from the War Diary, Seaforth Highlanders of Canada. Library and Archives Canada. RG 24, vol.15256 (1943/12 to 1944/07).

...but the only one that mentioned it Roy, *The Seaforth Highlanders*, 270.

Ellaschuk still had his Interview by Dr. R.L. McDougall with Don Harley and Clifford Wood, Toronto, June 7, 1961. Seaforth Highlanders of Canada Archives. Box 998.135.118.

5 — Weds. [January 1944] Diary of Major Roy C.H. Durnford, Chaplain (P). Seaforth Highlanders of Canada Archives. Box 998.135.118.

15 Canadian Captives of Germans Douglas Amaron, "15 Canadian Captives of Germans in Peril as Own Men Raid House," *Montreal Gazette*, January 11, 1944, p.16.

7 — Fri. 14 Diary of Major Roy C.H. Durnford, Chaplain (P). Seaforth Highlanders of Canada Archives. Box 998.135.118.

Early on Boxing Day Roy, *The Seaforth Highlanders*, 270.

1 Bill's fragmented storytelling and open debate with himself recall Neimeyer's observation that trauma narratives are often marked by a "ruminative struggle with radically contradictory images and emotions," as the traumatic experience has disrupted "the thematic assumptions on the basis of which the person has lived" (Neimeyer,

"Fostering Posttraumatic Growth," 55). When it is hard for the interviewer to follow the story, this is sometimes because "critical aspects of the plot structure of the traumatic narrative . . . remain hidden, unintegrated, and without social validation and support" (ibid., 56). The unfolding of Bill's story also evokes Kirmayer's view that "traumatic experience is not a story but a cascade of experiences, eruptions, crevasses, a sliding of tectonic plates that undergird the self" (Kirmayer, "Landscapes of Memory," 181). Bill's account mirrors this metaphor; the articulation of one remembered fragment seemed to draw forth another in quick succession, forming a kind of involuntary cascade.

2 The term for this rhetorical structure is *chiasmus*. A famous literary example of its use in dissolving distinctions between apparent moral opposites is the line in Shakespeare's *Macbeth*, "Fair is foul, and foul is fair."

3 Evidence that Padre Durnford was opposed to ruthless treatment of the Germans was his disturbed reaction to a "blood-thirsty" speech by Major-General Chris Vokes—see Chapter 10.

4 Indeed, the Seaforths' commander in Ortona, Lieutenant Colonel Syd Thomson, seems to have heard a very different version of the story. In an interview with regimental historian R.L. McDougall, the transcript of which is found in the Seaforth Archives, Thomson said:

> Also in the WD [War Diary] it doesn't give the picture of SGT Elaschuk… he was actually taken prisoner, and the Germans couldn't get him out; so they let him go, but he had to promise that he wouldn't come back during the war… my understanding is that he never did.

In a later book, R.L. McDougall fictionalized Thomson's story, writing it up as if it were the testimony of a Canadian soldier who was there as a prisoner and who witnessed all that happened. That fictionalized version by McDougall has been unwittingly accepted by some Canadian military historians who have republished it as a real eye-witness account (McAndrew, *Canadians and the Italian Campaign*, 80; Geroux, "The Urban Battle of Ortona," 142-3). McDougall's made-up story is in the form of a letter home by a Seaforth private:

> Dear John… I'm an escaped prisoner of war, believe it or not! . . . We took another house that afternoon… something went wrong, I don't know what, and the next thing we knew the place was full of German paratroopers, Schmeissers in our faces, and that was that. But it wasn't to be the end in the way we expected. For some reason they kept us in the house. It was like going backstage, seeing them like that, young fellows, lean-faced, going about their business. Came down, Capt. Harley I guess came to check our position, got fired on, put in an attack with the rest of the company, and we became surplus to the Germans, who needed every man to fight back. So they did a deal with Sgt. Elaschuk, there's hardly a section in the company doesn't have at least one many can speak German—said they would let us go if we promised not to fight again. Johnny promised, and we went. I don't know whether that kind of promise is covered in the rules of war, but while they're figuring it out we're going back. Suits me. (McDougall, *A Narrative of War*, 153-4.)

McDougall explains in his book's introduction that he has written these fictional letters from a fictional private "to bridge a gap in narrative which I would otherwise be at a loss to know how to span" (11). Clearly, McDougall's inspiration for this one was the story that Syd Thomson told him. (As for historian Bill McAndrew's acceptance and republication of the story as a real testimony, McAndrew's source for that is McDougall's unpublished draft of his book; perhaps in that draft, McDougall didn't include the clarifying note about fictionalization.)

Thomson's source for the story is unknown. I think it belongs to the category of "bullshit stories" that some of the Edmonton veterans told me to beware of—unbelievable tall tales that some of their comrades were notorious for telling (like the one about a German paratrooper who mocked the Canadians in the midst of a firefight by walking fearlessly into the middle of the street and putting down a flower pot, as if to show that the Canadians couldn't shoot straight). However, in the case of this story about the captives that Thomson heard and repeated to McDougall, this might be more than a mere bullshit story; it might be a fantasy version of events in the house that was made up by some of the men who were there in order to comfort themselves about the violence that actually happened.

Thomson's credulity is a bit puzzling. As noted earlier, the Seaforth padre evidently heard and recorded a more realistic version that's a closer fit with what was remembered by Bill and reported by Canadian news correspondent Douglas Amaron. And it's hard to believe that Thomson, the commanding officer, would have agreed to allow one of his sergeants to opt out of future combat just because of a promise the sergeant had supposedly made to a German. Perhaps Thomson told the story in a playful spirit that was misunderstood by McDougall.

5 Rudolf Hess was a long-time Nazi Party leader and Hitler's Deputy Führer. In May 1941, sidelined by Hitler and troubled by the plan to invade the Soviet Union before ending the war with Britain, Hess undertook a bold solo mission. Without informing anyone, he flew from Germany to Scotland, landed in a field, and told the farmhand who discovered him that he had an urgent message for the Duke of Hamilton. British officials who interrogated Hess found he had little to offer beyond what Hitler had already conveyed: that Britain could not win the war and should join Germany in its fight against Bolshevism. When Hitler learned of Hess's unauthorized mission, he was deeply shaken and swiftly disavowed his deputy. A broadcast to the German people declared Hess mentally ill.

In his haste to distance himself, Hitler had failed to consult his chief propagandist, Joseph Goebbels, who later pointed out the implausibility of the "mental illness" story: "It's rightly asked how such an idiot could be the second man after the Führer" (Kershaw, *Hitler*, 613). Many ordinary Germans found the official story hard to believe. Some felt sorry for Hitler. Others mocked the regime. "'That our government is mad is something we've known for a long time,' Berliners were reported as saying, 'but that they admit it—that's something new!'" (Evans, *The Third Reich at War*, 170.)

As for Churchill's illness, which the German paratroopers reportedly mentioned to their Canadian captives in the house in Ortona, that was very recent news at the time.

On December 14, 1943, while in Carthage to meet General Eisenhower, Churchill became ill and was diagnosed with pneumonia. The following day, he suffered a mild heart attack. His family was summoned; he and his doctor both feared his death might be imminent. On December 16, he began to recover, but still didn't rise from his sickbed until December 24—just a little more than a day before the Germans brought it up with Bill and his comrades. (Holland, *The Savage Storm*, 437-38, 442; Atkinson, *The Day of Battle*, 307-11.)

6 It's possible that Bill's memory gap around Christmas was the result of a dissociative response to a traumatic experience. Dissociation is an adaptive response to "acute stress and trauma" (Seligman and Kirmayer, "Dissociative Experience," 32) whereby individuals mentally and emotionally detach themselves (their sense of self) from what is happening around them and to them, to the point that they may be left with "gaps in awareness, memory, or identity" (Kirmayer, "Pacing the Void," 92). As for Bill's mistaken belief that his captivity in the house with the Germans happened on Christmas Day, this could be a case of what Portelli calls "chronological displacement," the unconscious reordering of events in our memory from their historical dates to other times where they make a better fit according to the meanings we assign to those events (Portelli, *The Death of Luigi Trastulli*, 15).

CHAPTER SIX

Canadian, German Vets May Gather "Canadian, German Vets May Gather For An Historic Christmas Eve Dinner," *Edmonton Journal*, August 10, 1998.

In the weeks that followed, I tracked the progress Peter Goldring, "Liberal Grinch Steals Christmas From Canada's Ortona Veterans," News Release, August 12, 1998. Earl McRae, "Vets Inch Forward in Battle of Ortona, Part II," *Ottawa Sun*, September 5, 1998. Earl McRae, "Put Up or Shut Up For Ortona Vets," *Ottawa Sun*, September 16, 1998. Earl McRae, "People's Army Fights For Ortona," *Ottawa Sun*, September 18, 1998.

Goldring's fundraising appeals provided mixed messages Peter Goldring, "Liberal Grinch Steals Christmas From Canada's Ortona Veterans," News Release, August 12, 1998. Peter Goldring, "Open Letter to Minister of Defence Art Eggleton," August 17, 1998. Peter Goldring, "Open Letter to All Members of Parliament and Senators," August 20, 1998. Peter Goldring, "Letter to Constituents," December 1, 1998.

...his original letter to Veterans Affairs Edmund Griffiths, Letter to Veterans Affairs Canada, undated, 1997.

'I am here to remember' Rosie DiManno, "The Survivors. Fifty-five years after fighting to the death, old enemies meet," *Toronto Star*, December 24, 1998, p.A25.

The German government doesn't wish Rosie DiManno, "Old enemies make peace at last. Canadian, German veterans sit down together for Christmas dinner," *Toronto Star*, December 26, 1998, p.A3.

The Canadians have been treated Rosie DiManno, "War vet goes AWOL from scripted tour," *Toronto Star*, December 28, 1998, p.D1.

One had to make a pilgrimage Dave Brown, "Christmas Eve Dinner Held For War Veterans," *The Record*, December 28, 1998, p.12.

And, now it had come Earl McRae, "Reconciliation in Italy. Canadian and German WWII foes break bread," *The Saturday Sun*, December 26, 1998, p.10.

As for the CBC's story CBC (Canadian Broadcasting Corporation), "Return to Ortona." 25 mins. February 1, 1999. http://www.cbc.ca/archives/categories/war-conflict/second-world-war/reports-from-abroad-matthew-halton/return-to-ortona.html, accessed September 21, 2013.

"Tells a story here," I said Stevens, *A City Goes to War*, 279-80.

1 The war cemetery in Ortona is managed by the Commonwealth (formerly Imperial) War Graves Commission. All commonwealth war cemeteries follow the same design that was established shortly after the end of World War I. In the following passage, I'm describing the cemetery from the perspective of someone who is seeing it for the first time. For more on the history and design of the cemeteries, see Zuehlke, *Through Blood and Sweat*, 39-45, 112-5, 165-8; Vance, *Death So Noble*, 60-6; and Wood and Swettenham, *Silent Witnesses*.

2 Ted's plan was to send thirty Canadian veterans to meet an equal number of Germans. The Canadian contingent included six men from each of the following units: Ted's own 12th Armoured (Three Rivers) Regiment, the Loyal Edmonton Regiment, the Seaforth Highlanders of Canada, the Royal 22e Régiment ("Van Doos"), and the No. 1 (RCMP) Provost Company. Though he acknowledged that the entire 1st Canadian Division had contributed to the capture of Ortona, he limited participation to just these five. (Why not invite any veteran who was interested, regardless of their original unit? Perhaps he was adhering to military tradition—organizing the group by regiment, and ensuring that each had enough members to represent its history and identity.)

His criteria for selecting units were a bit puzzling. First, he wanted to prioritize those who had fought inside the town. This meant excluding the 1st Brigade—the 48th Highlanders, Royal Canadian Regiment, and Hastings and Prince Edward Regiment—despite their costly engagement with the German paratroopers just four kilometres west of Ortona during the same week in December. Yet he included the Royal 22e, which had neither fought in the town nor engaged in any significant action during that week.

The Royal 22e is a French-speaking regiment from Quebec, commonly known as the "Van Doos"—a phonetic rendering of *vingt-deuxième*, French for "twenty-second." Their main action near Ortona was the battle for Casa Berardi, a key farmhouse southwest of the town, on December 14-15. After capturing the house, the Van Doos were surrounded and suffered heavy casualties, but held their ground through the night until reinforcements arrived. For his leadership, Captain Paul Triquet was awarded the Victoria Cross.

Ted could argue that Casa Berardi was vital to the eventual capture of Ortona – but the same could be said for the 1st Brigade's efforts. More likely, he was swayed by the prestige of Triquet's VC and the national attention the Van Doos received as a result.

He made one other exception to his criteria: John Matheson, a veteran of the Royal Canadian Regiment, former Liberal politician, member of the Order of Canada, and prominent public figure known for helping design Canada's flag.

As for the RCMP Provost Company—virtually absent from historical accounts—Ted explained that they handled traffic control and prisoner custody during the battle, and they lost more men in Ortona than in the rest of the Italian Campaign combined (Griffiths, *Dare to be True*, 359). He may have been particularly attuned to their contribution—and inclined to invite them—given his own personal ties to the police.

3 Joseph L. Wilhelm was Archbishop of the Archdiocese of Kingston, Ontario from 1966 until his resignation in 1982. He died in 1995.

4 Carl Bayerlein's brief memoir of Ortona was later translated and published in *Canadian Military History* ("Parachute Engineers in Combat, Ortona 1943: A German Perspective").

5 Di Tullio is the author of *1943: The Road to Ortona*, a graphic history of the battle told from the civilian point of view. Another important local assistant to the 1998 Reconciliation was Angela Arnone. In 2021, Arnone was awarded the Canadian Governor General's Meritorious Service Medal for her advocacy and liaison work for commemorations of the battle.

6 The monument was created by Ortona artist Tommaso Cascella and was inaugurated on October 24, 1965. It was originally placed in the square in front of San Tommaso Cathedral. Some time between then and the late 1980s it was moved to the cemetery entrance.

CHAPTER SEVEN

We parked the Humber Comfort, *Artist at War*, 112-4.
I could not possibly paint Ibid., 114.
There is only one issue Griffiths, *Dare to be True*, 353.
...trying to turn our trip Ibid., 361.
Goldring rather childishly Ibid., 363.
When he saw Ibid., 365.
...continued to plague Ibid., 366-7.
Surette had initially offered Ibid., 356.
Our 'free' statue Ibid., 358.
Ted got stuck with the cost Ibid., 362.
I am not a person of infinite patience Ibid., 360.
Both parties recognized each other Ibid., 364.
...it was to be a memorable Ibid., 364-5.
Prior to being seated Ibid., 365.
Sadly, the only fly Ibid., 365.
On my going Ibid., 411.
Christmas Day, 1943, is a day Ibid., 135-6.

Narrator: On Christmas morning CBC (Canadian Broadcasting Corporation), "Return to Ortona." 25 mins. February 1, 1999. http://www.cbc.ca/archives/categories/war-conflict/second-world-war/reports-from-abroad-matthew-halton/return-to-ortona.html, accessed September 21, 2013.
This mad dance Griffiths, *Dare to be True*, 139.
Recalling the visual Ibid., 139.
The Canadian Army history Ibid., 130, quoting Nicholson, *Official History*, 324.
The Seaforths and 'A' Squadron Griffiths, *Dare to be True*, 130-5.
In Freud's definition Freud, "Screen Memories," 19.
The church I partly Griffiths, *Dare to be True*, 346-7.
When I think of the joys Ibid., 347.
After a quick wash Ibid., 134.

1 Comfort was one of thirty-two artists hired in February 1943 by the Canadian War Records Committee and embedded within the Canadian army, navy, and air force. With the armed forces in the field, the artists did sketches and watercolours; large scale paintings were done later at studios in London and Ottawa. The artists were tasked with portraying "significant events, scenes, phases and episodes in the experience of the Canadian Armed Forces" (CWRC instructions to artists quoted in Brandon, "'Doing Justice to History,'" 1; see also Brandon, "Veracity and Expectation in Charles Comfort's War Art").

Prior to the war, Comfort was a commercial artist known especially for his murals depicting Canadian industry in the Toronto Stock Exchange building. With the 1st Canadian Infantry Division in Ortona, he was accompanied by fellow war artist Lawren P. Harris, son of Group of Seven member Lawren S. Harris..

2 Comfort, *Artist at War*, 113. In his history of the Canadian army in the Italian Campaign, Dancocks quoted Comfort's description of San Tommaso but mistakenly wrote "deer" instead of "steer" (Dancocks, *The D-Day Dodgers*, 186). I think Dancock's misreading of Comfort's word is understandable in light of the frequent use of hunting imagery in accounts of the battle.

3 While the dome of San Tommaso was fully reconstructed, its frontispiece was not. In the immediate aftermath of the battle, about half of the frontispiece was still standing. This might have been the reason that Mel felt, when he returned, that there was something very new about the cathedral; the dome is much more noticeable without the frontispiece. The half-remaining frontispiece might also be the source of his mistaken belief that "the tower was still standing" at the time of the battle but now it was gone.

4 My use of the term "main story" is informed by BenEzer's analysis of trauma signals in life stories. BenEzer, an anthropologist and clinical psychologist, observes that "an event which was not narrated in the main story" sometimes gets shared later in response to probing by the interviewer or as an apparent afterthought by the narrator—"accompanied by distressing emotions such as mourning, grief, shame or guilt which were not previously expressed during the telling of the story" ("Trauma Signals in Life

Stories," 34). In Ted's case, these emotions were already present in his main story (of the church) but were hard to make sense of until Ted shared his previously hidden story (of the Christmas Eve German).

5 In other words, the church functioned for Ted as a compromise-formation. According to Westen, compromise-formations are psychodynamic mechanisms that "allow the expression of repressed individual (or social) desires . . . while cloaking them in a form acceptable to the 'collective consciousness'" (Westen, *Self and Society*, 249). Westen suggests that myths may serve this function; I would add that key symbols of a culture (such as the church) are especially amenable to this purpose.

6 The phrase "still small voice" comes from 1 Kings 19:12 in the King James Version of the Bible. It refers to how God spoke to the Prophet Elijah on Mount Horeb. In both Jewish and Christian traditions, the story is often interpreted as a lesson about the subtlety of divine communication. Modern interpretation sometimes equates it with the inner voice of conscience.

7 The Salesians of Don Bosco is an order of Catholic priests whose mission is the care and education of young people.

8 Portelli, *The Death of Luigi Trastulli*, 1-26 discusses how apparent mistakes in the chronology of events in personal narratives can be motivated by the meanings that the narrator wishes (or in Ted's case, perhaps, does not wish) to make of them.

9 The War Diary of the Seaforth Highlanders mentions tanks firing on Santa Maria delle Grazie only on December 25: "The Church had been taken, but conceded back to the enemy due to the heavy pounding it had received from our supporting tanks 75 MM guns." After the 25th, the Seaforth diary doesn't mention the church.

However, the War Diary of Ted's Three Rivers Regiment notes that the tanks fired on the church on both December 25 and 26. On December 25: "No. I troop, under the command of Lieut. F.W. Simard, advanced to the 2nd Main Square, turned left and advanced to the hospital - church Square. These buildings and the square was shelled by the tanks and covering fire given while the infantry advanced and occupied the buildings." On December 26: "No. I troop, under the command of Lieut. F.W. Simard, advanced again to the hospital - church Square. It was learned that the enemy had infiltrated during the night and recaptured the hospital and church buildings. Supporting fire was given to the infantry and H.E. [high explosive] fire brought to bear on these buildings." This raises another possibility: Ted shot the church on both days and remembered it as a single event.

10 When Canada's war artists returned to their studios in London and Ottawa, they were encouraged by army historical officers to consult photographs and War Diaries along with their own field sketches and watercolours in order to paint "Action Episodes"—scenes the artists hadn't witnessed firsthand. Such paintings are works of "imagination, rearrangement, and synthesis" and are "to a large extent, fictional," writes Laura Brandon, former curator of war art at the Canadian War Museum. Even so, Brandon adds, the paintings may "convey more fully the meaning and implication" of the soldiers' experiences ("'Doing Justice to History,'" 3-4).

CHAPTER EIGHT

...an article he'd written for *The Forty-Niner* Maurice D. White, "Ortona 1999: 55th Anniversary and Pilgrimage Trip to Italy, October 1-13, 1999," *The Forty-Niner* 102 (1999):77-78.

The monument entitled Griffiths, *Dare to be True*, 368.

I was honoured to deliver Ibid., 368-9.

A recent message Ibid., 370.

The months following our trip Ibid., 367-8.

A deliberate, low-key Ibid., 370.

In 2004, the Canadian government Parks Canada, "The Government of Canada Unveils a Plaque to Commemorate the National Historic Significance of the Battle for Ortona, Italy," News Release, October 28, 2004. http://www.pc.gc.ca/APPS/CP-NR/release_e.asp?id=841&andor1=nr, accessed March 2, 2014.

The price of peace is staggering Adrienne Clarkson, Speech on the Occasion of a National Historic Sites Plaque Unveiling Ceremony. Ortona, Italy, October 27, 2004. http://archive.gg.ca/media/doc.asp?lang=e&DocID=4298, accessed March 2, 2014.

In Ortona's Piazza del Plebiscito Peter Goldring, "Price of Peace," Speech in House of Commons, November 1, 2011. http://www.parl.gc.ca/HousePublications/Publication.aspx?DocId=5221043, accessed January 10, 2014.

It is on the battlefield Griffiths, *Dare to be True*, 369.

Underneath the brutality Ibid., 410.

In 2008, a massive youth pilgrimage to Ortona Dan Black, "Into Ortona Then and Now," *Legion Magazine*, March 2, 2009; Martha Sarmatiuk, "For Students, War Graves a Touching Sight," *Winnipeg Free Press*, December 28, 2008: A10; Laura Byrne Paquet, "Exploring the Battlefields," *Legion Magazine*, September 25, 2009. Reports on the number of Remembering Ortona Tour participants were inconsistent, ranging between 1,200 and 1,500. The higher figures may have been including the accompanying teachers, organizers, and other support staff.

Once again we have a generation Steven Hills quoted in Dan Black, "Into Ortona Then and Now," *Legion Magazine*, March 2, 2009.

...a symbolic cleansing Dave Robinson quoted in Martha Sarmatiuk, "For Students, War Graves a Touching Sight," *Winnipeg Free Press*, December 28, 2008: A10.

An online slideshow Laura Byrne Paquet, "Exploring the Battlefields," *Legion Magazine*, September 25, 2009; John McRae Secondary School, "Road to Ortona" (Video Slideshow) http://www.schooltube.com/video/ d460636a3a7f65e1e491, accessed March 2, 2014.

I have a sad story Natalie Salat, "Tears in Italy," *Legion Magazine*, January 1, 2005.

I shot a German Philippe Gohier, "So This is Christmas? Maurice White, On the Front Line," *Maclean's*, November 10, 2010. This same version of Maurice's story was also included in the book *We Were Freedom*, a collection of Canadian wartime personal narratives edited by the Historica-Dominion Institute with text by historian Tim Cook.

1 Private William Thomas Wychopen was killed in action on December 16, 1944 and is buried in the Ravenna Commonwealth War Cemetery.

2 In *The Fight for History*, Tim Cook describes the popular revitalization of Canadian war remembrance that started in the mid-1990s after decades of relative indifference. On remembrance programs for youth in this time period, see Carr, "War, History, and the Education of (Canadian) Memory"; Iqbal, "Enacting Remembrance Day in the Public Sphere"; and Cosh, "Killing Matters," 91-106.

3 This use of remembrance activities to forge connections between youth and presently-serving Canadian armed forces happened in the context of the Canadian military's public relations campaign, launched in 2006, called "Operation Connection" (and nicknamed "Recruit the Nation" by Chief of Defence Staff Rick Hillier). The purpose of the Operation was to increase military recruitment and bolster public support for the military's combat role in Afghanistan. See Dupuis-Déri, *L'Armée Canadienne n'est pas l'Armée du Salut*; Fremeth, "Searching for the Militarization of Canadian Culture"; McCready, "Tie a Yellow Ribbon 'Round Public Discourse"; McKay and Swift, *Warrior Nation.*

CHAPTER NINE

The forward localities Alon M. Johnson, "The Last Patrol in Ortona," *The Forty-Niner* 94 (1991), 35-38.

This is Matthew Halton Matthew Halton, CBC Radio broadcast, January 4, 1944, CBC Radio Archives.

The official civilian death toll Sources for the following multi-page narrative of civilian suffering are di Tullio, *1943*; Iubatti, *Testimonianze*; and Giannetti et al., *La Battaglia di Ortona*, 148.

Code-named "Morning Glory" Zuehlke, *Ortona*, 226.

Precisely at 0800 hours Ibid., 229-30.

Comic relief was provided War Diary, 12th Canadian Armoured Regiment (Three Rivers Regiment), December 27, 1943. RG24, vol. 18206 (1943/11 to 1944/04).

I think before leaving Ortona James Riley Stone: My Army Recollections (Reel 1, Side 2). Interview by William Thackray, May 13, 20, and June 3, 10 and 17, 1980. University of Victoria Canadian Military Oral History Collection, Reginald H. Roy Collection.

A. Staples, Letter to Reginald Roy Seaforth Highlanders of Canada Archives. Box 998.135.118.

The tragic consequences "Italian Civilians," 1 Can Div Intelligence Report, 9 Jan 44. In appendices to TRR War Diary, RG24 vol.18206. See also Cavasin, "Hai Visto i Canadesi," 72.

The railway yards were crowded The source for this paragraph and the next is di Tullio, *1943*, 49-52.

Meanwhile the Germans Di Luzio, *Ortona Guerra e Dopoguerra*, 54-5.

In the air it feels Ibid., 56-7.

A. Staples, letter to Reginald Roy Seaforth Highlanders of Canada Archives. Box 998.135.118.

It was the last day of 1943 Johnson, *Action With the Seaforths*, 225-6.

This is a gray morning Iubatti, *Testimonianze*, 83-4.

1 The time period and numbers of dead were specified in the Italian Presidential decree of June 16, 1959 that conferred on Ortona the Gold Medal for Civilian Valour for its suffering during the war. See also Zuehlke, *Ortona*, 375.

2 Di Tullio, *1943*, 80. The man was actually a former Italian soldier who had acquired the sweaters in trades with British prisoners whom he had guarded at a POW camp.

3 Denis must have been picturing San Tommaso, because Santa Maria delle Grazie (the church in Piazza San Francesco/Dead Horse Square) did not have a dome. Also, the crushed body could not have been at San Tommaso. There are multiple testimonies from Seaforth veterans locating the body near where they fought in Dead Horse Square; it was not the Seaforths but the Edmontons who fought in front of San Tommaso; and during the battle, the square in front of San Tommaso was impassable to Canadian tanks.

4 In 1998, political scientist Piero Ignazi surveyed AN members who attended the party's pivotal congress of that year. He found that 61% agreed that "fascism was overall a good regime." As for the party's electoral appeal, AN voters were disproportionately male (55%) and young (50% under the age of 40). The AN had a slight edge of support among students, entrepreneurs, and the self employed. Its regional strengths were in Rome and in the *Mezzogiorno*, Italy's historically underdeveloped south (which includes Ortona's region of Abruzzo). While most political analysts considered the AN to be "far-right," its ideology was not as xenophobic as most European parties with that label. Ignazi, *Extreme Right Parties in Western Europe*, 50-2. See also Griffin, "The 'Post-Fascism' of the Alleanza Nazionale"; Griffin, *Fascism,* 103-5; and Ginsborg, *Italy and its Discontents*, 288-300.

In 2009, the AN dissolved and merged with Silvio Berlusconi's centre-right Il Popolo della Libertà (People of Freedom). In 2012, a number of former AN leaders broke away from Berlusconi's party and founded Fratelli d'Italia (Brothers of Italy), a new party that positioned itself as a continuation of the MSI and AN political tradition. The FdI showed that alignment very clearly by adopting the old MSI and AN tricolour flame as its symbol. One of the FdI founders, Giorgia Meloni, had started her political career in the MSI youth wing in Rome. In Italy's 2022 national election, the FdI won a plurality of seats and Meloni became Italy's prime minister. For a thorough English-language history of Italy's post-WWII far-right politics, including the evolution of the MSI into the AN and the current FdI, see Broder, *Mussolini's Grandchildren*.

5 In my fieldnotes, I recorded that Tommaso's father was a railway worker. I don't have a note of it, but I remember Tommaso telling me that he came from a fishing family. It's possible that he was referring to earlier generations of his family, but it wouldn't be unusual if his father made a living from both fishing and wage labour at different times

in his life. Shortly after rejecting the Fascist Party and being fired, Tommaso's father died, and the family was left destitute.

6 The Italian word *paese* can mean either country or hometown. When used with reference to one's hometown, as Tommaso did here, it evokes a deep emotional sense of rootedness and belonging.

7 In Italy's streamed public school system, the *liceo classico* is the most prestigious, with a curriculum that emphasizes the humanities and the study of ancient languages and literature.

8 Some Ortonesi accounts mention that there were "Salò republicans" fighting alongside the Germans in Ortona. These would have been soldiers of the Italian Social Republic. As they were integrated with the German 1st Parachute Division, they may well have belonged to Fascist Italy's "most ferociously committed and destructive fighting force," the Folgore Parachute Division, most of whose members remained loyal to Mussolini and Nazi Germany after the armistice (see Morgan, *The Fall of Mussolini*, 46).

9 Giannetti et al., *La Battaglia di Ortona*, 147. Doctor Bernabeo dates this incident on December 24, not Christmas Day as Stefano Durante recalled. It isn't clear from Bernabeo's account if he was actually present in the hospital at the time. He may have written the story based on what he heard later from his nursing colleagues.

10 Ibid., 148. Bernabeo dates this December 26. The War Diary of the Three Rivers Tank Regiment observes it happening at 11:00 on December 27.

11 Adriano believed that the Canadians were going to carpet bomb Ortona on December 28 if the Germans had not retreated. I only noticed this detail while I was writing this book, and Adriano has since passed away, so unfortunately there's no chance to ask him more about it. (At the time, I thought he meant that the *Germans* were going to carpet bomb.) In my three months in Ortona, I never heard such a thing from anyone else. However, in his graphic history, Saverio di Tullio describes the threat that was supposedly made on Christmas Day: "With the outcome of the battle still uncertain, the Allies warn civilians and Germans [via an airdrop of leaflets] that a carpet bombardment of the city will be carried out at 10:00 on 28 December" (di Tullio, *1943*, 95). No source for this is given by di Tullio, but in a published collection of local testimonies, there's a story by Alberto Giuliani who claims that a Canadian soldier told him on December 28 that this is what they had planned to do. Giuliani cites another source that says, "On December 25, two reconnaissance planes dropped leaflets in which the British warned the Germans and the civilian population to evacuate the city by 10 am on December 28" (Università Frentana, *Affidandosi alla Memoria*, 49). Returning to Adriano's belief, I notice that he didn't mention this alleged threat of carpet bombing in his published memoir.

In the Canadian records that I've studied, there's no mention of any such plan. On the contrary, on the evening of December 27, Brigadier Bert Hoffmeister gave orders for the Princess Patricia's Canadian Light Infantry, which had been held in reserve, to move forward the next morning into Ortona, take over the attack from the exhausted Edmontons and Seaforths, and try to push the Germans out of the castle area and the cemetery (Zuehlke, *Ortona*, 345). On the morning of December 28, PPCLI troops were already advancing to these positions when reports began coming in that the Germans had left. Indeed, it was probably PPCLI troops who met Tonino and Uncle Guido at the cemetery church.

In any case, it's understandable if some Ortonesi feared imminent destruction by Allied bombardment. Everyone knew what had happened to Pescara. On August 31, 1943—while Italy was still officially at war with the Allies, though secret negotiations for an armistice were underway—Allied bombers attacked the city, levelling much of its centre and killing more than 2,000 civilians. On September 14, six days after the armistice, Allied bombers returned. Many residents initially cheered at the sight of them, believing they signalled the start of an Allied invasion that would free them from the Germans. In reality, the aim was to destroy more of Pescara's infrastructure, denying its use to the Germans; but in hitting the train station at a busy hour, the bombers killed hundreds more civilians (Serafini, *Danni di Guerra*, 22). Later, during the Eighth Army's November–December offensive up the Adriatic coast, Allied fighter-bombers flew "hundreds of sorties" in support. Six towns within twenty kilometres of Ortona were heavily bombed. According to the British official history, "Ortona was spared because of a hope that it would fall quickly and be useful as a rest-centre for troops during the coming winter, and as a port" (Molony et al., *The Mediterranean and Middle East*, 509).

12 According to the website of the German War Graves Commission: "In 1959 and 1960, the reburiers of the Volksbund [the Commission] recovered 20,076 bodies from countless smaller cemeteries and scattered field graves and interred them in Cassino." https://kriegsgraeberstaetten.volksbund.de/en/friedhof/cassino, accessed May 6, 2025.

CHAPTER TEN

[T]here is within Grossman, *On Killing*, 4.
Those who would not fire Ibid., 3-4.
Canadian soldiers normally fired Engen, *Canadians Under Fire*, 139.
...make sure of it – wait Canadian Army Training Memorandum No. 38 (May 1944) quoted in Engen, "S.L.A. Marshall and the Ratio of Fire," 45.
Immediately following the act Grossman, *On Combat*, 167.
In the air environment Grossman, *On Killing*, 110. See also Dyer, *War*, 57.
At mid-range distance Grossman, *On Killing*, 111.
When it comes to killing Ibid., 114-16.
At close range the resistance Ibid., 118.
Even harder is to kill Ibid., 122, 129-30.
Regardless of the distance Ibid., 112, 158.
Most soldiers do not 'kill' Ibid., 92.
In his later book Grossman, *On Combat*, 167-8.
...hatred and animosity toward the enemy Engen, *Strangers in Arms*, 94.
"Lili Marleen" had been banned Evans, *The Third Reich at War*, 575-6.

...genuinely a struggle Granatstein, *The Last Good War*, viii.

...a necessary war against evil Cook, *The Fight For History*, 434.

Seaforth veteran Bill Worton CBC, "Return to Ortona." 25 mins. February 1, 1999.

Soldiers don't make war "Former Enemies Reconcile: Battle of Ortona Vets Meet for Christmas Feast," *Kingston Whig-Standard*, December 26, 1998, 18.

On learning that the Germans Rosie DiManno, "Old enemies make peace at last. Canadian, German veterans sit down together for Christmas dinner," *Toronto Star*, December 26, 1998, p.A3.

It was just like in a boxing CBC, "Return to Ortona." 25 mins. February 1, 1999.

And yet there are those Levi, *The Drowned and the Saved*, 91. Levi described his arrest in Aosta in *The Periodic Table*, 127-38. His memoir of Auschwitz, *If This is a Man*, begins with his arrival in Fossoli.

[T]he war against the evils Griffiths, *Dare to be True*, 142.

My father's news Mowat, *And No Birds Sang*, 7.

Dark gore was still Ibid., 303.

Then Mowat found a Canadian Ibid., 303-4, 306.

Consider the following definitions Leydesdorff et al., "Introduction: Trauma and Life Stories," 1; Neimeyer et al., "Mourning and Meaning," 240; Hunt, *Memory, War and Trauma*, 7.

Writing in 2009, Brett Litz Litz et al., "Moral Injury and Moral Repair," 700, 702-4.

A moral injury may Molendijk, *Moral Injury*, 79.

The stories of Bob Ibid., 74-5.

The unsettled, self-contradictory Ibid., 75.

[M]any societies used to have rituals Ibid., 162, quoting B.J. Verkamp, *The Moral Treatment of Returning Warriors in Early Medieval and Modern Times* (Scranton: University of Scranton Press, 1993).

These traditions share Ibid., 162-3.

Importantly, what is absent Ibid., 161.

Finally, Molendijk found that Ibid., 163-4.

1 Durnford quoted in Roy, *The Seaforth Highlanders*, 130 note 32. In *The Generals*, Granatstein observes that "Vokes was a tough-talking officer" known for his "constant and colourful cursing and womanizing" (p.132). He adds, "soldiers who admired these traits thought highly of him" (p.265). Vokes' remark about scalping is quoted in Dancocks, *The D-Day Dodgers*, 28.

2 Engen, "Killing For Their Country," 125. Basically, the concern about Marshall's work is that he left no documentation of how he came up with his statistical data: "there is only Marshall's word that his claims regarding the ratio of fire were supported by the empirical evidence of his interviews." Engen's own research on Canadian rates of fire in World War II casts further doubt on Marshall's findings. See Engen, *Canadians Under Fire*, and Grossman's response, "S.L.A. Marshall Revisited . . .?"

3 Looking back, I think I became overly cautious; there were sensitive ways I could have asked the veterans for their thoughts about the war's moral purpose, and I could have

asked about that near the end of each interview after I'd given them plenty of neutral space to talk.

4 War Diary, Seaforth Highlanders of Canada, December 26, 1943. Library and Archives Canada. RG 24, vol.15256 (1943/12 to 1944/07). Granted, their youth may have contributed to the fact that they were captured—or killed. The British army war photographer Bill McConville took close-up shots of at least two dead German paratroopers in Ortona, both of whom appear to be teenagers. (Those images are in the archives of the Imperial War Museum.) The paratrooper shown on the title page of this chapter, photographed by Canadian army photographer Terry Rowe, looks similarly young, despite holding the rank of corporal. Of course, this focus on youthful subjects may also reflect selection bias on the part of the photographers.

5 Kesselring was tried and convicted in Venice in 1947. Initially sentenced to death by firing squad, his sentence was later commuted to life imprisonment. In 1952, he was released on compassionate grounds due to ill health. The trial summary is available at: https://www.worldcourts.com/imt/eng/decisions/1947.05.06_United_Kingdom_v_Kesselring.pdf. The British War Crimes Section report is available at: https://phdn.org/archives/www.ess.uwe.ac.uk/genocide/partisans1.htm.

A major recent initiative to document German war crimes in Italy is the project, "The German Massacres in Occupied Italy (1943-1945)" led by historian Dr. Carlo Gentile at the University of Cologne. It began work in 2019 with support from the German–Italian Future Fund—a bilateral initiative created by the governments of Germany and Italy to create a "shared culture of remembrance" with regard to Nazi and Fascist crimes. The project's findings are published at: https://www.ns-taeter-italien.org/en/. That site includes a page specifically on the German 1st Parachute Division: https://www.ns-taeter-italien.org/en/perpetrators/1fallschirm-jaeger-division. Descriptions of the Ardeatine, Civitella, and other major massacres can be found under the "Massacres" menu item. (All online sources accessed on June 28, 2025.)

6 The research project for the Atlas (*Atlante delle Stragi Naziste e Fasciste in Italia*) is directed by Dr. Paolo Pezzino, historian at the University of Pisa. For the list of documented crimes by the 1st Parachute Division, see: https://www.straginazifasciste.it/?page_id=297&ricerca=515. The Atlas is only available in Italian, but an English-language account of the Pietransieri massacre can be found at: https://www.ns-taeter-italien.org/en/massacres/pietransieri.

The Canadian Army's official history does not mention the Pietransieri massacre—the Canadians were probably unaware of it—but it does describe what the West Nova Scotia and Van Doos soldiers saw of the paratroopers' scorched earth tactics in villages throughout the valley: "With typical thoroughness the Germans had seized all food stocks and cattle, evicted the unfortunate inhabitants and then demolished and burned their homes . . . In all, ten villages were deliberately and systematically destroyed, with no house left standing. The enemy had spared little thought for the peasantry, who now homeless were trekking, some with carts and mules, into the brigade's forward areas, blocking the roads and bringing with them the problem of their care and transportation to the rear areas. . . . They brought pathetic stories of ruthless destruction and of women being held as hostages because their menfolk refused to work on the German defences" (Nicholson, *Official History*, 280-3).

7 The Francavilla massacre is documented at https://www.straginazifasciste.it/?page_id=38&id_strage=2583. One of the researchers was Ortona historian Andrea di Marco.

8 Stories of four of the German veterans who were on the Reconciliation trip can also be found in two history books—but these are limited to their wartime experiences and don't mention the Dinner of Reconciliation nor their ways of remembering more generally. Fritz Illi, Willy Fretz, and Carl Bayerlein contributed stories to Zuehlke's *Ortona*. Joseph Klein makes a few appearances (as Jupp Klein) in Holland's *The Savage Storm*.

9 Mowat, *And No Birds Sang*, 303-6. In *My Father's Son*—a later memoir reflecting on his wartime service—Mowat credited his commanding officer, Lieutenant-Colonel Bert Kennedy, with possibly saving his life. In early January 1944, recognizing the danger posed by Mowat's deteriorating mental state, Kennedy pulled him "out of the line" and got him assigned to brigade headquarters as a junior liaison officer. "Not to mince matters," Mowat recalled, "I was saved." With deliberate understatement, he described his mental condition as "burn out," invoking his father's euphemistic term for World War I comrades so psychologically broken they effectively committed suicide. As his father put it, "They didn't even know what was the matter with them and there wasn't anybody to tell them because we were all too inexperienced to see" (Mowat, *My Father's Son*, 33-8).

While Mowat described his breakdown as occurring outside Ortona on Christmas Day, historian Mark Zuehlke suggests it had been building since Sicily, where Mowat was deeply shaken by the slow deaths of grotesquely wounded Germans—men who'd been shot by his own company commander (*Through Blood and Sweat*, 205-7).

10 Mowat, quoted in King, *Farley*, 320-1. Mowat had not wanted to write an epilogue. He only did so at the insistence of his American publisher, Peter Davison at Atlantic Monthly Press, who believed the book's ending was "too abrupt." The book's Canadian publisher, McClelland and Stewart, agreed with Mowat that an epilogue wasn't necessary. As a result, the epilogue only appears in American (and possibly some foreign language) editions; it's mostly unknown to Canadian readers. I discovered it from reading Chris Hedges' *War is a Force That Gives Us Meaning* where it's quoted on page 21.

Mowat's biographer James King observes that Davison—determined to get an epilogue after months of Mowat's resistance—actually wrote the first draft of it which then was "extensively revised" into the final version by Mowat. After consulting Mowat's archived correspondence with his publishers (McMaster University Archives, Farley Mowat fonds, Twelfth accrual, Box 302, file 4) I would add that Davison's first draft may have been a paraphrase of Mowat's comments to him over the phone. In a letter to Mowat on May 2, 1979, Davison wrote: "Soon I will be nudging you by telephone if you don't write the epilogue telling your American readers What Became of Gracious You." On May 29, Mowat replied: "I simply won't work on the damn book anymore—not a word, not a line. Me poipes is full o fog, me son. Right full! Thank God we have three seeing eye dogs." Davison's draft of the epilogue is dated June 14. Mowat sent Davison his revision of it on July 9 and mentioned their recent phone conversation.

Regarding the passage that I've quoted here, there are two points of overlap between Davison's draft and Mowat's revised and final version. First, in the draft, there's the line: "For decades my war has been so wrapped in the cotton-wool of protective forgetfulness, that unwrapping it has been enough to recall the boy that I was, and the man I began to become." In his revision, Mowat put more emphasis on his desire to bury traumatic memories, and suggested that he only "unwrapped" them because he felt the need to speak out against war. Second, the draft states: "What matters, I suppose, is only my firm conviction that there are, and can be, no good wars. My war was one of the best and a bloody damn thing it was." In his revision, Mowat strengthened his conviction to "absolute" and more strongly hedged the exception he was willing to make for World War II.

11 Srebrenica is known as the site of a 1995 massacre during the Bosnian War, where more than 8,000 Bosnian Muslim men and boys were killed by Bosnian Serb forces. It's widely considered the worst atrocity to occur in Europe since World War II, and was ruled a genocide by the International Court of Justice. Dutch UN peacekeepers, stationed there to protect the "safe area," failed to prevent the massacre. The causes of that failure were hotly debated. In 2002, the Dutch government resigned after an official report concluded it had sent troops on an ill-prepared mission.

12 The redesign of Canadian Heroes Square was completed in February 2021. Veterans Affairs Canada contributed 30,000 euros toward the project, which cost a total of 200,000 euros. The project was managed by the municipal government in collaboration with the Lions Club of Ortona. "Ortona: Apre la Nuova Piazza degli Eroi Canadesi," *Il Giornale di Chieti*, February 18, 2021. https://www.ilgiornaledichieti.it/news-il-giornale-di-chieti/ortona-apre-la-nuova-piazza-degli-eroi-canadesi/

CHAPTER ELEVEN

...lines by the World War II veteran Hynes, *The Soldier's Tale*, 8, 27.

1 The book was Charles Monroe Johnson, *Action with the Seaforths*. A quote from it appears in Chapter 9. I have Norman (and his son) to thank for that reference.

Bibliography

INTERVIEWS

Canada

Alon Johnson. September 20, 2000.
Angus (Gus) Campbell. December 10, 1999 and October 9, 2000.
Bill (Pseudonym). October 5, 2000.
Bill Shaw. December 10, 1999.
David I. Fairweather. September 27, 2000.
Denis Meade. September 29, 2000.
Ernest W. (June) Thomas. September 19, 2000.
Jack Birmingham. December 10, 1999.
Maurice D. White. December 2, 1999.
Melville A. McPhee. November 27, 1999 and October 10, 2000.
Norman Tweedhope. September 22, 2000.
Roland L. (Rollie) Castagner. December 10, 1999 and October 9, 2000.
Samuel Lenko. November 29, 30, and December 1, 1999.
Wilf Gildersleeve. September 28, 2000.

Italy and Germany

Adriano di Luzio. April 13, 2000.
Angelo Tenisci. April 9 and 11, 2000.
Antonio Falcone. March 18, 2000.
Antonio (Tonino) Catena. May 11, 2000.
Fritz Illi. June 3, 2000.
Giordano Angelone. March 17, 2000.
Luisa di Luzio. April 13, 2000.
Nicola Bottega. April 13, 2000.

Nicola Del Ciotto. May 4, 2000.
Rosilda Giambuzzi. May 14, 2000.
Stefano Durante. April 15, 2000.
Tecla Garzarelli. May 14, 2000.
Tommaso Sorino. April 11, 2000.
Willy Fretz. May 16, 2000.

ARCHIVES

City of Edmonton Archives
Loyal Edmonton Regiment Collection
Library and Archives Canada
War Diary, Loyal Edmonton Regiment. RG24, vol.15114 (1943/09 to 1944/01)
War Diary, Seaforth Highlanders of Canada. RG24, vol.15256 (1943/12 to 1944/09)
War Diary, 12th Canadian Armoured Regiment (Three Rivers Regiment). RG24, vol.18206 (1943/11 to 1944/04)
McMaster University William Ready Division of Archives and Research Collections
Farley Mowat fonds
Seaforth Highlanders of Canada Archives
Box 998.135.118
University of Victoria Special Collections and University Archives
Military Oral History Collection

WORKS CITED

Atkinson, Rick. *The Day of Battle: The War in Sicily and Italy, 1943–1944*. New York: Picador, 2007.

Basti, Gaetano, ed. *Ortona Ricorda: Luoghi e Momenti della Vita Ortonese dalla Fine dell'800 alla Metà del '900 Ricostruiti Attraverso Documenti e Immagini*. Ortona: Edizioni Menabò, 1994.

Bayerlein, Carl, Alex MacQuarrie, and Dean Oliver. "Parachute Engineers in Combat, Ortona 1943." *Canadian Military History* 8, no. 4 (1999): 47–50.

Beevor, Antony. *The Second World War*. New York: Little, Brown and Co., 2012.

Behar, Ruth. *The Vulnerable Observer: Anthropology That Breaks Your Heart*. Boston: Beacon Press, 1996.

BenEzer, Gadi. "Trauma Signals in Life Stories." In *Trauma and Life Stories: International Perspectives*, edited by Kim Lacy Rogers, Selma Leydesdorff, and Graham Dawson, 29–44. London: Routledge, 1999.

Bercuson, David Jay. *Maple Leaf Against the Axis: Canada's Second World War*. Calgary: Red Deer Press, 1994.

———. *Our Finest Hour: Canada Fights the Second World War*. Toronto: HarperCollins, 2014.

Bernard, H. Russell. *Research Methods in Anthropology: Qualitative and Quantitative Approaches*. 6th ed. Lanham, MD: Rowman & Littlefield, 2017.

Besnier, Niko. "Language and Affect." *Annual Review of Anthropology* 19 (1990): 419–451.

Bosworth, R.J.B. *Mussolini's Italy: Life Under the Fascist Dictatorship, 1915–1945*. London: Penguin, 2005.

Brandon, Laura. "Veracity and Expectation in Charles Comfort's War Art, 1940–1948: The Hitler Line in Perspective." In *Take Comfort—The Career of Charles Comfort*, edited by Mary Jo Hughes, 53–56. Winnipeg: The Winnipeg Art Gallery, 2007.

———. "'Doing Justice to History': Canada's Second World War Official Art Program." *Canadian War Museum*. Accessed July 31, 2025. https://www.warmuseum.ca/cwm/exhibitions/artwar/essays/artandwar-canadas_2nd_world_war_art.pdf.

Broder, David. *Mussolini's Grandchildren: Fascism in Contemporary Italy*. London: Pluto Press, 2023.

Brown, Sean R.G. "'The Rock of Accomplishment': The Loyal Edmonton Regiment at Ortona." *Canadian Military History* 2, no. 2 (1993): 9–24.

Carr, Graham. "War, History, and the Education of (Canadian) Memory." In *Memory, History, Nation: Contested Pasts*, edited by Katharine Hodgkin and Susannah Radstone, 57–78. New York: Routledge, 2003.

Case, G.C. "Trial By Fire: Major-General Christopher Vokes at the Battles of the Moro River and Ortona, December 1943." *Canadian Military History* 16, no. 3 (2007): 13–28.

Catena, Tonino. *Mi Ricordo: Ortona*, 1940–45. Ortona: Self-published, n.d.

Cavasin, Zachary David. "Hai Visto i Canadesi? A Study of the Social Interactions Between Canadian Soldiers and Italian Civilians Before, During, and After the Battle of Ortona." MA thesis, University of Ottawa, 2010.

Comfort, Charles Fraser. *Artist at War*. Toronto: Ryerson Press, 1956.

Cook, Tim. *We Were Freedom: Canadian Stories of the Second World War*. Toronto: Key Porter Books, 2010.

———. *The Necessary War, Volume 1: Canadians Fighting the Second World War, 1939–43*. Toronto: Penguin, 2014.

———. *The Fight for History: 75 Years of Forgetting, Remembering, and Remaking Canada's Second World War*. Toronto: Allen Lane Canada, 2020.

Copp, Terry. *No Price Too High: Canadians and the Second World War*. Toronto: McGraw Hill Ryerson, 1996.

Copp, Terry, and Bill McAndrew. *Battle Exhaustion: Soldiers and Psychiatrists in the Canadian Army, 1939–1945*. Montreal and Kingston: McGill-Queen's University Press, 1990.

Cosh, D. Ian. "Killing Matters: Canadian War Remembrance and the Ghosts of Ortona." PhD diss., York University, 2014.

Dancocks, Daniel G. *The D-Day Dodgers: The Canadians in Italy, 1943–1945*. Toronto: McClelland and Stewart, 1991.

di Luzio, Adriano. *Ortona Guerra e Dopoguerra*. Ortona: Editrice Soc. Coop. "Iniziativa Cristiana" Ortona, 1998.

di Paolo, Antonio. "Curare le Ferite di Guerra – Il Caso di Ortona." Public presentation slides from MArch thesis (Laurea Specialistica in Architettura), Università degli Studi "G. D'Annunzio" Chieti–Pescara, 2013. City of Ortona website. Accessed May 20, 2025. http://storico.comuneortona.ch.it/immagini/news/TAV56.pdf, http://storico.comuneortona.ch.it/immagini/news/TAV7_8.pdf.

di Tullio, Saverio. *1943: The Road to Ortona*. Translated by Angela Arnone and Alex MacQuarrie. Ottawa: Legas, 1998.

Dupuis-Déri, Francis. *L'Armée Canadienne n'est pas l'Armée du Salut*. Montreal: Lux, 2010.

Dyer, Gwynne. *War*. New York: Crown Publishers, 1985.

Engen, Robert. "Killing for Their Country: A New Look at 'Killology.'" *Canadian Military Journal* 9, no. 2 (2008): 120–128.

———. *Canadians Under Fire: Infantry Effectiveness in the Second World War*. Montreal: McGill-Queen's University Press, 2009.

———. "S.L.A. Marshall and the Ratio of Fire: History, Interpretation, and the Canadian Experience." *Canadian Military History* 20, no. 4 (2011): 39–48.

———. *Strangers in Arms: Combat Motivation in the Canadian Army, 1943–1945*. Montreal: McGill-Queen's University Press, 2016.

Evans, Richard J. *The Third Reich at War, 1939-1945*. London: Penguin, 2008.

Ewing, Katherine Pratt. "Clinical Psychoanalysis as an Ethnographic Tool." *Ethos* 15, no. 1 (1987): 16–33.

———. "Is Psychoanalysis Relevant for Anthropology?" In *New Directions in Psychological Anthropology*, edited by Theodore Schwartz, Geoffrey M. White, and Catherine A. Lutz, 251–268. Cambridge: Cambridge University Press, 1992.

———. "Revealing and Concealing: Interpersonal Dynamics and the Negotiation of Identity in the Interview." *Ethos* 34, no. 1 (2006): 89–122.

Fentress, James, and Chris Wickham. *Social Memory*. Oxford: Blackwell, 1992.

Finnegan, Ruth. *Oral Traditions and the Verbal Arts: A Guide to Research Practices*. London: Routledge, 1992.

Francis, Daniel. *The Imaginary Indian: The Image of the Indian in Canadian Culture*. 2nd ed. Vancouver: Arsenal Pulp Press, 2011.

Fremeth, Howard. "Searching for the Militarization of Canadian Culture: The Rise of a Military-Cultural Memory Network." *Topia* no. 23–24 (2010): 52–76.

Freud, Sigmund. "Screen Memories." In *The Uncanny*, edited and translated by David McLintock, 3–22. London: Penguin, 2003 [1899].

Friedman, Herbert A. "The Allied 'Passierschein' Safe Conduct Passes of WWII." Psywarrior website, n.d. https://www.psywarrior.com/GermanSCP.html.

Galloway, Strome. *A Regiment at War: The Story of the Royal Canadian Regiment, 1939–1945*. s.l.: s.n., 1979.

Geroux, Jayson. "The Urban Battle of Ortona." MA thesis, University of New Brunswick, 2020.

Geroux, Jayson, and Lee Windsor. "Urban Anchor on the Gustav Line: Ortona, December

1943." In *Urban Battlefields: Lessons Learned from World War II to the Modern Era*, edited by Gregory Fremont-Barnes, 47–84. Annapolis, MD: Naval Institute Press, 2024.

Giannetti, Elio, Nicola Iubatti, and Dino Pacaccio, eds. *La Battaglia di Ortona: Momenti di una Tragedia, 1943–1944*. Pescara: Tipolitografia G. Fabiani, 1983.

Ginsborg, Paul. *A History of Contemporary Italy: Society and Politics, 1943–1988*. London: Penguin, 1990.

———. *Italy and Its Discontents: Family, Civil Society, State, 1980–2001*. London: Allen Lane, 2001.

Gooderson, Ian. "Assimilating Urban Battle Experience: The Canadians at Ortona." *Canadian Military Journal* 8, no. 4 (2007): 64–73.

Granatstein, J. L. *The Generals: The Canadian Army's Senior Commanders in the Second World War*. Calgary: University of Calgary Press, 2005.

———. *The Last Good War: An Illustrated History of Canada in the Second World War, 1939–1945*. Vancouver: Douglas and McIntyre, 2005.

Greenhous, Brereton. "Would It Not Have Been Better to Bypass Ortona Completely. . .?" *Canadian Defence Quarterly* 18, no. 5 (1989): 51–55.

Griffin, Roger. "The Post-Fascism of the Alleanza Nazionale: A Case Study in Ideological Morphology." *Journal of Political Ideologies* 1 (2007): 123–45.

———. *Fascism*. Medford, MA: Polity Press, 2018.

Griffiths, E.R.M. *Dare to be True: An Odyssey of Hope and Challenge*. Ottawa: Adsum Publications, 2000.

Grossman, Dave. *On Killing: The Psychological Cost of Learning to Kill in War and Society*. Boston: Back Bay Books, 1996.

———. *On Combat: The Psychology and Physiology of Deadly Conflict in War and Peace*. NP: PPCT Research Publications, 2004.

———. "S.L.A. Marshall Revisited . . .?" *Canadian Military Journal* 9, no. 4 (2008): 112–13.

Hedges, Chris. *War is a Force That Gives Us Meaning*. New York: Public Affairs, 2002.

Hollan, Douglas. "Developments in Person-Centered Ethnography." In *The Psychology of Cultural Experience*, edited by Carmella C. Moore and Holly F. Matthews, 48–67. Cambridge: Cambridge University Press, 2001.

Holland, Dorothy, and Naomi Quinn, eds. *Cultural Models in Language and Thought*. Cambridge: Cambridge University Press, 1987.

Holland, James. *The Savage Storm: The Battle for Italy, 1943*. New York: Atlantic Monthly Press, 2023.

Hollway, Wendy, and Tony Jefferson. "The Free Association Narrative Interview Method." In *The SAGE Encyclopedia of Qualitative Research Methods*, edited by Lisa M. Given, 296–315. Sevenoaks, CA: Sage, 2008.

Hunt, Nigel C. *Memory, War and Trauma*. Cambridge: Cambridge University Press, 2010.

Hynes, Samuel. *The Soldiers' Tale: Bearing Witness to Modern War*. New York: Penguin, 1997.

Ignazi, Piero. *Extreme Right Parties in Western Europe*. New York: Oxford University Press, 2003.

Iqbal, Noor. "Enacting Remembrance Day in the Public Sphere." *Constellations* 2, no. 1 (2010): 87–102.

Iubatti, Nicola, ed. *Testimonianze: 50° Anniversario della Battaglia di Ortona*. Ortona: Associazione Archeologica Frentana, 1994.

Johnson, Charles Monroe. *Action with the Seaforths*. New York: Vintage Press, 1954.

Kershaw, Ian. *Hitler*. London: Penguin, 2008.

King, James. *Farley: The Life of Farley Mowat*. Toronto: HarperCollins, 2002.

King, Thomas. *The Truth About Stories: A Native Narrative*. Toronto: House of Anansi Press, 2003.

Kirmayer, Laurence J. "Pacing the Void: Social and Cultural Dimensions of Dissociation." In *Dissociation: Culture, Mind, and Body*, edited by D. Spiegel, 91–122. Washington, DC: American Psychiatric Press, 1994.

———. "Landscapes of Memory: Trauma, Narrative, and Dissociation." In *Tense Past: Cultural Essays in Trauma and Memory*, edited by Paul Antze and Michael Lambek, 173–198. New York: Routledge, 1996.

Kondo, Dorinne K. *Crafting Selves: Power, Gender, and Discourses of Identity in a Japanese Workplace*. Chicago: University of Chicago Press, 1990.

Levi, Primo. *The Periodic Table*. New York: Schocken Books, 1984.

———. *If This Is a Man; and, The Truce*. London: Abacus, 2003 [1947].

———. *The Drowned and the Saved*. London: Abacus, 2013.

LeVine, Robert A. *Culture, Behavior and Personality: An Introduction to the Comparative Study of Psychosocial Adaptation*. 2nd ed. New York: Aldine, 1982.

Levy, Robert I., and Douglas W. Hollan. "Person-Centered Interviewing and Observation." In *Handbook of Methods in Cultural Anthropology*, edited by H. Russell Bernard, 333–364. Walnut Creek, CA: Altamira Press, 1998.

Leydesdorff, Selma, Graham Dawson, Natasha Burchardt, and T.G. Ashplant. "Introduction: Trauma and Life Stories." In *Trauma and Life Stories: International Perspectives*, edited by Kim Lacy Rogers, Selma Leydesdorff, and Graham Dawson, 1–26. London: Routledge, 1999.

Linde, Charlotte. *Life Stories: The Creation of Coherence*. Oxford: Oxford University Press, 1993.

Litz, B.T., N. Stein, E. Delaney, L. Lebowitz, W. P. Nash, C. Silva, and S. Maguen. "Moral Injury and Moral Repair in War Veterans: A Preliminary Model and Intervention Strategy." *Clinical Psychology Review* 29, no. 8 (2009): 695–706.

Loyal Edmonton Regiment Military Museum. "About the Battle of Ortona Painting." *Loyal Edmonton Regiment Military Museum*. Accessed August 19, 2025. https://www.lermuseum.org/about-the-battle-of-ortona-painting.

Malinowski, Bronislaw. *Argonauts of the Western Pacific: An Account of Native Enterprise and Adventure in the Archipelagoes of Melanesian New Guinea*. New York: Dutton, 1960 [1922].

McAndrew, Bill. *Canadians and the Italian Campaign, 1943–1945*. Montreal: Éditions Art Global, 1996.

McCready, A.L., "Tie a Yellow Ribbon 'Round Public Discourse, National Identity and the War: Neoliberal Militarization and the Yellow Ribbon Campaign in Canada." *Topia* (23–24) (2010): 28–51.

McDougall, Robert L. *A Narrative of War: From the Beaches of Sicily to the Hitler Line with the Seaforth Highlanders of Canada, 10 July 1943—8 June 1944*. Kemptville: Golden Dog Press, 1996.

McKay, Ian, and Jamie Swift. *Warrior Nation: Rebranding Canada in an Age of Anxiety*. Toronto: Between the Lines, 2012.

McLeod, John. *Narrative and Psychotherapy*. London: Sage Publications, 1997.

Molendijk, Tine. *Moral Injury and Soldiers in Conflict: Political Practices and Public Perceptions*. London: Routledge, 2021.

Molony, C.J.C., et al. *The Mediterranean and Middle East*. Vol. 5, *The Campaign in Sicily and the Campaign in Italy. History of the Second World War.* London: Her Majesty's Stationery Office, 1973.

Montgomery, Adam. *Invisible Injured: Psychological Trauma in the Canadian Military from the First World War to Afghanistan*. Montreal and Kingston: McGill-Queen's University Press, 2017.

Morgan, Philip. *The Fall of Mussolini: Italy, the Italians, and the Second World War*. Oxford: Oxford University Press, 2007.

Mowat, Farley. *Aftermath: Travels in a Post-War World*. Toronto: Key Porter Books, 1995.

———. *Otherwise*. Toronto: McClelland and Stewart, 2008.

———. *And No Birds Sang*. Vancouver: Douglas and McIntyre, 2012 [1979].

———. *My Father's Son*. Madeira Park, BC: Douglas and McIntyre, 2015.

Neimeyer, Robert A. "Fostering Posttraumatic Growth: A Narrative Elaboration." *Psychological Inquiry* 15, no. 1 (2004): 53–59.

Neimeyer, Robert A., Holly G. Prigerson, and Betty Davies. "Mourning and Meaning." *American Behavioral Scientist* 46, no. 2 (2002): 235–251.

Nicholson, G.W.L. *The Official History of the Canadian Army in the Second World War*. Vol. 2, *The Canadians in Italy, 1943–1945*. Ottawa: Queen's Printer, 1956.

Ochs, Elinor. "Narrative Lessons." In *A Companion to Linguistic Anthropology*, edited by Alessandro Duranti, 269–289. Malden, MA: Blackwell, 2004.

Ochs, Elinor, and Lisa Capps. *Living Narrative: Creating Lives in Everyday Storytelling*. Cambridge, MA: Harvard University Press, 2001.

Pacaccio, Dino. *Tommaso: Uno dei dodici*. Edited by Vittorio Polsoni. Ortona: Azienda Autonoma di Soggiorno e Turismo di Ortona, 1996.

Pandian, Anand, and Stuart J. McLean, eds. *Crumpled Paper Boat: Experiments in Ethnographic Writing*. Durham, NC: Duke University Press, 2017.

Politi, Antonio. *I Giorni del Martirio: Ortona 1943*. Ortona: Tip. Centobeni, 1948.

Portelli, Alessandro. *The Death of Luigi Trastulli and Other Stories: Form and Meaning in Oral History*. Albany: SUNY Press, 1991.

———. *The Battle of Valle Giulia: Oral History and the Art of Dialogue*. Madison, WI: University of Wisconsin Press, 1997.

Peacock, James L., and Dorothy C. Holland. "The Narrated Self: Life Stories in Process." *Ethos* 21, no. 4 (1993): 367–383.

Popular Memory Group. "Popular Memory: Theory, Politics, Method." In *Making Histories: Studies in History-Writing and Politics*, edited by Richard Johnson, 205–252. London: Hutchinson, 1982.

Rabinow, Paul. *Reflections on Fieldwork in Morocco*. Berkeley: University of California Press, 1977.

Roy, Reginald H. *The Seaforth Highlanders of Canada, 1919–1965*. Vancouver: Seaforth Highlanders of Canada, 1969.

Samuel, Raphael. "Perils of the Transcript." In *The Oral History Reader*, edited by Robert Perks and Alistair Thomson, 389–392. London and New York: Routledge, 2003.

Seligman, Rebecca, and Laurence J. Kirmayer. "Dissociative Experience and Cultural Neuroscience: Narrative, Metaphor and Mechanism." *Culture, Medicine and Psychiatry* 32 (2008): 31–64.

Serafini, Lucia. *Danni di guerra e danni di pace: Ricostruzione e città storiche in Abruzzo nel secondo dopoguerra*. Villamagna: Tinari, 2008.

Stacey, C. P. *A Date with History: Memoirs of a Canadian Historian*. Ottawa: Deneau Publishers, 1983.

Stevens, George Roy. *A City Goes to War: History of the Loyal Edmonton Regiment (3PPCLI)*. Brampton: Charters Publishing Co., 1964.

Strauss, Claudia, and Naomi Quinn. *A Cognitive Theory of Cultural Meaning*. Cambridge: Cambridge University Press, 1997.

Taylor, A.J.P. *The Origins of the Second World War*. New York: Simon and Schuster, 2005 [1961].

Thomson, Alistair. *Anzac Memories: Living with the Legend*. Oxford: Oxford University Press, 1994.

———. "Anzac Memories: Putting Popular Memory Theory into Practice in Australia." In *The Oral History Reader*, edited by Robert Perks and Alistair Thomson, 300–310. London and New York: Routledge, 2003.

Tonkin, Elizabeth. *Narrating Our Pasts: The Social Construction of Oral History*. Cambridge: Cambridge University Press, 1992.

Università Frentana della Terza Età. *Affidandosi alla Memoria: Ricordi dei Giorni della Guerra 1940–1944*. Lanciano: Centro di Servizi Culturali, n.d.

Vaillant, George E. *Ego Mechanisms of Defence: A Guide for Clinicians and Researchers*. Washington, DC: American Psychiatric Press, 1992.

Vance, Jonathan. *Death So Noble: Memory, Meaning, and the First World War*. Vancouver: UBC Press, 1997.

Watson, Lawrence C., and Maria-Barbara Watson-Franke. *Interpreting Life Histories: An Anthropological Inquiry*. New Brunswick, NJ: Rutgers University Press, 1985.

Weiner, Annette B. *The Trobrianders of Papua New Guinea*. New York: Holt, Rinehart, and Winston, 1988.

Westen, Drew. *Self and Society: Narcissism, Collectivism, and the Development of Morals*. Cambridge: Cambridge University Press, 1985.

Wood, Herbert Fairlie, and John Swettenham. *Silent Witnesses*. Toronto: Hakkert, 1974.

Zuehlke, Mark. *Ortona: Canada's Epic World War II Battle*. Toronto: Stoddart, 1999.

———. *Through Blood and Sweat: A Remembrance Trek Across Sicily's WWII Battlegrounds*. Vancouver: Douglas and McIntyre, 2015.

Image Credits

Images are listed in order of appearance. Archival photographs retain the original captions assigned by military photographers at the time. Credits and sources follow each caption.

Abbreviations: CWM—Canadian War Museum; DND—Department of National Defence (Canada); LAC—Library and Archives Canada; IWM—Imperial War Museum (UK)

Front Matter

Map of Ortona, 1943. Created by Christina Lee in collaboration with Ian Cosh. Sources consulted: Map F in "Operations of 1 Cdn Inf Div and 1 Cdn Armd Bde in Italy, 25 Nov 43 – 4 Jan 44," Canadian Military Headquarters Report No. 165, Directorate of History and Heritage (DND); Antonio di Paolo, "Curare le Ferite di Guerra—Il Caso di Ortona"; Gaetano Basti, *Ortona Ricorda*; Tonino Catena, *Mi Ricordo*; Google Maps satellite and street view of Ortona, accessed July 2025.

Detail from "Ortona" poem by Mel McPhee. Author's collection.

'Doggerel'

Postcard of Ortona collected after the battle by Stan Chettleborough, Loyal Edmonton Regiment. Loyal Edmonton Regiment Military Museum, 1986.13.1.

Chapter 1

"Men of B Company, Seaforth Highlanders of Canada, filing along mined coastal path. Town of Ortona in distance." 21 December 1943. Photograph by F. G. Whitcombe. LAC, PA-152749. Cropped from original.

Postcard of Ortona collected after the battle by Rollie Castagner, Loyal Edmonton Regiment. Loyal Edmonton Regiment Military Museum, 2000.21.1.7.

"Ruins of unidentified church." 30 December 1943. Photograph by Terry F. Rowe. LAC, PA-136308.

Chapter 2

"Youthful prisoners of the 26 Panzer Reconnaissance Regt., who were captured during a night attack on the Ortona-Orsogna lateral road area. They all seem pleased to be well away from the constant shelling by the Indians, and R.A.F. straffing [sic]." 17 December 1943. Photograph by Bill McConville. IWM, NA-9988.

"Private T.M. Collins of The Carleton and York Regiment searching German prisoners, Enna, Italy." 18 July 1943. Photograph by Frank Royal. LAC, PA-169996. Cropped from original.

"Infantrymen of the Seaforth Highlanders of Canada searching German prisoners near the Moro River, Italy." 8 December 1943. Photograph by Terry F. Rowe. LAC, PA-167914.

Placemat from Mountain Pizza and Steakhouse, Whitecourt, Alberta. Author's collection.

Chapter 3

"Some of the men who took part in the action celebrate their victory. They are, left to right—Major J. Stone (49 Edmonton Regt.) of Peace River, Alberta, Sgt. Maj. R. Bowen, (49 Edmonton Rgt.) of Edmonton, Maj. [sic] E.W. Thomas (Seaforth Highlanders of Canada) of Vancouver, Pte. C.G. Rattrey [sic] (49 Edmonton Regt.) of Lavoy, Alberta, and Capt. J.W. Baldwin (Seaforth Highlanders of Canada)." 28 December 1943. Photograph by Bill McConville. IWM, NA-10384. Cropped from original.

"The tanks (of the 12 Canadian Tank Regt.) and infantrymen (of the Princess Patricia's Light Regt.) advancing through the streets for the last phase of the bitter Ortona fighting." 28 December 1943. Photograph by Bill McConville. IWM, NA-10372. Cropped from original.

"Personnel of 'B' Company, Edmonton Regiment, advancing." 21 December 1943. Photograph by Terry F. Rowe. LAC, PA-116852.

Chapter 4

"Men (of the 49 Edmonton Regt.) patrolling a side street in search of snipers. Left foreground is a German paratrooper hounded from his lair by the Canadians." 28 December 1943. Photograph by Bill McConville. IWM, NA-10390. Cropped from original.

Page of the War Diary of the Seaforth Highlanders of Canada. 22 December 1943. LAC, RG 24 vol.15256 (1943/12 to 1944/07). Photograph by Ian Cosh.

"A Sherman tank guarding the main sqaure [sic] of Ortona." 28 December 1943. Photograph by Bill McConville. IWM, NA-10380. Cropped from original.

Menu card, Men's Annual Ortona Dinner, Seaforth Highlanders of Canada. Author's collection.

Chapter 5

"General view of Brigade Headquarters at Christmas dinner." 25 December 1943. Photograph by Terry F. Rowe. LAC, PA-152839.

Menu card, Men's Annual Ortona Dinner, Seaforth Highlanders of Canada. Author's collection.

Detail of "General view of Brigade Headquarters at Christmas dinner." 25 December 1943. Photograph by Terry F. Rowe. LAC, PA-152839.

Chapter 6

"Private B.D. Flynn of the regimental Aid Party, The Seaforth Highlanders of Canada, giving a drink of water to a badly-wounded German prisoner inside a church, Catona [sic], Italy." 21 December 1943. Photograph by Terry F. Rowe. LAC, PA-141670.

Chapter 7

"All that remains of one of Ortona's finest churches, the Church of San Thomas [sic]." 28 December 1943. Photograph by Bill McConville. IWM, NA-10389.

Charles Fraser Comfort, *Chiesa di San Tomasso, Ortona, Italy*, January 1944. Watercolour on paper. 38.1 x 58.7cm. CWM, Beaverbrook Collection of War Art, 19710261-2168.

Charles Fraser Comfort, *Via Dolorosa, Ortona*, no date. Oil on canvas. 101.5 x 76.2cm. CWM, Beaverbrook Collection of War Art, 19710261-2308.

Chapter 8

"A sniper (of the Edmonton Regt.) firing from the window of a house." 22 December 1943. Photograph by Bill McConville. IWM, NA-10204. Cropped from original.

Maurice White at *The Price of Peace* in Ortona, October 1999. Photographer unknown. Author's collection.

Chapter 9

"An old woman whose home was wrecked by the shelling being carried to safety on a chair." 28 December 1943. Photograph by Bill McConville. IWM, NA-10399. Cropped from original.

"After five days of sheltering from the holocaust of war, Italian families return to their homes, along the main street of the town." 28 December 1943. Photograph by Bill McConville. IWM, NA-10368. Cropped from original.

"On the road leading to the town, a few civilians remain. Some of them pose for a picture." 22 December 1943. Photograph by Bill McConville. IWM, NA-10185. Cropped from original.

Chapter 10

"German corporal who was killed during fighting with the Loyal Edmonton Regiment." 21 December 1943. Photograph by Terry F. Rowe. LAC, PA-115188. Cropped from original.

Detail of "Major-General Christopher Vokes addressing personnel of the Hastings and Prince Edward Regiment." 13 May 1944. Photograph by C.E. Nye. LAC, PA-132770.

Chapter 11

Lake and forest. Photograph by Christina Lee. Author's collection.

Charles Fraser Comfort, *Boschink*, c.1925–1926. Etching on wove paper. 23.6 x 30.8cm. Winnipeg Art Gallery, Gift of Robert and Margaret Hucal, 2005-68.

Acknowledgments

My PhD research was supported by grants and scholarships from the Social Sciences and Humanities Research Council of Canada, IODE Canada, the Mariano A. Elia Chair, and York University's Faculty of Graduate Studies.

Staff at Library and Archives Canada, the City of Edmonton Archives, the University of Victoria Archives, and Toronto Reference Library provided valuable help during my fieldwork. While preparing the manuscript, I received generous remote assistance from Dylan Bremner at the City of Edmonton Archives, and Darcia Arndt and Marjory Olsen at the Loyal Edmonton Regiment Museum, who tracked down images and clarified details about material I had collected. Andrew Webb at the Imperial War Museum and Jacqueline Vincent at Chislehurst Digitization were great help in obtaining photographs for the book.

Jonathan Crago read the manuscript with care and offered valuable feedback—especially on creative forms of scholarly writing. Daphne Winland's encouragement and her example of engaged scholarship lifted me at a key moment. I also appreciated the insights and assistance provided by Bruce Walsh, Jennifer Bonnell, Jennifer Stephen, Andrew Gordon, Pamela Holway, Anne Brackenbury, Edmund Li, Leonard Wyma, and Douglas Hildebrand along the way.

Ken Whyte recognized the book's potential, understood its spirit, and made its publication possible. I'm grateful to Bruce Walsh for encouraging me to send the manuscript to Ken. Tim Rostron was a sharp and steady editor, bringing clarity, patience, and much-appreciated humour to the process. The entire team at Sutherland House has my thanks.

Malcolm Blincow, Veronica Schild, and Dan Yon have been generous mentors and companions over many years. Their example of intellectual honesty and political courage has been a constant source of inspiration. Jason Winkler offered perspective, insight, and steady encouragement through some of the more difficult stretches of writing. Christina Lee's support and companionship were profoundly important, making this long process much easier. I could not have done this without my sister Sarah and my parents, Iris and Dave—who supported me throughout the project and whose example has long grounded my curiosity and approach to the world.

Above all, this book exists because of the people who lived through these events and chose to speak about them. I've done my best to honour their decision to share.

Index